The SAT Master Class

By Alok Bhardwaj, Principal Tutor, Yale Tutors

A Mind Leap Publication

© Alok Bhardwaj 2009. All rights reserved. No part of this book may be reproduced, stored in a retrieval system or transmitted in any form or by any means, electronic, mechanical, photocopying, recording, scanning or otherwise, without prior written permission from the author and the publisher.

INTRODUCTION 9
   A Metaphor for SAT Test Preparation: Training for a Sporting Event 9
   How often and when should I take the SAT test? 9
   Creating an SAT Test Prep Schedule 10
      Each Week of SAT Preparation: 11
      Two to Four Weeks before the Test 19
      The Week before the Test. 19
      The Day before the Test 20
      Sample SAT Prep Schedules 20
   General Test–Taking and Test–Day Guidelines 22

CRITICAL READING SECTION: Overview 24
   Elimination and Precision: Our Two Fundamental Techniques 24
      Elimination 25
      Precision 25
      Precise, Meaningful, Cross–Out Marks 26

CRITICAL READING SECTION: Sentence Completion Problems 29
   Overview 29
      Make Precise Pencil Marks to Preserve Your Thoughts on Paper 29
      Never Eliminate a Word Just Because You Don't Know What it Means. 29
      Do Not Be Afraid to Pick Answers with Words You Don't Know. 30
   Three Key Methods to Find the Meaning of the Blanks 30
      Identify Positive/Negative Blanks & Words. 30
      Fill in Your Own Words 30
      Identify/Underline Critical Words/Source of Meaning of the Blanks 31
   Three Less Important but Still Helpful Strategies 32
      Simplify the Sentence 32
      Watch Out for Words that Reverse Meaning 32
      If All Else Fails, Read Sentence with Answers Plugged in. 32
   The Nine–Fold Path for Sentence Completion Success 33
   Two Blank Question Strategies 34
      Two Blank Questions: Eliminate Blank by Blank 34
      Two Blank Questions: Synonym or Antonym Elimination 43
      Hard Two Blank Questions: Eliminate two easy words. 45
   Single Blank Question Strategies 46
      Key Strategy: Identify the Meaning of the Blank within the Sentence 46

Practice, Practice, Practice 52

Critical Reading Section: Sentence Completion Problem Sets 53

Vocabulary Building 61
   Word Roots 61
   Good Vocabulary Building Habits for Life 61

Sentence Completion Recapitulation 63

CRITICAL READING SECTION: Reading Passages 65

Elimination and Precision: Two Fundamental Techniques. 65

How to Read Passages 73
   Do I Need to Read the Full Passages? Can I Skim Them? 73
   Never Re–Read a Passage. 74
   Active Reading: Use Your Pencil While Reading. 74
   Fact–Based or Argument Passages 75
   Narrative Passages 78

Reading Passage Question Guidance 79
   Answer Line Number Questions First. 79
   Outside the Scope of the Passage: Most Common Wrong Answer 80
   Dual Passages: Be Aware of Each Author's Position (who's pro and who's con) 80
   Line Number Questions 84
   Conclusion and Logical Reasoning Questions 89
   Meaning in Context/Most Nearly Means 95

Critical Reading Section: Reading Passage Problem Set 102

Reading Passages Recapitulation 110

MATH SECTION: Overview 112

Question Strategies 112

Guessing Strategy 114
   If You Eliminate Even One Choice, You Must Guess! 114
   Grid–In Problems: No Penalty for Wrong Answers 114

Work on Paper. 115

Write Down Everything You Know. 115

When Stuck, Move On. 115

Before You Bubble–in Your Final Answer 116
   Re–read the Question (before you circle your answer). 116

Practice, Practice, Practice 117

Three Key Problem-Solving Methods: Plugging In Numbers, Working Backwards, and Measurement *117*
    Plugging In Numbers 117
    Working Backwards from the Answer Choices 129
    Measurement 135

MATH SECTION: Algebra **137**

Algebraic Terms and Concepts to Know. *137*
    Equation. 137
    Inequality. 137
    Coefficient. 138
    Variable. 138
    Constant. 139
    Integers 139
    Rational Numbers 139
    Absolute value. 140
    Polynomial. 141
    Function. 142
    Degree of an equation. 145

Three Key Techniques for Algebra Problems *148*
    1. Plug In Numbers. 148
    2. Working Backwards from the Answer Choices 148
    3. Write Down Everything You Can about the Problem: Variables, Equations, Then Solve. 148

Solving Systems of Equations *150*

Multiplying Polynomial Expressions and FOIL *157*
    Multiplying Simple Polynomials 157
    Multiplying Quantities with Polynomials: FOIL (First Outer Inner Last) 158

Factoring Quadratic Equations *163*

Translating English into Equations *172*

Manipulating Inequalities *176*

Rate and Percentage Mixture Problems *183*
    Rate Problems 183
    Percentage Mixture Problems 186

Inverse and Direct Proportions/Ratios *190*

Functions: Graph Problems *196*
    Vertical Line Test 196
    Shifting Functions 196

Functions: Functions of Functions *201*

Functions: Inverse Functions *206*

Functions: Tables *209*

Two Fractions in an Equation *211*

Absolute Value Equations *213*

MATH SECTION: (mostly) Arithmetic **216**

Order of Operations (PEMDAS—P/E/MD/AS) *216*

New or Made-up Operators *226*

Elementary Number Theory: Prime and Composite Numbers *232*

Sequences and Series *242*
    Arithmetic Sequences 242
    Geometric Sequences 244
    Repeating Sequences.. 245
    Sums of Sequences: Series 251

Percentage Problems: *252*
    Percentage Basics 252
    Percentage Pay and Percentage Off... 255

Basic Combinatorics: Combinations & Permutations *258*

Probability *264*

Statistics *272*

Averages *277*

MATH SECTION: Geometry **280**

The Fundamental Method for Geometry Problems: Work from the Diagram *280*

Alternate Method to using "pure" Geometry: Measurement *280*

Equations are written in the front of each math section—still memorize them *281*

Coordinate Geometry *281*

Complementary and Supplementary Angles *284*

Parallel Lines Intersected by a Transversal: Alternate Interior/Exterior, Corresponding and Vertical Angles *285*

Analytical Geometry *287*
    Lines 287
    Slope 287
    Y-Intercept... 288
    Equation of a line... 289

    Parallel and Perpendicular Lines..291

Circles..*295*
    Definition of a Circle, Radius, and Diameter...295
    Area..296
    Circumference...296
    Volume of a Sphere and a Cylinder 298

Special Right Triangles..*299*
    3:4:5 Right Triangles..299
    30°–60°–90° Right Triangles 300
    45°–45°–90° Right Triangles 301
    Pythagorean Theorem..302
    More on Triangles..303

Polygons..*309*
    Sum of the Interior Angles of a Polygon 309

Solved Geometry Problems..*312*

Math Recapitulation *344*

WRITING SECTION: Multiple–Choice Questions Overview 346

Sentence Correction Problems..*347*

Sentence Revision and Paragraph Revision Problems..*349*

Our Approach to the Writing Multiple-Choice Section...*353*
    The same grammar rules are repetitively tested. 353
    Use your ear to hear grammatical mistakes..353
    Cross out extraneous parts of the sentence so that errors are easier to hear...354
    Shorter is often better..354

WRITING SECTION: Grammar Review 355

Parts of Speech: a Quick Review..*355*

Exercise: Practice Breaking Sentences Apart According to Their Parts of Speech 360

Grammatical Errors Tested..*361*
    Verb Tense..361
    Parallelism..362
    Subject–Verb Agreement 364
    Noun–Noun Agreement (subject–object or noun–pronoun)..............................366
    Pronoun Agreement 368
    Pronoun Case..369
    Pronoun Ambiguity 371
    Misplaced Modifier 372
    General Conjunction Errors 373

    Correlative Conjunction Errors 373
    Double Negative/Redundancy 375
    Proper Comparisons 376
    Comparisons: More/Most 377
    Idiomatic Errors/Wrong Preposition 378
    Incorrect Word 379
    Sentence Fragments 385
    Singular Nouns 386
    Adjective where an Adverb is necessary or vice versa 388

Punctuation Errors.. 389
    Separating Two Independent Clauses 389
    Colons 390
    Commas 391

Grammar Checklist: Possible Errors by Part of Speech 393

Writing Section: Grammar Review Problem Set 395

WRITING SECTION: Multiple-Choice Questions Solved and Analyzed 397

Sentence Revision Problems 397

Sentence Correction Problems 405

Paragraph Revision Problems 411

Writing Section Multiple Choice Question Problem Sets 417

Writing Recapitulation 426

WRITING SECTION: Essay 427

Your Four Musts 427

Introductions and Conclusions 429

Essay Content 430

Writing Tips 431

Outline Creation Practice 432

Concluding Thoughts 435

APPENDIX 1: Problem Set Answers 436

Critical Reading Section: Sentence Completion Problem Set Answers 436

Critical Reading Section: Reading Passage Problem Set Answers 438

Math Section: Overview Problem Set Answers 442

Math Section: Algebra Problem Set Answers..*448*

Math Section: (mostly) Arithmetic Problem Set Answers................................*475*

Math Section: Geometry Problem Set Answers..*500*

Writing Section: Grammar Review Problem Set Answers.............................*518*

Writing Section: Sentence Correction Problem Set Answers........................*522*

Writing Section: Sentence Revision Problem Set Answers...........................*526*

Writing Section: Paragraph Revision Problem Set Answers........................*531*

APPENDIX 2: Outline of the Master Class Methods for Easy Reference..... **534**

APPENDIX 3: How to Write an Essay: the PRO+CUPED METHOD............... **548**

APPENDIX 4: Word Roots and Origins **560**

Negative Prefixes..*560*

Positive Prefixes...*562*

Other Common Prefixes..*563*

Common Suffixes...*568*

More Roots..*569*

APPENDIX 5: SAT Subject Test Preparation Guidance **575**

APPENDIX 6: The Four Components of College Admissions..........................**577**

APPENDIX 7: Turn Out a Great College Application Essay. **582**

INTRODUCTION

A Metaphor for SAT Test Preparation: Training for a Sporting Event

The SAT is not an intelligence test. It's not at all clear what the test measures actually. The A in SAT at one point stood for aptitude but the College Board has long since dropped that and any other acronym.

Treat your SAT preparation as you would training for any sport—you have to practice and train hard to improve your score. There may not be anything meaningful about putting a ball through a hoop just as any particular SAT score doesn't mean anything, but it's important to respect the activity whether it's playing basketball or taking the SAT test as a challenge in order to do well.

Work hard to achieve your goals and to improve your score. Don't worry, though, about what your particular SAT score is or isn't; SAT scores have little predictive value (some studies have shown a correlation between college students' first semester grades and SAT scores…even those were weak). Being the best basketball player in the world or the best golfer in the world doesn't make one "the most athletic person in the world" nor does the highest SAT score make anyone "the most intelligent person" in the world.

Work hard and achieve your goals—and that's what your score improvement will reflect, that you can set, work towards and achieve goals. If you're able to do that, you'll be able to do most anything you want to in life.

How often and when should I take the SAT test?

The College Board approved a new score reporting policy (start date: March 2009) whereby you'll be able to choose which SAT I and SAT

Subject Test scores to send out to colleges. You're now able to take SAT tests as often as you like and only report your best test dates' scores. Given this change, we would also change our recommendations for students to something like *take the SAT early and take it often.*

With this new policy change, we'd recommend students take the SAT after roughly two months of intense preparation—we wouldn't recommend most students prepare for an extended period e.g. six months intensely without taking a real SAT test. After roughly two to three months of intense prep, you should feel relatively confident to take the test and may as well try your hand at a real test. In terms of timing, we generally recommend taking the SAT I test in the winter or spring of your junior year which gives you four test date options: January, March, May, and June. You should save at least one if not both of the May and June test dates for the SAT Subject tests…which leaves January and March as key SAT I test dates.

Keep in mind you'll also have the opportunity to take the SATs again in the fall of your senior year.

Creating an SAT Test Prep Schedule

You've got months (we hope) until test day. You need to develop a schedule and plan for preparation.

First off, we recommend starting sooner than later—if you reach your score goals early, you can always take a break. By early, we'd recommend doing some preparation in the summer before your junior year or in the early fall of your junior year in advance of the PSAT test. Ideally, you will have done roughly 2 months worth of preparation before your PSAT test in the fall of your junior year. That way, your PSAT scores which you'll get back in the winter will be a fairly accurate representation of where you're scoring. If they're lower than what you're aiming for, you'll have a few to several months in the late winter and spring to prepare for the real SAT test. Your PSAT test score, incidentally, doesn't count towards your college admissions—if you do really well, you may be eligible for a modest scholarship, that's it.

Each Week of SAT Preparation:

Mandatory: 4 hours per week to complete a full practice SAT test.

This is absolutely, no questions asked, mandatory. If you're doing extremely well on a particular section, say math or the essay, you could leave the math sections out or the essay out and even double–up the reading sections. As it gets closer to the test date, you must go back to taking complete practice tests with all three sections (math, reading and writing).

It's very important that you do complete, timed (you must time yourself) practice tests in a quiet place without any distractions with 100% of your attention and concentration. You have to train yourself to be able to do your best for four hours straight and build up your test–taking endurance.

You also have to become familiar with the test format and the types of questions asked on the test. To this end, we strongly encourage you to take College Board prepared practice tests. You can find 8 such practice tests in the College Board published book available in just about any bookstore *the Official SAT Study Guide*. You can get 7 more such practice tests via the College Board's online course at http://satonlinecourse.collegeboard.com.

Don't get over–ambitious and do all 15 tests in 2 weeks…once you've taken these tests, there aren't any more accurate and good practice tests to take! Do save at least 2 practice tests for the week or weeks before your actual test in case you're beginning preparation more than 4 months in advance of the test.

In case you run out of practice tests, you can try tests prepared by independent vendors such as Kaplan or the Princeton Review. Those books and tests usually have decent math and writing questions, but be wary of their reading comprehension questions, those are often off. If you use up the 15 College Board tests, use a mix of sources (e.g. Kaplan, Princeton Review and the GRE book, say) and you should be in decent shape. Don't rely on tests from a single vendor as any single vendor can misguide you and mis-prepare you. We sometimes have our SAT students use math and reading sections from ETS–prepared GRE tests (several practice tests can be found in the book: *GRE: Practicing to Take the General Test*). The GRE test is very similar to the SAT test (there are some question types that have been eliminated from the SAT, skip those).

Try to take your weekly practice test in the same 4 hour block of time every week. If it's not possible, it's not the end of the world, but it's best to get into a good training routine, you'll find it easier to stick to. If you can take your practice test either every Saturday or Sunday morning, that's ideal since you'll take the real test in one of those time–slots.

We can't emphasize this enough: the most important part of SAT test preparation is completing weekly College Board practice SAT tests.

<u>Mandatory: 1–3 hours per week for an intense and full review of your practice test.</u>

You have to set aside another 1 to 2 hour block of time for reviewing your weekly practice test. You may need more or less time depending on how well you're doing and your goals.

We emphasize intensity and focused thought and effort in test preparation. There's no use taking a dozen practice tests and continuing to miss the same types of problems over and over. You have to find out which problems you got wrong (and also the ones you got right) and analyze, why did I miss this (or get this right?)? And learn, learn, learn why you missed those problems and figure out an approach (with your own thought, with the help of this book, even with the help of others) to get those problems consistently right. *It's important to do a lot of problems and practice tests, but it's more important to review those tests intensely and figure out what approach and methods work for you and what doesn't.*

Always Keep In Mind As You Review Tests and Practice Problems that you need reliable ways to answer types of questions...the SAT has 50 or so types of questions which they use over and over. You need to be able to answer problems of each of those types generally and not just know how to answer a particular question or why the correct answer is correct for a particular problem (that's a start but not enough). You need a method to reliably arrive at the correct answer when encountering a similar but differently structured problem of that type again. You need methods which you feel comfortable and confident using which will reliably bring you to the correct answer. Our techniques, which you'll learn as you work through this book, will provide you with such methods and a framework for tackling every type of SAT problem.

When you review tests, thus, don't just look at the right answer and then "get it" and say "a–ha"...or go through some similar routine. That's not going to be helpful in the long run! You have to delve into what you were thinking, how you approached the problem and why your approach in this case led to you to the incorrect answer. It may be a sentence completion problem in which you eliminated 3 of the 5 answers and then had to guess (and had the bad luck to pick the wrong answer). In such a case, you did a pretty good job and you should probably ask yourself if there was any way you could have eliminated that single remaining wrong answer or if there was anything to suggest giving a little extra weight to what was the right answer. Or it may be you did your absolute best and you simply had to guess...and that's that.

So as you review problems ask yourself–why is the correct answer correct? Why are the wrong answers wrong? What makes each wrong answer wrong? (these two questions about wrong answers are critical to ask yourself for reading section problems). Most importantly ask yourself: if I encountered a similar problem, what's my method, my thought process, my approach to the problem which will reliably lead me to the correct answer? Test–taking is about thinking carefully through a problem and you have to do that again in your post mortem test reviews. Don't worry about getting any particular problem right or wrong, rather be circumspect and concerned about your methods and logic to approaching every problem.

To recapitulate, mandatory components of your SAT prep are to:
1. *Take a College Board Practice SAT Test Once a Week ideally in the Same Time–Slot (preferably Saturday or Sunday morning). Time Yourself. Do the test without taking any long breaks (4 hours straight roughly). No Distractions. 100% Concentration.*
2. *Review that Practice Test Intensely in a 1–2 hour block later.*

Optional: Address Weaknesses/Other Problem Sets/Secondary SAT Work

If your goals include 100+ point improvements for any particular section, you should (really must) supplement your core weekly practice test with additional SAT problem sets. You should schedule 1 or more additional 2–hour blocks of time into your weekly schedule for this additional work (if it's during the school year, a single 1 to 3 hour block of time should be sufficient).

The critical reading section is the most difficult section to get additional, good problems for (apart from the College Board prepared practice tests). You have options, though. Our preference would be to use reading sections from the GRE book *GRE: Practicing to Take the*

General Test, and the old book *10 Real SATs* (with older SAT and GRE tests—skip the antonyms and analogies questions which were removed from the current incarnation of the SAT test) for which you can find used copies available online at amazon.com. Though we prefer either older SAT or GRE reading passages for additional practice, you can also try reading comprehension problems from 2 or more independent vendors to supplement your core practice tests e.g. a Kaplan book, Gruber's book, et cetera. Independent vendors' books for reading comprehension are not very highly recommended but if you must use them, use more than one.

For the math section, particularly if you feel like you need to review one or more areas in some depth, there are a number of math workbooks such as the Princeton Review Math Workout, the Kaplan Math Workbook, etc. with good problem sets organized by type of math problem. Try to do 2–3 chapters and the problem sets associated with those chapters' topics in each book in a 2 hour block once a week (or more as time permits).

For the writing section, if you need more essay prompts, you can usually find more at the College Board's website. If you need more multiple choice questions to review, use 2 or more (never just 1) independent vendors' books such as Kaplan, Gruber, Princeton Review, etc.

Highly Optional: Tertiary SAT Prep Work

Vocabulary–Building.

Everyone should have good habits regarding vocabulary–building. Anytime you encounter a word you don't know, you should make a note of it and look it up at some point. If you're reading a book, it may break the flow of reading to look it up immediately which is why writing it down is a better option. Also, when you write a word down, you'll likely look at it and look it up more than once. You need to use the word and look it up multiple times to really learn it. Make an effort to use new words you learn—assimilate them into your working vocabulary. Ask your teachers or parents or anyone else if you're not sure how to use a particular word.

Connecting words to images or similar–sounding words are good ways to remember new words. When you have many words to learn, using index cards (word on the front/definition on the back) is a great idea— you can flip through the cards whenever you have 5 or 10 minutes free and the simple action of flipping a card actually helps you learn better and stay engaged versus reading a list of words off a page.

Beyond having good habits, we don't recommend you spend much time trying to build your vocabulary. The SAT test is much less a test of your mastery of English vocabulary than it used to be, and our techniques which you'll soon learn are very powerful.

If you'd still like to improve your vocabulary, do read over the word roots in Appendix 3 of this book. Knowing Greek and Latin word roots can help you learn more words in general and also guess at the meanings of unfamiliar words. We've put together a list of the most common and helpful word roots in Appendix 3. Further, we'd recommend that instead of trying to memorize words out of a book, try to read challenging essays and novels which will contain unfamiliar words to learn as well as "stretch" your brain to understand them.

Reading.

It's a good idea to read widely and this will help you do better on the SAT test. You can get recommendations from your teachers, and we also have a few which are good for both vocabulary–building as well as reading comprehension.

For non–fiction essays: the New Yorker which unlike Time and most other magazines is written at a high school or college (not middle school) reading level and their essays are available for free online.

Stephen Jay Gould's essays have been collected into various books. There are also many anthologies of essays which you can purchase online inexpensively. Essay–reading is probably the ideal SAT prep reading (in our opinion, more important than reading fiction).

For fiction, most of the so–called classic novels should be challenging as well as vocabulary–augmenting (e.g. Charles Dickens, Jane Austen, et cetera). Anthologies of classic short stories are a good choice to be exposed to many different writers and writing styles. If you're really hankering for a lot of obscure words and a difficult read, try one of Vladimir Nabokov's English novels like *Ada* or *Pale Fire* (be warned that they're difficult novels which may be hard to "get into" with lots and lots of difficult words).

Essay–Writing.

If you'd like to improve your essay or analytical writing skills in general, take a look at Appendix 2 for a full exposition of our PRO+CUPED method of essay writing. We've found PRO+CUPED to be an effective framework for writing analytical or critical essays for writing students. To improve your writing, try to write essays regularly, at least one or two per month, and revise them multiple times (complete at least two drafts per essay). You'll need an experienced writer or writers (two opinions are better than one) to read, edit and offer advice and comments on your essays; your teachers should be ready to help you in that capacity. Improving your general writing skills takes time, several months to years, so try to dedicate two or three blocks of time out of your week (e.g. Monday and Friday afternoons) to writing—in time you'll see improvement.

Mathematics.

If you'd like to study recreational mathematics with some idea to improving your SAT score, there are a few options beyond the SAT workbooks. You can try and solve rather difficult math problems—but problems of a similar nature to what you're used to from school. You could also try to improve your maturity as a mathematician and problem solver in general by studying some pure mathematics. In pure math, you'll try to create your own proofs or study proofs for various theorems in mathematics. Unfortunately, just about all of what you've been taught in school is what should be called applied mathematics, using mathematics to solve problems. There's a whole other, very rich and beautiful part of mathematics (what mathematicians actually would call "real mathematics") which is proving theorems in pursuit of truth. Proofs are not driven by a need to solve any real–world problem (like how to solve a percentage discount of a sweater) but rather to know the truth about certain things in mathematics (for instance whether the Pythagorean theorem is always true or if it's just almost always true).

Some books with hard math problems and a bit of pure mathematics include:

The USSR Olympiad Problem Book: Selected Problems and Theorems of Elementary Mathematics (published by Dover) by D. O. Shklarsky, N. N. Chentzov, & I. M. Yaglom
This is a fairly approachable book with problems and lucid solutions from many areas of mathematics. Many problems represent key theorems in elementary mathematics so there's a fair amount of pure mathematics covered. This book is easy to use in that you can just open it up and start trying to solve that problem—if you can't get it, you can read and study the solution, then start on another problem. This book has an advantage that there's no commitment needed to benefit from it! If you really enjoy this book and more difficult math problems, there are many books with mathematical contest questions and other tough problems available.

Journey through Genius: The Great Theorems of Mathematics by William Dunham is as the title indicates a book of a dozen or so classic proofs from mathematics. It's not an easy read but also not at all difficult. You can pick it up and read/work through a chapter in an hour to a few hours to learn each proof.

What is Mathematics by Richard Courant is a classic by a great mathematician which presents an introduction to many different fields in mathematics, mathematical concepts and key proofs, and mathematical thinking. It's a long book and while not difficult, it's also not easy. If you really want to learn some mathematics and are ready make a sustained effort, this is a good book. Incidentally, Einstein praised this book when it was first published in the 1940s.

Two to Four Weeks before the Test

You need to do full, College Board practice tests in each of the 2 to 4 weeks before the real test. Try to do them on Saturday or Sunday mornings at this point if it's at all possible. Again, these should be timed tests in a quiet place.

Also, your reviews of the practice tests should be intense and you should feel confident you've mastered our techniques and methods and know the test well.

The Week before the Test.

If you've been working hard and your practice test scores are where you want to be, relax and take it a bit easy that week. If you're not where you'd like to be in terms of scoring, try your best come test day and or think about changing your test date if it's possible for you. The College Board has a new policy that will allow you to choose which scores will go out to colleges—double–check that it applies to you—so you likely won't have to worry about your score if you don't feel entirely prepared. Also keep in mind you can cancel your scores—if you feel you haven't done well at the end of the test, tell the proctor and your test shouldn't be scored.

Try this week to review several of the practice tests you've taken in the past few months. Think through what you did right and how and why, where you went wrong and why. In your reviews, be intense but at the same time, don't stress yourself.

The Day before the Test

You have one critical job at this point: *get a good night's rest!*

Don't forget to get your pencils sharpened, a few pencils dulled (some dull pencils for bubbling), a pencil with accurate tic marks on the tip (for our measurement technique on geometry problems), erasers, a calculator, extra batteries or an extra calculator, and snacks for test–day ready.

In case you've just bought this book and your SAT test is tomorrow… read what you can here, the chapters on what you think you may need the most work in, and work through a practice test or two from the College Board.

Sample SAT Prep Schedules

Intense Preparation Schedule—100+ point gain goals in each of the three sections

Saturday Morning 10am–2pm: Full practice test.

Sunday Afternoon 4pm–6pm: Review of the previous day's practice test.

Tuesday Night 7pm–9pm: In the *Princeton Review Math Workout for the SAT* and *Kaplan Math Workbook*, read and solve problems in 2 chapters and complete all problems in the 2 associated problem sets.

Wednesday Night 8pm–9:30pm: Read some essay or articles from the New Yorker Online or from Stephen Jay Gould's *The Lying Stones of Marrakech*. Write a short 5 paragraph essay analyzing the argument of the essay I read.

Thursday Night 7pm–8pm: Additional reading comprehension passages for 1 hour (3 sections skipping antonyms and analogies problems) from GRE tests (found in the book, *GRE: Practicing to Take the General Test 10th Edition*).

Regular Preparation Schedule—50 point gain goals for each section

Sunday Afternoon 1pm–5pm: Full practice test.

Sunday Night 7pm–9pm: Review of the practice test.

Wednesday Afternoon 3pm–5pm: In the *Princeton Review Math Workout* book, read and solve problems in 2 chapters and complete all problems in the 2 associated problem sets.

As I have time, read *Bleak House* by Charles Dickens.

Relaxed Preparation Schedule—let's try some preparation but not go crazy about it

Friday Evening 4pm–8pm: Full practice test.

Sunday Afternoon 3pm–5pm: Review of the practice test.

General Test–Taking and Test–Day Guidelines

✓ ***Bubble in groups with a dull pencil***—bubble 5 or 10 answers at a time. You're less prone to making bubbling mistakes and this also saves a bit of time. Be sure to bring a dull pencil to the test with you just for bubbling purposes: a dull point on your pencil makes filling the circles faster. When you initially solve a problem, write the letter of the answer next to the problem number. After you've solved 5 to 10 problems, bubble them all in. As time starts to run out, bubble in each answer after you solve the problem.

✓ ***Eliminate and Guess.*** For any section, if you eliminate even one answer, you MUST guess.

✓ ***Time is Super–Precious. When Stuck, Move On.*** If you're stuck on a problem, come back to it later. Often when you come back to a question later, the answer will be clearer to you...if you're still stuck, eliminate and take a guess. Time is absolutely crucial, and you don't have time to agonize over any problem. Circle questions or the question number for questions you're stuck on or unsure of and come back to them when you've finished the other problems in the section.

✓ ***Work on paper... move your thoughts to paper.*** Working on paper helps keep your mind moving (so to speak). Moving a thought to paper frees your brain to move on to other thoughts and reduces the chances that you'll make a careless mistake. Studies have shown the brain can keep 7 plus or minus 2 things in short–term memory at any point in time. You want to keep moving thoughts about a problem out of your short–term memory and onto paper to free those 7 slots of short–term memory up. Also, the more detail/information you have for a question written down and thus preserved in your work, the less time you waste in re–thinking through a problem you come back to. You're able to write in the SAT test booklet and write all over SAT questions (many other tests are purely computer based so you can't write on the test questions themselves) so write away! The fact that the SAT test is a written test is something our techniques exploit, particularly for the reading section. For all sections, reading, writing and math, working on paper will help you be a better test–taker. Writing down all the steps of your solution for a math problem on paper will make you much less prone to making careless mistakes and much more prone to double–checking your work and catching careless mistakes. For the writing and reading sections, putting down your ideas about each problem on paper will help you eliminate your way to the correct answer (more on those techniques in the coming chapters).

✓ *Provisions*—take many, at least four pencils (one sharp to do your work with, a back–up sharp pencil, one dull pencil to bubble with, one marked pencil to use as a ruler), a silent watch to keep track of your time on each section, silent candies to eat quietly during the test, juice, and snacks for the break. For the pencil to use as a ruler, accurately make 1mm tick marks on its tip to use for geometry problems (we'll explain our measurement technique in the geometry section).

✓ *Sign up for tests as well in advance as possible*—slots fill quickly at convenient locations and the minimum advance notice to sign–up is approximately four weeks.

CRITICAL READING SECTION: Overview

Elimination and Precision: Our Two Fundamental Techniques

The Critical Reading section consists of two types of questions: sentence completion problems and reading passage problems. Both types of problems are highly comprehension-driven and only slightly to fairly vocabulary-driven (as opposed to older and now eliminated analogy and antonym problems which were highly vocabulary-driven). The SAT test was last changed in 2005 when analogy questions were eliminated which was in line with a decade long trend in the SAT test to depreciate testing vocabulary and focus more on testing comprehension.

As the test changes, so of course do our techniques. We do not recommend most students spend a lot of time trying to learn new vocabulary words as many did for older incarnations of the SAT test. We do emphasize a bit of work on your vocabulary and generally trying to keep growing your vocabulary—you're at an age when you're building what will be the bulk of your lifelong working English vocabulary so you should take pains to make your working vocabulary as precise and as big as possible. Don't kill yourself to memorize hundreds of new words just for the SAT test, though.

We have very powerful techniques for both sentence completion and reading passage questions that can help you considerably even when you don't know the meaning of all the words in the question. *These techniques are elimination and precision.*

They may seem vague or hard to understand at first, but these ideas should become clearer both in theory and in practice in the solved problems later in this chapter.

Elimination

For math problems, we generally solve them i.e. we find the right answer. It's a little strange to say that when given the problem 2+2, we eliminated all the other possible numbers and were left with the answer of 4. In math problems, we usually solve the problem and obtain the correct answer. Elimination is used infrequently on the math section.

In the reading section, our approach is different. We eliminate the wrong answers. This is because there are many ways to read or interpret any sentence or passage. There are often multiple answers which may have some aspect of "truth" or correctness to them among the answer choices. If we aren't careful, we may read an answer choice that has some aspect of correctness to it (but isn't as correct as other answers) and choose it even though it's the wrong answer. Even if you immediately read an answer and are sure it's correct, you should still read every other answer and eliminate them to be absolutely certain there's no better answer out there.

Moreover, elimination is what drives us in the reading section—think "what can I eliminate" when approaching problems. In the reading section, our task is to eliminate all the wrong answers...but how do we know what to eliminate?

Precision

The means by which we know what to eliminate and how to eliminate is the idea of precision. Precision guides us in how to eliminate answer choices for reading passage and sentence completion problems. You have to find the answer choice in which every word/phrase is made meaningful and thus true by the passage. The idea of precision is that the answer that requires "the least effort" to be true, the least imagination, is the correct answer. Give words a precise, clear, and unimaginative meaning. When you've done that to an answer choice (if it is supported by the passage in the case of reading passage problems), odds are it's the correct answer. To be sure, you should *always* eliminate the other choices—those answer choices that are not supported by the text to the necessary level of precision must be eliminated.

Precision also encompasses the fact that every word in an answer choice counts; every word must be given meaning. If an answer doesn't capture the entirety of what's being expressed, cross out the word(s) that makes that answer choice "not quite right" which effectively eliminates that choice. If you're not sure but you don't think some part of an answer choice is wrong, *cross the words out lightly*. If you're sure, cross that part of the answer choice out with a dark pencil mark.

Don't cross out entire answers or the letter of the answer choice to eliminate an answer unless the whole thing really is totally wrong, instead carefully cross out only the parts of the answer choice that are wrong—that helps you to think precisely and analyze answer choices better as well as preserve your thoughts on paper accurately.

Precise, Meaningful, Cross–Out Marks

To eliminate answer choices, we have to cross out either the whole answer choice or some part of it. We use precision to guide us in what to cross out. You should only cross out those words/terms that actually make the answer wrong; leave the rest of the words in that answer choice untouched.

This method has a number of advantages. It preserves your thought on the paper through that mark. It also helps keep open our short-term memory (continuously opening up those 7 slots without losing that knowledge or information). One way to move your discoveries about a problem out of your head and onto paper is through a precise pencil mark eliminating just those words that are wrong. If you ever come back to look at that answer choice, you'll most likely immediately remember what was wrong about those particular words. Once you've moved your thought to paper, your brain is free to move on to new thoughts and continue to analyze the problem.

Crossing out only what's wrong also forces your mind into precision–mode. You're forced to analyze the answer choice and figure out what *exactly* is wrong with it. We don't want to eliminate choices in the reading section because they sound wrong (though that's what we do in the writing section), but rather because they're not supported by the passage or they don't make the sentence in a sentence completion problem sensible.

Lastly, precise marks enable you to work like a detective on a reading problem. Through gathering small clues you solve the problem even though when you just looked at the problem and read it, you had no idea what was right or wrong. Treat solving reading section problems like you would the investigation of a crime—accumulate clues as to what's right and what's wrong and then you have to follow the outcomes of those clues (i.e. pick the answer choice with the least cross–outs, least question marks, and most check marks).

Marks to make include:

Hard/Dark cross–out: word(s) or even a full answer choice that's definitely wrong. Push your pencil down a tad hard to make a dark mark to cross out these word(s)/answer choices.
Light cross–out: word(s) or even a full answer choice that you think is wrong but you're not absolutely sure. Push your pencil down lightly to make a light mark in these cases.
Check marks: next to word(s) or answer choice(s) that work or are particularly good.
Question marks: next to word(s) or an answer choice that doesn't quite make sense, but you can't say that it's wrong hence no light cross–out mark.

*Remember **if you eliminate at least one answer choice**, you **must** choose an answer and take a guess on that problem. The odds will be with you!*

As we tackle problems, these ideas will become clearer. As you do problems on your own and practice tests, you must practice using these techniques. It'll take a little time to learn them and a little discipline to implement them, but they're powerful and are the best guide we know of when combined with your intelligence to bring you consistently to the correct answers.

CRITICAL READING SECTION: Sentence Completion Problems

Overview

Our techniques for the sentence completion problems are powerful. They'll aid you significantly even when you don't know the meaning of multiple words in a sentence. You must combine these techniques with a lot of practice doing College Board practice tests so that you get a good sense of the degree of precision that they're seeking in correct answer choices.

There are multiple guidelines to keep in mind—general guidelines that are critical for all sentence completion problems and guidelines based on what type of question it is (e.g. double-blank versus single-blank questions). Three quick rules to keep in mind are:

Make Precise Pencil Marks to Preserve Your Thoughts on Paper

If you eliminate one word of a pair, cross out only that one word. Use light and dark marks to indicate relative degree of confidence in elimination.

Never Eliminate a Word Just Because You Don't Know What it Means.

Never cross out a word just because you don't know what it means. If you're not sure what it means but you think it's say a negative word when we need a positive word, put a question mark by that word. If you have no idea what a word means, leave it alone, make no mark.

Do Not Be Afraid to Pick Answers with Words You Don't Know.

Our techniques make you work detective–like, accumulating clues as to what may be right and what may be wrong. If all the other answer choices have something crossed out or question marks, and you're left with a choice with a word or words you don't know, you must pick it—that's where our logic has led you and you have to stick with it!

Three Key Methods to Find the Meaning of the Blanks

Identify Positive/Negative Blanks & Words.

Many blanks will have a positive or negative "charge"—the sense that some negative or some positive word is needed. Try to identify if the blanks in a question are positive or negative and identify them as such by writing a plus, minus, or equal sign in the blank (equal sign for neutral blanks—neither positive nor negative).

Once you've identified blanks as positive/negative/neutral, then you can eliminate words based on that criteria (e.g. negative words are eliminated for positive blanks). For words you're not sure of, try to use word roots to guess at their meaning or at least their "charge" e.g. a word beginning with the "mal–" prefix will very likely be a negative word so if the blank requires a positive word you could put a question mark by it (maybe even use a light cross out mark if it sounds quite negative).

Fill in Your Own Words.

Trying to fill in your own words or phrases in the blanks is another technique for identifying the meaning of the blanks. *Cover up the answer choices* before you try to fill in any words to avoid being biased by the words in the answer choices.

Don't worry about thinking of the perfect or most elegant word for each blank, just *pick a word or some group of words or even phrase(s) which effectively express the meaning you think the blank requires.*

Read the sentence to yourself carefully to make sure it makes sense. Eliminate words which are far away (in meaning) from your words. If a word is slightly away from your word or phrase but not terribly far away, you must keep that word or at most put a question mark next to it (only cross out or eliminate words that are far away). Cross out those words which are really far away from the meaning of the word you've chosen, but be careful particularly on a first pass about eliminating words which are at all close to your words. Put a check mark next to any words that are really close in meaning to the word you've picked. Remember, *this technique is used not so much to arrive at the correct answer, but to eliminate wrong answers.*

Identify/Underline Critical Words/Source of Meaning of the Blanks

Particularly for single blank questions, there is some word or group of words which together imply the meaning of the blank in question. The answer thus is generally a synonym or an antonym for that word or group of words. As you identify the word or words that impinge on the blank, draw arrows from them to the blank. Then you can fill in the blank with the word or words that are giving that blank a meaning as well as give the blank a charge (+/–). From there, eliminate your way to the correct answer.

Three Less Important but Still Helpful Strategies

Simplify the Sentence

If the sentence is a bit bulky, cross out unnecessary modifiers and prepositional phrases. This helps you perceive the meanings of the words in the blanks better and lets you read the sentence to yourself faster. Be careful not to cross out any words that may be crucial to the meanings of the words in the blanks.

Watch Out for Words that Reverse Meaning

Words such as however, but, though, et cetera reverse the meaning of a blank—so be very careful and cognizant of such words when you encounter them. It's a good idea to circle such words to make sure you don't forget about them.

If All Else Fails, Read Sentence with Answers Plugged in.

For all problems, you'll need to occasionally plug your own words or answer choices in and read the sentence to yourself to make sure it makes sense. It's a good idea to always plug in your answer into the sentence and read it to yourself once to be sure the sentence makes sense. For some problems, you may be at a loss to identify blanks as positive or negative and as to what the blanks could mean. In such cases, you may have no choice but to plug in the answer choices and see whether the sentence makes sense or not with those words. Still work by elimination—plug in all the choices and eliminate wrong answers. Use this approach only when nothing else is working as it requires too much time otherwise and isn't as effective as the other techniques.

The Nine–Fold Path for Sentence Completion Success

1. Make Precise Cross-Out and other Marks to preserve your thoughts on paper
2. Never Eliminate a word just because you don't know what it means.
3. Do not be afraid to pick answers with words you don't know if the others have been eliminated.
4. Identify Positive/Negative/Neutral Blanks & Words.
5. Cover Up the Answer Choices. Fill in Your Own Words.
6. Identify & Underline Critical Words or the Source of Meaning of the blanks
7. Simplify the Sentence
8. Watch Out for Words that Reverse Meaning
9. If all else fails, read the sentence with the answer choices plugged in.

Two Blank Question Strategies

Two Blank Questions: Eliminate Blank by Blank

Are two blank questions easier than single blank questions, and if so, why?

If you said yes and because there's twice as much to eliminate, you're exactly right. The more we have to eliminate, the better our approach works so rejoice when you see two–blank questions.

You should tackle these questions blank by blank: eliminate words via the first blank then move on to eliminating words via the second blank. After you've eliminated via each of the blanks, it's likely only one or two answer choices without anything marked out will remain (so the correct answer will be close at hand).

Let's solve some problems and see how our techniques work together to help us arrive at the correct answers. Notice that we tend to be conservative, particularly on a first pass. If we're not sure but we think a word doesn't work, we'll just put a question mark next to it. We're, particularly on our first pass, hesitant to cross anything out we're not pretty sure is really far off from the appropriate meaning.

Solved Problem 1

The Indian dish has an unmistakably ____ taste—from its bitterness, you can immediately ____ it even when it's prepared with honey and sugar.

(A) acrid ... consume
(B) tart ... expose
(C) delicious ... distinguish
(D) acerbic ... detect
(E) healthy ... apply

Let's assume that we've tried to fill in our own words into the blanks and couldn't think of anything. We have to move to a blank–by–blank analysis. The first blank has something to do with the taste of something. There's a critical word in the sentence which has to do with taste that tells us the meaning of the blank: 'bitterness.' The blank, thus, is related to 'bitterness' and is likely either a synonym or an antonym of 'bitterness.' In this case, there are no words that would imply an antonym is needed (words like however, though, but, etc.). Write in 'bitter' into the blank so we remember what the blank has to mean.

> The Indian dish has an unmistakably <u>bitter</u> taste—from its bitterness, you can immediately ____ it even when it's prepared with honey and sugar.

Let's eliminate words that are far away in meaning from bitter. 'Delicious' is pretty far away—hard cross out—and 'healthy' is also quite far away, hard cross out. I'm not sure what acrid and acerbic mean—so we have to leave them. 'Tart' means a bit bitter so let's put a check next to it.

Now we're left with:

    (A) acrid ... consume
    (B) tart √ ... expose
    (C) ~~delicious~~ ... distinguish
    (D) acerbic ... detect
    (E) ~~healthy~~ ... apply

We're already down to three choices—let's see what we can eliminate via the second blank. For the second blank, let's assume that we can't quite identify any words in the sentence that give it a meaning. We have to try plugging in answer choices. Cover up all the choices in the first blank while you're plugging in the second blank words. This prevents you from being biased by the first blank (e.g. you may have fallen in love with 'tart' for the first blank and thus may not be objective in analyzing its companion word, for tart's case 'expose'). Before we start plugging in, can we simplify the sentence? We can—the whole last part is essentially irrelevant to the meaning of the blank so we can cross it out which saves us from having to read it several times as we analyze the answer choices.

> The Indian dish has an unmistakably bitter taste—from its bitterness, you can immediately ____ it ~~even when it's prepared with honey and sugar.~~

For (A), plugging in 'consume' into the sentence, does the second half of the sentence make sense? It kind of makes sense—so we can't eliminate it. It doesn't sound particularly convincing, though, so let's put a question mark by it. What about 'expose' in (B)? '...you can immediately expose it.' Expose doesn't make sense—dark cross out. We're running a bit low on time since we have to plug in the second answer choice directly into the sentence, let's skip (C) and (E) for now and tackle (D)'s 'detect'. Does 'detect' make sense? '...you can immediately detect it...' sounds decent to good—let's leave it.

Now we're left with:

    (A) acrid ... consume ?
    (B) tart √ ... ~~expose~~
    (C) ~~delicious~~ ... distinguish
    (D) acerbic ... detect
    (E) ~~healthy~~ ... apply

We're running out of time. We're down to (A) and to (D). The *no marks* of (D) beats *the single question mark* of (A) so we *have* to choose (D). Pick (D) and move on. Is (D) correct? Indeed, it is! We didn't know the meaning of the first words in either (A) or (D), but with the analysis that 'consume' was an awkward choice for the second blank, we were able to narrow it down to (D)...and that was enough (after the choices were eliminated) to solve the problem!

Our methods for tackling sentence complete problems are quite powerful—with practice you'll be able to use our methods to solve many problems reliably that at first glance look quite difficult with multiple, unfamiliar words in the answer choices.

Solved Problem 2

> Never _____ even when their work didn't sell demonstrated the artists' _____: they were determined and could not be deterred from realizing their ideas.
>
> (A) happy ... kindness
> (B) relaxed ... single–mindedness
> (C) discouraged ... malleability
> (D) daunted ... superfluousness
> (E) disappointed ... indomitability

After reading the sentence, you hopefully have the intuition that both blanks are positive words—the second half of the sentence particularly clues us in. There are two key phrases that give us the meaning of the blanks: 'determined' and 'could not be deterred.' 'Could not be deterred' corresponds well to 'never ____' in that both are negation followed by a word, so let's put 'deterred' into the first blank. The second blank, then, we can fill with a noun form of 'determined'; let's use determination.

Here's our sentence with our words, read it to yourself to be sure it makes sense. It doesn't have to read like a sentence out of Shakespeare, but the words you've chosen have to make sense! We've also written in plus signs to indicate we've identified that positive words have to go in each blank.

> Never +, *deterred* even when their work didn't sell demonstrated the artists' +, *determination*: they were determined and could not be deterred from realizing their work.

If you've read the sentence again, you should've noticed a problem. The first blank, deterred, is not actually a positive word. It feels positive since it's not deterred, but actually the blank requires a negative word (like deterred)! Be on watch for words like never, hardly, not, etc. which change the meaning of a blank. Here's the corrected sentence:

> Never −, *deterred* even when their work didn't sell demonstrated the artists' +, *determination*: they were determined and could not be deterred from realizing their work.

Now we eliminate blank by blank. First, eliminate words from the first blank that are either neutral, positive or far away from 'deterred.' Happy and relaxed are positive—hard cross outs. I'm not sure what daunted means—leave it. Discouraged and disappointed are both pretty close to deterred—let's check them.

(A) ~~happy~~ ... kindness
(B) ~~relaxed~~ ... single–mindedness
(C) discouraged √ ... malleability
(D) daunted ... superfluousness
(E) disappointed √ ... indomitability

On to the second blank, we can eliminate negative words, neutral words, and words far, far away from 'determination.' I'm not sure what indomitability and malleability mean—leave them. Superfluousness is a negative word—strong cross out. Kindness is far away from 'determination': light cross out. Single–mindedness is a good synonym for determination: check.

We're now left with:

    (A) ~~happy~~ ... ~~kindness~~
    (B) ~~relaxed~~ ... single–mindedness √
    (C) discouraged √ ... malleability
    (D) daunted ... ~~superfluousness~~
    (E) disappointed √ ... indomitability

We're down to two choices but they're both tied with a single check each. You have to take a guess by picking one and moving on. If you had a bit of time, you could try using word roots or other words to analyze 'malleability' and 'indomitability' to try to determine if either has a good chance of being a negative and thus wrong, or positive and thus right.

Guessing, we've got a 50/50 shot at it which is pretty good. If you were lucky, you would've guessed (E) which is correct. Malleability means flexibility and thus makes (C) incorrect. Notice that if we had crossed out words we didn't know like 'malleability' and 'indomitability', we would certainly have gotten the problem incorrect.

Solved Problem 3

    While I didn't end my friendship with her, I immediately _____ direct communication and only sent messages to her through _____.

    (A) processed ... entities
    (B) stopped ... competitors
    (C) allowed ... agents
    (D) began ... acquaintances
    (E) ceased ... intermediaries

Let's try to figure out the meanings of the blanks. A key word in the sentence is 'while.' It indicates in this case that the person did something negative with respect to her friend. Now that we know the first blank is negative, the next step is to cover up the blanks and try to fill in our own words. For the first blank, 'didn't keep having' makes sense and is milder than end—it doesn't sound that great (it's a bit wordy) but that doesn't matter. When you fill in your own words, you have to just be certain your word, words or phrase express the correct meaning that's intended for the blank. For the second blank, 'others' works well as it indicates that she's put some distance between her and her friend. So we've got:

> While I didn't end my friendship with her, I immediately —, *didn't keep having* direct communication and only sent messages to her through *others*.

Let's eliminate choices for the first blank. We have to cross out any word that's really far away from 'didn't keep having'. Processed is pretty far away—light cross out. Stopped is a better way of saying 'didn't keep having'—check it! Allowed is the opposite of 'didn't keep having' and began is also very far away—hard cross outs. Ceased is another word for 'didn't keep having'—check it.

    (A) ~~processed~~ ... entities
    (B) stopped √ ... competitors
    (C) ~~allowed~~ ... agents
    (D) ~~began~~ ... acquaintances
    (E) ceased √ ... intermediaries

Let's assume we're running low on time. We'll only evaluate (B) and (E) then. Is either competitors or intermediaries far away from others? Competitors is somewhat far away and doesn't quite make sense in the sentence—question mark. Intermediaries is a better word for others as it indicates other people who are relaying messages for me—check!

(A) ~~processed~~ ... entities
(B) stopped √ ... competitors ?
(C) ~~allowed~~ ... agents
(D) ~~began~~ ... acquaintances
(E) ceased √ ... intermediaries √

Two checks beats a check and a question mark. We have to pick (E), and (E) is correct.

Solved Problem 4

Studying computer science was the most popular major for seven years, but the ____ job market for programmers ____ new batches of students from studying it.

(A) burgeoning ... encouraged
(B) weak ... promoted
(C) collapsing ... dissuaded
(D) impressive ... prevented
(E) static ... supplemented

Let's try to fill in our own words. The word 'but' signals to us that the second half of the sentence is negative (as opposed to the first clause in which studying computer science had been 'popular', a positive characteristic). We, because of 'but', know that the second half of the sentence has to indicate something negative. What's something negative that can happen to a job market? Cover up the answer choices before you take a guess (to prevent them from influencing you). A *declining* or *shrinking* job market is a bad thing—not a market we want to be in. Let's write them in the first blank. What word, then, works in the second blank—we already thought that we wouldn't want to be in a declining job market. The students then would be *deterred* from studying computer science by the poor job market. Let's write deterred in as well.

We've got:

> Studying computer science was the most popular major for seven years, but the _–, declining, shrinking_ job market for programmers _–, deterred_ new batches of students from studying it.

Let's eliminate choices blank by blank. Eliminate any positive or neutral words in the first blank. Impressive is positive—strong cross out. Static is neutral—light cross out. I'm not sure what burgeoning means—leave it. Weak and collapsing are negative and fairly close to declining or shrinking: checks.

> (A) burgeoning ... encouraged
> (B) weak √ ... promoted
> (C) collapsing √ ... dissuaded
> (D) ~~impressive~~ ... prevented
> (E) ~~static~~ ... supplemented

Let's eliminate second blank choices (eliminate anything positive or neutral). Encouraged, promoted and supplemented are all positive: strong cross outs. Leave dissuaded and prevented which are both negative words.

> (A) burgeoning ... ~~encouraged~~
> (B) weak √ ... ~~promoted~~
> (C) collapsing √ ... dissuaded
> (D) ~~impressive~~ ... prevented
> (E) ~~static~~ ... ~~supplemented~~

(C) is the only choice without anything crossed out—we have to pick it....and (C) is indeed correct. Notice we put charges in the blanks (negative) as well as filled in our words to be certain we were eliminating correctly.

Use multiple techniques together on a problem to help you solve problems! The accumulation of small insights into the sentence and answer choices methodically guided us to the correct answer!!!

Two Blank Questions: Synonym or Antonym Elimination

For some double–blank questions, you may be able to identify that the two blanks must be synonyms in which case both words have to be either positive or negative (+ + or – – for both blanks), or that they're antonyms (+ – or – + for both blanks), or that they're unrelated (both blanks can not be synonyms nor antonyms).

If you can identify that the words in the blanks have to be synonyms or antonyms, you can use that knowledge to eliminate answer choices. Thus, if you know the words have to be antonyms, you can eliminate any answer choices that have pairs of words with a mostly synonymous or unrelated relationship.

When you eliminate words this way, you're essentially eliminating the words as a pair. *Make an appropriate pencil mark that represents the idea that you eliminated the words as a pair: a straight line that goes through both words.* If you cross out one then the other word, you won't know if you eliminated each word blank by blank or if you eliminated both words as a pair.

Solved Problem 1

Auto accidents kill thousands every month and despite the new laws designed to ____ defensive driving education, the number of monthly fatalities is ____.

(A) curb ... growing
(B) reduce ... relenting
(C) shrink ... abating
(D) promote ... mushrooming
(E) identify ... debilitating

From 'despite', we know that the two blanks are related to each other—either synonyms or antonyms. We also know that each blank is a word like increase or decrease. Plugging in increase in the first blank, we can also figure out that increase needs to go in the second blank as well—despite increasing education, fatalities are increasing. That makes sense. The blanks have to be synonyms—we can eliminate any answer choices as a pair if they're either antonyms or unrelated. When you eliminate an answer choice as a pair, cross the whole answer choice out (so you'll be able to figure out why you eliminated it if you ever re–analyze the problem).

(A) is a pair of antonyms—dark cross out. (B) are synonyms—check. (C) are also synonyms—check. (D) are synonyms—check. (E) are unrelated—light cross out.

(A) ~~curb ... growing~~
(B) reduce ... relenting √
(C) shrink ... abating √
(D) promote ... mushrooming √
(E) ~~identify ... debilitating~~

We're left with three pairs of synonyms. There's one small shortcut we could use to eliminate two answer choices. *It's impossible for there to be two correct answer choices—so if two choices are saying the same thing, they both have to be wrong since they both can't be right.* In this case, both (B) and (C) are synonyms of negative words...since there can't be two right answers, both (B) and (C) have to be wrong.

We're then left with (D) which happens to have words quite close to our own word (increase) for the blanks. Let's plug (D) into the sentence to see if it makes sense. Would the government promote education—that makes sense. And despite promoting driving education, fatalities are mushrooming—that's correct as well because of the critical word 'despite'. (D) is thus correct.

Hard Two Blank Questions: Eliminate two easy words.

If it's the last or second to last sentence completion question and it's a double–blank question, the answer is very likely not going to be two easy words. You can then eliminate double-easy words in an answer choice in a hard double-blank question, but still do double–check the easy words to see if they in fact make any sense in the sentence.

We don't recommend this technique for single blank questions because often an easy word will have a secondary or tertiary meaning which is being used in a difficult question (and thus must be carefully considered).

So if you're down to a few answer choices for a hard two blank question and you're stuck, eliminate a choice if it has two easy words.

Single Blank Question Strategies

Key Strategy: Identify the Meaning of the Blank within the Sentence

For single blank questions, identifying the meaning of the blank via words and phrases in the sentence is the essential strategy. You can almost always identify the meaning of the blank that way. The problem then becomes to figure out which word in the answer choices has that meaning. Use your knowledge of the degree of precision required by the College Board in sentence completion questions and elimination to identify the correct answer choice.

Let's see how our techniques work together to help us solve single–blank questions.

Solved Problem 1

The purpose of the boar's digging was ____, though he was digging fervently we could not identify why.

(A) immeasurable
(B) inscrutable
(C) visible
(D) discernible
(E) salubrious

Let's assume we couldn't come up with our own word or words for the blank. It's a single blank question, and the critical method for those problems *is identifying the words in the problem that determine the meaning of the blank.* Let's underline (you can also circle) the words that give us the meaning of the blank for this problem.

> The purpose of the boar's digging was _____, though he was digging fervently we <u>could not identify why</u>.

'Could not identify why' is the meaning of the blank—so we need a word that means that; the simplest and most obvious word to use is unidentifiable. That works. Can we assign a +/–/neutral value to 'unidentifiable'? It's more neutral, maybe slightly negative (we'll use an = sign to represent neutral). We can, thus, eliminate any choices that are strongly negative or positive—as well as any words that are far away from unidentifiable.

> The purpose of the boar's digging was *unidentifiable, =*, though he was digging fervently we <u>could not identify why</u>.

None of the answer choices are strongly negative or positive so I can't eliminate any that way. Immeasurable is not too far away from unidentifiable so I can't eliminate it. Visible and discernible mean essentially identifiable—hence they're antonyms of unidentifiable and can be eliminated—dark cross outs. I'm not sure what inscrutable and salubrious mean, so I have to leave them.

We're left with:

(A) immeasurable
(B) inscrutable
(C) ~~visible~~
(D) ~~discernible~~
(E) salubrious

We're down to three choices of which I know the meaning of just one. Let's first tackle the choice I know the meaning of, (A) immeasurable. Does immeasurable work in the sentence to the degree of precision that the College Board usually requires? 'The purpose of the boar's digging was *immeasurable*' sounds a bit strange as we don't usually measure a purpose...so we can eliminate it.

(A) ~~immeasurable~~
(B) inscrutable
(C) ~~visible~~
(D) ~~discernible~~
(E) salubrious

We're left with (B) and (E) whose words we don't know the meaning of. Let's see if we can analyze the words and try to assign a slightly positive or negative charge to either of them. Since unidentifiable has a slightly negative to neutral sense, does either choice seem positive? If so, I can put a question mark next to it—I can't cross out either (B) or (E) since I'm not sure what either means. Salubrious sounds a little positive—let's put a question mark by it.

(A) immeasurable
(B) inscrutable
(C) ~~visible~~
(D) ~~discernible~~
(E) salubrious ?

Let's try to break down inscrutable and see if we can analyze it further. Inscrutable, through breaking down the word, means not scrutable. Could scrutable mean identifiable? Perhaps—that seems plausible. That's a slight plus for choice (B) and we already have a slight negative for (E), so choice (B) beats choice (E). We have to pick (B), and (B) is, lucky for us, correct.

The key to solving this problem was identifying as much as we could about the blank and using those details to eliminate choices. This problem would be the hardest sentence completion question in a section so being left with two hard words is a likely outcome and even taking a blind guess between the two would've been pretty good. In this case, we did a bit more sleuthing by analyzing the words' meanings and charge (negative, positive, neutral) and were left with the correct choice.

Solved Problem 2

> After his defeat in the debate, the politician was obsessed with making _____, retaliatory accusations against his opponents.
>
> (A) reparations
> (B) lucubrations
> (C) jeremiads
> (D) diatribes
> (E) solicitations

This is another hard problem. It's a single blank problem—so let's identify the phrase or words which give the blank meaning.

> After his defeat in the debate, the politician was obsessed with making _____, <u>retaliatory accusations</u> against his opponents.

Retaliatory accusations is strongly negative—so let's fill in the blank with a negative sign.

> After his defeat in the debate, the politician was obsessed with making _−_ , <u>retaliatory accusations</u> against his opponents.

Now, we have to eliminate choices that are neutral, positive or far away from retaliatory accusations in meaning. Reparations and solicitations are neutral to positive words—strong cross out. I'm not sure what lucubration or jeremiad means—leave them. A diatribe is a kind of speech which attacks someone or something—that's pretty close to retaliatory accusations—check it with a small check mark since a diatribe doesn't necessarily contain accusations.

> (A) ~~reparations~~
> (B) lucubrations
> (C) jeremiads
> (D) diatribes √
> (E) ~~solicitations~~

We're left with three choices now. Let's try to analyze (B) and (C) to see if I can eliminate one or both of them. Does either sound positive or negative? It's hard to say—so we have to leave them. Can we break either word into its roots? 'Luc' may be from Latin meaning light—so lucubrations may have something to do with bringing light to something. Bringing light is pretty far away from retaliatory accusations—let's put a question mark next to lucubrations.

    (A) ~~reparations~~
    (B) lucubrations ?
    (C) jeremiads
    (D) diatribes √
    (E) ~~solicitations~~

We're left with nothing for (C) and a small check for (D). We know that diatribe means a very negative attack or denunciation which is quite close but doesn't quite mean retaliatory accusation. A word that means retaliatory accusation is recrimination—unfortunately it's not one of our answer choices. Is diatribes close enough that we should pick it, or is it sufficiently imprecise that we need to pick jeremiads? In this case, very negative attacks have a strongly accusatory sense—so diatribes is quite close and we should pick it. Moreover, a check beats the question mark and the blank so we had to pick (D). The correct choice is in fact (D).

On the test, the best word for the blank may not be one of your answer choices—as in this problem. You have to pick the most appropriate choice among the five answer choices—which will still be very close in meaning to the best word you may have independently found. As you take College Board prepared practice SAT tests (in their book), you'll get a good sense of the level of precision needed for an answer choice to be correct.

Solved Problem 3

> The announcement of the election results that he had lost badly was such a disappointing ____ that he broke into tears.
>
> (A) outcome
> (B) affront
> (C) ruse
> (D) appraisal
> (E) assessment

Using our fundamental single blank technique of identifying the words which give the blank meaning, it's not clear what words in the sentence give meaning to the blank. It seems like putting in 'announcement' itself works. Try reading the sentence with announcement in the blank: it does work. So the blank gets its meaning from the subject of the sentence, 'announcement' and the blank means some kind of announcement, probably a negative announcement.

We can also simplify the sentence a little bit by crossing out the prepositional phrase 'of the election results' and the following dependent clause 'that he had lost badly.'

> The <u>announcement</u> ~~of the election results~~ ~~that he had lost badly~~ was such a disappointing *announcement* that he broke into tears.

Let's eliminate words which are far away from 'announcement.' Outcome is different from announcement, but still reasonably close, keep it. I'm not sure what affront and ruse mean, leave them. Appraisal and assessment aren't that far away from announcement as well, leave them. We unfortunately haven't made any progress—we haven't been able to make any marks by any answer choices!

(A) outcome
(B) affront
(C) ruse
(D) appraisal
(E) assessment

Let's try plugging the words we know ((A), (D), and (E)) into the sentence and see if any make sense—using the sentence as we simplified it won't take much time to test each choice. Outcome sounds great—two checks. Appraisal isn't bad but not great—small check. Assessment is also not great but not bad—small check. We've now got:

(A) outcome √√
(B) affront
(C) ruse
(D) appraisal √
(E) assessment √

Notice that we're getting sophisticated in how well tuned our assessment of the answer choices is—we're now using varying sizes and numbers of check marks to accurately reflect our analysis! In this case, the two big checks is strongly affirmative; we have to pick (A). It beats out (D) and (E), and it's unlikely that (B) or (C) would be a better choice even though we don't know what they mean. If this were the hardest problem in the section (the last problem), then we'd have to be a bit more circumspect before choosing (A) as it's slightly less likely that an easier word like 'outcome' would be the correct answer of the hardest problem in a section. In this case, though, (A) is correct.

Practice, Practice, Practice

We hope that reading through the solved problems has given you a good idea of how to implement our ideas and techniques for sentence completion problems, and how to think through and approach these problems. Our methods are very powerful—for many problems, we didn't know multiple words in the answer choices but still managed to answer the problems correctly.

The first time you try to use these techniques for Sentence Completion problems on your own it may take you a relatively long time but with practice these techniques become second-nature and can be applied quickly. Practice using these techniques and you'll solve problems quickly, efficiently and more accurately. Questions that looked hopeless previously you'll be able to get correct.

Speaking of practice...let's start now!

Critical Reading Section: Sentence Completion Problem Sets

Practice our sentence completion techniques with the problems below. Feel free to look back at our techniques and solved problems to model your own work, approach and thinking process.

Answers are in Appendix 1 on page 436.

Single-Blank Questions

1. The new German words were ___, joined together from other words and roots.

    (A) concatenated
    (B) opinionated
    (C) fragmented
    (D) garnished
    (E) expressed

2. Boris began his service with a ____ act, graciously rebuilding the burnt–down home of one of his parishioners.

    (A) lengthy
    (B) benevolent
    (C) hostile
    (D) indolent
    (E) personal

3. Passing the bill was ____; it immediately ended the debates on alternative courses of action.

    (A) extralegal
    (B) political
    (C) peremptory
    (D) fulfilling
    (E) erratic

4. Her hair was so ____ that it reflected enough light back to the camera to obscure her face.

    (A) exposed
    (B) long
    (C) refined
    (D) lustrous
    (E) deprived

5. Because of the reported dangers, he prepared for what he expected would be a _____ journey.

   (A) modest
   (B) inspirational
   (C) intrusive ?
   (D) provocative ?
   (E) treacherous

6. The peace activists were _____ by the public, denigrated for refuting the war mongers' reasons for starting a new war.

   (A) pilloried ?✓
   (B) celebrated
   (C) disclosed
   (D) isolated ✓
   (E) delegated ✓

7. Keep churning the mixture until it's _____ , of the same consistency and appearance.

   (A) similar ✓ ✗
   (B) homogenous ?✓
   (C) iridescent ?
   (D) discrete ?
   (E) visible ✓

8. Everyone wept a great deal and felt terribly sad at the ____ event.

    (A) incompatible
    (B) vicarious
    (C) lugubrious
    (D) reticent
    (E) indelible

9. Delivering a concession speech and admitting defeat was such an ____ proposition that the candidate refused for hours to give it.

    (A) appealing
    (B) affirmative
    (C) earnest
    (D) unsavory
    (E) apathetic

10. Eager to regain a simple life without the burdens of governing the nation, the ruler was apt to ____ and relieve himself of his powers.

    (A) regress
    (B) denounce
    (C) surmise
    (D) divulge
    (E) abdicate

Double–Blank Questions.

Be sure to follow our techniques, carefully making precise pencil marks. Feel free to look back at our techniques and at solved problems to model your own work and thinking.

Answers are in Appendix 1 on page 437.

11. At times ____ reigned supreme, and at times it was ____; but always the pageant was imposing.

    (A) gaiety .. sadness
    (B) happiness .. joy
    (C) fear .. inquietude
    (D) truth .. falsehood
    (E) kings .. queens

12. Although the sculpture was begun in an ____ manner, it wasn't until ten years later that it was ready for ____.

    (A) enthusiastic .. appropriation
    (B) indifferent .. display
    (C) interesting .. novelty
    (D) energetic .. exhibition
    (E) ornate .. casting

13. There was ____ in the air, but the queen ____ continued her normal activities mainly managing the construction of a new fountain at the palace.

    (A) revolution .. fearfully
    (B) comfort .. proudly
    (C) danger .. carefully
    (D) insurrection .. indifferently
    (E) extravagance .. cheerfully

14. Napoleon ____, but finally ____ the building plan which gladdened the architect.

    (A) deferred .. denied
    (B) lauded .. affirmed
    (C) hesitated .. approved
    (D) supported .. retracted
    (E) consented .. regretted

15. Amid all this ____ there is, however, an undeniable, ____ charm

    (A) disarray .. unpalatable
    (B) beauty .. attractive
    (C) ugliness .. impulsive
    (D) ingratitude .. immune
    (E) disorder .. inexplicable

16. The unattractive Bertha ____ her critics with the statement that since her company ____ the emperor there was nothing more to be said.

    (A) aggravated .. feared
    (B) silenced .. pleased
    (C) taunted .. supported
    (D) persuaded .. restrained
    (E) gladdened .. delighted

17. The slightest ____ would ____ him, rendering him visibly irritated and saddened.

    (A) recognition .. encourage
    (B) praise .. irritate
    (C) criticism .. strengthen
    (D) error .. infuriate
    (E) reproach .. unnerve

18. With the many ____ from her fans, she was ____ to make a sequel to her hit film.

    (A) opinions .. criticized
    (B) entreaties .. coaxed
    (C) threats .. induced
    (D) requests .. prepared
    (E) fears .. dissuaded

19. Threes of ____ from its neighbor ____ the country into giving up its land and resources to the invaders.

    (A) criticism .. influenced
    (B) resignation .. soothed
    (C) obliteration .. cowed
    (D) boons .. terrified
    (E) alarm .. alerted

20. Our ____ concern as educators is for the ____ of our students' intellectual and moral capacities.

    (A) paramount .. advancement
    (B) benign .. perversion
    (C) critical .. fulfillment
    (D) foremost .. suppression
    (E) trivial .. edification

Vocabulary Building

The techniques that you now know are very powerful and when you practice them, you'll find yourself getting many problems right without knowing all of the words in them. We thus don't recommend most students spend a lot of time trying to memorize or learn a lot of new vocabulary words. We rather have two recommendations for all our students which are 1. to make a brief study of some key word roots which can help you guess at the meaning of unfamiliar words (Appendix 3 has a list of them) and 2. to have good vocabulary building habits in general (always write down and look up unfamiliar words you encounter).

Word Roots

We highly recommend studying the word roots list in Appendix 3. You'll enjoy learning more about the origins of the words you use regularly, and you'll have some valuable tools for guessing the meaning of unfamiliar words. Moreover, learning a few roots can help you learn many, many words—so you get a pretty good return on your effort. Making index cards of the roots and studying them in the context of words you already know will help you learn them pretty quickly.

Good Vocabulary Building Habits for Life

You're at an age where *you're building the vocabulary you'll use your whole life*. Try to build it up as much as you can by learning new words and assimilating them into your working vocabulary.

Develop good habits. Anytime you encounter a word you don't know, write it down, look it up and start using the word that day and henceforth in your working vocabulary. Write new words down somewhere and come back to them—you have to use and encounter a word several times before you really "learn" it.

A few ideas for learning and remembering new words are (no need to use just one of them, try using two, three or all four in conjunction to learn new words!):

1. **Homophones.** Think of similar–sounding words and phrases and relate them to the new word. For example, for remonstrate which means to say or plead in protest or disapproval, you could try to remember *remonstrations at the demonstrations*
2. **Think of a Picture.** Think of a picture, something memorable so preferably kind of crazy or funny, for each new word. For example, for perfidious which means treacherous or deceitful, imagine the word hideous with perforations or holes in it (perf–hideous is kind of how perfidious is pronounced, and holes or perforations in the word hideous can represent hiding or obscuring e.g. treachery).
3. **Learn Words in Groups.** You can learn related words in groups; this helps you get a sense of how to use different words and a better grasp on the precise meaning of words. For example, it can help you learn whether a word has a pejorative (negative) or positive or neutral connotation. For example, both erudite and pedantic basically meaning bookish; they have a very similar meaning in terms of their literal content. Erudite, though, has a positive connotation, it's a good thing to be called (and thus means learned, well–read), while pedantic has a pejorative connotation, it's an insult to be called pedantic (meaning more by–the–book in such a way as to be semi brain–dead). Learning words in groups helps you keep track of what sort of connotation different words have and how to use them precisely.
4. **Index Cards.** Write words on index cards with the words on the front and their definitions on the back. The action of flipping the cards will help you learn better than just staring at a sheet of paper (particularly for kinesthetic learners). It's easy to carry around index cards, and you can flip through the cards giving yourself a quick quiz anytime you have five or ten minutes free.

Sentence Completion Recapitulation

Practice our sentence completion methods and techniques, they're very powerful as we've seen from the solved problems in this section! Here they are in summary form:

The Nine–Fold Path for Sentence Completion Success

1. Make precise pencil marks to preserve your thought on paper

2. Never eliminate a word just because you don't know what it means.

3. Do not be afraid to pick answers with words you don't know if the others have been eliminated.

4. Identify Positive/Negative Blanks & Words.

5. Cover Up the Answer Choices. Fill in Your Own Words.

6. Identify/Underline Critical Words/Source of Meaning of the blanks

7. Simplify the Sentence

8. Watch out for words that reverse meaning

9. If nothing else is working, read the sentence with each of the answer choices plugged in.

Single–Blank Questions

- ✓ **Identify the Source of Meaning of the Blank (circle it and draw a line from it to the blank)**

Double–Blank Questions.

- ✓ **Solve Blank by Blank (eliminate answer choices based on the first blank then the second blank).**

- ✓ **For Hard Double–Blank Questions, Eliminate Answer Choices with Two Easy Words**

- ✓ **Eliminate Answer Choice(s) as a Pair Based on Synonyms / Antonyms / No Relationship.**

CRITICAL READING SECTION: Reading Passages

Elimination and Precision: Two Fundamental Techniques.

The same two ideas we use to tackle sentence completion problems we also use for reading passage problems: elimination and precision. The idea of precision is that the answer that requires the least effort or the least imagination to be made true by the passage is the correct answer.

For reading passage problems, precision also encompasses the idea that every word counts. Every word in the answer choice must be given meaning—every word or phrase in the answer choice must be made true by the reading passage.

Any word or phrase that isn't supported by the passage must be crossed out (by you!). For any answer choice or some part of an answer choice which isn't supported by the passage or is outside the scope of the passage, cross out just that word or words that make that answer choice incorrect. If you're not sure, make a light pencil mark.

You'll learn the twin methods of precision+elimination by using them. Below are two solved problems to illustrate how to use precision+elimination and how they provide a framework for thinking about critical reading questions.

Solved Problem 1

It is a very difficult matter to tell how men came to know anything of iron, and the art of employing it. We are not to suppose that they should of themselves think of digging it out of the mines, and preparing it for fusion, before they knew what could be the result of
5 such a process. On the other hand, there is less reason to attribute this discovery to any accidental fire, as mines are formed nowhere but in dry and barren places, and such as are bare of trees and plants, so that it looks as if nature had taken pains to keep from us this secret. Nothing therefore remains but the extraordinary
10 circumstance of some volcano, which, belching forth metallic substances ready fused, might have given the spectators a notion of imitating that operation of nature.

According to the author, what was most likely responsible for the initial human experiments with iron

(A) the successful, previous imitation of natural phenomena
(B) finding readily fused iron near a volcano
(C) an accidental fire
(D) discovering iron underground
(E) knowing that iron could be useful for making machines

Elimination is our key method for solving reading problems. Let's see if there's anything we can eliminate in each answer choice.

Choice (A) is the most common wrong answer: outside the scope of the essay. Nowhere in the passage does it mention any previous, successful imitation of natural phenomena. We'll strongly cross out "successful, previous" since that's the part of the choice that's wrong and write O.S. (outside the scope of the essay) to the right of it. Choice (E) is also outside the scope of the essay. Nowhere in the essay does it discuss the uses of iron. Let's strongly cross out "machines" and write in O.S.

(A) the ~~successful, previous~~ imitation of natural phenomena   O.S.
(B) finding readily fused iron near a volcano
(C) an accidental fire
(D) discovering iron underground
(E) knowing that iron could be useful for making ~~machines~~   O.S.

(B) has support in the essay in line 10—a volcano may belch forth iron already fused which may give humans (spectators in line 11) the idea to imitate that idea. Finding fused iron thus could've been responsible for the initial human experiments with iron. If we wanted to take the author literally, finding iron may not be sufficient, humans may have needed to be witness to the volcano itself. Still, (B) is close enough that we have to keep it, and it's actually sufficiently supported by the text to warrant a check.

(C) is repudiated in the passage. In lines 5–6, the author directly writes "there is less reason to attribute this discovery to any accidental fire." Thus, we can eliminate (C) as being a likely cause of the human discovery of iron working—strong cross out.

(D) is also repudiated in the passage directly in lines 3–4 where the author writes that "we are not to suppose that they [early human beings] should of themselves think of digging it out of the mines." In other words, the author considers it highly unlikely human beings would've had some idea to start digging for iron on their own without any other influence. Strong cross out.

(A) the ~~successful, previous~~ imitation of natural phenomena   O.S.
(B) finding readily fused iron near a volcano √
(C) ~~an accidental fire~~
(D) ~~discovering iron underground~~
(E) knowing that iron could be ~~useful for making machines~~   O.S.

We have to pick (B)—the four other choices have something strongly crossed out in them. Though (B) wasn't perfect as we analyzed, it's the closest to what the author believes and most importantly, has nothing wrong in it. The other four choices have something in them that based on the passage is incorrect. We, thus, have to pick (B) and (B) is correct.

It's very important to notice that (A) in some ways contains more plainly the main idea of the author that humans got the idea for how to work iron by imitating a natural phenomenon, namely the expulsion of iron from a volcano. The problem with (A), though, is that it cites something that isn't discussed at all by the author—the previous imitation of nature. Thus, there is an aspect to (A) which reflects the author's idea, but if any small part of an answer is wrong (in this case, the part refers to something outside the scope of the essay), that whole answer is wrong. That's the nature of precision in reading comprehension problems.

Solved Problem 2

It is a very difficult matter to tell how men came to know anything of iron, and the art of employing it. We are not to suppose that they should of themselves think of digging it out of the mines, and preparing it for fusion, before they knew what could be the result of
5   such a process. On the other hand, there is less reason to attribute this discovery to any accidental fire, as mines are formed nowhere but in dry and barren places, and such as are bare of trees and plants, so that it looks as if nature had taken pains to keep from us this secret. Nothing therefore remains but the extraordinary
10 circumstance of some volcano, which, belching forth metallic substances ready fused, might have given the spectators a notion of imitating that operation of nature.

The author cites that "nature had taken pains to keep from us this secret" to make the point that:

(A) it was too expensive to advance metallurgy
(B) previous discoveries of iron had been purposefully hidden
(C) the search for knowledge of iron–working had excluded natural phenomena
(D) it would only be by accident that one would get the idea to employ and work iron
(E) iron was hidden underground

There's no mention of the expenses of developing metallurgy—cross out "expensive" in (A). There's no mention of any "previous discoveries of iron." Also, there's no mention of anyone purposefully hiding anything—the author writes that it looks as though nature tried to hide the secret from humans, but it's too big a leap to interpret nature as being able to "purposefully" hide anything. We can, then, cross out "purposefully" as well as "previous discoveries of iron" in (B). There's no mention of any previous searches for knowledge of iron–working— let's cross out "search for knowledge" in (C). Choices (D) and (E) are both supported by the passage; let's leave them for now. We're left with:

(A) it was too ~~expensive~~ to advance metallurgy
(B) ~~previous discoveries of iron~~ had been ~~purposefully~~ hidden
(C) the ~~search for knowledge~~ of iron–working had excluded natural phenomenon
(D) it would only be by accident that one would get the idea to employ and work iron
(E) iron was hidden underground

Which of the choices, (D) or (E), best coheres with the author writing that "nature had taken pains to keep from us this secret [of iron making]?" If it was only by accident that one could get the idea of how to work with iron, then that knowledge would seem to be hidden: check (D). If iron was hidden underground, that would seem like

69

nature had kept that secret from us well–hidden. Let's check (E). We're still stuck with (D) and (E) both having checks! If you were in a rush, take a guess and pick one of them and move on.

Assuming we have time, we have to now ask ourselves which of the choices (D) or (E) is best supported by the passage as why it would seem that nature has hidden knowledge of iron from us. Is it the fact of iron being underground the key knowledge that's hidden from us? No. According to the author the key knowledge humans lacked was that iron exists and how to work with iron not so much where it is. Thus, the most important knowledge is to be gleaned by the accident of seeing forged iron come out of a volcano (or more safely recovering forged iron from a recent volcanic explosion). From there, humans would learn how to work iron (extreme heat) as well as what iron was (an extremely hard substance). The author doesn't discuss whether getting the thought to dig for iron is particularly hidden or not—but we might infer that it isn't assuming that the hardest step was being witness to forged iron being belched from a volcano. The correct answer is thus (D). Notice how closely we stuck to the text of the passage! Stick as close to the text of the passage as possible—for both elimination and affirmation of answers.

Solved Problem 3

I conceive of two species of inequality among men; one which I call natural, or physical inequality, because it is established by nature, and consists in the difference of age, health, bodily strength, and the qualities of the mind, or of the soul; the other which may be
5   termed moral, or political inequality, because it depends on a kind of convention, and is established, or at least authorized, by the common consent of mankind. This species of inequality consists in the different privileges, which some men enjoy, to the prejudice of others, such as that of being richer, more honored, more powerful,
10 and even that of exacting obedience from them.

What pair of terms best describes the origin of each of the species of inequality?

(A) health and moral
(B) inherited and environmental
(C) from chance and earned
(D) natural and artificial
(E) inborn and societal

This is a bit of a big picture question—it assumes we've understood the critical idea of the passage. Let's use our idea of precision to see what we can eliminate. From the passage, keep in mind that the first species of inequality is "natural or physical...because it is established by nature" and the second species is "moral or political...because it is...authorized by the common consent of mankind."

For choice (A), moral describes the second species of inequality well since it's one of the author's key terms for it along with political (in line 5), but health describes only one aspect of the first species. Let's check moral and put a question mark by health.

Choice (B) has the problem that both inherited and environmental describe the first type of inequality, natural or physical inequality. One could stretch environmental to perhaps mean the political environment—but that's a bit of a stretch. Let's put a question mark by (B).

From chance describes natural or physical inequality but it also describes the second species of inequality as well—the author doesn't indicate that the 'different privileges' in line 8 are earned—let's cross out earned then.

Natural describes the first type of inequality well—check it. Artificial doesn't quite indicate moral or political inequality or inequality via the 'consent of mankind'—let's put a question mark by it.

Inborn describes well natural or physical inequality in that one is born with a certain nature, physical characteristics, quality of mind, et cetera. Societal also works fairly well in describing inequality that results from the 'consent of mankind.' Let's check both terms in (E).

(A) health ? and moral√
(B) inherited and environmental ?
(C) from chance and ~~earned~~
(D) natural√ and artificial?
(E) inborn √ and societal √

We've got two checks for (E) which beats a check and a question mark for (A) and for (D). We have to pick (E) which also reflected well what we thought the passage was arguing: that there are two species of inequality, one which originates from one's blessings at birth and the other that originates from the blessings of society. (E) is correct.

Solved Problem 4

Problem 8, Section 3, Test 4, page 589, the Official SAT Study Guide Book.

Here's an analysis of a dual passages problem about the biologist Linnaeus in *the Official SAT Study Guide.* Read the passages and answer the problem on your own before reading our analysis (you have to read the passage and questions in your own copy of the book as the College Board refused to give us permission to republish any problems from their book).

We can eliminate choices (C), (D), and (E) as being outside the scope of both essays. There's no mention in either passage of reviving interest in biology, resolving disputes or the discoveries upon which Linnaeus built.

Analyzing the remaining choices (A) and (B) is a good example of our idea of precision and how it relates to the type of reading comprehension the College Board tests. Even though we'd be inclined to say that the point about limiting science is emphasized much more in both passages, we can't pick (B) since that point is never made with reference to the 'present–day.' We can thus cross–out 'present–day' in choice (B). We have to pick (A) as both authors do cite their respect for Linnaeus even though that point is not nearly as central to either passage as discussing how Linnaeus's work and his followers' work limited science.

Note again the nature of "SAT reading comprehension" and precision—if there's a single word that's not supported by the passage e.g. present-day then that makes the answer choice wrong even if the rest of the choice is accurate.

How to Read Passages

Do I Need to Read the Full Passages? Can I Skim Them?

We generally recommend most students read the full passages. From reading a passage, you'll get an idea of what the passage is about, what it's arguing, and what evidence and facts it's presenting. Moreover, if you read at a reasonable pace, you will have time to read the full passages. If you're a good skimmer, then go ahead and skim fact–based passages (more on them later).

If you feel that it takes you a lot of time to read the passages or that you have a lot of trouble concentrating on the passages when you try to read them, consider not reading one or more of the passages and immediately going to the questions. We've found many students go directly to the questions and still do quite well on the critical reading section. We'll mention this again later but if you follow this (or any other) strategy of skipping/skimming the passages, be sure to answer the line–number detail questions first (even if you read the full passage, we recommend you still answer all the line–number questions first).

Never Re–Read a Passage.

If you get stuck or bored while reading a passage, never go back and never re–read the passage. You need to get to the questions relatively quickly, and while answering the questions you'll be forced to effectively re–read most of the passage anyway.

Active Reading: Use Your Pencil While Reading.

To Keep Your Eyes Moving. Use your pencil to guide your eyes, to focus your attention and to keep your eyes moving. The action of moving your pencil keeps your eyes reading and moving through the passage; also the pencil is right there to underline key words and circle main ideas...keeping your mind attentive.

Circle and Underline. Even if you don't use your pencil to guide your eyes, do keep your pencil in a position ready to make notes immediately. You should be prepared to underline or circle key words, facts or arguments in the passage—particularly words or phrases that indicate a change in tone or argument.

Summarize Paragraphs. It's also not a bad idea to take a few moments to summarize a paragraph after you've read it. If the paragraph was full of facts about the moon, for example, circle those facts and jot down quickly 'facts about moon.' If the paragraph made a new argument that the original explanation of the origin of the moon could be wrong, jot down 'new argument: alternative moon origin explanation.' It takes you a few moments but when you're answering the questions, your notes can save you time by immediately guiding you to key points in the passage. Making small notes also helps force you to synthesize the passage and put the passage's ideas together in your mind; it also helps you stay engaged while reading.

Fact–Based or Argument Passages

Just a Few Ideas, Get Them and Move on to the Questions.

You're not expected (ever) to remember every last detail of any essay or story you read. You're expected instead to get the ideas, the key ideas most importantly, from the passage. This includes for an argument or fact–based passage what the structure of the argument is and what the ideas are which are used to make the argument. In a fact–based passage, there will be a few critical ideas; once you identify those and how they fit together in the argument, your work is done (the work of reading the passage itself that is).

If you're ever short on time, try reading just the first sentence of each paragraph in a fact-based passage. This is often sufficient to get the basic argument of the passage (which again is all you're supposed to get from reading such a passage).

Example:

Try to summarize the main argument(s) or idea(s) of the following passage from reading only the first sentence of every paragraph:

      Fee-based net prejudice (the position of being anti-"net neutrality"), what telecommunications and internet service companies are arguing they should be allowed to continue informally and begin more formally to practice, would allow your internet service provider to charge websites an extra fee which would enable a website which pays to reach you faster than other websites. Suppose Yahoo agrees to pay your service provider some fee and Google doesn't—then Google, who doesn't pay this fee, would load up on your computer later than Yahoo, who does pay, even though you clicked on them at the exact same time.

If your first instinct is that this sounds more like a bribe (from Yahoo) than an actual service that's been provided—that's exactly right. While there are scenarios in which fee-based net prejudice could lead to genuine investment and services, when the design and the current state of the internet is examined, there is overwhelming evidence and reason to believe that fee-based net prejudice will have only pernicious outcomes without any benefits and massive harms for consumers and the world.

The essential difference is that there are various ways an internet service provider could provide "better service," but based on the design of the internet it almost certainly would not. It could actually deliver websites to you faster or it could artificially slow down certain websites that you've also requested to give the illusion that other websites are getting to you faster. The realities of the design of the internet are such that building out special cables that go to every home (which is where the bottlenecks lie) for the providers who are willing to pay is so exorbitantly costly that no provider could afford to do it.

On your own, write down a summary of what you would predict each paragraph and the passage is arguing based on the first sentence of each paragraph (reproduced below), then compare it with our summaries below.

First Sentence of Paragraph 1: net prejudice is allowing internet providers to charge a fee
First Sentence of Paragraph 2: this fee is basically a bribe and not a real service
First Sentence of Paragraph 3: there could be an alternative where there's a legitimate service offered but it's too expensive

To summarize the passage then from just those three sentences: opponents of net neutrality support something we can call net prejudice which could in theory lead to investment and genuine services for users but in reality because of the design of the internet will function as receiving bribes from websites without providing any valuable service. Pretty good, right? For fact-based passages, you just have to get the key idea or ideas of what each paragraph is about and often those can be found in the first sentence or two of each paragraph.

More practice with College Board SAT passages:

From the Official SAT Study Guide, take the essay on bats in section 5 of test 2 (page 469), try reading just the first sentence of each paragraph and then predicting the argument of the passage. Then read our summary gleaned from the first sentences of each paragraph below.

From the first sentence, we get the idea that the first paragraph is likely full of facts about bats. From the second paragraph's first sentence, we get the idea that things that live at night are thought to be abnormal. From the final paragraph's first sentence, we get the claim that bats have figured in human culture as supernatural and frightening creatures. Putting the last two ideas together, we can guess at the argument of the last two paragraphs: bats have been considered frightening because they live at night. We've got the key argument of the passage from just those three sentences (all we're missing are the facts in the second half of the first paragraph that argue that bats in and of themselves shouldn't inspire fear which is somewhat important).

Here are some more essays you can use to practice this technique in the Official SAT Study Guide. Again, try to summarize the main argument(s) or idea(s) of the following passages using just the first sentence of every paragraph:
    Each of the dual passages on environmentalism in section 7 of test 4 (page 608).
    The passage on scent in section 2 of test 6 (page 712).

Read Fact-Based or Argument Passages Relatively Quickly

If you've gotten the ideas of the passage, you're done—don't waste time trying to memorize facts or details. In fact-based or argument passages, every word doesn't necessarily express something important....there are just a few key ideas, get those and then move to the questions.

Don't Memorize Facts, Just Know Where They Are.

Not only is it not practical to try to memorize all the facts in a fact-based passage, it's not necessary. You only have to know how to find them quickly. To that end, make a quick note ('facts about X') whenever you encounter some group of facts which will enable you to immediately find them later when answering questions.

Narrative Passages

Many Ideas!

There can be many, many ideas in a narrative passage. Every phrase or even word could express some aspect of what the narrator is thinking or feeling. There is usually, though, some main idea(s) or concern(s) of a narrator which it's helpful to identify, but it's not as straightforward as breaking down an essay into an argument.

Relative to fact-based or argument passages, read narrative passages more carefully.

Narrative passages demand more careful reading and attention than fact–based or argument passages. Since ideas may be subtly expressed through tone, word choice, poetic devices, et cetera—it's not as easy to get the main ideas or points out of narrative passages as it is for fact–based passages. Try to thus read them a little more carefully than you would a fact–based passage—but still never re–read a passage or spend too much time reading any passage.

Practice: Write a Summary of the Passage, Identifying Thesis and Key Ideas

As an exercise for some practice tests that you take, try to write quick summaries of the passage and/or pull out the logical structure in an outline form. If you do this week after week for passages on practice tests, by the time the real test rolls around, you'll do this automatically. For fact–based essays, each paragraph will have an idea, try to know the idea for each paragraph. For narrative essays, each paragraph will usually as a whole express or move the narrative somewhere—try to get an idea of how each paragraph and passage is working and jot down a quick summary after reading it.

If you want to do this exercise for practice tests, give yourself a little extra time to do these summaries. Also be sure to write quick summaries in outline form, no need to re–state the ideas in a lot of detail.

Reading Passage Question Guidance

Answer Line Number Questions First.

Save main–idea questions for the end. Answer questions which cite some particular line number first. By the time you've answered the line–number questions, you will have effectively read the passage a second time and thus will be better prepared to answer the main–idea question(s).

Outside the Scope of the Passage: Most Common Wrong Answer

The most common wrong answer in SAT reading passages are 'outside the scope of the essay.' Answers that are outside the scope of the essay are exactly that—answers that discuss something which is not in the essay. These wrong answers will mention facts or ideas that are never discussed in the passage.

If you don't find any reference to an answer choice in the passage, ask yourself if it's really relevant to what the essay is about—it's very likely that the answer choice is wrong and is outside the scope of the essay.

Dual Passages: Be Aware of Each Author's Position (who's pro and who's con)

Generally, one author will be for something and the other author will be against it. The authors, though, like good debaters will often grant their opponents (of whom the other author is presumably one such person) certain claims or arguments—thus, it's usually a black & white (or pro and con) distinction between the two authors with a bit of grey in the middle. Be aware of which author is for the idea in question and which author is against it.

Knowing that, for example, the author of the second passage is generally against idea X can help you eliminate: any answer choices which imply that the author of second passage would be in favor of idea X have to be wrong and can be eliminated.

Here are analyses of two problems from dual passages about Colonial Williamsburg from *the Official SAT Study Guide*. Read the dual passages and answer the problems on your own before reading our analyses.

Solved Problem 1

Problem 17, Section 9, Test 8, page 875, Official SAT Study Guide by the College Board.

We first have to identify that the author of the first passage had a positive view towards the improvised speeches being given by guides in Williamsburg. We can also from that guess that the author of the second passage is going to take exception to and have a negative view of much of what the first author praises which in fact the author of the second passage does. The very first sentence of the second passage confirms this: 'The replacement of reality with selective fantasy is characteristic of....themed entertainment.' In other words, improvised speeches are a kind of *entertainment* (pejorative or bad thing in this case) in which the guides engage in *selective fantasy* (pejorative or bad thing again in this case). We've thus confirmed our instinct that what the author of Passage 1 favors, the author of Passage 2 is against. We can conclude that the correct answer choice for problem 9 is going to be negative, and we can thus eliminate any answers which are positive in nature.

(A) and (C) are both positive so we can eliminate them. (B), though negative, is probably not the most likely reason for the second passage's author to be against these improvised speeches. The second passage's author would likely concede that such speeches may actually generate interest in history as the first passage's author claims, but the second passage's author would criticize such speeches for being historically inaccurate. We can thus cross out (B) or if you want to be conservative, you could just put a question mark by it. (D) is outside the scope of passage one which doesn't discuss architecture (even though the second passage's author discusses architecture a great deal) and more than that, the guide's speeches don't have anything to do with architecture and 'architectural integrity.' Strong cross out of 'architectural integrity' (D). (E) is what we'd expect the author of passage two to say, that the guides' improvised speeches may not describe reality or historical facts accurately. Check it.

The check mark for (E) beats the question mark for (B)...so we have to pick (E) which is the correct answer.

Solved Problem 2

Problem 9, Section 9, Test 8, page 874, Official SAT Study Guide by the College Board.

This problem illustrates how to use an author's position to eliminate answer choices. It's also a good example of why to read above and below the cited line. It's important to read the whole paragraph (lines 28–34) which contain the lines in question (31–32) to get a sense of how the author feels about the European museum 'ribbon' and 'sign' (negatively) and the Williamsburg experience (positively). The paragraph as a whole expounds the idea that Williamsburg has a unique way of presenting history that engages visitors which is absent from European museums.

While the Williamsburg experience seeks to bring people into the experience, the European experience represented by the 'ribbon' and the 'sign' is going to have some negative or limiting aspect to it. Let's try to eliminate answer choices.

(A) would mean that the 'ribbon' and 'sign' are positive things, that they are 'helping people.' We know, though, that the author views them as negative things so (A) has to be wrong—cross out. (B) is too literal--(the question is asking of the author's purpose in citing the sign not the sign's creator's purpose)! Be careful of questions in which words are used a bit metaphorically or expansively, but the answer choice is the literal definition or usage of the phrase or word. (B) is wrong in that while the 'ribbon' and 'sign' surely do intend to prevent damage to the antiques, that's not the author's purpose in citing them. Moreover, it's never mentioned in the passage that the purpose of the 'ribbon' and 'sign' is to prevent damage, rather the author implies that they mar the user experience. Cross out (B) then. (C) is outside the scope of the essay—no mention of architects anywhere in passage 1. Cross out 'architects' and write O.S. at the end of (C). (D) is a negative point about the "ribbon" and 'sign', and it has to do with limiting the visitor experience: good, check it. (E) is also outside the scope of the passage in that the wealth of Williamsburg is never discussed—the wealth of the current U.S. is mentioned in line 41 but that's a separate matter. Cross out "wealth" and write O.S. at the end of (E).

Since every other choice has something crossed out in it, we're left with (D). We liked (D) and checked it so we have to pick it...and (D) is in fact correct.

Line Number Questions

Always read a few lines above and a few lines below the line numbers cited in order to get the context of the lines. Oftentimes the correct answer is sitting right there a few lines before or after the line numbers in question!

The following solved problems illustrate the importance of recognizing outside the scope of the passage wrong answers, reading above and below cited lines for line number questions, and using precision+elimination, our two key methods for the critical reading section.

Solved Problem 1

I conceive of two species of inequality among men; one which I call natural, or physical inequality, because it is established by nature, and consists in the difference of age, health, bodily strength, and the qualities of the mind, or of the soul; the other which may be
5 termed moral, or political inequality, because it depends on a kind of convention, and is established, or at least authorized, by the common consent of mankind. This species of inequality consists in the different privileges, which some men enjoy, to the prejudice of others, such as that of being richer, more honored, more powerful,
10 and even that of exacting obedience from them.

In context, the word "species" (line 1) is used in order to imply that:

(A) there are different species of human beings
(B) inequality can be systematically studied as animals are in biology
(C) inequality is part of nature
(D) it's possible for inequality to become extinct
(E) many animals exhibit the same traits

Let's begin eliminating.

Choice (A) is outside the scope of the passage—there's no discussion of different species of human beings, only different species of inequality. Cross out 'of human beings.' Species has to do with biology—so let's leave (B) for now. Species are also part of nature—leave (C) for now as well. Choice (D) is outside the scope of the passage—there's no discussion of extinction or of ending inequality. Let's cross out 'extinct.' There's also no discussion of other animals or traits—we can cross out 'animals' and 'traits' in choice (E) then.

We're left with:

- (A) there are different species ~~of human beings~~ O.S.
- (B) inequality can be systematically studied as animals are in biology
- (C) inequality is part of nature
- (D) it's possible for inequality to become ~~extinct~~ O.S.
- (E) many ~~animals~~ exhibit the same ~~traits~~ O.S.

We're left with (B) and (C). If you were short on time, pick (B) and move on. Let's analyze the content of (B) and (C) and see what we can eliminate based on the passage. (C) makes a claim that we can test—does the author ever argue that inequality is part of nature? No...eliminate (C) by crossing out 'part of nature.'

Does the author argue that inequality can be systematically studied? Not directly but the author actually begins a systematic study himself by breaking inequality into two different types (natural or physical inequality and moral or political inequality) and then describing the nature of each type. Could species as a term be used to indicate that inequality comes in different forms and can be studied in each respective form? Yes, that makes sense and coheres with the author's subsequent description of the two forms of inequality. (B) is correct.

Solved Problem 2

> I conceive of two species of inequality among men; one which I call natural, or physical inequality, because it is established by nature, and consists in the difference of age, health, bodily strength, and the qualities of the mind, or of the soul; the other which may be
> 5 termed moral, or political inequality, because it depends on a kind of convention, and is established, or at least authorized, by the common consent of mankind. This species of inequality consists in the different privileges, which some men enjoy, to the prejudice of others, such as that of being richer, more honored, more powerful,
> 10 and even that of exacting obedience from them.

"Moral, or political inequality" in line 5 refers to differences in:

(A) genetic makeup
(B) prestige and possessions
(C) intelligence
(D) family values
(E) character

This question illustrates the critical importance of reading above and below the cited lines. We can eliminate everything in the passage above that line, as it refers to natural or physical inequality. We can check everything in the passage below that line as that refers to characteristics of moral or political inequality. The answer is actually right there in line 9…but let's still systematically analyze each answer choice.

There's no mention of genetic makeup in the passage, but it would be most related to physical or natural inequality and differences in health or bodily strength (lines 2–3)—thus we can cross out (A). Prestige and possessions correspond fairly well to honor and riches mentioned in line 9—these are part of moral and political inequality. Check (B). Intelligence is related to qualities of the mind in line 4—part of natural or physical inequality not moral or political inequality—eliminate (C).

Family values is related literally to morality so be on guard as it's a literal meaning; family values are not mentioned anywhere in the passage and thus it's ambiguous if it would be related to either type of inequality. Question mark for (D). Character would be part of the qualities of the mind in line 4—part of natural or physical inequality. Eliminate (E).

We've eliminated everything other than (B) and (D). The check for (B) beats the question mark of (D)—pick (B) which is correct. Remember to always read above and below the cited line in line number questions. We confirmed fairly quickly via line 9 that differences in prestige and possessions are a big part of moral or political inequality. *Often times, the answer is sitting right there in a line above or below the cited lines in the question!*

Solved Problem 3

 I am at present a middle–aged man of a broadish build, in cords, leggings, and a sleeved waistcoat the strings of which is always gone behind. Repair them how you will, they go like fiddle–strings. You have been to the theatre, and you have seen one of the violin–
5 players screw up his violin, after listening to it as if it had been whispering the secret to him that it feared it was out of order, and then you have heard it snap. That's as exactly similar to my waistcoat as a waistcoat and a violin can be like one another.

 The author uses the comparison of coat–strings to fiddle–strings in line 3 to indicate?

(A) the comic appearance of his coat
(B) he can use his waistcoat like a musical instrument
(C) his waistcoat makes sounds similar to the fiddle
(D) he wears the waistcoat when attending musical concerts
(E) he needs to get his waistcoat fixed

This is a narrative passage from a work of fiction. It's important to get an idea of the tone of such passages. In this case, it's humorous. If the passage didn't strike you as humorous, read it again paying attention to comic phrases such as 'fiddle–strings', 'whispering the secret to him…', and 'as a waistcoat and a violin can be like one another.'

Realizing that the passage is humorous, we immediately check (A). Let's see what we can eliminate or check in the remaining answers. Both (B) and (C) are too literal and miss that the passage is being humorous in comparing coat strings to a violin's strings. Eliminate both (B) and (C). (D) is outside the scope of the passage—there's no mention of attending musical concerts. Choice (E) is also both a bit literal and outside the scope of the passage—use of the word repair is not meant to be taken literally that the coat needs to be fixed. Moreover, there's no mention that the coat is literally damaged or broken in some way, the author just can't keep the coat strings in proper order.

   (A) the comic appearance of his coat √
   (B) ~~he can use his waistcoat like a musical instrument~~
   (C) ~~his waistcoat makes sounds similar to the fiddle~~
   (D) he wears the waistcoat when ~~attending musical concerts~~ O.S.
   (E) he needs to get his waistcoat ~~fixed~~

We're left with (A) which coheres well with the humorous tone of the passage: the author is being humorous in comparing his coat with a violin and it emphasizes a comic appearance to his coat. Be cognizant of tone, particularly with narrative passages! Also, all SAT passages aren't serious, there is the occasional humorous or sarcastic passage. (A) is the correct answer.

Conclusion and Logical Reasoning Questions

There will be a number of questions for longer passages in which you'll be asked what the author's main point is or what the implication of the whole argument is. These are conclusion or main idea questions. Save these questions for the end—solve line number and detail type questions first. In this way, you will have read virtually the whole passage a second time by the time you're asked to evaluate the whole passage in a meaningful way.

There are also some questions which will ask you to categorize or analyze the type of reasoning or argument being made in the passage or some part of the passage.

Use elimination+precision for these problems. Keep in mind that more general or "big picture" type answer choices will (obviously) more often be correct for big picture or conclusion type questions than detail-oriented answer choices. Here's a sample problem that models a bit of the thinking and approach to follow for eliminating answer choices.

Solved Problem 1 (Conclusion)

It is a very difficult matter to tell how men came to know anything of iron, and the art of employing it. We are not to suppose that they should of themselves think of digging it out of the mines, and preparing it for fusion, before they knew what could be the result of
5 such a process. On the other hand, there is less reason to attribute this discovery to any accidental fire, as mines are formed nowhere but in dry and barren places, and such as are bare of trees and plants, so that it looks as if nature had taken pains to keep from us this secret. Nothing therefore remains but the extraordinary
10 circumstance of some volcano, which, belching forth metallic substances ready fused, might have given the spectators a notion of imitating that operation of nature.

Based on his reasoning, the author would most likely agree with which proposition:

(A) Humans pursue pure science heartily without thought of its possible utility.
(B) Humans will not on their own dig and explore their surroundings.
(C) Humans are afraid of new technologies.
(D) Humans are reluctant to expend effort without knowing in advance the outcome
(E) Humans are natural experimenters and will never cease to try to use new things imaginatively

Before we think about what the author would agree with—let's eliminate what we're pretty certain the author would disagree with. Particularly, we can eliminate outside the scope of the essay answer choices. This includes (C), there's no mention of fear in the passage, and (E), there's no mention of humans being 'natural experimenters.' On a first pass, we also find support for (B) in that the author does seem to assume that humans won't dig everywhere, otherwise they might have discovered iron from digging—so let's check 'will not on their own dig' in choice (B). For the other choices, (A) and (D), we can't on the face of it say what the author's opinion would be without further analysis so we have to leave them.

(A) Humans pursue pure science heartily without thought of its possible utility.
(B) Humans will not on their own dig√ and explore their surroundings.
(C) Humans are ~~afraid~~ of new technologies.
(D) Humans are reluctant to expend effort without knowing in advance the outcome
(E) Humans are ~~natural experimenters~~ and will never cease to try to use new things imaginatively

Let's analyze the passage further and the author's argument to see if we can eliminate either (A) and or (D). The author argues that

90

humans most likely discovered how to work iron through the accident of witnessing a volcanic eruption and finding fused iron from one. The author doesn't think that humans would've thought to dig it on their own nor prepared iron for fusion without some external inspiration. From that assumption, it's implied that humans will not experiment greatly without having some idea of what to do and what will happen i.e. without having witnessed it being done. That's quite close to (D)—if humans have to see iron forged from a volcano before trying it themselves then assuming that they're reluctant to work without knowing that there is a good chance of success is a reasonable conclusion. Let's check (D). What about (A)? It's roughly the opposite of (D) so we can eliminate it—particularly 'without thought of its possible utility'—humans according to the author need to know in advance of the possible success or utility of their efforts or they won't try them (e.g. we have to see iron forged by a volcano before trying it ourselves).

- (A) Humans pursue pure science heartily ~~without thought of its possible utility.~~
- (B) Humans will not on their own dig√ and explore their surroundings.
- (C) Humans are ~~afraid~~ of new technologies.
- (D) Humans are reluctant to expend effort without knowing in advance the outcome√
- (E) Humans are ~~natural experimenters~~ and will never cease to try to use new things imaginatively

We're down to (B) and (D). Which one is more of a big picture type of conclusion—which one is more general? It's (D)…so if we were pressed for time, we ought to pick it and move on. (D) is correct as it is more general and thus a more appropriate answer than (B). There is also a problem with (B)—we can eliminate 'explore their surroundings' in that the author discusses a range of areas such as forests and volcanoes thus the author doesn't assume that humans won't explore. He rather makes a more general assumption that significant effort won't be expended until one has seen the strong possibility of success and value in the effort. (D) is thus correct.

Solved Problem 2 (Type of Argument)

I conceive of two species of inequality among men; one which I call natural, or physical inequality, because it is established by nature, and consists in the difference of age, health, bodily strength, and the qualities of the mind, or of the soul; the other which may be
5   termed moral, or political inequality, because it depends on a kind of convention, and is established, or at least authorized, by the common consent of mankind. This species of inequality consists in the different privileges, which some men enjoy, to the prejudice of others, such as that of being richer, more honored, more powerful,
10   and even that of exacting obedience from them.

The passage makes its argument through:

(A) personal experiences
(B) relay data to support an argument
(C) comparison of two competing explanations
(D) presentation of a new phenomenon
(E) definition of terms to distinguish two ideas

Let's use precision+elimination to eliminate some choices. Does the author describe any personal experiences? No, the author doesn't mention anywhere in the passage any personal experiences—strong cross out of 'personal experiences'. Does the author relay any data in the passage? No, no data is presented—strong cross out of 'data'. Does the author present two or more competing explanations? The author does present two types of inequality—let's keep (C). Does the author present a novel theory or any theory for that matter? Not really, the author presents 'two species of inequality' but inequality is not a new phenomenon. Let's lightly cross out "phenomenon" in (D). Does the author define terms to distinguish two ideas? The author does discuss two types of inequality—let's keep (E).

(A) ~~personal experiences~~
(B) relay ~~data~~ to support an argument
(C) comparison of two competing explanations
(D) presentation of a ~~new phenomenon~~
(E) definition of terms to distinguish two ideas

We're down to (C) and (E). Does the author present two explanations or does the author define terms to distinguish two ideas? The author describes two types of inequality and spends most of the passage defining each type of inequality. The author doesn't really explain anything—two types of inequality are presented but why and what these definitions of inequality explain if anything are not presented in the passage. We can, thus, eliminate (C) and select the correct answer (E).

Notice that elimination was quite effective in solving the problem. Also, notice that the first sentence of the passage was critical in telling us the structure of the argument in the passage and thus critical to solving the problem—details aren't important for this type of problem. We have to try to understand the logical structure of how the author is making an argument—whether through personal observations supporting an argument, whether through comparisons, whether as in this passage through detailed definitions, or through some other method.

Solved Problem 3 (Logical Reasoning)

It is a very difficult matter to tell how men came to know anything of iron, and the art of employing it. We are not to suppose that they should of themselves think of digging it out of the mines, and preparing it for fusion, before they knew what could be the result of
5 such a process. On the other hand, there is less reason to attribute this discovery to any accidental fire, as mines are formed nowhere

but in dry and barren places, and such as are bare of trees and plants, so that it looks as if nature had taken pains to keep from us this secret. Nothing therefore remains but the extraordinary
10 circumstance of some volcano, which, belching forth metallic substances ready fused, might have given the spectators a notion of imitating that operation of nature.

Select the discovery or phenomenon most analogous to the discovery of working iron as described in the passage above.

(A) Seeing birds fly, build wings to try to fly
(B) Noticing that successful people are early–risers, resolve to become an early–riser
(C) Start drinking tea after scientific studies indicate it lowers risk of a heart attack
(D) Build an irrigation system to get more water to crops after observing that crops receiving more water grow faster than those receiving less water
(E) Start playing tennis after friend describes how much fun playing tennis is

Our standard method of text-based elimination+precision isn't very helpful for this problem. Rather, we have to find the argument and pare it down to its essential idea. The discovery of iron according to the author was spurred by persons who saw iron spewed out of a volcano i.e. after seeing a natural process, man imitated it. The answer choice following that pattern is (A) in which man observing birds who have wings fly, builds wings to try to fly. Choices (B) and (E) involve observing and copying other human beings not some other natural process or part of nature. Choices (C) and (D) involve data and analysis rather than the direct observation and imitation of nature. Choice (A) then best mimics the author's theory of the discovery of working iron.

Meaning in Context/Most Nearly Means

Here are a few techniques to keep in mind when answering questions which ask you what a word "most nearly means" or what a word means "in context." *Plug the answer choice into the sentence in question and see if the word makes the sentence make sense.* If it doesn't, eliminate the word. Another technique we can use, borrowed from our sentence completion problem techniques, is to circle the phrase or words or sentence in the passage that gives meaning to the word in question.

Solved Problem 1

I conceive of two species of inequality among men; one which I call natural, or physical inequality, because it is established by nature, and consists in the difference of age, health, bodily strength, and the qualities of the mind, or of the soul; the other which may be
5   termed moral, or political inequality, because it depends on a kind of convention, and is established, or at least authorized, by the common consent of mankind. This species of inequality consists in the different privileges, which some men enjoy, to the prejudice of others, such as that of being richer, more honored, more powerful,
10 and even that of exacting obedience from them.

"Privileges" in context most nearly means?

(A) achievements
(B) character traits
(C) benefits
(D) developments
(E) improvements

Let's simplify the sentence then plug in the answer choices into the sentence to see which one(s) make sense.

'…which some men enjoy…' is not really necessary, and we can cut off the ending after "more powerful." We're left with:

This species of inequality consists in the different privileges, ~~which some men enjoy, to the prejudice of others,~~ such as that of being richer, more honored, more powerful, ~~and even that of exacting obedience from them.~~

Let's plug in the answer choices into the blank.

This species of inequality consists in the different achievements, ~~which some men enjoy, to the prejudice of others,~~ such as that of being richer, more honored, more powerful, ~~and even that of exacting obedience from them.~~

Being richer and more honored are achievements of a sort. We have to keep (A).

This species of inequality consists in the different character traits, ~~which some men enjoy, to the prejudice of others,~~ such as that of being richer, more honored, more powerful, ~~and even that of exacting obedience from them.~~

Being richer and more honored aren't character traits, they don't describe one's personality or self. Hard cross–out.

This species of inequality consists in the different benefits, ~~which some men enjoy, to the prejudice of others,~~ such as that of being richer, more honored, more powerful, ~~and even that of exacting obedience from them.~~

Being rich, honored and powerful are benefits—but benefits of what exactly…we'll analyze it later, for now benefits can work so we have to keep (C).

This species of inequality consists in the different <u>developments</u>, ~~which some men enjoy, to the prejudice of others,~~ such as that of being richer, more honored, more powerful, ~~and even that of exacting obedience from them.~~

Developments sounds awkward. Becoming richer would be a development, but being richer or more honored is less of a development and more of a type of status. It sounds a bit awkward and its meaning doesn't quite work but it's not that far off—question mark.

This species of inequality consists in the different <u>improvements</u>, ~~which some men enjoy, to the prejudice of others,~~ such as that of being richer, more honored, more powerful, ~~and even that of exacting obedience from them.~~

Improvements is similar to developments but it sounds a bit better since being richer or more honored is an improvement to being less honored, say. Let's keep (E).

We're left with:

    (A) achievements
    (B) ~~characteristics~~
    (C) benefits
    (D) developments ?
    (E) improvements

From plugging the words into the sentence and seeing how they sound, we could roughly eliminate two choices. We'll have to analyze the sentence and the passage now to eliminate further choices. A critical word that gives us the sense of 'privileges' in the sentence is 'inequality'—it's inequality that gives rise to these privileges. Inequality fundamentally has less to do with the positive aspects of what someone does and more with societal norms and the structure of society, what the author describes in line 6 as 'convention' or later as 'the common consent of mankind.' Thus, 'privileges' from inequality would not be earned in some positive sense by the recipient. We can, then, eliminate both achievements in (A)—since achievements implies that someone has earned the privileges of being richer, more honored, etc. The idea of inequality, though, is that such 'privileges' aren't earned. Achievements, thus, isn't what the author's expressing—eliminate it. Benefits doesn't have any implication of being earned—a benefit is something one enjoys and may or may not have been fairly earned. Let's check benefits. Improvements can be eliminated along the lines of eliminating achievements. It's ambiguous where the improvements would be coming from, but the implication that the person who is richer and more honored has improved himself or herself defeats the idea of inequality and thus should be eliminated. We're left with (C) which is correct.

It's important to understand the author's idea in this passage. He's arguing that there are two sources of difference between human beings (which is what he calls inequality): one source is natural gifts or benefits such as being a fast runner or having a photographic memory, and the other source is the design of society to award riches, honors, etc. to some occupations rather than others. For example a doctor on average earns more than a shoe salesperson. A shoe salesperson may work longer hours than a doctor and thus be working as hard or harder than the doctor but he or she would likely not earn more than the doctor—that is described by the author as a type of inequality. The doctor's 'being richer' and 'more honored' from the author's perspective aren't earned (since the shoe salesperson is working as hard or harder) but rather are benefits from the structure of a society that favors doctors.

Solved Problem 2

I am at present a middle-aged man of a broadish build, in cords, leggings, and a sleeved waistcoat the strings of which is always gone behind. Repair them how you will, they go like fiddle-strings. You have been to the theatre, and you have seen one of the violin-
5 players screw up his violin, after listening to it as if it had been whispering the secret to him that it feared it was out of order, and then you have heard it snap. That's as exactly similar to my waistcoat as a waistcoat and a violin can be like one another.

Repair in context most nearly means?

(A) Display
(B) Sew
(C) Instruct
(D) Play
(E) Arrange

Let's simplify the sentence and plug in the answer choices. There's not much to simplify, but replacing the pronoun with its antecedent makes the meaning clearer to us. So let's replace 'them' with the 'strings of my waistcoat' which is what 'them' refers to.

<u>Repair</u> ~~them~~ *the strings of my waistcoat* how you will, they go like fiddle-strings.

Now let's plug in the answer choices and eliminate those that sound awkward and whose meaning doesn't cohere in the sentence.

<u>Display</u> *the strings of my waistcoat* how you will, they go like fiddle-strings.

Display sounds fairly awkward and doesn't quite make sense—one doesn't really display a waistcoat when one is wearing it—let's cross it out.

<u>Sew</u> *the strings of my waistcoat* how you will, they go like fiddle-strings.

The literal use of the word 'repair' would indicate that the strings may need to be fixed and thus would need to be sewed. If there were some way to truly 'repair' his coat, the author would've mentioned as much but there is no discussion of it in the passage and no mention of sewing in the passage. Cross out sew. *The word in question in meaning in context questions will usually not be used according to its literal meaning*—so be on guard when you encounter any answer choices with the literal meaning of the word. Most of the time, the word you're asked to analyze will **not** be used literally.

<u>Instruct</u> *the strings of my waistcoat* how you will, they go like fiddle-strings.

Though instruct may work poetically to describe what needs to be done to the strings, it's not literally possible to 'instruct' strings. Light cross out.

Note that the word in question in most nearly means questions will usually not be used literally, but the answer choices will generally be used literally! It's very unlikely then that the word in question, repair, is being used literally which is partly how we eliminated 'sew', and it's very unlikely that an answer choice will be used poetically which is how we eliminated 'instruct.'

<u>Play</u> *the strings of my waistcoat* how you will, they go like fiddle-strings.

Play sounds quite awkward—one can play violin strings but not coat strings! Strong cross out.

<u>Arrange</u> *the strings of my waistcoat* how you will, they go like fiddle-strings.

Arrange reads well, and its meaning is appropriate. The author will arrange his coat strings in different ways, but every time, the strings will go awry. Check for arrange.

We're left with:

   (A) ~~Display~~
   (B) ~~Sew~~
   (C) ~~Instruct~~
   (D) ~~Play~~
   (E) Arrange √

We're left with choice (E)...and it's correct.

Practice, Practice, Practice

You may be growing tired of hearing this refrain but it is a simple truth that the more you practice anything, the faster and better you become at doing it (well generally anything) and that's most certainly true for using our reading comprehension techniques. The first time you use these techniques it may take you some time to feel like you're using them properly, but with practice over time using them will be second nature and you'll solve problems quickly and accurately. Let's start practicing now!

Critical Reading Section: Reading Passage Problem Set

Practice our reading passage techniques with the problems below. Feel free to look back at our techniques and solved problems to model your own work and thinking.

Answers are in Appendix 1 on page 438.

The principles of agriculture were known a long time before the practice of it took place, and it is hardly possible that men, constantly employed in drawing their subsistence from trees and plants, should not have early hit on the means employed by nature for the generation of vegetables; but in all probability it was very late before their industry took a turn that way, either because trees, which with their land and water game supplied them with sufficient food and did not require their attention; or because they did not know the use of corn; or because they had no instruments to cultivate it; or because they were destitute of foresight in regard to future necessities; or in fine, because they wanted means to hinder others from running away with the fruit of their labors.

1. The phrase "hit on" in context most nearly means:

    (A) created
    (B) discovered
    (C) pushed
    (D) beaten
    (E) required

2. The following are all reasons the author would agree could be responsible for the late onset of agriculture by human beings EXCEPT for:

   (A) Focused on satisfying short–term needs
   (B) Did not need additional food sources
   (C) Lacked effective farming tools
   (D) Didn't realize that agriculture could generate substantial quantities of produce
   (E) Were afraid of others stealing their crops

On many accounts I regarded that beautiful city with affectionate veneration. There were more than local attractions to render it interesting. The same river ran on as it had run on before, but the cheerful faces that had been once reflected in its stream had passed away. I saw things once familiar as I saw them before; but "the fathers, where were they ?" I was in this respect like one awaked from the slumber of an age, who found himself a stranger in his own land.

There were the recollections of those who ceased in the interval to be denizens of this world. These could not but breathe sadness over the noble edifices that recalled men, conversations, and convivialities which, however long departed, shadowed upon the mind its own inevitable destiny.

3. What does "shadowed upon the mind its own inevitable destiny" refer to?

   (A) The author had had those thoughts before
   (B) The author's fate was to rule the city
   (C) A reminder of mortality
   (D) Memories of buildings that are now gone
   (E) Re–experiencing happy moments from the past

4. Why is the narrator "a stranger in his own land"?

   (A) The author's friends are no longer in the city
   (B) The city looks familiar but actually is new to the author
   (C) The author is lost and not sure where to go.
   (D) Everyone pretends not to remember the author
   (E) There are new buildings in the city.

Such was, or must have been, had man been left to himself, the origin of society and of the laws, which increased the fetters of the weak, and the strength of the rich; irretrievably destroyed natural liberty, fixed forever the laws of property and inequality; changed an artful usurpation into an irrevocable title; and for the benefit of a few ambitious individuals subjected the rest of mankind to perpetual labor, servitude, and misery. We may easily conceive how the establishment of a single society rendered that of all the rest absolutely necessary, and how, to make head against united forces, it became necessary for the rest of mankind to unite in their turn. Societies once formed in this manner, soon multiplied or spread to such a degree, as to cover the face of the earth; and not to leave a corner in the whole universe, where a man could throw off the yoke, and withdraw his head from under the often ill-conducted sword which he saw perpetually hanging over it.

The civil law being thus become the common rule of citizens, the law of nature no longer obtained but among the different societies, in which, under the name of the law of nations, it was qualified by some tacit conventions to render commerce possible, and supply the place of natural compassion, which, losing by degrees all that influence over societies which it originally had over individuals, no longer exists but in some great souls, who consider themselves as citizens of the world, and forcing the imaginary barriers that separate people from people, after the example of the Sovereign Being from whom we all derive our existence, make the whole human race the object of their benevolence.

5. In last sentence of the passage, what could "natural compassion" replace in theory according to the author?

   (A) system of law
   (B) trade with other people
   (C) belief in a Supreme Being
   (D) civil liberty
   (E) inequality

6. The author's attitude towards the establishment of society and laws is primarily one of?

   (A) cautious approval
   (B) unabated celebration
   (C) regretful dissatisfaction
   (D) objective indifference
   (E) full condemnation

7. The formation of a single society forced other groups of people to similarly organize into societies in order to?

   (A) trade competitively
   (B) defend themselves
   (C) join the comity of nations
   (D) exploit natural resources
   (E) preserve natural liberty

The glamour of history when engaged through cultural artifacts would be considerably dimmed if everything was explained, and a very seamy block of marble may be chiseled into a very acceptable statue if the workman but knows how to avoid the doubtful parts. An itinerary that follows not only the ridges, but occasionally plunges down into the hollows and turns up or down such crossroads as may have chanced to look inviting, is perhaps more interesting than one laid out on conventional lines. A shadowy something, which for a better name may be called sentiment, if given full play encourages these side-steps, and since they are generally found fruitful, and often not too fatiguing, the procedure should be given every encouragement.

8. In the second sentence of the passage, "itinerary" could most likely refer to:

   (A) the steps to make an acceptable statue
   (B) a plan of travel for a new place
   (C) acquiring explanations of the meaning of cultural objects
   (D) the blueprint for a new road to be built
   (E) a path of exploration for historical art and architectural works

9. What would be an example of "sentiment" as mentioned in the last sentence of the passage?

   (A) following conventional wisdom
   (B) visiting less appreciated artworks
   (C) traveling on unpaved or unfinished roads
   (D) understanding completely the purpose and design of a building one visits
   (E) making a sculpture which contains doubtful parts

These gardens of Louis XV were more fantastic, and followed less the lines of traditional good taste. Shapes and forms were complicated and indeed inexplicably mixed into a melange that one could hardly recognize for one thing or another, certainly not as examples of any well–meaning styles which have lasted until to–day. The straight line now disappeared in favor of the most dissolute and irrational curves imaginable, and the sober majesty of the gardens of Louis XIV became a tangle of warring elements, fine in parts and not uninteresting, effective, even, here and there, but as a whole an aggravation.

10. The author's attitude towards the gardens of Louis XIV and those of Louis XV, respectively, can best be described as

    (A) avant–garde and postmodern
    (B) organized and hodgepodge
    (C) optimistic and disorienting
    (D) inexplicable and aggravating
    (E) classical and effective

11. The author would most likely describe which of the following as an effective example of a garden

    (A) one executed with an unidentifiable style
    (B) one which combines elements from multiple styles
    (C) one that follows an internal logic consistently
    (D) one that experiments creatively with different elements
    (E) one with rational curves and straight lines

I shall say scarcely anything that those will not know who are somewhat familiar with bees. The notes and experiments I have made during my twenty years of beekeeping I shall reserve for a more technical work; for their interest is necessarily of a special and limited nature, and I am anxious not to over–burden this essay. I wish to speak of the bees very simply, as one speaks of a subject one knows and loves to those who know it not. I do not intend to adorn the truth, or merit the just reproach Reaumur addressed to his predecessors in the study of our honey–flies, whom he accused of substituting for the marvelous reality marvels that were imaginary and merely plausible. The fact that the hive contains so much that is wonderful does not warrant our seeking to add to its wonders. Besides, I myself have now for a long time ceased to look for anything more beautiful in this world or more interesting, than the truth; or at least than the effort one is able to make towards the truth.

12. In the second to last sentence of the passage, "add to its wonders" is used to indicate that

    (A) the author will not adorn additional wonders to bees and the beehive
    (B) Reaumur should not have made any exaggerations about bees
    (C) bees are wondrous and marvelous creatures
    (D) the author will not add any new facts to our knowledge of bees in the work
    (E) one should use imagination in describing the natural world

13. The passage is most likely written for:

    (A) insect experts
    (B) biology enthusiasts
    (C) truth seekers
    (D) aviation engineers
    (E) beekeepers

For each hive has its own code of morals. There are some that are very virtuous and some that are very perverse; and a careless bee–keeper will often corrupt his people, destroy their respect for the property of others, incite them to pillage, and induce in them habits of conquest and idleness which will render them sources of danger to all the little republics around. These things result from the bee's discovery that work among distant flowers, whereof many hundreds must be visited to form one drop of honey, is not the only or promptest method of acquiring wealth, but that it is easier to enter ill–guarded cities by stratagem, or force her way into others too weak for self–defense. Nor is it easy to restore to the paths of duty a hive that has become thus depraved.

14. The primary device used by the author to describe the bees is

    (A) metaphor
    (B) simile
    (C) personification
    (D) synecdoche
    (E) comparison

15. According to the author, "little republics" of bees may come into conflict primarily because

    (A) visiting flowers is hard work
    (B) a hive always wants to control other hives
    (C) mating requires acquiring a queen from another hive
    (D) bee–keepers encourage war between hives
    (E) creating honey themselves wastes a lot of time

> **An Exercise: Identify Passage Line Numbers**
>
> As an exercise to practice making sure you're reading passages precisely and paying close attention to the text, try this exercise. When you eliminate answer choices for reasons other than their being outside the scope of the passage, write down the line number from the passage which supports the elimination of that answer. This exercise helps force you to read passages carefully and only make claims or assumptions that supported by the passage.

Reading Passages Recapitulation

- ✓ **Eliminate, Eliminate, Eliminate. A mantra to repeat to yourself while tackling reading section problems:** *what can I eliminate, what can I eliminate...*

- ✓ **Precision+Elimination: Use Precise Analysis of the Text to Eliminate Answer Choices.**

- ✓ **Never Re-Read a Passage—Get to the Questions.**

- ✓ **Active Reading—Read with a Pencil in Hand ready to jot down quick notes and or keep your eyes moving ahead.**

- ✓ **Never try to Memorize Facts. For Fact-Based passages, learn the key one, two or three ideas presented in the passage then move on to the questions.**

- ✓ **Read Narrative-Based passages relatively more closely than Fact-Based passages.**

- ✓ **Just the Ideas—Don't Try to Memorize the Facts or Details in a Passage.**

- ✓ **Line Number and other Detail Type Questions First. Big Picture Type Questions Last.**

- ✓ **Above and Below—Read Above and Below any Cited Lines in Line-Number Questions.**

- ✓ **Expect Many 'Outside the Scope of the Passage' Wrong Answers.**

- ✓ **"Most Nearly Means" Questions: Plug in Answer Choices.**

- ✓ **Dual Passages: Be Aware of which Author is for the Idea in Question and which Author is Against It.**

MATH SECTION: Overview

We'll cover all the math content, and the test–taking and problem–solving methods you need to know for the SAT math section in these chapters. We feel that our approach for every type of math problem on the test represents the best approach—best in the sense of being easily learned, reliable, and widely applicable for the SAT problem type. If you've learned a way to solve certain math problems which is different from how we solve them, it's fine. Do continue to use your old method if it works for you or you could try our method if you don't feel comfortable with what you were taught before. Better yet—use your old method and also learn our method so that you have two tools with which to tackle math problems of that type!

Question Strategies

Easy, Medium, Hard Questions

The math section can be divided according to difficulty into three categories of questions: easy, medium and hard with the questions coming in that order. If there are 24 questions in a section, the first 8 will be easy, the next 8 medium, and the last 8 hard.

The math sections are thus ordered such that the easiest questions are first then the medium ones then the hard ones. Use this to your advantage. If an easy question seems easy, that's fine because it's supposed to be easy. If the last question in the section seems really easy, something's wrong—it's not supposed to be easy!

Order Strategy

500–600 range scorers

If you're aiming to score in the 500–600 range on the math test, don't try to solve any of the hard questions until you've done your absolute best on the easy and medium questions. As you do practice tests, don't worry about the hard questions as much as being certain that you've solved all the easy and medium questions correctly. If when taking practice tests, you don't get to any of the hard questions, it's okay, skip them. Just make sure you can get just about all the easy and medium questions correct. If time permits, quickly gauge which hard questions you feel you can get and solve them!

700–800 range scorers

If you're aiming for the 700–800 range on the math section, you absolutely must double-check, even triple-check your work. Careless mistakes are very costly in this score range. All test-takers no matter what your score goal, though, should keep that in mind: double-check your work. Every problem is worth 1 raw point whether it's the first problem and presumably the easiest on the test or the last problem and presumably the hardest. Spend an extra 10 seconds or more time on an easy problem to be absolutely sure you've gotten it correct. Two careless mistakes can cost you as much as 50 points in your final math score particularly for higher scorers—so you can not afford to make any careless mistakes. For problems with multiple steps, a common mistake is to do 2 of the 3 steps and mark that intermediate result as the answer (when there was some final and usually simple step left). Be certain you're always answering what the question is asking and always always double-check your work.

Guessing Strategy

If You Eliminate Even One Choice, You Must Guess!

This goes for all three sections. If you've eliminated even a single answer choice, it's statistically in your favor to guess... so you must make a guess! If you can't solve the problem, try to eliminate answers. If you eliminate even one answer choice, you must guess. When you take a guess, circle the problem as well so that if you have time at the end, you can come back and try to solve the problem again.

Grid–In Problems: No Penalty for Wrong Answers

Grid–in math problems are those in which you bubble in the actual solution and aren't given five multiple choice answers to choose from. If you arrive at any answer for a grid–in problem, grid it in even if you're uncertain of your answer. Always mark in your answer for grid–in problems because you don't lose any points for incorrect answers. You've got nothing to lose—if your answer is wrong, there is no penalty for the grid–in problems. There's no use in taking a blind guess as that just wastes time, but if you've done work and think you've solved the problem, write and bubble in your answer.

Work on Paper.
Write Down Everything You Know.
When Stuck, Move On.

You should be prepared and practiced enough when you take the test that the methods for solving problems come to you immediately without much thought—do enough practice tests and supplemental problem sets to get to the point where you're at that comfort level. For example, when you see variables in answer choices and recognize the problem as an algebra word problem, you should immediately ask yourself *can I plug in numbers* and fairly quickly analyze the problem to answer yourself (yes or no)!

Never sit and meditate on a problem. Math problems are solved by working them out on paper, not by looking and thinking. When you're solving a math problem, write down the givens, then write down your ideas, then try to write equations, etc. Eventually the insight(s) should come to you as to how to solve the problem as you work it out. Don't meditate on a problem—it wastes too much time even in the unlikely event a solution occurs to you. If you get stuck, move on. Circle the problem number and if you have time later, you can come back to the problem. Time is precious on the test, and you can't afford to spend 2 minutes sitting and thinking about a math problem.

Work on paper. Do not work out math problems in your head. Work on paper. Don't meditate on a problem. Work on paper. Write down your ideas, your thoughts, everything you know on paper. For geometry problems, work from the diagram—once you write everything you know in, you'll likely get the insight(s) necessary to solve it. For algebra problems, make sure you write each step out on paper and keep your work neat. It takes a few extra seconds but it means fewer careless mistakes and you'll have an easier time double-checking your work.

For the math section, work actively and work on paper. When you're stuck on a problem, don't dwell on it, move on.

Before You Bubble-in Your Final Answer

Check your answer's Reasonableness and Double-Check your work

Always take a quick look at your answer and make sure that it seems reasonable. Also, look at your work which should be neat and easily checked—be sure that you haven't made any calculation mistakes and that your equations follow or are verbatim from the question.

There are usually at least 2 ways to solve every math problem on the test—using your knowledge of mathematics e.g. geometry, algebra, et cetera, and using another problem-solving method such as working backwards from the answer choices or plugging in numbers. If you're aiming for a 700+ score, after you solve a problem you should re-solve the problem with a different method to be absolutely sure your answer is correct.

Re-read the Question (before you circle your answer).

What are you being asked for? Always re-read what you're being asked for once you're ready to choose your final answer to a question. Many problems require multiple steps and a common mistake is to put down an intermediate answer rather than what's actually being asked. Every question is worth a single point so invest a few seconds double-checking/triple-checking every question to make sure you're answering what's being asked.

Always double-check that you're answering the question, double-check your work, and check your answer for "reasonableness."

Practice, Practice, Practice.

There are twenty to thirty different types of problems that are tested in the math section—the more you practice them, the more adept you'll be at solving these types of problems and the better your mastery of the few, tested mathematical concepts.

If you need more practice than the weekly practice test, use independent vendors' books with titles like 'Math Workout for the SAT' or 'SAT Math Workbook' to get more problem sets to practice. Independent vendors usually write decent math problems so solving problem sets in those books will only help you.

Three Key Problem–Solving Methods: Plugging In Numbers, Working Backwards, and Measurement

You can always use pure algebraic methods or geometric techniques, say, to solve a math problem. It's sometimes easier and faster, though, to use other methods for solving SAT math problems. Here are three key methods to practice and master for solving math problems on the SAT: plugging in numbers, working backwards from the answer choices, and measurement.

Plugging In Numbers

A new mantra for you: whenever I see variables, I can (almost always) plug in numbers. Whenever I see variables, plug in numbers. Whenever I see variables, plug in numbers.

Whenever you see variables, you can most likely plug in numbers for those variables. This is particularly useful when variables are in the answer choices. This strategy is primarily for algebra and arithmetic problems, but it can be helpful for the occasional geometry problem which has variables.

There are three steps to plugging in numbers.

1. *Pick your numbers.* Identify the variables and equations for the problem, and pick numbers for the variables. It doesn't matter which numbers you pick, but try to pick easy–to–work–with integers like 2, 3, 5, et cetera.
2. *Plug in the numbers* you picked *into the problem* or into the equations, and solve.
3. *Plug in the numbers* you picked *into the answer choices* (if the answer choices have variables) and see which answer choice corresponds to your solution.

When there are variables in the answer choices, always plug your numbers into each answer choice. If you try (A), and it works, do not immediately pick (A). Make sure that none of the other answer choices work. You have to check that no other answer choice works because sometimes the numbers you pick may by chance work for multiple answer choices (even though those choices aren't correct). What happens if multiple answer choices yield the correct answer? In that case, pick new numbers, plug them in, and see if they make only one of the two remaining answer choices correct (let's hope they do).

It's a good idea to double–check your work by picking a second set of numbers to make sure your answer still works after you initially solved the problem—you can't afford any careless mistakes. Let's tackle some problems and see how plugging in numbers works.

Solved Problem 1

If a and b are positive integers and a − b = 18, then (18 + b) / a = ___ ?

(A) −1
(B) 1
(C) 5
(D) a − b
(E) a + 2

We notice variables in the question and in the answers so we think: plug in numbers. Will plugging in numbers work? Looks like it—I can pick a number for only one of them though, a or b, since once I pick a number for a, then b will be set and vice versa.

Step 1: Pick my numbers.

a = 20, then b = 2. (because 20 − 2 = 18)

Step 2. Plug my numbers into the problem. Solve the problem in terms of my numbers.

The problem's asking us to solve for (18 + b) / a so we need to plug our numbers into it:

(18 + b) / a   =
(18 + 2) / 20 =   (20) / 20   =   1

Step 3: Solve the answer choices in terms of my picked numbers OR find the picked number in the answer choice.

In this problem, (B) 1 corresponds to our solution. Neither a − b nor a + 2 equals 1 (a − b for our numbers yields 18 and a + 2 for our numbers yields 22), so we must choose (B). To be safe, it's a good idea to pick another set of numbers (say a = 25 and b = 7) and make sure that you still get a solution of 1. Try it...you will get 1 again. (B) is correct.

Solved Problem 2

What is the average of the following four terms: $10 - x$, 8, $10 + x$, 20?

(A) 8
(B) 12
(C) $20 - x$
(D) 22
(E) 24

More variables—let's plug in numbers again.

Step 1: Pick my numbers.

$x = 5$. Why 5? No particular reason except that it's easy to work with!

Step 2. Plug my numbers into the problem. Solve the problem in terms of my numbers.

$10 - 5$, 8, $10 + 5$, 20
5,   8,   15,   20

Let's now solve the average.

$$\frac{5 + 8 + 15 + 20}{4} = \frac{48}{4} = 12$$

Step 3: Solve the answer choices in terms of my picked numbers OR find the picked number in the answer choice.

In this problem, (B) 12 corresponds to our solution. 20 − x is equal to 15 which is not correct so we can eliminate (C). We have to thus pick (B), but again it's a very good idea to pick another set of numbers (say x = 0) and make sure that you still get a solution of 12.

The correct answer is (B) 12.

Solved Problem 3

Jim earns x cents for every newspaper he sells. He works four days a week and sells eighty newspapers a day. How many dollars will Jim earn in a year?

(A) $\dfrac{80x}{100 \times 4}$

(B) $52 \times 80 \times 100 \times x$

(C) $4 \times 52 \times 80 \times 100 \times x$

(D) $\dfrac{4 \times 52 \times 80 \times x}{100}$

(E) $\dfrac{4 \times 52 \times 80 \times 100}{x}$

Just looking at the answer choices, we can guess that deriving the proper equation looks pretty complicated. What's my alternative…when we're dealing with variables, particularly variables in the answer choices: it's to plug in numbers!

Step 1: Pick my numbers.

Let's say Jim earns forty cents for each newspaper he sells. So x= 40.

Notice that x equals 40 not .40. Jim earns 40 cents per newspaper which would also be equal to .40 dollars per newspaper (as we'll show in step 2) but the unit given in the question for x is cents so x is 40.

Step 2. Plug my numbers into the problem. Solve the problem in terms of my numbers.

In this case, we have to solve for how many dollars Jim earns in a year. From step 1, we know Jim earns forty cents for each newspaper sold. We need to convert that to dollars per newspaper sold, and then multiply that by how many newspapers he sells in a year. So

$$\frac{40 \text{ cents}}{1 \text{ newspaper}} \times \frac{1 \text{ dollar}}{100 \text{ cents}} = \frac{40 \text{ dollars}}{100 \text{ newspapers}} = .40 \text{ dollars/newspaper}$$

We need to now calculate how many newspapers Jim sells in a year.

Let's first calculate how many days a year he works. He works 4 days a week, and there are 52 weeks in a year. Jim, thus, works 4 x 52 or 208 days per year.

Jim sells, as the problem tells us, 80 newspapers a day.
So he sells 208 days x 80 newspapers/day or 16,640 newspapers a year.

Finishing up the problem, 16,640 newspapers/year x $.40/newspaper = $6656. Jim thus earns 6656 dollars per year.

A few additional things to note

If you were actually solving this on the SAT, you should keep your units as a double–check and your equations/work should look something like this:

$$\frac{4 \text{ days}}{1 \text{ week}} \times \frac{52 \text{ weeks}}{1 \text{ year}} \times \frac{80 \text{ newspapers}}{1 \text{ day}} = \frac{16{,}640 \text{ newspapers}}{1 \text{ year}}$$

$$\frac{16{,}640 \text{ newspapers}}{1 \text{ year}} \times \frac{\$.40}{1 \text{ newspaper}} = \frac{\$6656}{1 \text{ year}}$$

Notice that we can cross out the units to be sure we've done our work correctly. In the first equation, days and day cancel out as do weeks and week so that we're left with newspapers per year which is correct. In the second equation, newspapers and newspaper cancel out to leave us with dollars per year. Use units in the fractions as a double–check.

You hopefully remember the idea of a conversion fraction from doing stoichiometry in chemistry class. A conversion fraction is something you can multiply a quantity by to change its units—to convert it from one unit to another. In the first equation, we multiplied 4 days per week by the conversion fraction 52 weeks / 1 year in order to change our units from days per week to days per year (week and weeks cancel out). 52 weeks and 1 year are equivalents so we don't change the given value per se but we convert it from one unit to another (in this case from weeks into years). Think of it like changing your clothes. You wear (we assume) different clothes everyday but that doesn't make you a different person—you're the same person in different clothes. In the same way, when we multiply a quantity by a conversion fraction (as we did 4 days per week to convert it into days per year) we're changing the way the fraction looks but not its inherent value.

Step 3: Solve the answer choices in terms of my picked numbers OR find the picked number in the answer choice.

We need to find which answer choice gives us 6656 when x = 40.

Let's plug 40 into them and see what we get:

(A) $\dfrac{80 \times 40}{100 \times 4}$ = $\dfrac{3200}{400}$ = 8

(B) $52 \times 80 \times 100 \times 40$ = 16,640,000

(C) $4 \times 52 \times 80 \times 100 \times 40$ = 66,560,000

(D) $\dfrac{4 \times 52 \times 80 \times 40}{100}$ = 6656

(E) $\dfrac{4 \times 52 \times 80 \times 100}{40}$ = 41,600

6656, our answer choice, is there. The answer is (D)!

Math Section: Plugging-In Numbers Problem Set

Practice Plugging-In Numbers to solve the following problems. Answers are in Appendix 1 on page 442.

1. Reduce the following where b and a are not equal to either 1 or –1:

$$\frac{\frac{1}{(b-1)}}{a + \frac{1}{(b-1)}}$$

(A) (b – 1) / a (b – 1)
(B) (a) / (b – 1)
(C) (ab – a) / (a + 1)
(D) 1 / (ab – a + 1)
(E) (b – 1) / (ab – a)

2. James earns x cents for each book he sells. He sells y books per day, and works g days per week. Which of the following correctly represents James's yearly earnings in dollars?

(A) 100 × 52 × x × y × g
(B) (52 × x × y × g) / 100
(C) (100 × x) / (52 × y × g)
(D) (52 × x × y) / (100 × g)
(E) (100 × g) / (x × y)

3. If k percent of 50 is equal to 60 divided by m, then what's the value of km?

(A) 70
(B) 90
(C) 110
(D) 120
(E) 130

4. If $x^{11} = j$ and $x^{15}=m$, what must be equal to x^7?

(A) jm/2
(B) j^2/m
(C) $(j^2)(m)$
(D) $(j)(m^2)$
(E) m^2/j

5. If 7a / (8x −3y) = ¾ , then 14a / (32x −12y) = ???

(A) 3/8
(B) 1/2
(C) 5/6
(D) 9/8
(E) 5/4

6. When x is divided by 7, the remainder is 2. What's the remainder when x+10 is divided by 7?

(A) 1
(B) 2
(C) 3
(D) 5
(E) 6

7. To make your own pizza, it costs a flat fee of j dollars plus m cents for every extra topping and n cents to have a thick crust pizza. What formula gives us the cost in dollars for a thick crust pizza with x toppings?

(A) $100 \times j + n + x \times m$
(B) $j + 100 \times n \times m$
(C) $j + n + x \times m$
(D) $j + ((n + x \times m)/100)$
(E) $(j + n + x \times m) / 100$

8. If $5x + y = 9$ and $x + y = 5$, then $4x = ?$

(A) $-2y$
(B) y
(C) $x + y$
(D) $2x + y$
(E) $-x + 2y$

9. The expression $(15 - x + y)$ is how much less than the expression $(y - x + 50)$?

(A) 25
(B) 30
(C) 35
(D) 40
(E) 45

10. Wole is six years older than Jean who is twice as old as Doris whose current age is x. In three years, Wole will be how old?

(A) $x + 6$
(B) $2x - 3$
(C) $2x + 3$
(D) $2x + 6$
(E) $2x + 9$

Working Backwards from the Answer Choices

When we plug in numbers, our last step is to plug in our numbers into the answer choices. When we work backwards, we start with the answer choices and plug them into the problem! You plug the answer choices into the problem to determine which answer is correct. This method works particularly well when there are numerical values in the answer choices. Always start with the middle value so that you have to try a maximum of three answers (e.g. if you plug in the middle term and it's too small, you know to try only answer choices (D) and (E) which should be bigger).

Solved Problem 1

If four times a number is the same as 15 plus that number, what is that number?

(A) 4
(B) 5
(C) 6
(D) 8
(E) 9

We've got numerical values in an algebra word problem—when you encounter algebra problems with numerical values in the answer choices, think *I can work backwards!*

Let's Work Backwards. First we have to translate the problem which is in English into a mathematical equation. Four times becomes 4 x; a number becomes x; the same as becomes = (an equal sign); 15 plus is of course 15 +; that number is x again... which gives us:

$4 \times x = 15 + x$

We'll start with the middle term which is (C) 6. Does plugging in 6 for x make our equation true? No. 24 is not equal to 21! It's close, though, so let's go for the number closest to 6 which is (B) 5.

$4 \times 5 = 15 + 5$
$20 = 20$

Check! So the answer is 5 or (B).

Notice there were two steps to solve this problem: first converting the English sentence (the problem) into a mathematical equation and then plugging in the answer choices into the equation.

Solved Problem 2

What are the possible values of $k + 1$ given the following:
$kx = k^3x$

(A)   0 and 1 only
(B)   1 and 2 only
(C)   0 and −1 only
(D)   0, 1 and −1 only
(E)   0, 1, and 2 only

This is a two–step problem. First, we have to figure out which values of k make the given equation true. Then, we have to calculate $k + 1$ and choose the correct answer.

In the answer choices, there are four possible values for $k + 1$: 0, 1, 2 and −1. There are thus 4 possible values for k: −1, 0, 1, and −2. Let's *work backwards* and plug in the possible values of k to see which work. Plugging in 0, we get

$0 \times x = 0 \times x$

Is that a true statement? Yes, so 0 is a possible value of k.

Plugging in 1, we get

$1 \times x = 1 \times x$

This is also a true statement so 1 is a possible value of k.

Plug in –1:

$-1 \times x = (-1)^3 \times x$
$-x = -x$

This is also a true statement (–x = –x), so –1 is a possible value of k.

Plug in –2:

$-2 \times x = (-2)^3 \times x$

$-2x = -8x$

This is NOT a true statement, so –2 is NOT a possible value of k.

So the answer is (D) 0, 1, and –1, right? No!! Always re–read what the question is asking for before you answer it!!! Don't forget that last step to turn the values of k that work into k + 1—always double–check that you're answering the question.

We're asked not for k, but for the possible values of k + 1. So the answer isn't –1, 0, 1 but rather each of those plus one or (E) 0, 1 and 2.

Math Section: Working Backwards Problem Set

Solve each of the following problems by Working Backwards (after solving the problem by Working Backwards, for additional practice try solving it using algebra, arithmetic, et cetera.).

Answers are in Appendix 1 on page 446.

1. If $2x^2 - kx - 12 = (x + k)(2x - 6)$, what's the value of k?

(A) −4
(B) −3
(C) 2
(D) 4
(E) 6

2. You bought $45 worth of pencils and pens. Each pen cost $2 and each pencil $1. For each pen purchased, you bought three pencils. How many pens did you buy?

(A) 9
(B) 10
(C) 11
(D) 12
(E) 13

4. A computer previously for sale at 75% of its retail price is discounted an additional 25% to a final price of $675. What was its original price?

(A) $800
(B) $900
(C) $1000
(D) $1100
(E) $1200

5. If $\dfrac{14}{x+4} = \dfrac{7}{6}$ what's the value of x?

(A) 7
(B) 8
(C) 9
(D) 10
(E) 11

6. If 7a – 15 = 4a then 2a = __?

(A) 5
(B) 8
(C) 9
(D) 10
(E) 12

7. What's the largest integer in the group of seven consecutive integers whose sum is 154?

(A) 17
(B) 19
(C) 20
(D) 24
(E) 25

8. If $x^2 - 3x + 15 = 5x$, then what is one possible value of $x/2 = $?

(A) −2.5
(B) −1
(C) 1.75
(D) 2.5
(E) 3

Measurement

With algebra problems, there are usually at least two ways of solving the problem between using pure algebra, plugging in numbers and working backwards. For geometry problems, we have a technique that can occasionally be used to supplement pure geometry: a neat and fairly simple technique of measurement.

Let's say you need to figure out the length of one side of a triangle given the length of some other side of the triangle. You could use our measurement technique to measure the length of the given side and the to–be–determined side in terms of pencil tick marks. Then, you can solve a ratio of given units to tick marks to get the exact length of the to–be–determined side. To use this technique, you'll need to turn one of your pencils into a makeshift ruler by making equally spaced marks on the pencil tip.

This is a sample illustration (from a problem at the end of this chapter) of how to use your tick marked pencil to "measure" your way to an answer. We first count how many tick marks on the pencil correspond to units given in the diagram. We, then, use that ratio (pencil tick marks to given diagram units) to solve for the unknown lengths.

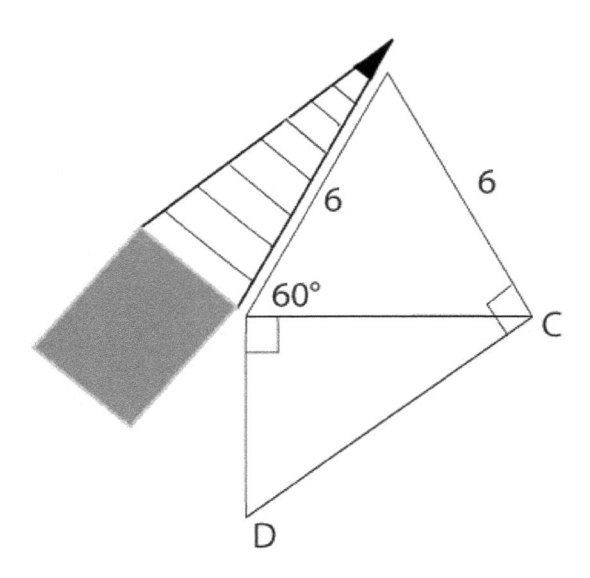

If you need to estimate an angle, draw a 90 degree angle over the shape itself (a square corner basically) and then draw a line that bisects that angle to make it into two 45 degree angles and from there estimate.

If any diagram is not drawn to scale (it will say so somewhere in the diagram) and it looks quite a bit off, re–draw the diagram and then use our measurement technique.

MATH SECTION: Algebra

Algebraic Terms and Concepts to Know.

Equation.

A mathematical statement in which two expressions are equal. Equations on the SAT will almost always have one or more variables. An equation is written mathematically with an equal sign. Usually, we'll need to solve an equation which means solving for the value of a variable in the equation. To manipulate and solve an equation, it's crucial to remember this rule: any operation done to one side of the equation must be done to the other side of the equation (in order to keep both sides of the equation balanced or equal). Here are some examples of equations:

$3 + x = 37$

$x + 3x = 387$

$y = x^2 - 3x$

Inequality.

An inequality is a mathematical statement in which one quantity is stated to be greater than (>) or lesser than (<) some other quantity. There are two other signs: $\geq$ means greater than or equal to, and $\leq$ means less than or equal to. It's important to think of an inequality as an equation but with some different symbols instead of an equal sign ($<, >, \leq, \geq$). We can manipulate inequalities basically the same way we manipulate equations with only one difference: when we multiply or divide both sides of an inequality by a negative constant, the inequality sign flips. Here are some examples:

$7 \geq 3$
$1 \leq 1$

The above inequalities are true since 7 is greater than or equal to 3, and 1 is less than or equal to 1. Below are some more inequalities.

$y \leq 2x^3 + 8x$

$x > 7x + 83$

Coefficient.

The number or constant that multiplies a variable. Here are some examples:

$7x$ (the coefficient is 7)

$23 + 8x = 93$ (the coefficient of 8x is 8)

$9x^7$ (the coefficient of $9x^7$ is 9)

Variable.

A variable is a mathematical value than can change. In the problems we solve on the SAT, a variable is usually what we solve for and thus represents some not–yet–discovered value. In mathematics, we use some symbol like x to represent a variable. The most common variables are x, y and z.

Constant.

A constant is some fixed number. It's a number that can't change unlike a variable. Coefficients are the key example of constants on the SAT. The idea of a constant gets confusing as a constant could be unknown and thus represented as "k" (usually we use k or a, b, or c to represent constants whose values we may need to solve).

Small Note for the Curious: So if k can be a constant it seems like it's a variable since we don't know the value and thus its value could be anything, right? Well, not really...even though we don't know the value of the constant k, whatever that value is can not change once it's fixed which makes it different from a variable—this idea is not important to understand for the SAT but very important when you study calculus and yes it's perplexing!

Integers

The set of numbers with decimal portions equal to zero that differ by steps of 1 from negative infinity to positive infinity: .... , −3, −2, −1, 0, 1, 2, 3, ...

Rational Numbers

The set of numbers each of which can be expressed as a fraction of integers. Every rational number must be able to be put into the form a / b where a and b are both integers. The rational numbers include all repeating decimal numbers (examples include: 3.12121212..., 4.33333..., 3.123123123...) and terminating decimal numbers (any number which stops e.g. 3.125, 4.753, 3.234984, 4.5, etc.).

More examples of rational numbers include −11, 0, 15, 2 / 3, − .7348, and −3 / 1292.

Absolute value.

The absolute value of a number is the magnitude of the number—for a positive number it's the number itself and for a negative number, it's that number made positive. Two straight lines | | are used to indicate that you should take the absolute value of a number. Basically you take the number in the brackets and make it positive if it's negative and leave it if it's already positive.

$| \ 3 \ | = 3$

$| -3 \ | = 3$

We treat absolute value signs like parentheses if there are other operations involved: solve what's inside them first before you take the absolute value and then solve what's left outside them.

$7 - | -18 + 4 \times -2 \ | =$

$7 - | -18 + -8 \ | =$

$7 - | -26 \ | =$

$7 - \ \ 26 \ \ = -19 \ .$

It's also important to know what a graph of an absolute value function looks like.

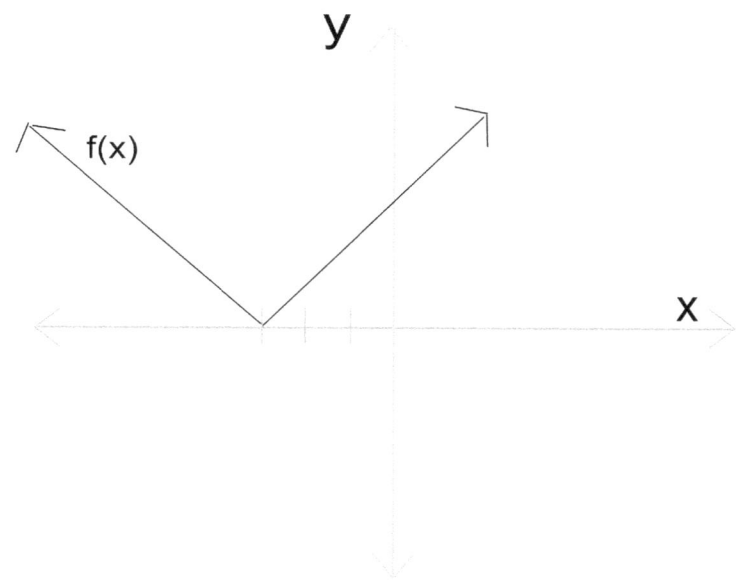

Graph of the Absolute Value Function: f(x) = | x + 3 |

Notice that the graph of a linear absolute value function (linear because there's just an x to the power of one, no x squared or cubed, etc.) is two rays that meet at a point and form a right angle between each other. Also notice that the function is symmetrical about a vertical line, for the above function the line y = –3.

Polynomial.

A polynomial for our purposes is essentially a combination of coefficient multiplied by a variable to some exponential power. It's important to remember that any variable can be expressed as a polynomial expression, thus:

$$x = 1x^1$$

Remember that x has the implied coefficient of 1 and an implied exponent of 1, so that even x can be written as a polynomial expression (as we did above)!

Three more examples of polynomials:

$$3x^6 \qquad\qquad -83y^2 \qquad\qquad 42xy$$

Function.

There are a few different ways to think of a function. One way is to think of a function as a machine. We give the machine an input (the independent variable) and it gives us an output (the dependent variable). Let's take an example of a function which is written in the form of an input/output table:

x	y
1	3
2	4
3	5
4	6
5	7

In this function, if we input 2, we get the output of 4 (look for 2 in the x column, and next to it is 4 in the y column). If we input 4, we get 6.

Functions can also be thought of as the association or mapping of every element in one set with one and only element in some other set. So, in the above table, we've associated 1 with 3, 2 with 4, et cetera…alternatively we can say that 1 has been mapped to 3, 2 mapped to 4. Thinking of a function as a mapping is, then, another way to think of a function.

You have to remember one special rule for functions which is that there's one and only one output for any given input. Thus, 5 gives us the output of 7. If there was another entry which listed 5 in the x column and 10 in the y column, then the input of 5 would yield two outputs both 7 and 10...then we wouldn't have a function.

The vertical–line test tells us if a graph represents a function or not. If you can draw a vertical line that passes through more than a single point on the graph of an equation, then that's not a function. If any vertical line you can draw passes through one and only point on the graph—then you do in fact have a function.

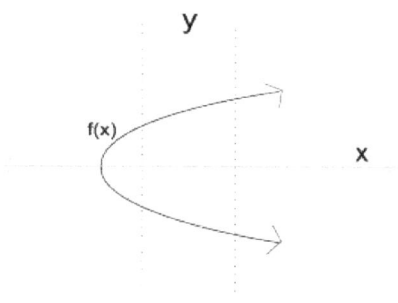

Vertical lines pass through two points of this function (the parabola rotated 90 degrees) so it IS NOT a function (it doesn't pass the vertical line test).

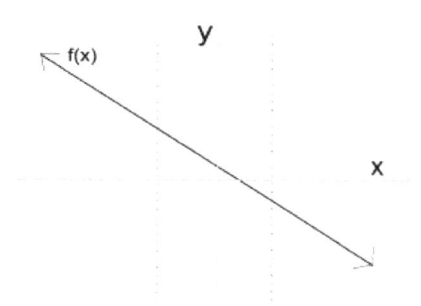

Vertical lines pass through a single point each of this function (a line) so it IS a function (it passes the vertical line test).

Functions are often written in algebraic form. The typical notation for a function in algebraic form uses f(x) notation:

$f(x) = x^2 + 3x + 7$

The input is what's in the parentheses, in this case the x variable. You can always replace f(x) with y. Thus the equation would look like:

$y = x^2 + 3x + 7$

Replacing f(x) with y helps us clearly see that a function is an equation of two variables.

You may be asked to solve a function for certain inputs.

e.g. what's f(10)?

For such a question, the number in the parentheses should be substituted for x—and then we fill in that number in every place in the function where there's an x. We plug in the input (x is always the input variable and then we calculate the output, y or f(x)). Remember you can always replace f(x) with y—for the problem below, y and f(10) are just different names for the same thing, the output value of the function for the input value of 10.

$f(x) = x^2 + 3x + 7$
Solve the above function for f(10).

$f(10) = x^2 + 3x + 7$
$y = x^2 + 3x + 7$

We have to now substitute 10 for x.
$y = (10)^2 + 3(10) + 7$

Now we can solve for y or f(10).
$y = (100) + (30) + 7$
$y = f(10) = 137$

Degree of an equation.

The degree of an equation is the numerical value of the greatest exponent of any variable in the equation. The degree of an equation is important because it tells us the maximum number of solutions for an equation which also represent the maximum number of points of interception of the equation by the x–axis.

Let's take $x^3 + x^2 = 78^6$. The degree of this equation is 3 since that's the value of the largest exponent of a variable in the equation (x^3). Though 78 is to the 6th power, 78 doesn't count since it's a not a variable. 78 could be to any power without affecting the degree of the equation.

For $y = x + x^2 + 15^4$, the degree is 2. Also, remember that any variable that doesn't have an exponent (y and the x in that equation for example) has an implied exponent of 1. This is because any number to the exponent of 1 is equal to itself so $7^1=7$.

Math Section: Algebra Concepts Problem Set

Insure that you know Algebra Concepts by solving the following problems.

Answers are in Appendix 1 on page 448.

1. Classify each of the following numbers as an integer and or a rational number:

    5

    0

    .78932

    −3

    ½

    −2.669

2. Identify the variable and coefficient for each polynomial expression below:

$4x^{-3}$

$-82y^6$

y

$22z^4$

3. Solve the following absolute values:

$|-8| =$

$|9 - 8 \times -3| =$

$|(-7 \times 6 / 3 + 1)| =$

$|(-9 + 3) / -3| =$

4. Explain what a function is and how both the below equation and table each represents a function.

$f(x) = x^2 - x + 2$

x	y
1	2
2	4
3	8
4	14
5	22

5. What's the degree of each of the below equations?

$x^4 - x^6 = 85$

$x^2 - x^3 + x^4 = 98$

$x^2 + 2x^2 - 4x^2 = -9.5$

6. What does the degree of an equation tell us?

7. What's the one difference between manipulating an inequality versus manipulating an equation?

Three Key Techniques for Algebra Problems

1. Plug In Numbers.

Plugging In Numbers for Variables is a key technique as discussed earlier. You *must* practice it.

Remember the three steps:
1. **Pick numbers.**
2. **Solve the problem in terms of the picked numbers.**
3. **Solve answer choices in terms of the picked numbers.**

2. Working Backwards from the Answer Choices

Working Backwards is another key technique. You *must* practice it. Top scorers will solve algebra problems algebraically and then double-check them by working backwards or plugging in numbers.

3. Write Down Everything You Can about the Problem: Variables, Equations, Then Solve.

For math problems in general, we **work on paper!** For a tough algebra problem, you may have to solve it using pure algebra. In such cases, you need to follow a method, and we suggest the following three steps. Write down everything you know that could help you solve a problem (equations, etc.) as well as write down everything given to you in the problem. From there, you need to write and manipulate equations until you get to the point where you have as many equations as you do variables. Once you're at that point, manipulate and solve the equations.

Here are the three steps again:
1. *Write down everything you know and everything that's given in the problem.* Write down the givens, the unknowns/define variables, any equations you know (e.g. the Pythagorean theorem, the three angles add up to 180° rule, etc. for a problem involving triangles, or distance = rate x time for such an algebra problem).
2. *Create/write equations.* You need to have as many variables as you have equations. One tip to get more equations, try to define variables in terms of other variables.
3. *Solve, once you have as many equations as you do variables.* If you have more variables than you do equations and you're stuck, try defining one variable in terms of another variable (this will generate another equation).

For hard algebra problems, you're going to have to use this method because there are too many steps to "see" the solution all at once. Work on paper! Memorize and practice doing tough algebra problems using these steps.

Solving Systems of Equations

A system of equations is a set of two or more equations and more than one variable which you need to solve for. You need to have as many equations as you have variables in order to solve a system of equations. Typically, you'll find two equation/two variable problems on the SAT.

There are two methods to solve a system of two equations: using substitution and adding/subtracting equations. It's important to know both methods, though **adding/subtracting equations is generally the faster method.**

Substitution Method

The idea of the substitution method is to solve the first equation for one of the variables and then substitute whatever that variable is equal to into the second equation.

Problem: we need to solve for x and y and we've got two equations.
$7x + 8y = 18$
$3x - 2y = 15$

First Step: Solve for a single variable in one of the equations
Add 2y to both sides of the second equation to isolate x. Remember that anything we do to one side of an equation, we *have* to do to the other side of the equation (to keep the equation balanced).
$3x - 2y + 2y = 15 + 2y$
$3x = 15 + 2y$
Divide both sides of the equation by 3 to get:
$x = 5 + (2/3)y$

Second Step: Plug the solved equation in for that variable in the other equation.
The other equation is: $7x + 8y = 18$
We need to plug $(5 + (2/3)y)$ in for x in that equation, so it becomes:

7[5 + (2/3)y] + 8y = 18

Third Step: Now we've got a single equation with a single variable. We can solve for that variable.
35 + 14/3 y + 8y = 18
38/3 y = −17
y = − 51 / 38

Fourth Step: We plug in the value we found for y into either equation and solve for x.

3x − 2y = 15
3x − 2(− 51 / 38) = 15
3x + (102/38) = 15
3x = 468/38 or 234/19

Divide both sides of the equation by 3 and we get:
x = 78/19 which as a mixed fraction is 4 2/19

Adding/Subtracting Equations Method.

The idea of the adding/subtracting equations method is that we add or subtract the equations so that one of the variables cancels out and we're left with an equation with just a single variable in it which we can solve. This is a crucial method to understand and learn (it's faster to use than substitution!).

Problem: we need to solve for x and y and we've got two equations.
7x + 8y = 18
3x − 2y = 15

First Step: Multiply one of the equations by a constant so that the variables cancel out via addition or subtraction of the two equations.

Let's multiply the second equation by 4, then the y terms will cancel out.
4 × [3x − 2y = 15]
12x − 8y = 60

We now have two equations:
7x + 8y = 18
12x − 8y = 60

Second Step: Add or subtract the two equations so that one of the variable terms cancels out.

Since both sides of an equation are equal, the sum of the two sides of the equations must equal the sum of the other two sides of those equations. Thus we get:

$$\begin{array}{r} 7x + 8y = 18 \\ +\ 12x - 8y = 60 \\ \hline 19x + 0\ = 78 \end{array}$$

19x = 78

Third Step: We now have a single equation with a single variable which we can solve...so let's solve it.

19x / 19 = 78 / 19
x = 78/19

Fourth Step: We can plug in the value we found for x into either equation and solve for y.

7x + 8y = 18
7 (78/19) + 8y = 18
546/19 + 8y = 18
8y = 18 − 546/19
8y = −204/19

y = –25.5/19 which becomes –51/38 (a proper fraction doesn't have a decimal point in it)

Generally, adding/subtracting equations is the faster and simpler method, but understand and practice both methods so that you feel comfortable using either one to solve a system of equations.

Math Section: System of Equations Problem Set

Use both the substitution and adding/subtracting equations methods to solve the problems (try adding/subtracting equations first as it's the easier method and the key method to practice).

Be sure to write out all your work/all the steps you take to solve the problem neatly.

Answers are in Appendix 1 on page 450.

1. $17x - 15y = 46$
    $24x + 60y = 20$

2. $3x + 4y = 5$
    $5x + 12y = 13$

3. $15x - 25y = 45$
    $35y - 15x = 20$

4. $-11x - 22y = -33$
   $4x - 15y = 45$

5. $-20x + 20y = 40$
   $10x + 40y = -40$

6. $16x - 16y = 32$
   $3x + 8y = -16$

7. If $x + 2y - z = 2$ and $2x + y + z = 13$, then $x + y = $??

(A) 3
(B) 5
(C) 7
(D) 8
(E) 9

8. If $3x - 2y - z = 12$ and $x + y + z = 11$ then, $4x - y = ?$

(A) 7
(B) 9
(C) 12
(D) 17
(E) 23

Multiplying Polynomial Expressions and FOIL

You need to know how to multiply polynomial expressions for the test.

Multiplying Simple Polynomials

To multiply two simple polynomial expressions, we have two steps:
1. Multiply the coefficients
2. Add the exponents of like variables. For different variables, the exponents don't change but must be kept.

Solved Problem 1:

$3x \times 17x = ?$

$3x \times 17x =$
$3x^1 \times 17x^1 =$
$(3 \times 17)(x^1 \times x^1) \quad = \quad (3 \times 17)(x^{1+1}) \quad = \quad 51x^2$

Notice we wrote in the exponent of 1 for each x. That's a good practice as it makes it easier to solve the problem and also helps us make sure that we're adding up all the exponents and not forgetting any.

Solved Problem 2:

$14x^2y \times 17y = ?$

$14x^2y \times 17y =$
$14x^2y^1 \times 17y^1 =$
$(14 \times 17)(x^2)(y^{1+1}) \quad = \quad (238)(x^2)(y^2) \quad = \quad 238x^2y^2$

So to multiply polynomial expressions, we multiply the coefficients then add the exponents of like variables!

Multiplying Quantities with Polynomials: FOIL (First Outer Inner Last)

To multiple two quantities which contain polynomial expressions (polynomials in parentheses with terms separated by plus or minus signs), we use a method you were likely taught called FOIL which stands for First Outer Inner Last. We multiply the first terms together, then the outer terms, then the inner terms, and then the last terms—then we add up any like terms to simplify.

When doing FOIL, we recommend students first get rid of any minus or subtraction signs in the expressions by turning them into the addition of a negative quantity. This helps you to avoid making any careless errors.

Solved Problem 1:

$(3x - 7) \times (4x + 2) =$

Turning the minus sign into adding a negative number gives us:
$(3x + -7) \times (4x + 2) =$

Using FOIL to multiply all the terms (we multiply each term by every other term e.g. 3x by 4x and by 2, also −7 by 4x and by 2):

   First   Outer   Inner   Last
$(3x^1 \times 4x^1) + (3x \times 2) + (-7 \times 4x) + (-7 \times 2) =$

Finally, multiplying it out gives the usual single x^2 term, two x terms and a constant so we're pretty sure we've done our FOIL correctly:
$12x^2 + 6x + -28x + -14 =$

Lastly, we add like terms to show the product in most reduced form. In this case, we add the like terms 6x and −28x to get −22x.
$12x^2 + -22x + -14$

Notice we didn't use subtraction signs. Instead of writing subtraction, we always wrote it as adding a negative number (equivalent to subtracting)—doing only addition makes us less likely to make any careless mistakes.

Sometimes you may have to multiply a sum of two terms by a sum of three terms, here the acronym FOIL itself won't lead you to the correct answer. You have to use the idea of FOIL which is that every term in the first expression must be multiplied by every term in the second expression. Then we have to add those terms up. The next problem is such an example.

Math Section: FOIL Problem Set

Practice FOIL by solving the following problems.

Answers are in Appendix 1 on page 454.

1. $(x - 4)(x + 8) =$

2. $(x - 7)(x - 8) =$

3. $(x + 5)(x + 5) =$

4. $(x - 9)(x + 9) =$

5. $(x - 3)(x - 4) =$

6. $(x + 7)(x + 6) =$

7. $(x - 2)(x + 2) =$

8. $(x + 7)(x - 4) =$

Solved Problem: More Difficult FOIL

$(x - 4)(x^2 - 3x - 7) = ?$

Before we do anything else, let's get rid of the subtraction signs by turning them into addition of a negative number:
$(x + -4)(x^2 + -3x + -7) = ?$

Now to solve the problem, we have to multiply every term in the first expression by every term in the second expression. Let's take x in the first expression: we have to multiply it by x^2, $-3x$, and -7. We have to do the same thing for -4. Then we add the terms, reduce, and we're done.

$(x + -4)(x^2 + -3x + -7) = ?$

You can draw 'arches' from each term to every other term in the adjacent expression to know what to multiply together:

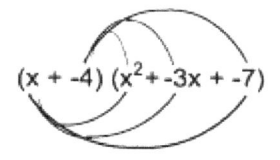

$$(x + -4)(x^2 + -3x + -7)$$

Multiplying out the terms by each other (2 terms in the first expression by 3 in the second expression), we get 6 terms so we know we're correct:
$(x^1 \times x^2) + (x^1 \times -3x^1) + (x \times -7) + (-4 \times x^2) + (-4 \times -3x) + (-4 \times -7) =$

Now solving the terms:
$(x^{1+2}) + (-3x^{1+1}) + (-7x) + (-4x^2) + (12x) + (28) =$
$(x^3) + (-3x^2) + (-7x) + (-4x^2) + (12x) + (28) =$

Adding up the terms to show the product in most reduced form:
$(x^3) + (-3x^2 + -4x^2) + (-7x + 12x) + (28) =$
$x^3 + -7x^2 + 5x + 28$

Math Section: Advanced FOIL Problem Set

Further practice FOIL by solving the following problems.

Answers are in Appendix 1 on page 454.

1. $(2x - 7)(x - 2) =$

2. $(2x - 3)(3x + 3) =$

3. $(3x - 6)(4x + 11) =$

4. $(4x + 5)(6x + 7) =$

5. $(x - 8)(2x + 3) =$

6. $(2x + 6)(3x - 17) =$

7. $(x + 3)(x^2 - 5x + 12) =$

8. $(2x + 2)(x^2 - 17x + 15) =$

9. $(x - 5)(2x^2 - 8x + 31) =$

Factoring Quadratic Equations

You'll need to know not just how to multiply polynomial expressions, but also how to break them up or factor them, particularly quadratic equations.

A quadratic equation is an equation with a single variable with a degree of two. A quadratic equation that you'll see on the SAT will most likely be some variant of this form:

$ax^2 + bx + c = 0$ where a, b, and c are constants.

To factor such an equation means to show how two expressions multiplied yield it:

$ax^2 + bx + c = (dx + e)(gx + h) = 0$ where a, b, c, d, e, g, and h are constants.

Notice in the above equation that:
c = h × e
a = d × g
b = (e × g) + (d × h)

So the last term, c, is the product of the two terms without any variables. The coefficient of the x^2 term is the product of the coefficients of the two x terms. The middle term b is the sum of two products.

Understanding b in particular is easier using a simpler version:

$x^2 + bx + c = (x + e)(x + h) = 0$ where b, c, e, and h are constants.

From this, try to see that b = e + h. You can work it out by multiplying the expressions to see that bx is the sum of ex plus hx, so b has to be equal to the sum of e and h.

Remember the middle coefficient b or the coefficient multiplying the x term is the sum of the two factors without any variable. This is true in the case when the coefficients for x are both 1 (hence a=1); if a is equal to anything other than 1, this isn't true.

Also remember, the last term (c) without any variable is the product of those same two terms, e and h, the terms without any variables.

So for any equation of the form: $x^2 + bx + c = (x + e)(x + h)$
$b = e + h$
$c = e \times h$

The middle term is the sum of the two factors.
The last term is the product of the two factors.

How we factor quadratic equations

Let's first consider examples of this form: $x^2 + bx + c = 0$.

We need to figure out which two numbers, e and h, will add or subtract to equal b and will when multiplied equal c. To do this, we first write down all the factors of c, and then see which set of factors add up or subtract to equal e and multiply to yield c. Let's try some problems to see how factoring works.

Solved Problem 1:

What are the solutions for the equation: $x^2 + 6x + 8 = 0$?

Since it's + +, we know the form will be (x + __)(x + __), so we need to figure out what two numbers sum to 6 and multiply to 8.

Let's write down the factors of 8:
     2 and 4 multiply to get 8,
     8 and 1 multiply to get 8.

Which set when added equals 6...2 and 4 of course. We've just about solved the problem.

It's $(x + 2)(x + 4) = x^2 + 6x + 8 = 0$.

You can always multiply out the expressions to make sure that it's the correct factorization.

Now, let's find the solutions. We've factored the initial equation into:

$(x + 2)(x + 4) = 0$.

To figure out the solutions, we have to know what values of x make the equation true. We know that there's only one way to multiply two numbers and get a product of 0 (as dictated by the right side of the equation being 0 and the left side of the equation being the product of two numbers): one or both of the numbers multiplied in the left side of the equation has to be zero. So either $(x + 2)$ is zero OR $(x + 4)$ is zero—solving those two will give us the solutions.

$x + 2 = 0 \quad x = 0 + -2 \quad x = -2$
$x + 4 = 0 \quad x = 0 + -4 \quad x = -4$

So $x = -2$ or -4.

Good Advice: Use a Table to Organize Your Work

We can make a table in which write out all the possible factors of c (8 in the above problem) and see which set of factors sums to equal b (6 in the problem above):

c (e × h)	e (factor of c)	h (factor of c)	b (e + h)
8	4	2	6
8	-4	-2	-6
8	8	1	9
8	-8	-1	-9

We first wrote in the c value, our given. Then we wrote in the possible e and h pairs whose product equals c i.e. all the sets of integers which when multiplied equal 8. Finally, we see which pair of e and h sums to 6 (our desired b value). From our table, the top row yields the correct b value of 6, so the equation factors to 4 and 2 or (x + 4) (x + 2).

You can always make a table to organize your work and to make sure you're not missing any possible factors!

Solved Problem 2:

Factor $x^2 - 4x - 12 = 0$.

Since the equation is − − (minus minus), we know that the equation when factored must be in the form (x + __) (x − __), so we need to figure out what two numbers have a difference of 4 and multiply to be 12.

Let's write down the factors of 12:
       1 and 12 multiply to get 12,
       3 and 4 multiply to get 12,
       6 and 2 multiply to get 12.

Which of these pairs has a difference of 4? 6 and 2. We've nearly solved the problem now. Let's insert 6 and 2, but we need to make sure all our signs in the proper place.

$(x - 6)(x + 2) = x^2 - 4x - 12 = 0$.

−6 x 2 is equal to −12 so that's correct. −6 plus 2 equals −4 which is also correct. We've solved the problem. The equation factors into:

$(x - 6)(x + 2) = x^2 - 4x - 12 - 0$

Solved Problem 3:

Find the solutions of: $x^2 - 11x + 42 = 18$.

Uh oh, this equation isn't equal to 0, what do we do? If you said, subtract 18 from both sides, you're exactly right. Then we'll have an equation equal to zero which we can then factor and solve.

$x^2 - 11x + 42 + (-18) = 18 + (-18)$

$x^2 - 11x + 24 = 0$

Since the given equation is $-$ $+$, we know we have to factor it into: (x $-$ __) (x $-$ __) =0. This is because two numbers have to have a product of 24 (two negative numbers multiplied together yield a positive number), and the same numbers summed have to equal -11 (two negative numbers summed yield a negative number).

The negative factors of 24 are:
    -24 and -1
    -8 and -3
    -6 and -4.

-8 and -3 also add up to -11, so they are our choices and we've now factored the initial equation.

$(x - 8)(x - 3) = 0$.

The solutions are what make each of the parenthetical expressions of (x -8) and (x $-$ 3) equal to 0 respectively. The solutions for this problem, then, are 8 and 3.

Solved Problem 4:

Find the solutions of $3x^2 - 3x - 6 = 0$.

Uh oh, this problem has a coefficient other than 1 in front of the x^2 term. That makes this problem a tad more complicated to solve than the previous examples...but we'll still get it, don't worry. We have to figure out what combination of coefficients for the first x^2 and what factoring of –6 together yield the middle term (–3).

For these problems, we have to multiply the factors of the coefficient of x^2 (in this case 3) with the factors of the constant term (–6 in this case), and then add those two products to yield the middle term's coefficient (–3 in this case). It sounds a little complicated but when we solve the problem, it will make sense.

This comes from our original generic quadratic equation:
$ax^2 + bx + c = (dx + e)(gx + h) = 0$
for which:
$c = h \times e$
$a = d \times g$
$b = (e \times g) + (d \times h)$

The factors of the first term's coefficient (3): 3, 1 or –3, –1
The factors of the last term (–6): –3, 2 or 3, –2 or –6, 1 or 6, –1

At this point, it takes a bit of trial and error to figure out which pairs are correct. Let's try 3,1 for the first term and 6, –1 for the second term. Once you pick two pairs to try, there are actually two ways to try it to see if we can get the middle term of –3.

$(3 \times 6) + (1 \times -1) = 17$ (not correct)
$(3 \times -1) + (1 \times 6) = 3$ (not correct but pretty close)

We've almost got the middle term's coefficient of –3, but instead we got 3. So if we can reverse the signs of one pair, we'll have the correct pairs. We can't reverse 3 and 1; we have to change both of them to –3 and –1 or not change them at all. Thus, we have to change –1 and 6 to 1 and –6—we can do that (it's one of the pairs we listed).

Our correct pairs thus should be 1 and 3 for the coefficient of x and 1 and –6 for the factoring of the last term. Let's be sure they yield the middle term of –3:

$(3 \times 1) + (-1 \times 6) = 3 + -6 = -3$

Check. So we have the correct pairs (1, –6 and 1,3), so we're very close to the correct answer. We've factored the original equation.

$3x^2 - 3x - 6 = (3x - 6)(x + 1)$

You should double-check that the factors and coefficients are in the correct place by multiplying out $(3x - 6)(x + 1)$ to make sure it equals $3x^2 - 3x - 6$. After we're sure our factoring is correct, we can solve the two solutions of the equation.

Solution 1: We'll set the first parenthetical expression equal to zero.
$3x - 6 = 0$ becomes $3x = 6$ so $x = 2$

Solution 2: we have to now set the remaining parenthetical expression to zero.
$x + 1 = 0$ so $x = -1$

The solutions are 2 and –1.

Important Final Note: $x^2 - y^2$ always factors to $(x + y)(x - y)$!

A required insight for some problems is to realize that you can factor an expression of a squared term minus some other squared term. So remember how it gets factored:

$x^2 - y^2 = (x + y)(x - y)$

Math Section: Factoring Problem Set

Practice Factoring by solving the following problems.

Answers are in Appendix 1 on page 455.

1. $x^2 - 5x + 6 = 0$

2. $x^2 + 18x + 45 = 0$

3. $x^2 - 2x - 15 = 0$

4. $x^2 - 5x + 6 = 0$

5. $x^2 + x - 20 = 0$

6. $x^2 - 7x - 30 = 0$

7. $x^2 + 8x + 12 = 0$

8. $x^2 - 2x - 3 = 0$

9. $x^2 + 11x - 12 = 0$

10. $2x^2 + 16x - 18 = 0$

11. $3x^2 + 20x + 25 = 0$

12. $4x^2 - 10x - 14 = 0$

Translating English into Equations

Many algebra word problems will require you to translate sentences in English into mathematical equations. With a bit of practice, you'll realize how words translate into mathematical symbols, e.g. 'is' into '=', 'more than' into '+', et cetera. Let's take on some sentences.

Solved Problem 1

Find the value of any one of three integers where:
the sum of three integers is ten less than the sum of two of the integers.

$$(x + y + z) \quad = (-10) \quad + \quad (x + y)$$

We thus have the equation:
$x + y + z = (x + y) - 10$

To solve the problem we subtract x and y from both sides of the equation which yields: $z = -10$.

Solved Problem 2

There are 42 more children enrolled at the school (total students = 100) than adults. How many children attend the school?

We can use that statement to define the variables for both children and adults in terms of each other.

C = children = A + 42
A = adults   = C − 42

Note that the above is really a single equation. If we add 42 to both sides of the equation (A = C − 42), we get the equation (A + 42 = C).

We need one more equation since we have two variables. We need a second equation…most likely it should use some information given in the problem that we haven't made use of yet namely that there are 100 total students. We know that there are two types of students at the school, adults and children, so combined they have to equal the total, thus:

A + C = 100

We can now solve the problem.

A = C − 42
A + C = 100

Let's substitute C − 42 from the first equation for A into the second equation yielding:

(C − 42) + C = 100

2C − 42 = 100
2C = 142
C = 71

We've solved the problem. 71 children attend the school.

Solved Problem 3

A number is divided by 7, and the result is the same when 11 is added to that number.

$$x \; / \; 7 \; = \; 11 \; + \; x$$

So:
x / 7 = 11 + x

Let's solve this equation. First, multiply both sides by 7.

$7 \times (x / 7) = 7 \times (11 + x)$
$x = 77 + 7x$

Subtracting x from both sides yields:

$0 = 77 + 6x$

Subtracting 77 from both sides yields:

$-77 = 6x$

Dividing both sides by 6 yields:

$x = -77 / 6$

Math Section: Translating English into Equations Problem Set

For each problem below, translate the problem (from English) into an equation then solve for the missing number or value.

Answers are in Appendix 1 on page 456.

1. Four less than a number is the sum of three plus the square of two.

2. The product of five and another number is equal to the absolute value of the difference of five hundred and seven hundred.

3. A number is divided by 8, and the result is the same when that number is subtracted from seven.

4. Twice the sum of three integers is equal to twice the sum of negative sixteen and two of the integers. Find the value of any one of the three integers.

5. With attendance at night lecture totaling fifty, there are sixteen more women than men. How many men and how many women attend night lecture?

Manipulating Inequalities

Inequalities have an inequality sign (<, >, ≤, or ≥) instead of an equal sign (=) in them. They're manipulated just like ordinary equations (that have an equal sign) with one very important exception: *If you multiple or divide an inequality by a negative number, the sign flips.*

Graphing Inequalities
When you graph an inequality, there are two steps to take.
1. Graph the inequality as though it were an equation e.g. graph the line or parabola, etc. which its graph would be if instead of an inequality sign, it had an equal sign. *If your inequality sign is < or >, you should graph the line as a dotted line. If your sign is ≤ or ≥, then you should graph it as a solid line.*

So for y > –7, let's first graph y = –7 but with a dotted line since it's only greater than (not greater than *or equal to*) which looks like:

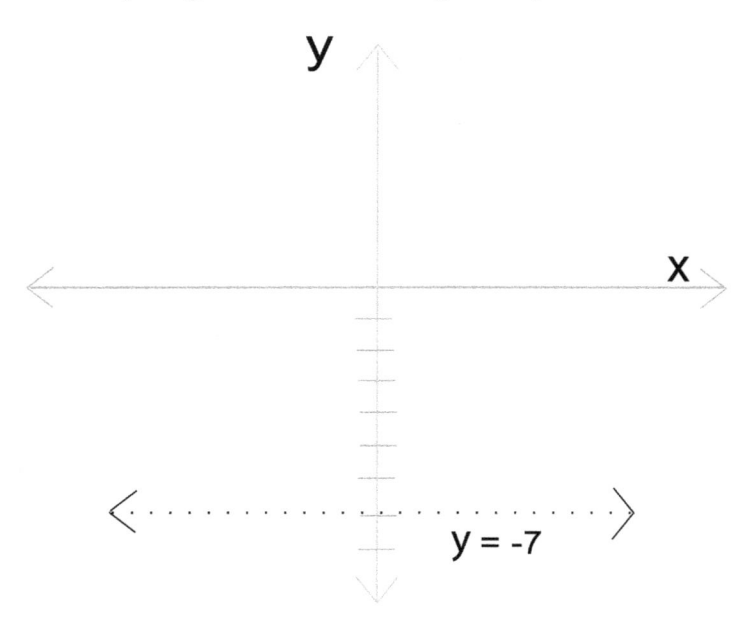

Notice that the line was dotted above because the inequality had a > sign. To finish our graph of y > –7, we need to shade the appropriate region either above or below the line. *For greater than, we shade the region above the line since any value above that line will satisfy the inequality.*

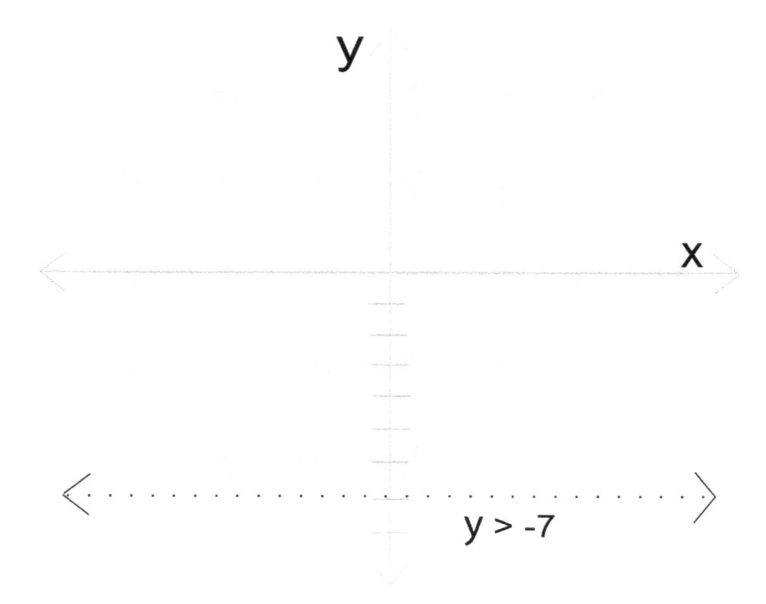

y > -7

That's the graph of y > –7. Keep in mind that the dotted line and the shading above it go on forever!

Let's graph one more inequality: x ≤ 7.

1. We'll again start with a graph of x = 7 but this time, we'll need to make sure the line is solid not dotted (since it's less than *or equal to*). The vertical line represents all values when x equals 7.

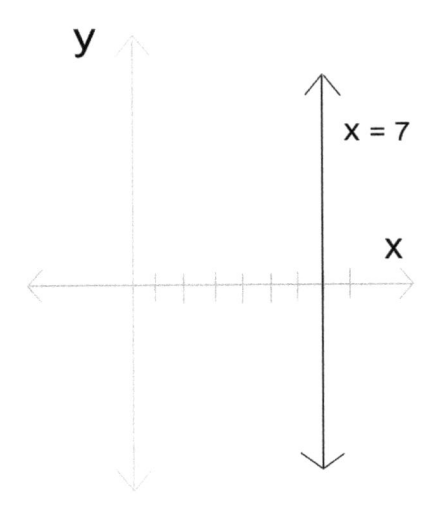

2. Shade a region either to the left or to the right of that line. For x is greater than (> or ≥), you always shade the region to the right of the line, and for less than (< or ≤), you always shade the region to the left of the line. For y is greater than (> or ≥), you always shade the region above the line, and for less than (< or ≤), you always shade the region below the line. In the case of x ≤ 7, all values of x either equal to 7 or less than 7 satisfy the inequality, hence we have a solid line at x = 7 and the left region of all small x values shaded. Here's the graph of x ≤ 7 with the region to the left of x=7 appropriately shaded:

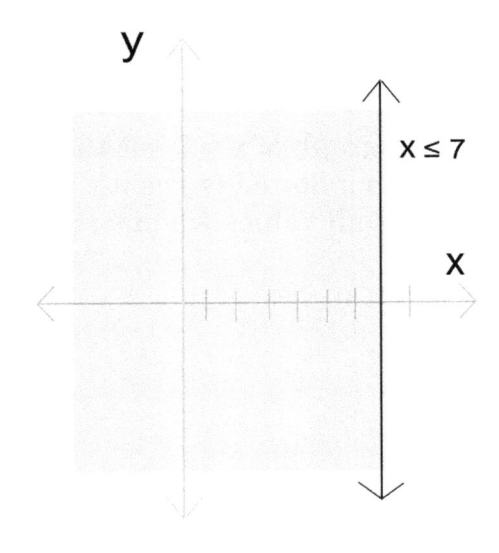

Why do these methods work?

Why does the sign flip in an inequality when you multiple or divide by a negative number? This happens because positive and negative numbers behave inversely in respect to magnitude and size. The magnitude of a number is its absolute value so that the magnitude of both –10 and 10 is 10. The greater the magnitude for a positive number, the bigger it is (i.e. 15 is bigger than 10). The greater the magnitude of a negative number, though, the smaller it is (i.e. –15 is smaller than –10). Multiplying or dividing by a negative number we can think of as taking numbers say that were positive or negative and switching them; we thus have to switch our treatment of their size as well.

Why is the line we graph either dotted or solid? For greater than *or equal to* and less than *or equal to*, the line is solid because of the 'equal to.' That equal to means that we have both a line or equality and an inequality. Thus the line is solid. For greater than or less than, the values can not be equal to the line we graph (but can be infinitely close to it) hence the line is dotted (and dotted means that points on the dotted line do not satisfy the inequality).

Why do we shade a region above or below the line? We shade the region above the line for greater than inequalities because all values greater than that line satisfy the inequality i.e. all values greater than that make the inequality true. That's analogously why we shade the region below the line for the less than sign, because all values less than that line make the inequality true.

Here are some examples of inequalities and how to solve and graph them:

Solved Problem 1

−7y − 8 > 23

Let's add 8 to both sides yielding:

−7y > 31

Divide both sides by −7 which triggers a sign flip

y < −31 / 7

We've 'solved the inequality. Let's graph it. We first have to draw the dotted line y = −31 / 7—it's dotted since it's less than (not less than or equal to). We can now shade the area beneath that dotted line which represents all possible values of y less than −31 / 7.

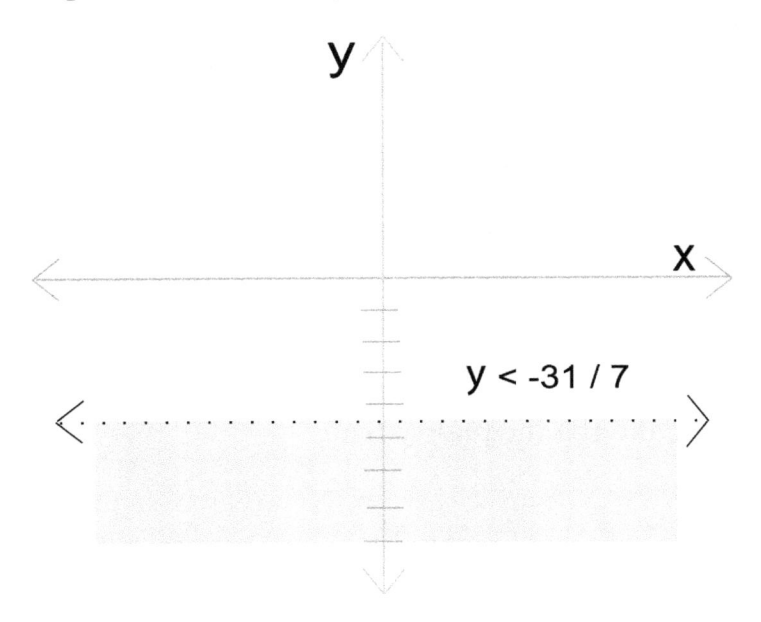

y < -31 / 7

Solved Problem 2

$7y - x \leq -11$

We need to manipulate the equation to get it into slope-intercept form ($y = mx + b$) which we can then easily graph.

Add x to both sides.

$7y \leq -11 + x$

Let's divide both sides by 7 (notice that since 7 is positive, the inequality sign doesn't flip):

$y \leq (-11 / 7) + (x / 7)$

We've solved the inequality. Let's graph it. First we need to draw the line. The first point we can label is the y-intercept (0, −11 / 7), and then we can find the next point using the slope of 1 / 7—we can go up 1 and to the right 7 from the y-intercept and graph the second point (7, − 4 / 7). From there, we can draw our solid line (solid because it's less than *or equal to*) and then shade the area below the line.

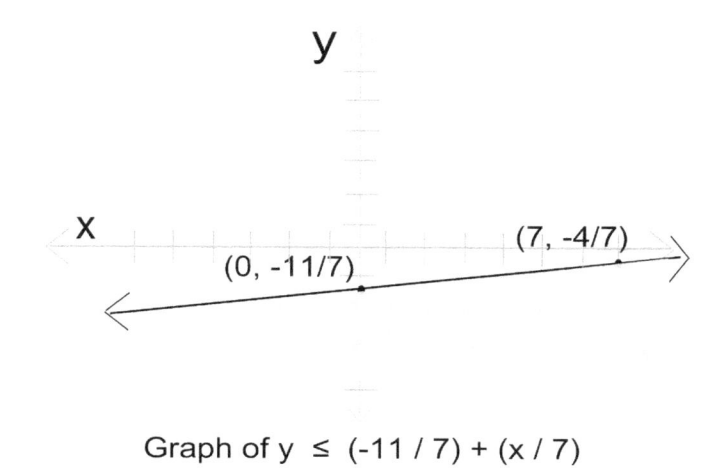

Graph of $y \leq (-11 / 7) + (x / 7)$

Math Section: Inequality Problem Set

Solve the Following Inequalities.

Answers are in Appendix 1 on page 457.

1. $-x - 1 > -1$

2. $-3y \leq -3$

3. $5x - 15 \geq 25 - 3x$

4. $-2x - 8 > 15$

5. $-7x - 8 > 20$

Solve and Graph the Following Inequalities.

6. $x - y > 8$

7. $17y < -9 + 3x$

8. $-2y \leq -16 - 4x$

Rate and Percentage Mixture Problems

Three key methods:
- Keep units as a double-check
- Use conversion fractions—units of desired answer indicate how to set up fractions
- *Use a table for these problems*

Rate Problems

Key equation: **Distance = Rate × Time**

Use a table—it makes it a lot easier to solve problems and keeps your work organized! Let's see how it works to solve a problem.

> John's office is 20 miles away. He spends 90 minutes commuting everyday. Due to heavy traffic, his speed coming home is 15 miles per hour. What's his speed in the morning going to work?

We first make a table with columns for distance, rate and time. We, then, fill in all the data from the problem, putting in variables for unknowns.

	Distance =	Rate ×	Time
Morning	20 miles	x	y
Evening	20 miles	15 miles/hour	z
Total	40 miles	---	y + z

At this point, we've got two equations with three variables:

20 miles = x × y
20 miles = 15 mph × z

That's a problem as we need to have as many equations as we have variables in order to solve a problem. So we need one more equation since we have three variables. Is there any information from the problem that we haven't used yet, that didn't go into the table?

Yes, that 90 minutes round–trip time. We can turn that into one more equation: it represents the total time thus $y + z = 1.5$ hours. Notice we've converted the 90 minutes into 1.5 hours—units in all our equations have to be consistent! If you're using hours in other equations, use hours (and not minutes or seconds) in all your equations!

We can use conversion fractions to convert minutes into hours:

Our conversion fraction is 60 minutes / 1 hour. We're given 90 minutes. Let's convert it.

$$\frac{90 \text{ minutes}}{1} \times \frac{1 \text{ hour}}{60 \text{ minutes}} = 1.5 \text{ hours}$$

We had to flip the conversion fraction so that minutes and minutes would cancel out and we'd be left with 'hours' as our only units.

Back to the problem: we now have three equations and three variables. We can solve the problem.

1. 20 miles = $x \times y$
2. 20 miles = 15 mph $\times z$
3. $y + z = 1.5$ hours.

It's actually a little tricky to solve a system of three equations. We're going to solve the problem using substitution, so make sure your work is really neat to avoid any careless errors.

Solve equation 3. for z:
$z = 1.5$ hours $- y$

Plug in our value for z into equation 2.:
20 miles = 15 mph × (1.5 hours − y)

Solve equation 2. for y
20 miles = 22.5 (miles [mph × hours becomes just miles]) − (15 mph × y)
20 miles = 22.5 miles − (15 mph × y)

Subtract 22.5 miles from both sides of the equation:
−2.5 miles = −15 mph × y

Divide both sides of the equation by − 15 mph:
−2.5 miles / −15 mph = y
y = 2.5 miles / 15 miles/hour = 2.5 / 15 hours = 1 / 6 hours

Now that we've solved y, let's plug that value in for y in equation 1 and solve for x:
20 miles = x × (1 / 6 hours)

Divide both sides by 1 / 6 hours:
20 miles / (1 / 6 hours) = x

x = ((20 x 6) miles) / (1 hours) = 120 miles per hour

We've thus solved the problem (finally!): John drives at 120 miles per hour in the morning to get to work every day (which means he must be really good at avoiding speeding tickets!).

Note again key steps we took to solve the problem:
- *Using the equation distance = rate × time*
- *Using a table*
- *Writing down as many equations as we have variables*

Percentage Mixture Problems

In percentage mixture problems, you'll be given a mixture of various percentage components (e.g. 20% salt and 30% alcohol by weight) and will be asked to solve for the new percentages given some change in the mixture. For percentage mixture problems, making a table, as we did for the rate problem above, is very helpful. Let's solve a problem to see how.

Solved Problem

2 pounds of a solution is 30% saline by weight. How many pounds of salt should we add to make it 80% saline by weight?

We can think of this problem as having an initial and a final condition. Let's first write down everything we know and what we have to solve.

We started out with 2 pounds of a 30% saline solution. If 30% is salt (saline means salt), then 70% is water. Thus, we have .6 pounds of salt and 1.4 pounds of water initially. Let's put that into our table. We know that we're only adding salt—so the amount of water won't change—so the final water is the same as the initial water or 1.4 pounds. The final salt will be the initial .6 pounds plus the x pounds we add—so final salt is .6 pounds + x. Let's put all of that also into our table.

	Initial	Final
Water	1.4 pounds	1.4 pounds
Salt	.6 pounds	.6 pounds + x
Total	2 pounds	2 pounds + x

We've got one variable—we now need an equation to solve it. Is there any data in the problem we haven't yet used? Yes—that the final solution should be 80% salt. What does 80% salt mean or equal? It means that if we have 100 pounds of solution, then 80 pounds will be salt. To convert a percentage into a decimal which we can use to make an equation, we divide a percentage by 100 so 80% becomes 80/100 or .8.

.80 salt = # pounds of salt / # pounds of total solution

We've added x pounds of salt to the total salt as well as x pounds to the total solution (hence we added x to both the numerator and the denominator). Filling in our values for pounds of salt and total solution from the table (the final values), we get the equation:
.80 salt = .6 + x pounds of salt / 2 + x pounds of total solution

Let's solve the equation. First let's cross–multiply the fractions.
.80 / 1 = .6 + x / 2 + x

1.6 + .8x = .6 + x
1 = .2x
x = 1 / .2 = 5

We need to, then, add 5 pounds of salt to the initial solution to yield an 80% saline solution.

Double–check: If we add 5 pounds of salt, we'll end up with 7 pounds of total solution of which 5.6 pounds will be salt. If our answer is correct, then 5.6 pounds of salt divided by 7 pounds of total solution should be 80% (since we're supposed to have an 80% salt solution). 5.6 / 7 is in fact .8...we're correct!

Math Section: Rate and Percentage Mixture Problem Set

Make a table to solve each problem!

Answers are in Appendix 1 on page 460.

1. 5 pounds of a solution is 25% saline by weight. How many pounds of salt should we add to make it 60% saline by weight?

2. Your office is 50 miles away. You spend 200 minutes commuting everyday. Due to heavy traffic, your speed coming home is 25 miles per hour. What's your speed in the morning going to work?

3. 12 gallons of a mixture are 45% cow's milk and 30% goat's milk by volume. If we add 4 gallons of goat's milk to the mixture, what percentage of the resulting mixture will be cow's milk?

4. You drive at 55 miles per hour to a concert at night. You're only able to travel back home from the concert at 40 miles per hour. If the distance from your home to the concert venue is 220 miles, how much total time did you spend traveling to and from the concert?

Inverse and Direct Proportions/Ratios

Proportions or ratios are often tested on the SAT. A proportion is a way of fixing the relationship between two things. For example, we can say that for every 2 green M&Ms that you get, I'll get 3 brown M&Ms. That's an example of a direct proportion or ratio, and it fixes the relationship between your green M&Ms and my brown M&Ms. There are also inverse proportions in which when one number goes up, the other goes down. For example, the more people we have to write a program, the less time it will take to develop the software.

There are thus two types of proportions: direct and inverse.

Direct Proportion: Two Fractions or Division. When x goes up, y also goes up.

$$X_1 / Y_1 = X_2 / Y_2$$

Inverse Proportion: Multiplication. When x goes up, y goes down.

$$X_1 \times Y_1 = X_2 \times Y_2$$

X represents one variable and Y the other. They are numbered 1 and 2 because we use a proportion to calculate how many X and Y we have at some point in time (X_2 and Y_2 should be thought of as X and Y at time 2) based on some fixed ratio or original point of time (represented by X_1 and Y_1).

When you encounter a problem that involves ratios or proportions, first determine if it's a direct or an inverse proportion—ask yourself if one quantity increases, does the other increase or decrease? If it increases, it's a direct proportion and if it decreases, it's an inverse proportion. After that, use the appropriate equation/relationship to solve the problem.

Solved Problem 1

It takes 100 people 75 days to build a house. How many days should it take 150 people to build the same house?

Since the problem describes how two variables (men and days) relate to each other, it's a proportion problem. The first thing to ask yourself is: is this a direct or an inverse proportion? When the number of people goes up, does the number of days required to build the house go up or down? The *more* people we have working, presumably the *less* time it takes. Thus, this is an inverse proportion. Let's write down our inverse proportion relationship.

$$X_1 \times Y_1 = X_2 \times Y_2$$

First, let's replace X with people and Y with days.

(original people) × (original days) = (new people) × (new days)
(100 people) × (75 days) = (150 people) × (Y_2)

Our variable, we know from the Y_2, is new days. We now have a single equation with a single variable, let's solve it.

100 people × 75 days = 150 people × Y_2
7500 people–days = 150 people × Y_2
7500 people–days = 150 people × Y_2

Divide both sides by 150 people yields:

$$\frac{7500 \text{ people–days}}{150 \text{ people}} = \frac{150 \text{ people} \times Y_2}{150 \text{ people}}$$

50 days = Y_2

Thus, it should take 150 people 50 days to build the same house that it would have taken 100 people 75 days to build.

Solved Problem 2

A pound cake requires 2 cups of sugar and 3 eggs. If we have unlimited sugar but only 20 eggs, how many cakes can we bake?

You should recognize that this is a proportion or ratio problem since we're relating or fixing two variables together (eggs and sugar). Is this a direct or an inverse proportion? If we add more sugar, do we also need to add more eggs? Yes, when eggs go up, so does the sugar we need....so it's a direct proportion. Let's write down our direct proportion relation which we know are two fractions.
$$X_1 / Y_1 = X_2 / Y_2$$

We can plug in sugar and eggs for X and Y so:
    2 cups sugar / 3 eggs = x cups sugar / y eggs

We have 20 eggs, but if we plug in 20 eggs in the equation, we'd be solving for cups of sugar. But we need to solve for cakes!? How do we figure out how many cakes we can make?

We need another ratio with cakes in it. We know that for every 2 cups sugar and 3 eggs, we can bake one cake. If eggs are our limiting factor, then we have the ratio 1 cake: 3 eggs. Let's set up a new relation:
    1 cake / 3 eggs = x cakes / 20 eggs

We can solve for x since we have a single equation and a single variable.

Multiplying both sides by 20 yields:
20 / 3 cakes = x
x = 6.667 cakes.

Presumably we can't make 2/3rds of a cake so the answer would likely not be 6.667 cakes but rather 6 cakes!

Solved Problem 3: A Mixture Problem

In a mixture, the ratio is 3 almonds to 5 cashews to 2 walnuts (3:5:2). In such a mixture of 350 nuts, how many almonds and cashews are there?

Note: Ratios (direct proportions) are often written with a colon like the above.

Key Point to Remember: The total number of things in a mixture or ratio has to be a multiple of the sum of the ratio! So in the above problem, the total number of nuts has to be a multiple of the sum of the ratio which is 10 (3 + 5 + 2).

The mixture has to be some multiple of 10 (3 + 5 + 2) which 350 is, and the fewest number of nuts we could have in a mixture according to that ratio is 10. The reason the mixture has to come in steps of 10 nuts is that every time we add 3 almonds to the mixture, we have to also add 5 cashews and 2 walnuts (i.e. a total of 10 nuts). We can't just add 2 cashews and 1 walnut willy–nilly or the ratio would be broken. The only way to preserve the ratio is by always growing our mixture by steps of 10 nuts which are broken down according to our ratio (10 nuts= 3 almonds + 5 cashews + 2 walnuts).

In a mixture of 350 nuts, then, we know we have 350 / 10 or 35 steps. In each step there are 3 almonds + 5 cashews = 8 almonds and cashews.

The total number of almonds and cashews then is:
35 steps × (8 almonds and cashews / step) = 280 almonds and cashews.

Math Section: Proportions/Ratios Problem Set

Answers are in Appendix 1 on page 462.

1. It takes 10 girls 5 days to clean the garage. How long will it take 25 girls to clean the same garage?

2. It takes 16 minutes to fill the bucket with 800 liters of water. How long will it take to fill the bucket with 350 liters of water?

3. A cake requires 3 eggs and a hundred grams of sugar. How many cakes can you make with 10 eggs and five hundred grams of sugar?

4. In a mixture of dried fruit, there are 2 banana chips to 3 dried apricots to 5 prunes. How many dried apricots are in such a mixture of 770 pieces of dried fruit?

5. If it takes 5 boys 6 days to mow the golf course, how long will it take 2 boys to mow the whole golf course?

6. We have a bag of chocolate bars. There were 15 children at the party and each child was going to get 6 chocolate bars. Three more kids showed up, however, and there are now 18 children at the party. If we give each child the same number of chocolate bars, what's the maximum number of chocolate bars we can give to each child?

7. There are 10 blue marbles and 9 red marbles in a jar. What's the least number of marbles we can ADD to the jar to get the ratio of blue marbles to red marbles to be 3:2.

8. x is directly proportional to y such that when $x = 10$, $y = 6$, what does y equal when $x = 15$?

9. z is directly proportional to q such that when $z = 20$, $q = 5$, what does z equal when $q = 50$?

10. The volume of vinegar to oil in a certain salad dressing is 3 to 5. To make 6 liters of the dressing, how many liters of vinegar do we require?

Functions: Graph Problems

Vertical Line Test

If you're ever shown a graph of something and asked if it's a function or not, there are three words to remember: vertical line test! If you can draw a vertical line that intercepts more than a single point of the graph, then it is *not* a function.

Shifting Functions

You may encounter problems in which you'll be shown a graph of a function and then asked to identify the graph of the function shifted.

The original function will often be identified simply as f(x) and the shifted function will be in the form f(x + j) + k where j and k are positive or negative integers.

For functions in the form f(x + j) + k,

k values shift the function up and down so that f(x) + 4 will shift the function f(x) up four, and f(x) − 3 will shift f(x) down three.

j values shift the function left and right: f(x + 1) shifts the function f(x) to the left one, and f(x − 5) shifts f(x) to the right five.

Notice that positive j values shift the function to the left (the negative direction) and negative j values shift the function to the right (the positive direction), but positive k values shift the function up (the positive direction) and negative k values shift the function down (the negative direction).

Let's look at an example. Below is a graph of f(x).

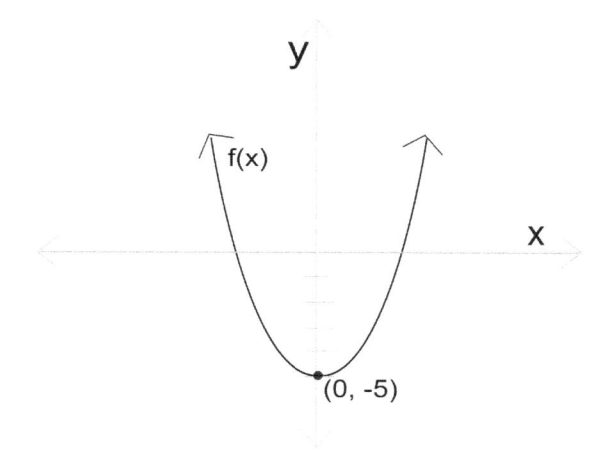

[Graph showing a parabola f(x) with vertex at (0, -5)]

Below is our original function f(x) shifted...it's now f(x) + 2 whose graph is f(x) shifted up two.

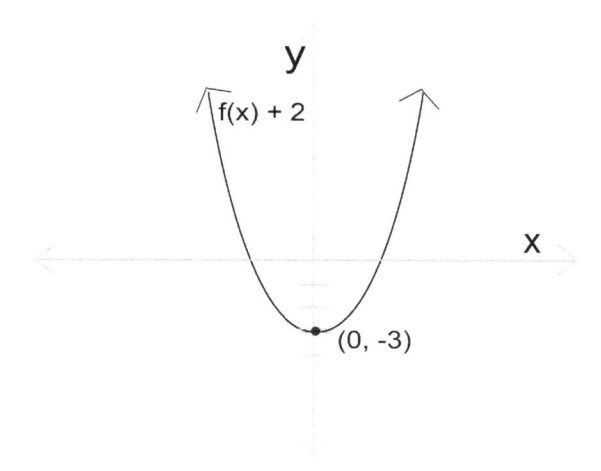

[Graph showing a parabola f(x) + 2 with vertex at (0, -3)]

The reason adding a constant to a function shifts it up or down is that now every single y value in that function has been increased or decreased by that constant (which for every point results in the whole function's graph moving up or down the amount of that constant).

Below is a graph of f(x + 2) whose graph is f(x) shifted two to the left.

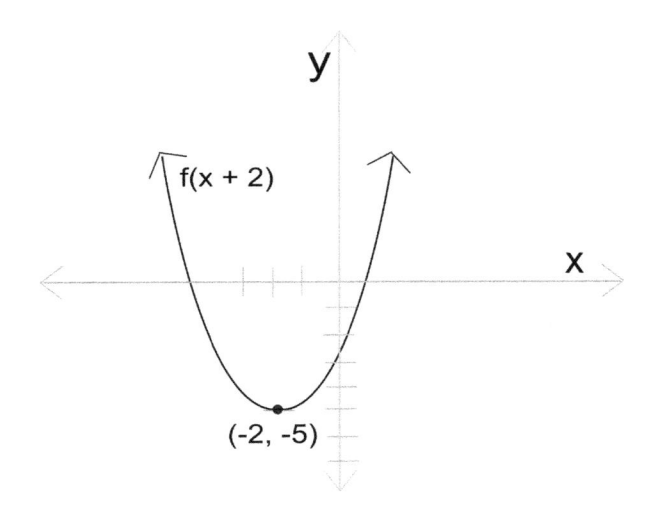

To understand why adding constants to x shifts the function to the left or right is a little more difficult. Let's consider the vertex of the function f(x) which was (0, −5). For the vertex point, the x–value we need to input is 0 to get the lowest y–value which is −5. If instead of x, we now have x + 2, then we still need to get 0 for that quantity and to get it we need to plug in −2 for x. Plugging in −2 for x yields 0 for the quantity x + 2 which is our input into the function, and the input 0 yields our vertex. Hence, the new x–coordinate of the vertex is −2 and all our other x–coordinates similarly shift two to the left.

Shifting Functions Summary:

f(x + j): j values shift f(x) in the opposite x–direction e.g. positive j values shift f(x) to the left (the negative x–direction) and negative j values shift f(x) to the right.

f(x) + k: k values shift f(x) in the same y–direction e.g. positive k values shift f(x) up (the positive y–direction) and negative k values shift f(x) down

Math Section: Function Graph Problem Set

Answers are in Appendix 1 on page 465.

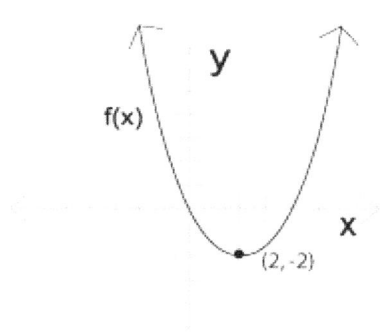

[Graph of f(x), an upward parabola with vertex at (2, -2)]

Using the above graph of f(x) with vertex at the point (2,–2), draw the following shifted functions:

1. Draw the graph of f(x) + 3

2. Draw the graph of f(x – 4)

3. Draw the graph of f(x) − 2

4. Draw the graph of f(x + 7)

5. For the graph of f(x) over the domain of −2 < x < 6, for how many values of x does f(x) = −1?

Functions: Functions of Functions

You may be asked to solve problems which involve multiple functions and taking a function of a function. Let's first review how a function works to understand how we can use another function as the input for a function.

Consider these two functions:
f (x) = 2x –3
g (x) = 17 – 4x

g (10) = ???

Remember that the above means our input is 10 and the output will thus be g (10). Another way to think about it is that whatever is in the parentheses should be substituted for x in the function's definition. So there's a single x in the definition of g(x) as 17 –4x…let's substitute 10 there and solve the problem:

g (10) = 17 – 4 (10)
g (10) = 17 – 40
g (10) = – 23

In the same way that we took the function g(x) for x=10, we can solve for a function where the variable x equals some other function.

To notate that we want to solve the function for 10, we write g(10). To notate that we want to solve the function by plugging in another function, we'll use one of the below two notations:

g (f (x)) =

> means plug in the function f(x) into the function g(x), or alternatively there's the notation:

$f \circ g =$

$f \circ g = f(g(x)) =$

which means plug in the function g(x) into the function f(x)

This is known as a function of a function or a composite function. There are occasionally such problems on the SAT, and they usually aren't difficult once you understand how functions work. If you follow the "instructions" of the function, they should be fine. Also remember to always follow the arithmetic orders of operation for such problems. Let's solve a few problems and see how these problems work:

Solved Problem 1:

$f(x) = 2x - 3$
$g(x) = 17 - 4x$

For the above two functions, solve for f (g (5)).

Following our order of operations, we do the innermost parentheses first which is solving for g(5).

$g(5) = 17 - 4 \times (5)$
$g(5) = 17 - 20$
$g(5) = -3$

Now, instead of g(5), we can write −3. So we're left with:

$f(g(5)) = f(-3) = ?$

Let's solve f (−3):

$f(-3) = 2x - 3$
$f(-3) = (2 \times (-3)) - 3$
$f(-3) = -6 - 3$

$f(-3) = -9$

And we're done: $f(g(5)) = -9$.

We followed our arithmetic rules for order of operations as well as our rules for solving functions and arrived with a little work at the correct answer.

Solved Problem 2:

$f(x) = 2x - 3$
$g(x) = 17 - 4x$

For the above two functions, solve for a new function: $f(g(x))$.

This problem is a little more difficult than the first problem since we have to solve it in the abstract. It's still not difficult. Instead of solving for a numerical value of g(x) and plugging that numerical value into $f(x)$ as we did for problem 1, here we have to simply plug the whole $g(x)$ function into $f(x)$ and reduce.

$f(g(x))$ tells us that wherever there's an x in the $f(x)$ function, we have to plug in the $g(x)$ function.

$f(x) = 2x - 3$

Since $g(x) = 17 - 4x$, for that single x in $f(x)$ we have to plug in $17 - 4x$. So instead of plugging in a single value, we plugged in a function.

$f(g(x)) = f(17 - 4x) = 2(17 - 4x) - 3$

Now we have to reduce the new composite function.

$f(g(x)) = 2(17 - 4x) - 3$

f (g(x)) = 34 − 8x − 3
f (g(x)) = 31 − 8x

And we're done, the solution is that f (g (x)) = 31 − 8x

Doublecheck: Plug in the values from the first problem which we solved manually (plugging values into one then the other function) and make sure our new composite function gives us the correct answer.

According to problem 1, f (g (5)) = −9. Let's solve for f (g (5)) with our just−solved composite function, f (g (x)) = 31 − 8x

f (g (5)) = 31 − 8x
f (g (5)) = 31 − 8 × 5 = 31 − 40 = − 9.   Correct. Our answer is confirmed!

Math Section: Functions of Functions Problem Set

Answers are in Appendix 1 on page 467.

For the two functions:
$f(x) = 4x^2 - 7x + 16$
$g(y) = 17 - y$

1. Solve for f(g(5))

2. Solve for g(f(– 10))

3. What's the composite function f(g(y)) = ?

4. What's the composite function g(f(x)) = ?

For the three functions:
$f(x) = -x^2 + 10x - 8$
$g(z) = 5z + 15$
$h(x) = 25 - x$

5. Solve for f(g(h(2)))

6. Solve for f(g(h(2x)))

7. What's the composite function f(g(h(x))) = ?

Functions: Inverse Functions

You may have to solve an inverse function—these problems are not too common but may pop up.

There are two steps to figuring out an inverse function for a given function. The first step is to invert the variables: replace x's with y's and y's with x's.
The second step is to manipulate the new equation so it's in the form y=___ (y equals something).

Solved Problem:

What's the inverse function, f^{-1}, of $f(x) = -12x + 32$?

Step 1: Invert x's and y's in the function or equation.

Let's first replace f(x) with y.

$y = -12x + 32$

Now we replace y with x, and the x's with y's.

$x = -12y + 32$

Now we have to manipulate the equation ($x = -12y + 32$) into the form $y = $ ___ (y equals something!).

Subtract 32 from both sides:

$x - 32 = -12y$

Divide both sides by -12

$(x - 32) / (-12) = y$

$y = (x - 32) / -12$

We've solved for the inverse function. Let's replace y with the inverse function symbol to finish the problem up:

$f^{-1}(x) = (x - 32) / -12 = -x/12 + 32/12$

Let's see the graph of our solved equation:

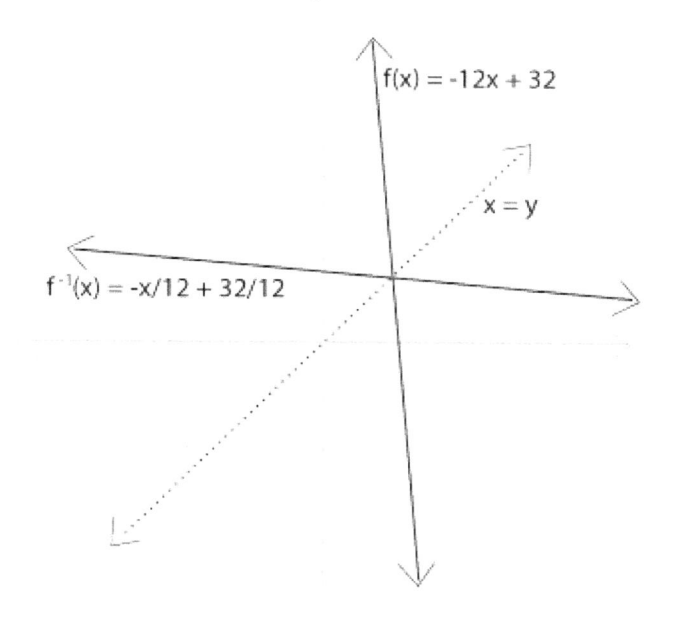

[Graph showing $f(x) = -12x + 32$, $f^{-1}(x) = -x/12 + 32/12$, and the line $x = y$]

Note that the graph of an inverse function is the reflection of the graph of f(x) across the line y = x!

Math Section: Inverse Functions Problem Set

Answers are in Appendix 1 on page 470.

What's the inverse function (f^{-1}) of the following functions:

1. $f(x) = 10x + 8$?

2. $g(x) = 81 - 5x$

3. $f(x) = -3x + 18$

4. $f(x) = 42 - 2x$

5. $f(x) = x - 3$

Functions: Tables

There are occasional problems in which functions will be represented by a table. Remember a function is a kind of machine in which we are given an input (x value) which is linked to some output (y or f(x) value). Thus a table of x and y values represents a function. For the below table, imagine that our input is 3 (x value), then our output would be 5 (the y value next to 3).

x	f(x)
1	2
2	−7
3	5
4	36
5	−11

Solved Problem

What's f(f(1)) based on the above function (the table above)?

We have to solve the innermost parentheses or f(1) first. Looking in the x column, 1 is the first entry, and the f(x) entry to its right is 2.

Thus, f(1) = 2. We can thus replace f(1) with 2.

Now we're left with: f(f(1)) = f(2) = ?

To solve for f(2), we go to next row in the x column and find 2, next to it is −7 in the f(x) column. Thus f(f(1)) = −7.

Math Section: Function Tables Problem Set

Answers are in Appendix 1 on page 471.

x	f(x)	g(x)
1	5	−5
2	4	−4
3	3	−3
4	2	−2
5	1	−1

1. $f(5) = ?$

2. $g(3) = ?$

3. $g(f(4)) = ?$

4. $f(-g(2)) = ?$

5. Using the same table for the functions f(x) and g(x) above, solve for x in the below equation.
$$x - f((-2 \times g(5))^2) = g(f(3)) \times g(f(2))$$

6. Using the same table for the functions f(x) and g(x) above, solve for y in the below equation.
$$g(f(4)^2) = y - 4 \times -g(3) + f(3)$$

Two Fractions in an Equation

If you encounter an equation which has two fractions equal to each other, think *cross–multiply*!! An equation with two fractions: I cross–multiply. An equation with two fractions: I cross–multiply. An equation with two fractions: I cross–multiply.

Solved Problem:

$$\frac{7x}{17} = \frac{8}{3x}$$

We've encountered an equation of two fractions, cross–multiply (remember when you encounter an equation of two fractions, *think cross–multiply*).

$7x \times 3x = 17 \times 8$
$21x^2 = 136$

Dividing both sides of the equation by 21,
$x^2 = 136 / 21$

Lastly, taking the square root of both sides (you'll have to use your calculator for the right side) yields the answer:

x ~ 2.5 OR –2.5

Remember there are two possible solutions for any square root, the negative root and the positive root. That ~ sign means 'is approximately equal to.'

A new mantra: **when I have an equation with two fractions I cross–multiply. When I have an equation with two fractions I cross–multiply.**

Math Section: Fractions in Equations Problem Set

Solve for x in each of the problems below.
Answers are in Appendix 1 on page 472.

1. $\dfrac{5x}{15} = \dfrac{8}{6x}$

2. $\dfrac{4}{9x} = \dfrac{48x}{27}$

3. $\dfrac{14x}{9} = \dfrac{70}{3x}$

4. $\dfrac{3}{32x} = \dfrac{27x}{8}$

5. $\dfrac{8x}{81} = \dfrac{16}{18x}$

Absolute Value Equations

Key technique to remember: turn absolute value equations into two equations (negative/positive)!

You may have to solve and or graph absolute value functions and equations. There's one important method to remember when solving an absolute value equation: to get rid of the absolute value sign, we split the equation into two equations. This is because positive values as well as negative values make an absolute value equation true. Thus we have to solve for which positive values make the equation true, and which negative values make it true.

Solved Problem

$|x - 8| = 5$

Both $(x - 8)$ and $-(x - 8)$ make the absolute value true—since the absolute value of $-(x - 8)$ is just $(x - 8)$. Remember that the negative sign disappears when we take the absolute value e.g. $|-5| = |5| = 5$.

To solve $|x - 8| = 5$, we have to turn it into two equations which we'll solve separately:

1. $(x - 8) = 5$
2. $-(x - 8) = 5$

That's the key step in solving absolute value equations: turn the absolute value equation into two equations, one in which the absolute value quantity is positive and the other in which it's negative...just as we did above.

Now we have to solve both equations.

Solve 1. by adding 8 to both sides

x = 13

Solve 2. by first multiplying both sides by −1

x − 8 = −5

Now, add 8 to both sides

x = 3

We've now solved the given absolute value equation; there are two solutions.

x = 3 or 13

Double–check: let's plug our solutions into the original equation to make sure they're correct.
Original equation: $|x - 8| = 5$

$|(3 - 8)| = 5$
$|-5| = 5$
$5 = 5$
Check.

$|(13 - 8)| = 5$
$|5| = 5$
$5 = 5$
Check. Our answer works and is correct.

Math Section: Absolute Value Problem Set

Answers are in Appendix 1 on page 473.

1. $|x + 3| = 9$

2. $|2x - 3| > 5$

3. $|3x - 9| = 5$

4. $|15 - x| < 75$

5. $|x| = 58 - 38 + x$

6. $|2x| = 17 - 8$

MATH SECTION: (mostly) Arithmetic

Order of Operations (PEMDAS—P/E/MD/AS)

You may have forgotten this acronym, PEMDAS, which you likely learned in early middle school, but it's a very helpful pneumonic for remembering the arithmetic order of operations.

In solving equations or arithmetic problems, there are rules for the order in which we do mathematical operations for consistency and other reasons. The order goes as follows:

Parentheses: what's in parentheses is calculated first, beginning with the innermost parentheses and working our way out to the outermost parentheses. Again, we calculate what's in the innermost parentheses first, then what's in the next innermost set of parentheses, until there are no more parentheses left. Inside a set of parentheses, we follow EMDAS: solve exponents first then multiplication & division, and lastly addition & subtraction.

Exponents: after anything that's in parentheses, we solve exponents.

Multiplication & Division: after exponents, we do multiplication and division from left to right i.e. the left–most multiplication or division first and then move on to the next left–most one, etc.

Addition & Subtraction: after everything else is done, we do addition and subtraction from left to right.

Solving an order of operations problem should elucidate how to use PEMDAS.

Solved Problem

$(8 \times 5 / 10 - 2^3)^2 + 3/3 - 4/2 \times 2^4 = ?$

P for parentheses first. Within the parentheses, exponents first.

$(8 \times 5 / 10 - 8)^2 + 3/3 - 4/2 \times 2^4 = ?$

We've still got to finish up the parentheses: after exponents comes multiplication & division from left to right.

$(40 / 10 - 8)^2 + 3/3 - 4/2 \times 2^4 = ?$
$(4 - 8)^2 + 3/3 - 4/2 \times 2^4 = ?$

Still in the parentheses: after multiplication & division comes addition & subtraction from left to right.

$(-4)^2 + 3/3 - 4/2 \times 2^4 = ?$

No more arithmetic to do within parentheses (we've kept the parentheses around −4 so we don't get confused as to whether it's $(-4)^2$ or whether it's $-(4)^2$ which are two different numbers).

We're onto E for exponents.

$(-4)^2 + 3/3 - 4/2 \times 2^4 = ?$
$16 + 3/3 - 4/2 \times 16 = ?$

MD for multiplication & division from left to right

$16 + 1 - 4/2 \times 16 = ?$
$16 + 1 - 2 \times 16 = ?$
$16 + 1 - 32 = ?$

AS for addition & subtraction from left to right

$16 + 1 - 32 = ?$

17 − 32 = ?
− 15

PEMDAS has (after many calculations!) led us to the solution: −15.

Notice that it's crucial to follow PEMDAS. For example, had we not done multiplication and division before addition and subtraction and or not done multiplication/division from left to right—we would've gotten a different result.

Math Section: PEMDAS Problem Set

Answers are in Appendix 1 on page 475.

1. $8 - 4 + 5 \times 3^2 / -15 = ?$

2. $(15 - 3) \times 2 / -2 + 3 - 4^2 \times -1 = ?$

3. $(24 / 6 \times -5 / 10 - 5)^2 / (12 \times 3 - 12 / 2) = ?$

4. $(3 \times 15 / 9 - 5) + (12 / 3 - 8 / 2) = $?

5. $(-3 \times 4 / 2 - 1)^2 + 2 / 4 - 8 / 4 \times 3^3 = $?

6. $(((2 - 3 + 4^2) \times -2) - 8) + (5 \times 4 - 9 / 3) = $?

Radicals/Roots/Powers

You need to know the rules for manipulating radicals and exponents for the SAT.

Exponents, which you should be familiar with, are usually powers. For example, 2^3 we say as 2 to the third power or 2 cubed which means 2 times 2 times 2. 2 we call the base and 3 we call the exponent. 7^4 is seven to the fourth power which is 7 times 7 times 7 times 7. 8^2 is 8 squared or 8 to the second power which means 8 times 8.

You probably are also familiar with roots. Most likely the square root and the cube root. We often write roots with radical notation. Thus, $\sqrt{4}$ means the square or second root of 4 (which happens to be 2 since 2×2 is 4). $\sqrt[3]{8}$ means the cube or the third root of 8 (which also happens to be 2 since 2×2×2 is 8). $\sqrt[7]{5}$ means the seventh root of 5 i.e. what number times itself times itself times itself times itself times itself times itself equals five (yes, that was 7 times). For $\sqrt[7]{5}$, we call 7 the root, and the symbol over top of the 5 is called the radical—we read it as the seventh root of five. $\sqrt[7]{5}$ is approximately 1.26 incidentally.

Exponents can also be fractional which allows us to integrate the ideas of roots and powers into a single mathematical operation: exponents! The numerator of a fractional exponent is the power, and the denominator of a fractional exponent is the root.

$20^{3/4}$ means the fourth root of 20 to the third power. In radical notation, it looks like this: $\sqrt[4]{20^3}$

When you see problems in fractional exponent notation or radical notation on the SAT, always think that you can convert them into either notation. Sometimes, it's easier to solve a problem in fractional exponent form and sometimes it's easier when it's in radical form. We'll solve a few problems to demonstrate this shortly.

There are a few exponent rules you need to learn.

1. **Same base multiplied: Add Exponents.** When we have the same based multiplied by itself, add the exponents.
   $x^7 \times x^8 = x^{15}$

2. **Same base divided: Subtract Exponents.** When we have the same base divided by another expression with the same base, subtract the exponents.
   $\dfrac{x^{15}}{x^3} = x^{12}$

3. **Exponent to an exponent: Multiply them.** When we have an exponent to an exponent (or a power to a power), multiply the exponents.
   $(x^3)^4 = x^{12}$

4. **Same exponent: Multiply the Bases.** When we have two expressions multiplied by each other which have the same exponent, multiply the bases together.
   $3^5 \times 6^5 = 18^5$

Try to work out yourself why these rules are true by using the definition of an exponent (expanding the exponent). Remember that you can always expand an exponent—this can help you re–derive the rules if you ever forget them. Here's a demonstration of why adding exponents works when you have the same base multiplied by itself.

$x^7 \times x^8 = x^{15}$
$x^7 = x \times x \times x \times x \times x \times x \times x$
$x^8 = x \times x \times x \times x \times x \times x \times x \times x$
Thus,
$x^7 \times x^8 = (x \times x \times x \times x \times x \times x \times x) \times (x \times x \times x \times x \times x \times x \times x \times x)$

And
$(x \times x \times x \times x \times x \times x \times x) \times (x \times x \times x \times x \times x \times x \times x \times x) = x^{15}$

We've thus just shown that $x^7 \times x^8 = x^{15}$ is true.

First Important Note: Use Your Calculator!!!! Remember that you have and can use your calculator—check your work and if in trouble, try to solve radical and exponent problems by plugging in numbers and solving via your calculator!

Second Important Note: Break Bases Up into Their Prime Factorizations!! You'll see how useful this is for reducing radical and exponent expressions in the solved problem.

Solved Problem

$32^{1/2} \times \sqrt{18} = ??$

Many problems on the SAT will require you to reduce radical and fractional expressions. There are a few ways to do this which we'll use in this problem which you should make a mental note of. Note first of all that you could solve this particular problem with a calculator pretty quickly...we'll solve it using arithmetic manipulation though...

Let's first put the whole problem into fractional exponent form. The square root of 18 means 18 to the root 2 and to the power 1 (any number to the first power is just itself, so if no power is indicated the power is implicitly 1).

$32^{1/2} \times 18^{1/2} = ??$

Aha, we have two bases multiplied with the same exponent. This should remind you of something. Namely one of our exponent rules that we can multiply bases together when they have the same exponent. Even though we hope you remembered that rule, let's not use it for now... Let's break down the bases into their prime factorization. 32 is 2 to the 5th power, while 18 is made up of 3 times 3 times 2. Thus we can rewrite the equation above:

since $2^5 = 32$ and $2 \times 3^2 = 18$
$(2^5)^{1/2} \times (2 \times 3^2)^{1/2}$

We have exponents to exponents—according to our rule, let's multiply them. We have to distribute the power to both bases in the second expression.

$(2^5)^{1/2} \times (2 \times 3^2)^{1/2}$
$(2^{5/2}) \times (2^{1/2} \times 3^{2/2})$

Since $2/2 = 1$, we can reduce $3^{2/2}$ to 3^1.

$(2^{5/2}) \times (2^{1/2} \times 3^1)$
$(2^{5/2} \times 2^{1/2} \times 3)$

We now have two expressions with the same base, let's add their exponents.

$(2^{5/2} \times 2^{1/2} \times 3)$
$(2^{5/2 + 1/2} \times 3)$
$(2^{6/2} \times 3)$

We're just about done now. We just have to simplify and solve.

$(2^{6/2} \times 3)$
$(2^3 \times 3)$
(8×3)
(24)

We've got the answer. $32^{1/2} \times \sqrt{18} = 24$.

Surprising...but correct!

Key things to remember: you can use fractional exponent or radical form for solving root/exponent problems and taking the prime factorization of bases helps in reducing expressions. Memorize the four exponent rules.

Math Section: Radicals/Roots/Powers Problem Set

Solve these at first without using your calculator (then after solving them, practice solving them with your calculator)!

Answers are in Appendix 1 on page 477.

1. $5^{2/3} \times \sqrt[3]{125^2} =$

2. $\sqrt[4]{32^{11} \times 128^{19}} =$

3. $243^{1/3} \times \sqrt[3]{9} =$

4. $\sqrt[5]{128} \times \sqrt[10]{(8 \times 32)^2} =$

5. $18^{1/3} \times 9^{2/3} \times 12^{1/3} =$

6. $\sqrt[2]{32} \times 4^{3/4} =$

7. $\sqrt[4]{27} \times 27^{1/2} =$

8. $\sqrt[2]{(2^{20} \times 4^{40})} =$

New or Made-up Operators

You'll sometimes encounter problems with some funny looking symbols you've never seen before like:

x ◊ 7 = ?
or
7 † 4 = ??

If they asked 7 + 4 or 7 × 4, how many students out of a 100 would get the question correct? 100!! 100 would get it right since everyone knows the standard operations of arithmetic like addition (+), subtraction (–), division (/), and multiplication (×). On the SAT test, thus, they can't give you such a straightforward arithmetic question even though these made-up operator questions boil down to simple arithmetic.

These questions will define some new operation like (◊) or (†) in terms of the arithmetic operations you already know (+, –, /, ×). If you just follow the instructions they give and our general rules for doing arithmetic (particularly the order of operations PEMDAS), you won't have any trouble.

There will be some definition for each new operation: follow that definition!

For instance, let's take:

7 † 4 = ??
where
x † y = x² + y

From the definition, we know now that x † y means that we square the first number (x) and add the second number (y) to that sum.

In the given problem, 7 is the first number we'll plug in for x, and 4 is the second number which we'll plug in for y.

$7 † 4 = 7^2 + 4$
$= 49 + 4$
$= 53.$

Let's solve a few more problems:

Solved Problem 1

$x ◊ 7 = ?$
where
$x ◊ y = xy + 3$

We have to plug in x and 7 into the definition of this operation so we get:

$x ◊ 7 = xy + 3$
$x ◊ 7 = (x)(7) + 3$

It's pretty easy plugging x in, since we don't have to do anything (just leave the x alone!). We plugged in 7 for y since it's the second number or the value on the right–side of the diamond. Let's simplify:

$x ◊ 7 = (x)(7) + 3$
$x ◊ 7 = 7x + 3$

We're all done, the answer is 7x + 3!

Solved Problem 2

Given:
x ☺ y = $x^2 + xy + y$

Solve this equation:
z ☺ −10 = (−1 ☺ (4 ☺ 2))

This is a slightly complicated question. Let's first solve the right side of the equation
[(−1 ☺ (4 ☺ 2))]. We have to follow our PEMDAS rules and solve the innermost parentheses first (4 ☺ 2). Since 4 is to the left of the smiley face it's our x value and 2 is our y value which we have to plug into the given definition: $x^2 + xy + y$.

(−1 ☺ (4 ☺ 2)) =
(−1 ☺ (4^2 + 4×2 + 2)) =
(−1 ☺ (16 + 8 + 2)) =
(−1 ☺ (26)) =

We've solved (4 ☺ 2), now we have to solve the −1 ☺ 26 since 26 = (4 ☺ 2) as we just found above.

(−1 ☺ 26) =
(−1 ☺ 26) = $(−1)^2$ + −1×26 + 26
(−1 ☺ 26) = 1 + −26 + 26
(−1 ☺ 26) = 1

SO
(−1 ☺ (4 ☺ 2)) = 1

We've solved the right side of the equation, let's plug it in and solve the left side of the equation now.

z ☺ −10 = (−1 ☺ (4 ☺ 2)) = 1

SO
z ☺ −10 = 1

Lets expand z ☺ −10:

$z^2 - 10z + (-10) = 1$

Aha, this is a quadratic equation. Let's get it into the form $ax^2 + bx + c = 0$ and solve it!

$z^2 - 10z - 10 = 1$

Add −1 to both sides.

$z^2 - 10z - 11 = 0$

Let's factor it:

$(z - 11)(z + 1) = 0$

z = 11 or −1

We've got it, z = 11 or −1.

Math Section: New or Made-Up Operators Problem Set

Answers are in Appendix 1 on page 479.

1. $4 \blacksquare -3 = ?$ where $x \blacksquare y = x \times y + x$

2. $7 \spadesuit (6 \spadesuit 5) = ?$ where $x \spadesuit y = 2x - 4y$

3. Is $(-4 \odot -2) = (-2 \odot -4)$ where $x \odot y = y^x - 4$

4. $(z + 1) \star 1 = ?$ where $x \star y = xy - y$

5. $(x \# (y \# 8))$ where $x \# y = x - 5y$

230

6. $(5 \square (5 \square (5 \square 5)))$ where $x \square y = x^2 - 5y$

7. Solve for x in this equation: $x \top -5 = 7 \top x$
$$\text{where } x \top y = x^2 - 2xy + y^2$$

8. $6 \uparrow (8 \uparrow 9)$ where $x \uparrow y = xy + 5x$

9. $((-5 \blacksquare 5) \text{ x } (x \blacksquare x^2))$ where $x \blacksquare y = x^3 - xy$

Elementary Number Theory: Prime and Composite Numbers

Have you ever heard of something called Number Theory? Unless you're a recreational math enthusiast, we doubt it. Virtually no high school in the country teaches a course or even a topic that's identified as number theory. It's a little unfair, then, that there are number theory questions on the SAT, no?

Don't worry, even though you haven't heard of it, you've most likely studied a bit of number theory in elementary and middle school without knowing it.

Number theory is the branch of mathematics that studies the properties of numbers. It may be a little strange to think that numbers have properties the same way living creatures, say, have properties…but numbers do. In biology, if we came across some strange creature, to study it and understand it we'd try to figure out its properties such as what kind of skin does it have, is it warm or cold blooded, does it give birth to live young or lay eggs, et cetera. In the same way, numbers have properties that we can study: being even or odd, prime or composite, negative or positive, et cetera. The most crucial property in number theory is that of being prime. The prime numbers are the most studied numbers in mathematics. The greatest problem in all of mathematics involves trying to figure out what the pattern and distribution of the prime numbers is (it's called the Riemann Hypothesis incidentally). Most of what are widely considered the most beautiful proofs in mathematics are in number theory (and many aren't too difficult to understand as well).

Exercise: Write out the first twenty or thirty prime numbers. Try to find a pattern or some formula that generates those prime numbers. Don't spend too much time doing this—thousands of mathematicians have spent centuries trying to find a pattern to the primes without any luck!

2, 3, 5, 7, 11, ... are all **prime**. A **prime number** is a number that's divisible only by 1 and itself.

4, 6, 9, 10, 12 ... are all **composite**. A **composite number** is divisible by itself, 1, and some other set of numbers. We call non–prime numbers composite numbers because we can think of them as 'composed' of prime numbers as we'll soon see.

The **fundamental theorem of arithmetic** states that every positive integer except for 1 is either prime or the product of a unique set of prime numbers. To restate the theorem, every composite number is the product of a set of unique prime numbers. This means that there's one and only way to multiply prime numbers together and get that particular composite number.

$10 = 2 \times 5$
$15 = 3 \times 5$
$50 = 2 \times 5 \times 5 = 2 \times 5^2$
$20 = 2 \times 2 \times 5 = 2^2 \times 5$

Each of the above composite numbers has been written out in its **prime factorization.** In the prime factorization of a composite number, we write out the prime numbers which 'compose' that number—which prime numbers when multiplied together yield that composite number. In this way, we can think of prime numbers as the building blocks of the composite numbers. Breaking down a composite number into its prime building blocks is useful for many problems.

Use a prime factor tree to create a prime factorization of a composite number. To make one, you start with the composite number at the top of the tree and then keep breaking it into factors until you reach a prime number at which point the branch ends. You're finished when every branch in the tree ends in a prime number—and the product of all the prime numbers should be the number you started with (the original composite number) so you've then got the prime factorization.

Here's an example of a prime factorization tree (you probably did these in 5th or 6th grade—hopefully it looks familiar):

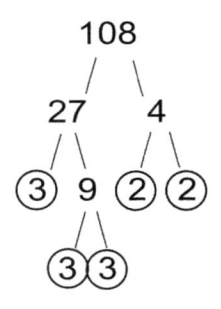

```
        108
       /   \
      27    4
     / \   / \
    ③  9 ② ②
       / \
      ③ ③
```

Thus, the prime factorization
of 108 is 3 * 3 * 3 * 2 * 2

You should also know a few other concepts:

Multiple: the multiples of 7 are 7, 14, 21, 28, 35, et cetera. The multiples of a number can be gotten by multiplying the given number by the positive integers in succession (e.g. the number times 1, then the number times 2, then the number times 3, etc.)

Least Common Multiple (LCM): the smallest number which two or more numbers can evenly go into e.g. the LCM of 14 and 20 is 140 since 140 is the smallest number into which both 14 and 20 go evenly.

Greatest Common Factor (GCF): the largest number which evenly goes into two or more numbers e.g. 7 is the GCF of 49 and 56 since both 49 and 56 can be evenly divided by 7 and not by any other larger common factor.

Remainder: you were hopefully taught division and remainders in elementary school. A remainder results from division of integers when one integer doesn't evenly divide the other e.g. 13 divided by 4 results in 3 remainder 1 or 29 divided by 11 results in 2 remainder 7. The remainder is how much is left over.

Solved Problem 1:

Three men yawn at 2pm. One man yawns every 12 minutes. The second every 8 minutes. The third every 18 minutes. At what time will all three men yawn in unison again?

The first thing to realize about this problem is that it's asking you to solve the LCM or least common multiple of 12, 8 and 18. The LCM represents the least number of minutes after the original three yawns when all three men will yawn together again.

How do we calculate the LCM?

Key step for all number theory problems: get the given numbers into their prime factorizations!

$8 = 2^3$
$12 = 2^2 \times 3$
$18 = 2 \times 3^2$

Okay, back to the previous question: how do we calculate the LCM?

We can think of the least common multiple as a number that has to contain 8, 12, and 18. Let's build that number, the LCM.

First put in 8. We don't, though, put 8 literally in—rather we put in the prime factorization of 8.

LCM = 2^3 (includes 8 in it)

Let's put 12 in now. $12 = 2^2 \times 3$. So we need two 2's and a 3. We've already got three 2's in our LCM...so we don't need any more 2's, just a single 3! We have to leave out any superfluous or unnecessary numbers otherwise we won't end up with the *least* common multiple.

LCM = $2^3 \times 3$ (includes 8 and 12 in it)

We have to put 18 in lastly. 18 = 2×3^2. We need a single 2 and two 3's. We've already got three 2's in our LCM so that's taken care of. We also have one 3...but we need two 3's...so let's put in one more 3.

LCM = $2^3 \times 3^2$ (includes 8 and 12 and 18)

Our LCM is then $2^3 \times 3^2$. = 8×9 = 72

Let's look at the LCM we've got in its prime factorized form and make sure it's correct. Are we sure that 8 is in it? 8 = 2^3 so it has to be a factor of the LCM and is thus in it since the LCM contains 2^3. What about 12? 12 requires two 2's and a single 3—all of which we've got. Do we need both 3's? Yes, for 18. It looks like 8, 12, and 18 are indeed three factors of our LCM and that our LCM is in fact the *least* common multiple.

LCM = $2^3 \times 3^2$

We have built the LCM using our prime number building blocks. Now we can multiply it out and get the answer: $2^3 \times 3^2$ = 8×9 = 72! Don't write in 72 yet...remember to always re–read the question and be sure that you're answering it!!! We've been asked at what time the three men will yawn in unison again, not how many minutes later. 72 minutes after 2pm is 3:12pm...so the very next time the three men will yawn in unison again is at 3:12pm.

*Key insight: for a number to be factor of another number, its prime components must be factors of that number. So for 8 to be factor of any other number, its prime factor components or 2^3 have to be among the prime factor components of the other number. Vice versa, any number which contains 2^3 among its prime components **has** 8 as a factor (as well as 2 and 4 which are also in 2^3).*

Solved Problem 2:

What's the largest positive integer that evenly divides 72 and 64?

This question is asking us to figure out the GCF, greatest common factor, of 72 and 64. What's the biggest number that goes into both 72 and 62?

From our key step above, let's first *write out the prime factorizations.*

$64 = 2^6$
$72 = 2^3 \times 3^2$

Second step for a GCF problem is to see which prime factors both (or all) numbers have in common. For 64 and 72, they both have three 2's. That's our GCF! That's the largest possible number that goes into both 64 and 72.

GCF = 2^3 = 8

Prime factorization is powerful! Taking the prime factorization of the given numbers helped us quickly and simply solve a problem that initially looked difficult.

Note for those who are starting to enjoy number theory: The fundamental theorem of arithmetic is a beautiful result when you think about it. The theorem, again, states that every positive integer except for 1 is either prime or the product of a unique set of prime numbers.

Imagine someone gave you all the prime numbers, and then asked you to give him all the positive integers. There would be a lot of gaps in the primes (between 3 and 5, between 5 and 7, etc.), how could we fill in each and every gap without ever double–filling any gap? We have to take the product of every possible combination of prime numbers! That would fill in each and every gap once and only once. That's what the fundamental theorem of arithmetic says.

The theorem isn't too difficult to prove—if you want to try, start with the assumption that the same composite number has two different prime factorizations and use that assumption to come up with some absurdity which proves then that our assumption has to be false (and that the fundamental theorem is correct).

Solved Problem 3:

When a certain two-digit positive integer is divided by 11 the remainder is 7, and when it's divided by 10, the remainder is 4. What is the number?

For these and any problems, we first want to see how the problem behaves i.e. let's start a list of two-digit numbers that when divided by 11 leave a remainder of 7. Here's the list of them:

18
29
40
51
62
73
84
95

Each of the numbers above when divided by 11 leaves a remainder of 7. We constructed the list by finding 18 first, then each subsequent number in the list is 11 greater than 18. We increment each number by 11 since if 18 leaves a remainder of 7 when divided by 11, if we add 11 to it then it will still leave the same remainder.

We actually went a bit beyond just seeing how the problem behaves into listing all the possible answer choices. For remainder problems, often this is your best strategy: work by hand! To finish up the problem, we have to find the number which when divided by 10 leaves a remainder of 4...it's 84.

Math Section: Elementary Number Theory Problem Set

Answers are in Appendix 1 on page 482.

1. The positive integer x is a two–digit number. When it is divided by 11, the remainder is 8, and when it is divided by 15, the remainder is 14. What is the value of x?

2. Jim has 123 cents. Jonah has 104 cents. Buying an artificial start tattoo costs 7 cents. Jonah and Jim each want to buy the same number of tattoos. What's the maximum number of tattoos Jim and Jonah can buy in total so that each individual owns the same number of tattoos?

3. What's the Greatest Common Factor of the following sets of numbers:

(a) 156 and 178?

(b) 24, 36 and 48

(c) 196 and 132

4. 56^{30} is divisible by all the following except:

(A) 14
(B) 16
(C) 28
(D) 84
(E) 112

5. What's the largest possible value for n for which 12^n is a factor of 360^{50}?

6. What's the least common multiple of the following sets of numbers:

(a) 32, 36 and 38

(b) 40, 45 and 48

(c) 42, 56 and 64

Sequences and Series

5, 7, 9, 11 ...

2, 1, ½, ¼ ...

There are some problems where there will be a pattern or rule that generates a sequence of terms. These are aptly called sequences.

Rule: Always write out the first several terms of a sequence

You have to write out the first several (at least the first five) terms of a sequence to see how the sequence behaves. Does the sequence repeat? Does each term increase by some fixed amount from the previous term?

There are three types of sequences. You should be familiar with and understand all three of them such that when you encounter a sequence, you can identify what category it falls in. You'll often be asked to find a particular term in a sequence e.g. the 17th term in a sequence. Each type of sequence has a method or equation for calculating any term in it (the nth term).

Arithmetic Sequences

Arithmetic sequences work by addition/subtraction. In an arithmetic sequence, successive terms increase or decrease by some fixed amount.

5, 7, 9, 11 ...

The above sequence is an arithmetic sequence since the second term is 2 bigger than the preceding or first term. The third term is 2 bigger than the second term or its preceding term, and so on... The sequence has a rule to generate all the terms: add 2 to get the next term.

You can use 'hats' from one term to the other to try to figure out how the sequence behaves—the rule that lets me get the next term from each previous term. Here's an example for the sequence 2, 8, 14, 20, et cetera.

$$\begin{array}{cccc} +6 & +6 & +6 \\ \frown & \frown & \frown \\ 2 \quad 8 & 14 & 20 \ldots \end{array}$$

All arithmetic sequences operate by some rule in the form of adding or subtracting a constant k to a term to get the next term.

The formula for getting the nth term (n can be any positive integer e.g. 3 or 5 or any other positive integer) **of an arithmetic sequence is:**

nth term = (first term) + ((n − 1) × k)

where k = constant which we add/subtract to get each term

For the above sequence, the first term = 5 and k = 2. The 17th term thus is determined by:

17th term = (5) + ((17− 1) × 2) = 5 + 32 = 37

The formula works because to get to any later term in the sequence, we have to start at the first term and then add the constant (which we're increasing each term by) n − 1 times to calculate the nth term.

Geometric Sequences

Geometric sequences work by multiplication/division. In a geometric sequence, successive terms are multiplied or divided by some fixed constant

2, 1, ½, ¼, ...

The above sequence is a geometric sequence in which each term is multiplied by ½ to get the succeeding term. Here's a diagram with 'hats':

$$\begin{array}{ccc} \times & \times & \times \\ 1/2 & 1/2 & 1/2 \end{array}$$

2   1   1/2   1/4 ...

All geometric sequences operate by a rule in the form of multiply or divide a term by some constant k to get the next term.

The formula for getting the nth term of an geometric sequence is:

n^{th} term = (first term) × ($k^{(n-1)}$)

where k = constant which we multiply/divide by to get each term

For the above sequence, the first term = 2 and k = ½ . The 4th term thus is determined by

4th term = (2) × ((1/2)$^{(4-1)}$) = (2) × ((1/2)^3) = 2 × 1/8 = 2/8 = 1/4

Exercise: For both the geometric and the arithmetic sequence formulas, try to figure out why they work. Why is it we use n – 1 and not n for example? Why is k to the power (n – 1)? Make sure you understand why every formula you use is correct!

Repeating Sequences

You may encounter sequences which repeat. You'll usually be given some rules which result in the same 3 or 4 terms repeating indefinitely.

5, 1, 3, 7, –1, 1, 3, 7, –1, 1, 3, 7, –1 ...

The above sequence after the first term repeats a set of four terms (1, 3, 7, –1). To figure out the nth term in a repeating sequence, you first have to figure out the number of terms that repeat (in this case 4) and if there are any extra terms at the beginning that aren't part of the repeating pattern (in this case there's a single term).

Let's define:
   p = the number of terms in the pattern
   j = the number of terms at the beginning of the sequence that aren't part of the pattern
   n = the rank of the term we seek i.e. the 7th term in the sequence, the 2nd term, etc.

The first step in solving any repeating sequence problem is to calculate:
the remainder of (n – j) divided by (p). We subtract j because those terms are not part of the repeating sequence, thus we have to get rid of them. (n – j) thus represents the number of terms in the repeated repeating sequence!

The second step is to figure out the value of the term. The remainder itself (the remainder of (n – j) divided by (p)) tells us which term in the repeating sequence it is. A remainder of zero indicates it's the last term in the sequence. A remainder of any number is that term in the sequence e.g. a remainder of 1 means we're on the 1st term in the repeating sequence or a remainder of 7 means we're on the 7th term in the repeating sequence.

If you're confused, don't worry, it will make sense when we solve a few problems.

Solved Problem 1

5, 1, 3, 7, –1, 1, 3, 7, –1, 1, 3, 7, –1 …

Calculate the 30th term in the above repeating sequence.

There's a single extra term at the beginning (j = 1), and the repeating pattern has 4 terms in it (p = 4). We need to find the remainder of (30 – 1) divided by (4) since we're seeking the 30th term, there was 1 term preceding the repeating pattern, and the pattern has 4 terms in it.

29 divided by 4 results in 7 remainder 1

Second Step: The remainder indicates the term in that place in the pattern. A remainder of zero means that it's the last value in the pattern (in this problem the last term is –1). Our remainder was 1 thus the 30th term is going to be 1st term in the pattern which is 1.

Solved Problem 2

1, 2, 3, 4, 7, 8, 9, 11, 7, 8, 9, 11, 7, 8, 9, 11, 7, 8, …

What's the 36th term in the above sequence?

There are four initial terms before a pattern sets in. So j = 4. The pattern of 7, 8, 9, 11 consists of 4 terms. So p = 4. We need to solve for the 36th term so n = 36.

First Step: Calculate the remainder of (n – j) divided by (p)

(36 – 4) divided by (4) results in (32) divided by (4) leaves a remainder of zero.

Second Step: Which term does the remainder point to.

A remainder of zero means that the term is the last term in the pattern which is 11. Thus the 36th term in the sequence is 11.

*Think through our approach to repeating sequences and be certain you understand **why** it works. That will help you remember it as well as tackle more difficult problems.*

Solved Problem 3

In the sequence T(n) where n is the nth term in the sequence, T(1) = 100 and T(n) = T(n – 1) + 1. What is the value of n when T(n) = 142?

First, we have to understand the notation of the problem. What exactly does T(n) mean or represent...T(n) represents the value of the nth term of the sequence. It's crucial to then understand that T(n – 1) represents the term before T(n) or T(n)'s preceding term or predecessor. Thus the formula T(n) = T(n – 1) + 1 can be translated into English as: each term in the sequence is equal to its preceding term plus one. While the notation is quite similar to that of function problems—be aware that there are slight differences (for example n in T(n) can only be an integer). We can now write out several terms in the sequence.

T(1) = the first term = 100
T(2) = the second term = its preceding term + 1 = 100 + 1 = 101
T(3) = the third term = its preceding term + 1 = 101 + 1 = 102
T(4) = the fourth term = its preceding term + 1 = 102 + 1 = 103

...and so on. We could calculate every other term in the sequence repeating this process which is called using iteration: applying the same method to each preceding term to get its succeeding term.

From our initial list of terms, we can see that the pattern of this sequence and write out the terms again.

Sequence Value: 100, 101, 102, 103, 104, ...
Nth Term in the Sequence: 1st 2nd 3rd 4th 5th, ...

We have to now recognize that this is an arithmetic sequence, each successive term is being raised by 1. We have a formula to determine the nth value of an arithmetic sequence, and we know the first term (100), the value of k (1), and the value of the term we're solving for (142). Let's plug them into our formula for arithmetic sequences.

Nth term = (first term) + ((n − 1) × k)

142 = (100) + ((n − 1) × 1)

142 = 100 + n − 1

43 = n

So 142 will be the 43rd term in the sequence.

The answer then, is 43.

Math Section: Sequences Problem Set

Answers are in Appendix 1 on page 486.

1. Each successive term of a sequence which begins with 2 is the square of its previous term divided by 2. What is the 17th term in this sequence?

2. Every even term of a sequence which begins with 5 is the three less than its previous term, and every odd term is the absolute value of the difference of the previous two terms. What is the 57th term in this sequence?

3. Every even term of a sequence which begins with 0 is the two greater than its previous term, and every odd term is four less than its previous term. What is the 57th term in this sequence?

4. What's the 8th term in the following geometric sequence?
81, 27, 9, 3, 1...

5. A sequence begins with 20. Every even term is the product of its previous term and −1, and every odd term is the sum of its previous term and −1. What is the 45th term in this sequence?

6. The sequence below begins with –20 and every successive term is determined by multiplying its predecessor by some positive integer x and adding some integer y. What is the sum of x and y?

–20, –25, –35, –55, –95, –175, …

7. In the sequence T(n) where n is the nth term in the sequence, T(20) = 47 and T(n) = T(n – 1) – 5. What is the value of n when T(n) = –8?

8. In the sequence T(n) where n is the nth term in the sequence, T(1) = 1/27 and T(n) = T(n – 1) × 3. What is the value of n when T(n) = 27?

9. The average price of a cup of coffee was $1.50 in 2005 and it's been increasing by $.10 a year ever since then. In what year will the price of a cup of coffee be $8.70?

10. The average cost of a doughnut was $1.00 in 2005 and it's been increasing by 10% a year since then. What will the price of a doughnut be in 2055?

Sums of Sequences: Series

You may (though it's unlikely) have a problem that involves calculating the sum of some sequence. When we have a sequence which we take the sum of, we call it a series. Series are used in mathematics a lot, and you'll see them in pre–calculus and calculus where they're fundamental. They're not often on the SAT, but we'll share a little trick that could be handy if you ever encounter such a problem on the SAT. This solution was supposedly arrived at by one of the great mathematicians, Carl Friedrich Gauss, when he was 10 years old. His teacher wanted to take a nap and gave the 10 year–olds a problem he was sure would take them at least fifteen minutes to solve: add up all the integers between 1 and 100. The teacher was surprised when a minute later young Gauss was at his desk with a solution.

Gauss discovered that instead of adding 1 + 2 + 3 + 4 +... which would've taken a long time, he could add the series as a set of pairs of terms. He paired 1 and 100, 2 and 99, 3 and 98, 4 and 97, 5 and 96, and so on. You can see where this is going. Each pair has a sum of 101 and there are 100 / 2 or 50 such pairs!

Thus the solution is 101 × (100 / 2) = 101 × 50 = 5050. The sum of the positive integers up to 100 is 5050.

The general formula for calculating the sum of an arithmetic sequence is:
 (sum of the first and last term) × (number of terms in the sequence divided by 2)

We have to calculate the sum of each pair (adding the first and last term gives us that) and then figure out how many pairs we have (the number of terms in the sequence divided by 2) and multiply those two numbers together. This method or equation works for all arithmetic sequences (no matter if they have an even or an odd number of terms).

This method may prove valuable on an SAT problem. If it doesn't, we still hope you enjoyed the anecdote about Gauss...

Percentage Problems:

Percentage Basics

Percentage is defined as part dividing whole, and it's represented by the math symbol %. A percentage is often written as the decimal multiplied by 100 e.g. 50% which in decimal form is .50—so to convert a percentage into a fraction or a decimal, divide by 100.

50% = 50 / 100 = .5

Remember the definition of a percentage, particularly in the form of an equation. Write down everything you know when you tackle a math problem and for percentage problems, that should include the definition of a percentage:

Percentage (%) = $\underline{\text{part}}$
 whole

Note that to get the percentage, we divide the part by the whole then we multiply it by 100 e.g. 1/2 = .5 = 50%. To put it in percentage form, we multiply the decimal value .5 by 100 to get 50 percent or 50%.

Tip for a Doublecheck: the units of the part and the whole should always be the same when you calculate a percentage. So, if your numerator is in terms of cents and your denominator is in terms of dollars, you've got a problem (convert the numerator into dollars or the denominator into cents).

Solved Problem

Calculate the percentage discount for a $40 shirt which has been marked down by $10 to a sale price of $30.

The dollar discount is the part ($10), and it's taken from the whole or the regular price ($40).

Percentage = $\dfrac{\text{Part}}{\text{Whole}}$ = $\dfrac{\$10}{\$40}$ = $\dfrac{1}{4}$ = .25

To put .25 into percentage form, we multiply it by 100

% form = decimal × 100 = .25 × 100

= 25%

We calculated the part over the whole and then multiplied our decimal solution of .25 by 100 to get the final answer in percentage form which is that the shirt has been marked down by 25%.

Math Section: Percentage Problem Set

Answers are in Appendix 1 on page 490.

1. If 15% of a number is equal to 300% of 50, then what is that number?

2. Shirts regularly priced at $40 each are marked down by 20%. If you were to buy three shirts, how much would you save in total (in dollars)?

3. If a baby's caloric intake grows an average of 10% each month, and in March a baby was eating 500 calories a day, how many calories would the baby eat in May?

4. A photo's height was reduced by 25% and its length increased by 20%. By what percentage, whether negative or positive, did the area of the photograph change?

Percentage Pay and Percentage Off

There are two ways to think about percentages—the percentage we pay for an item and the percentage off, what we're saving on an item. These are equivalent ways of representing the information a percentage expresses but sometimes it's easier to use one or the other method (we'll see that in the solved problem). For example, saying that you're paying 70% of the regular price is the same thing as saying you're saving 30%. In the solved problem on percentages, we could say that the $10 discount represents 25% off the $40 regular price or we could say that the $30 sale price represents paying 75% of the $40 regular price.

Almost all stores use only percentage off. You're unlikely to see a sign that says pay 80% of regular price, but you've probably seen hundreds of signs for 20% off, 10% off, etc. Why? It has nothing to do with mathematics since as we now know percentage pay and percentage off are equivalent descriptions. It most likely has something to do with the psychology of using the words 'buy' or 'pay' and 'save.' People are likely to buy something when they feel like they're 'saving', and not when they feel that they're 'paying.'

For many percentage problems, though, <u>percentage pay is very useful</u> and makes multi–step problems much easier. Let's see how.

Solved Problem

A bike was marked down by 40% a month ago. Two weeks later it was marked down another 25% to $100. What was the original price of the bike?

Define our variables
Original Price = O
First Sale Price = F
Final or Second Sale Price = $100

Write equations using the concept of percentage pay!
The original price was discounted by 40% which means that the first sales price was equal to 60% of the original price. Similarly, the second sales price is equal to 75% of the first sales price (since the discount was 25%). Notice that using the concept of percentage pay lets us immediately and simply write two equations.

1. $O \times .60 = F$
2. $F \times .75 = \$100$

1. $F = (.60)(O)$

Plug in $(.60)(O)$ for F in equation 2 yields:

$F \times .75 = \$100$
$(.60)(O) \times .75 = \$100$
$.45\, O = \$100$

Divide both sides by .45 yields:
$O = \$222.22$

We've solved the problem. The original price was $222.22. Notice again how easy the problem was to solve and the equations to set up— *all because we used the concept of percentage pay* (rather than percentage off).

Doublecheck. Let's apply the discounts to $222.22 to make sure we end up with a final price of $100. Applying a 40% discount to $222.22 results in a price of $133.33. Applying a further 25% discount to $133.33 brings the price down to $100. Our answer is confirmed.

Math Section: Percentage Pay/Percentage Off Problem Set

Solve each problem using Percentage Pay (instead of Percentage Off)! Answers are in Appendix 1 on page 491.

1. A shirt after a 30% discount costs $50. What was its original price?

2. You can buy a car for 70% of its list price in January with the price decreasing by another 10% in each month thereafter. What percentage of list price would you pay to buy the car in April?

3. The Beatles new single had sales of 60,000 which is 120% more than the average sales for a new single. The Rolling Stones single would have to sell how many more copies above the average sales for a new single to match the Beatles sales?

4. A new house is selling for $250,000 after being discounted 5% each month for the past three months. What was its original asking price?

Basic Combinatorics: Combinations & Permutations

Combinatorics is a branch of mathematics which studies, using more complicated strategies, the very first bit of mathematics you ever learned: counting. Combinatorics helps us do some pretty sophisticated counting. A little bit of combinatorics is tested on the SAT which we'll study now.

There are two types of calculations from combinatorics you may have to do on the SAT test: combinations and permutations. With permutations, order or arrangement matters. With combinations, order doesn't matter. Remember that!!

Permutations: order matters. Combinations: order doesn't matter.

You'll always have *more permutations than combinations*—since for combinations order doesn't matter, we count AB and BA (assuming A and B are two different elements) only once while for permutations we count them twice since they're both ordered differently. To calculate combinations, we first calculate the number of permutations and from there use that value to calculate the number of combinations.

For the kind of problems you'll find on the SAT, a *slots* metaphor is very useful. You'll be given problems in which you have to count how many different ways some number of elements can be placed in some number of slots.

> We have three nails on the wall. We have seven paintings. How many different ways can we arrange the paintings on the wall?

We thus have three slots—places where we put something—since we have three nails onto which we'll put paintings. We have seven paintings to put in those slots. Also, anytime you read the word "arrange", your mind should immediately think *permutations* (arrange implying that order does in fact matter) which are the number of ways to arrange the things.

To solve for the number of permutations, there are a few steps.

Step 1: Write down the number of slots in the problem (slots are always multiplied together so we can separate the slots with multiplication signs).

For the above problem, we have three slots: ___ × ___ × ___

Step 2: Write down the number of things, n, we have to place in the first slot, then (n–1) in the second slot, (n–2) in the third slot, etc.

<u>7</u> × <u>6</u> × <u>5</u>

Step 3: Multiply those three terms together and you've got the number of permutations.

Permutations = $7 \times 6 \times 5 = 210$.

There are 210 different ways to arrange the 7 paintings on the 3 nails.

Why do the steps work?
For the first slot, we have 7 possibilities. We have 7 paintings and can put any one of them on that nail. We, thus, have 7 possibilities for the first slot. For the second slot, one painting will be unavailable (it will have been put on the first nail), thus we have only 6 possibilities for the second slot. For the third slot, two paintings will have been placed, so there are only 5 possibilities.

To figure out how many ways we can put the paintings together, we use multiplication. Multiplication is the key arithmetic operation for combinatorics. Multiplication effectively puts together or calculates all the combinations and permutations for us. Thus, we multiply $7 \times 6 \times 5$ and come up with 210 permutations in this question.

Combinations

Follow the three steps and calculate the number of permutations. ...then add a step 4

Step 4: Divide the number of permutations by the number of slots factorial

Factorial is represented by the symbol !, and it's calculated by multiplying a positive integer by all positive integers less than itself.

For example, $5! = 5 \times 4 \times 3 \times 2 \times 1$
or $8! = 8 \times 7 \times 6 \times 5 \times 4 \times 3 \times 2 \times 1$

Let's solve a combinations problem.

There are 12 people trying out for the basketball team. Only 5 can make it. How many possible teams are there?

Let's think—does order matter in this problem? If we have a team of say Jack, Ted and Luke, should we count Ted, Jack and Luke as a separate team? No, right? For teams, ordering or arrangement doesn't matter and thus we need to solve for the number of combinations.

To do this, we first solve for the number of permutations.

Step 1: Write down the number of slots in the problem.

There are 5 slots since only 5 players can make the team.

Our 5 slots: __ × __ × __ × __ × __

Step 2: Write down the number of things, n, we have to place in the first slot, then (n–1) in the second slot, (n–2) in the third slot, etc.

Our 5 slots now filled: <u>12</u> × <u>11</u> × <u>10</u> × <u>9</u> × <u>8</u>

Step 3: Multiply those terms together and we've got the number of permutations.

12 × 11 × 10 × 9 × 8 =

= 95,040 permutations

Step 4 (for combinations): Divide the number of permutations by the number of slots factorial to calculate the number of combinations

Combinations = $\dfrac{\text{number of permutations}}{(\text{number of slots})!}$

We know there are 5 slots for players on the team, and from our previous calculation we found 95,040 permutations of groups of 5 people selected from a set of 12 people.

Combinations = Possible Teams = $\dfrac{95{,}040}{5!}$ = $\dfrac{95{,}040}{120}$ = 792

There are thus 792 combinations or 792 possible basketball teams when we have 12 applicants for 5 slots.

Optional: Why does the Combinations Formula work?
Why does dividing the number of permutations by the number of slots factorial yield the combinations? It works because the slots factorial equals how many times we're over-counting the arrangements of a single set of elements or the number of permutations of each combination of elements. Imagine we have 3 elements A,B, and C. To calculate their permutations we have to count every possible arrangement or ABC, ACB, BAC, BCA, CAB, and CBA. There are 6 permutations. Since there's just one single group of three elements, there's only one combination. 6 should thus equal 3!...and it does (3 × 2 × 1 = 6). Thus any set of permutations of 3 elements has to be divided by 6 (since every 1 combination yields 6 permutations of the elements) to calculate the number of combinations.

Math Section: Combinatorics Problem Set

Answers are in Appendix 1 on page 492.

1. You have 9 photographs and 6 picture frames. Assuming only a single photo can fit in each frame, how many possible photograph groups (each group consists of 6 photos in no particular order) could you make?

2. To make a doll, you choose two different colors out of six possible colors, and three different accessories out of seven different accessories. How many different dolls could you make?

3. Of the three digit numbers between 100 and 999, how many have exactly one digit equal to 8 e.g. 280 counts but 288 does not count since it has a digit of 8 twice?

4. From xville to yville there are 3 roads, from yville to zville there are 4 roads, and from zville to qville there are 5 roads. If you drive from xville to yville and then from yville to zville and then from zville to qville, how many different routes could you possibly take?

5. How many integers are there with different digits in the integers between 10 and 99 inclusive of 10 and 99?

6. You have to write a report on 3 different historical figures, and you have 11 historical figures to choose from. How many different combinations or groups of historical figures could you write about?

Probability

A probability is...let's use a definition which can be turned into an equation easily...**the number of desired outcomes divided by the number of possible outcomes.**

A probability tells us about the likelihood of something happening.

The Definition of a Probability

Probability of some event x or P(x) =
$$\frac{\textbf{number of desired outcomes}}{\textbf{number of possible outcomes}}$$

From the word "number" in both the denominator and the numerator of the fraction, you can guess we have to do some counting. To help us count, we may have to use the combinatorics we've learned!

There are a few key ideas to keep in mind when doing probability problems.

And/Or Statements in Probability

An *and* statement in a probability means we multiply the probabilities together.
An *or* statement in a probability means we add the probabilities together.

And: Multiply the probabilities.
Or: Add the probabilities.

If we were satisfied getting either a red ball or a blue ball, we add those two probabilities together. That makes sense in that we'd be satisfied with either one thus we add the probabilities together. If we need to get a red ball and a blue ball, then we have to combine those probabilities since we have to have both a red and a blue ball, and the way to combine probabilities mathematically is by multiplying them together.

To solve probability problems, turn the problem into a set of and/or statements. We can then turn the statements into mathematical symbols or an equation, and finally solve the problem. We'll see how this is done in the solved problems.

With or Without Replacement

It's important to recognize for any probability problem whether it's with replacement or without replacement. In a with replacement problem, after the item is chosen at random it's subsequently returned to be able to be chosen again. In a without replacement problem, after the item is chosen at random, it's left out and can not be chosen again.

We treat the two types of problems differently, namely:

With replacement problems: nothing gets reduced in the probability after a draw (e.g. after drawing a marble out of a bag) since the object gets put back in…so the probabilities do not change in a with replacement problem

Without replacement problems: we reduce the numerator and the denominator in the probability after a draw since what was taken out stays out…so the probabilities change after each draw in a without replacement problem

We'll see how these work specifically in a problem.

Solved Problem 1

You have 5 brown socks and 4 blue socks in your drawer. If you pull two socks out, what's the probability of getting a complete pair?

We could get either a brown pair or a red pair to be satisfied. This breaks the problem down a bit. It's already thus:

Brown pair OR Red pair.

We have to add both those probabilities (or means add!). We have to calculate each of the probabilities first, though. Keep in mind that there are actually two events (or at least we should treat them as two separate events even if we do them simultaneously): pulling out the first sock, then pulling out the second sock. Moreover, let's categorize this problem: is it a with replacement problem or a without replacement problem? When I draw a sock out, do I put it back in? No! Thus it's a without replacement problem (so both the denominator and the numerator of our probabilities should decrease)!

Probability of getting a pair of brown socks

Probability of a brown pair: first sock is brown AND the second sock is brown

= $\underline{\text{number of brown socks (1}^{st}\text{ draw)}} \times \underline{\text{number of brown socks (2}^{nd}\text{ draw)}}$
   $\ \text{number of socks (1}^{st}\text{ draw)}\text{number of socks (2}^{nd}\text{ draw)}$

The first probability represents the probability of drawing a brown sock in our first draw, and the second probability represents the probability of drawing a brown sock in our second draw. We multiply these together since they're separated by AND—we multiply and statements in probability problems (we need a brown sock AND another brown sock to have a pair). Since this is a without replacement problem, we know that the numerator and denominator should decrease.

Let's plug in our values. We know there are 5 brown socks and there are 9 total socks. Since we pull out one of the brown socks in the first draw, the numerator decreases to 4 in the second equation and the denominator also decreases to 8 since there are at that point there are only 8 total socks to be picked from.

$$P(\text{brown pair}) = \frac{\text{number of brown socks}}{\text{number of socks}} \times \frac{\text{number of brown socks}}{\text{number of socks}}$$

$$= \frac{5}{9} \times \frac{4}{8}$$

$$= \frac{20}{72} = 5/18$$

So the probability of drawing a brown pair of socks when you pull two socks out of the drawer is 5 / 18.

Probability of getting a pair of blue socks

We'll calculate the probability of getting a pair of blue socks using the same method we did for our calculation of the probability of drawing the brown pair.

Probability of a blue pair = first sock is blue AND the second sock is blue

$$P(\text{blue pair}) = \frac{\text{\# of blue socks (1}^{st}\text{ draw)}}{\text{number of socks (1}^{st}\text{ draw)}} \times \frac{\text{\# of blue socks (2}^{nd}\text{ draw)}}{\text{number of socks (2}^{nd}\text{ draw)}}$$

$$= \frac{4}{9} \times \frac{3}{8}$$

$$= \frac{12}{72}$$

$$= 1/6$$

Thus, the probability of getting a blue pair is 1 / 6

Probability of getting a pair of brown socks OR a pair of blue socks

The total probability of getting a matched pair is the probability of getting a brown pair OR a blue pair.

P (matched pair) = P (brown pair)   OR P (red pair)

Plugging in our values and replacing the OR statement with an addition sign (remember OR statements become plus signs, AND statements multiplication signs) yields:

P (matched pair) = $\frac{5}{18}$ + $\frac{1}{6}$

Getting a common denominator and then solving yields:

= 5/18 + 3/18 = 8/18 = 4/9

We've solved it. The probability of getting a matched pair of socks when we randomly pull out two socks is 4/9.

Solved Problem 2

If two positive integers less than 10 are randomly chosen, what's the probability that their product is a multiple of 3?

This is a multi–step problem. We first have to figure out how to know which products will be divisible by 3 (i.e. a multiple of 3), and then we have to calculate the probability of getting such a product.

From the fundamental theorem of arithmetic in number theory we studied, we know there's one and only one way a number can be a multiple of 3: it must have a 3 somewhere in it. Let's write out the positive integers less than 10 and identify which ones have 3 as a prime factor.

1, 2, 3, 4, 5, 6, 7, 8, 9

3, 6, and 9 have at least a single "3" in them (3 as a prime factor)...so products which are multiples of 3 have to have at least a single 3, 6, or 9 in them.

Let's start setting up our probability/combinations.

We have two slots in a sense: one for the first integer chosen and a second for the second integer chosen. There are 9 possibilities for each since this is a with replacement problem—I could choose 3 twice for example.

$\underline{9} \times \underline{9} = 81$ permutations of the positive integers less than 10.

Here's an important tip. *For many probabilities, when you're asked to calculate P(x) it'll often be easier to calculate P(not x) and subtract that from 1.*

Let's use it for this problem because it's otherwise quite difficult to count how many products have at least a single 3 in them. How many permutations are there which **don't** have 3 as a prime factor?

There are six integers without a 3 in them (without 3 as a prime factor). Thus the number of permutations is:

$\underline{6} \times \underline{6} = 36$

There are 36 permutations or products of the six integers which don't have 3 as a prime factor.

The probability of getting a product which is **not** a multiple of 3 is then 36/81, and the probability of obtaining a product which is a multiple of 3 is 1 − 36/81 or 45/81.

Our answer then is 45/81.

For fun, try to calculate 45/81 or the probability of obtaining a product which is a multiple of 3 outright without using P(not x) as we did above to solve the problem. It's not that difficult of a probability to calculate (hint: you'll have to subtract some double-counted possibilities). The most efficient way to solve the problem is still by calculating P(not x).

Probability Problems: Four Key Methods to Remember:

- ✓ *A probability is the number of desired outcomes divided by the number of possible outcomes*

- ✓ *There are always two ways to calculate a probability: calculate the probability directly, P(x), or calculate the probability of the event not occurring and subtract that from one, P(x) = 1 − P(not x).* The probabilities of an event occurring and not occurring have to add up to 1 (or 100%) since we know that there are only two choices for an event, either it happens or it doesn't. You can calculate the probability of event x not happening and subtract that from 1 to calculate the probability of x occurring. If your answer doesn't make sense when you calculate say P(x) directly, try calculating P(not x) and then subtract it from 1 to get P(x)

- ✓ *Is it a with replacement or a without replacement problem?*
    - o With replacement: nothing changes in subsequent probabilities
    - o Without replacement: both the numerator and denominator of the probability decrease by one

- ✓ *Turn the problem into a set of And/Or statements.*
    - o And = multiply
    - o Or = add

Math Section: Probability Problem Set

Answers are in Appendix 1 on page 494.

1. There are 7 green socks and 2 red socks in a bag. You draw two socks, one at a time. What's the probability that you have a matching pair?

2. There's a bag of marbles, and you have to draw a single marble out three times. After each draw, the marble's color is noted and the marble is returned to the bag. If you draw the same color marble all three times, you win a prize. There are 6 red marbles, 5 blue marbles, and 4 yellow marbles in the bag. What's the probability of drawing all three times marbles of the same color?

3. You've invited 14 guests over for dinner. Six guests have names beginning with the letter "c", three with the letter "d", and five with the letter "e." You have only six slices of cake. What's the probability that none of the guests with a name beginning with "c" will get a slice of cake if you distribute the slices at random to your guests?

4. There are 6 red socks and 6 blue socks in your drawer. What's the least number of socks you have to pick from the drawer to be certain you have at least a single blue sock?

Statistics

You may have some questions on statistics where you'll be asked to apply some statistical concept to a set of data.

The purpose of statistics is to analyze data: to perform some mathematical operation or calculation on the data in order to obtain some value(s) that tells us something about the data.

Four common methods used to tell us about the set of data are the mean, median, mode, and range.

We'll use the below sample data set to demonstrate how to calculate the mean, median, mode and range.

Sample Data Set: (–1, 3, 0, 2, –1, 4)

Mean:

The mean (or average) of a set of terms is the sum of every term in the set of data divided by the number of terms in the set of data.

For the above data set,

$$\text{mean} = \frac{\text{the sum of all the terms}}{\text{the number of terms}} = \frac{(-1 + -1 + 0 + 2 + 3 + 4)}{6} = \frac{7}{6}$$

Median:

The median is the middle term in the data when the terms are written in ascending order. If there are an even number of terms, the median is the mean of the middle two terms (sum the middle two terms and divide by two).

Let's write the set out in ascending order: (–1, –1, 0, 2, 3, 4). There are 6 terms, an even number of terms, so we take the two middle terms, 0 and 2. The mean of those two (0 + 2) / 2 = 1. The median is 1.

Mode:

The mode is the term that occurs the most often in the set of data.

There's only one term that occurs more than once: –1. The mode, then, is –1.

Range:

The range is the difference between the greatest and smallest term in the set of data.

The largest term is 4 and the smallest term is –1. The range for the above set of data, then, is (4) – (–1) which is equal to 5.

Optional: Standard Deviation:

You should also understand what a standard deviation is, even though you won't be asked to calculate it on the SAT test.

A standard deviation represents how far away most of the numbers in a set of data are from the mean of that set of data. Let's suppose that the mean of a set of normally distributed data is 50 and the standard deviation is 10. In that case, about 70% of the terms will be within one standard deviation of the mean and 95% will be within two standard deviations of the mean. That means that about 70% of the elements will be within the range of 50 plus or minus 10 or between 40 and 60. About 95% will be within two standard deviations or 50 plus or minus

20, between 30 and 70. The standard deviation thus tells us how dispersed the data is around the mean.

Don't worry about how to calculate the standard deviation, you definitely won't have to do that for the SAT—just try to have a basic understanding of the concept (though it's unlikely, there may be a question related to it on the SAT).

Line of best fit:

For a graph of a data set, the line of best fit is the line which best represents the data by which we mean it minimizes the average distance between the line and the points respectively. Don't worry about how to calculate such a line of best fit, but remember that it should go through the middle of the graphed points. It doesn't matter how many graphed points the line actually goes through. What matters is that line itself is as close as possible to as many points as possible—there should also be roughly an equal number of points above and below the line.

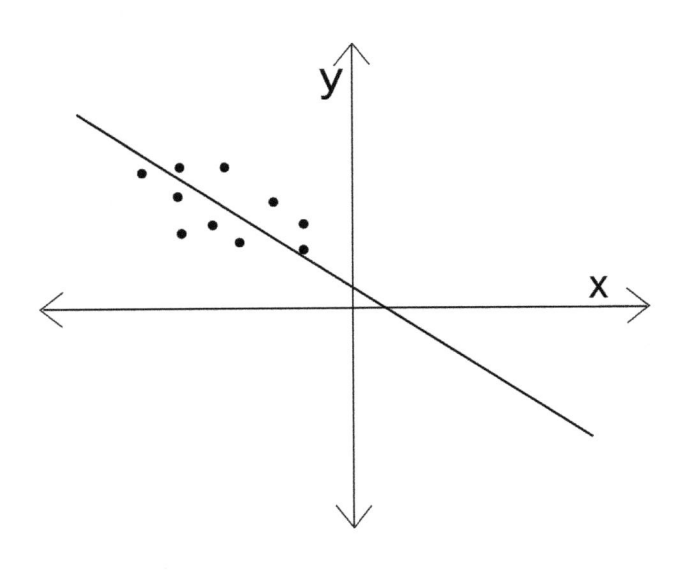

Notice that the line itself doesn't pass through any of the points. Also, there are an equal number of points above and below the line (five above and five below). The line is also relatively close to all the points, and it looks like if we tried to make the line closer to any particular point, it would move farther away from some other point (by a more than compensating distance).

Math Section: Statistics Problem Set

Answers are in Appendix 1 on page 496.

1. It rained every day the past five days and the average daily rainfall ranged between 2 inches and 15 inches. The median rainfall was 10 inches, and the mode was 15 inches. What is the least and greatest possible 5–day average or mean daily rainfall?

2. Draw a line of best fit on the following graph:

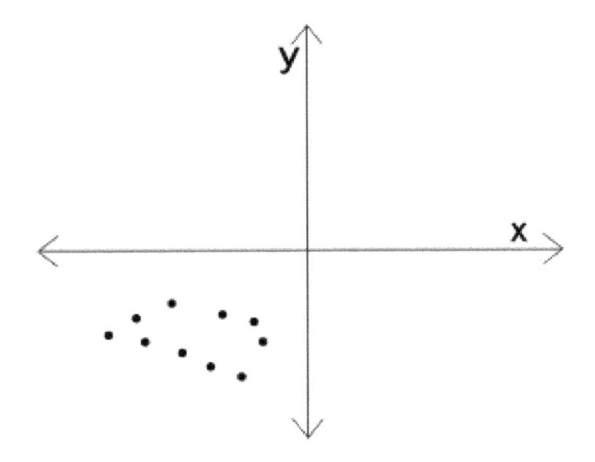

3. The median of a set of five distinct integers is five. The average of the set of integers is 4.8. The range of the set is three. The mode of the set appears three times. What is the mode of this set of integers?

4. For the following set of data: (0, 2, 0, 7, 3, 11, 9), find the mode, the median, and the mean.

5. For the following set of data: (−2, −1, 1, 1, 1, 7, 9, 11), find the mode, the median, and the mean.

Averages

Average for the SAT is the same thing as mean. To calculate the average of a set of data, sum up the terms and divide by the number of terms.

It's important to remember that definition which is also an equation.

Average = Sum of terms
 Number of terms

Remember a critical step in problem–solving: write down everything you know. Thus, when given any problem involving an average, write down the above equation which represents the definition of an average.

Sample Problem

Jill scored 78, 96, and 88 on the first three tests in her history course. Assuming that all tests are weighted equally, what does she need to score on the fourth and final test to have a 90 average?

Let's write down the definition of average as an equation.

Average = Sum of terms
 Number of terms

From the problem, we know:
Variable (what we have to solve for): x = 4th test score.
Average = 90.
Test Scores: 78, 96, 88, and x.
Number of terms or tests = 4

Lets plug these values into the equation.

Average = $\dfrac{\text{Sum of terms}}{\text{Number of terms}}$

$90 = \dfrac{78 + 96 + 88 + x}{4}$

We've got a single equation and a single variable. We can solve for x.

$90 = \dfrac{78 + 96 + 88 + x}{4}$

Multiple both sides by 4.
$90 \times 4 = 78 + 96 + 88 + x$

Simplify.
$360 = 262 + x$

Subtract 262 from both sides and we've solved the problem.
$x = 98$.

So Jill needs a 98 on her final exam to achieve a 90 average in the course.

Math Section: Averages Problem Set

Answers are in Appendix 1 on page 498.

1. What is the average of the following set of terms: 7, 11 − x, 12, 14 + x ?

2. To qualify as 'flame retardant' for country X, a jacket needs to survive an average temperature of 90° C without catching fire over four trials. In the first three trials, the jacket has withstood an average of 88° before catching fire. Up to what temperature does the jacket need to withstand heat in its fourth and final trial in order to qualify as 'flame retardant'?

3. The average of three numbers is 20. The average of another two numbers is 30. What's the average of all five of those numbers?

4. The average of six integers is 50. We want to add three more integers to the original six to raise the average to 60 for all nine integers from 50 for the six integers. What, then, should the sum of three additional integers be?

MATH SECTION: Geometry

The Fundamental Method for Geometry Problems: Work from the Diagram

Write in as much information as you can in the diagram no matter whether you think it's useful or not, keep putting in information, try solving for angles, sides, write down any and all equations that apply to the shapes...and gradually the insight necessary to solve the problem will come to you (let's hope!). If the diagram is too small or clearly not drawn to scale, redraw it.

Alternate Method to using "pure" Geometry: Measurement

Use your marked pencil as a ruler to make measurements of lengths. This often can bring you to the answer or at least help you narrow it down to two choices at which point you have to take a guess. You need to prepare a marked pencil to use when taking practice tests as well as for the real test.

You should make marks on the tip of your pencil that are evenly spaced and can thus be used to make measurements. We'll see how to use it to solve problems later. Here's what your marked pencil should look like:

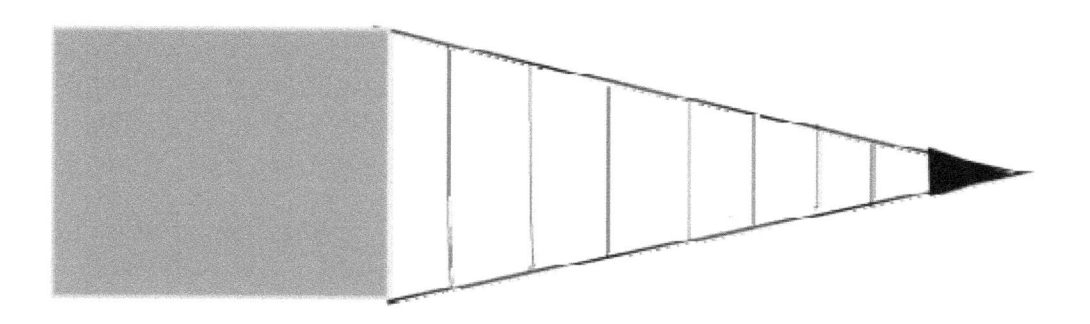

Equations are written in the front of each math section—still memorize them

In case you ever forget the Pythagorean theorem or the ratio of the sides in a 30–60–90 triangle, don't panic. They're written out in a row at the top of the first page in any math section in the SAT test. That being said, do try to have the equations and relationships memorized because they're easy to remember and knowing the equations and relationships cold will help you solve problems faster and more reliably.

Coordinate Geometry

Graphing Points and the Four Quadrants

You'll need to be able to graph points on what's called a Cartesian coordinate plane—a plane with an x and a y axis. Points will be in the form (x, y) where the first value, the x value, represents the number of spaces to move to the left or right and the second value, the y value, represents the numbers of spaces up or down to move to find the point.

For the x–axis, moving right is moving in the positive direction and moving left is the negative direction. For the y–axis, up is the positive direction and down is the negative direction.

There are also four quadrants in this coordinate plane. For all points in quadrant I, all x–values and y–values and positive. For all points in quadrant III, all x–values and y–values are negative.

Below is a Cartesian coordinate plane with the four quadrants shown and a point graphed. Notice that to graph the point (3, 5), we first move three spaces to the right (we move to the right since it's positive 3) and then five spaces up (up again since it's positive 5) to find the point (3,5).

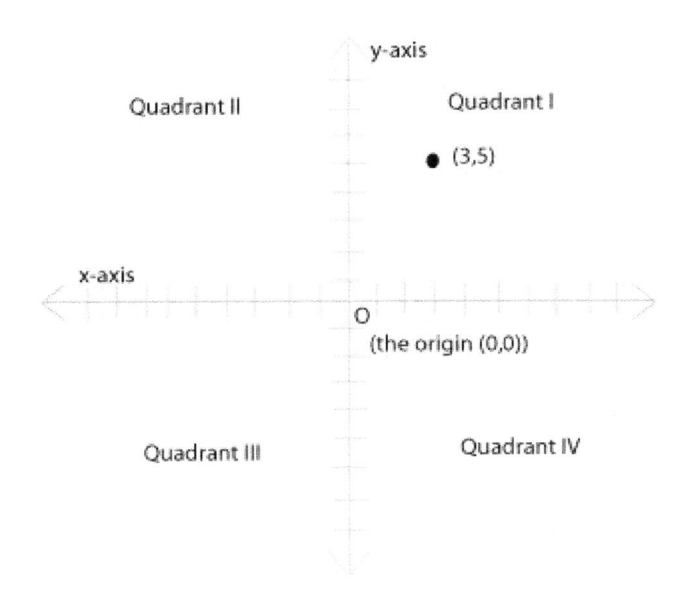

Story about the discovery of the Cartesian Coordinate Plane. This coordinate plane (the x and y axis plane) is named after the 17th century French mathematician and philosopher Rene Descartes. A story goes that he was lying in bed watching a fly hop on the ceiling in his room, perhaps lazing in bed—he slept in most mornings. Watching this fly hop around, he asked himself what's the simplest way I can describe the fly's position on the ceiling at any given moment? He postulated the idea of the Cartesian Coordinate Plane—fix some point (we'll call it the

origin (0,0)) and then describe the fly's position as being some number of steps both left/right (the x–direction) and up/down (the y–direction) from that fixed point (the origin). From that morning thought, the Cartesian Coordinate Plane was supposedly born.

Math Section: Graphing Points Problem Set

Answers are in Appendix 1 on page 500.

y

x

Graph the following points:

1. (2, 2)

2. (3, –3)

3. (4, 2)

4. (–2, 4)

5. Identify the four quadrants.

Complementary and Supplementary Angles

Complementary angles are two angles which together sum to 90 degrees.

Supplementary angles are a pair of angles which sum to 180 degrees.

The complement of a 40° angle is 50° (since 40° plus 50° equals 90°) and its supplement is 140° (since 40° plus 140° equals 180°).

It's important to note that complementary angles together make up a right angle, and supplementary angles together form a line (a line has a measure of 180°).

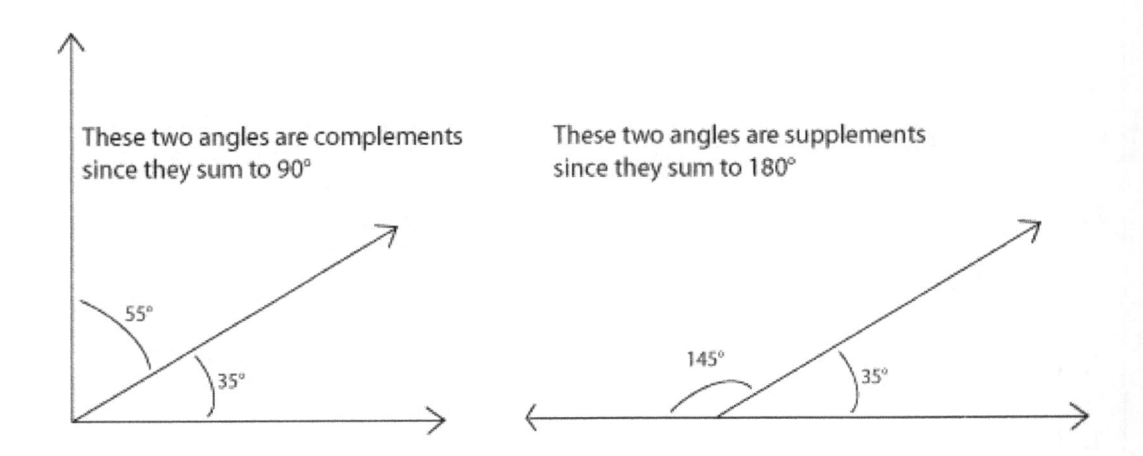

These two angles are complements since they sum to 90°

55°
35°

These two angles are supplements since they sum to 180°

145°
35°

Parallel Lines Intersected by a Transversal: Alternate Interior/Exterior, Corresponding and Vertical Angles

You may see a diagram of parallel lines or line segments intercepted by a transversal (a line or line segment which passes through both lines). In such a diagram, the angles have various relationships with each other which you should be familiar with.

There are four basic angle pairs in which both angles are equal. There are vertical angles which are angles opposite each other. Corresponding angles are angles that are in the same position on both parallel lines. Alternate interior angles are angles that are on opposite sides but interior to the two parallel lines. Alternate exterior angles are angles that are on opposite sides and exterior to the two parallel lines. Each angle in the pair has the same measurement so each angle of a pair of vertical, corresponding, alternate interior, or alternate exterior angles have the same measure.

In the diagram of the relationships below, be sure to be able to "see" intuitively the pair relationships and why the various angles have the same measure.

vertical angles: 1 and 4; 3 and 2; 7 and 6; 5 and 8.
corresponding angles: 1 and 5; 3 and 7; 2 and 6; 4 and 8.
alternate interior angles: 3 and 6; 4 and 5.
alternate exterior angles: 1 and 8; 2 and 7.

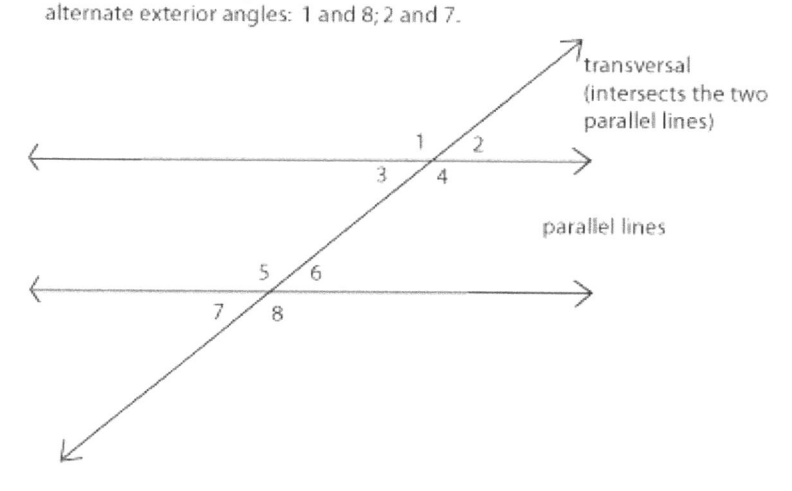

Math Section: Angles Problem Set

Answers are in Appendix 1 on page 500.

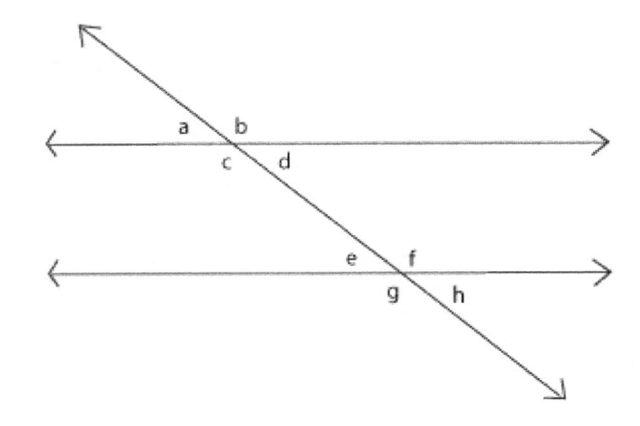

1. If Angle b = 150°, then

   Angle c = ?

   Angle g = ?

   Angle d = ?

   Angle h = ?

2. If Angles d, e, and g sum to 220°, what's the sum of Angles f and c?

3. If Angles h and e are complements, then what's the sum of Angles a, d, e, f, and g?

Analytical Geometry

Lines

You'll need to know analytical geometry as it applies to lines. Particularly, you need to know how to turn graphed lines into equations, linear equations into graphed lines and information about a line into an equation of a line. Analytic geometry enables us to do all those things!

Slope

We can think of lines as having a property of slope—literally how "sloped" or slanted the line is. Another way to think about the slope of a line is as instructions for how to construct the line. If you're given some starting point (any point in the line—the most useful for us will be the y–intercept), then you can use the slope of the line to find any other point on the line.

The slope is defined as *the rise over the run* or *the change in y over the change in x*. The numerator in the slope is thus the y-value or change in y value or the rise, and the denominator is the x-value or change in x value or the run. Suppose the slope of a line is 4/5. This tells us that if we're on some point on a line, we can find another point on the line by rising 4 and running 5—we have to always rise and run in that fixed ratio (4:5) in order to stay on the line. The slope is usually represented as a variable by the letter m.

$$\text{Slope} = m = \frac{\text{rise}}{\text{run}} = \frac{\Delta y}{\Delta x}$$

If you're given two points on the line, you can calculate the slope via this equation:

Given two points (x_1, y_1) and (x_2, y_2), $m = \dfrac{y_2 - y_1}{x_2 - x_1}$

You can remember that equation since it's the same as m equals the change in y (one y minus another y is the change in y, right?) over the change in x.

Y–Intercept

The y–intercept of a line is the y–coordinate of the point at which the line intercepts or touches the y–axis. The y–intercept point is always in the form (0, b)—the x–value is always 0 since the point intercepts the y–axis (to touch the y–axis, a point can not move either left or right so it has to move 0 in the x direction). The letter b typically is used to represent the y–intercept.

There are an infinite number of possible lines that have the same slope—so just knowing the slope of a line is not enough for someone to know what line you're referring to. You have to also know a single point on that line—for solving the equation of a line, the most convenient point to know is the y–intercept.

Typically, you'll solve for the y–intercept after you already have the slope of the line and some point on the line. In such a case, you can plug in the values for m, x and y into our generic equation for a line.

The generic equation for a line is:

y = mx + b
     where m is the slope of the line and b is the y–intercept.

Any and every point on the line is represented by x and y where x is the x–coordinate of a point and y is the point's y–coordinate.

To solve for b, we need to plug in values for m, x, and y. For m, we have to plug in the line's slope. For x and y, we plug in the coordinates for any point on the line. Thus if I know that the slope of a line was 7 and one point on the line was (–2, 8), I could calculate the y–intercept or b:

y = mx + b

8 = 7 × –2 + b

8 = –14 + b

22 = b

The y–intercept or b for the line is 22. Now, we can write the full equation for that line by filling in the values for m and b. The equation for that line is:

y = 7x + 22

Equation of a line

To "solve" a line, we try to write an equation for that line. The general form for an equation of a line, as we learned above, is y = mx + b; we need to find two things to "solve" a line and to determine its equation: m (the slope) and b (the y–intercept). Once we have m and b, we've "solved" the line—we've got the equation for that line. What does that let us do?

For one, we can now solve for whether any given point is on the line. Let's say that the equation of our line is y = ¾ x + 4. I want to know if the point (1,1) is on the line—can I use the equation to figure that out? Yes! Plug in (1,1) and see if it satisfies the equation—if it does, then that point is on the line. Let's suppose I want to know the y–coordinate of the point on the line for when x = 700,000. Can I use the equation to solve that? Yes—just plug in 700,000 for x, then solve for y. That's a lot easier than trying to draw a graph of the line and measure exactly what y is going to be when x reaches 700,000—turning a line into an equation is very powerful!!

The equation for a line is a beautiful thing. A simple equation of just a few symbols, y = ¾ x + 4, represents an infinity of points. Every single point that is on that line, an infinite number of points, makes the equation true and every single point not on the line makes that equation false.

To draw the graph of any line, we need two points on that line. To get the first point, graph the y–intercept—draw a point wherever b falls on the y–axis. For y = ¾ x + 4 which is in the form y = mx + b, it's pretty easy to identify that the y–intercept or b is 4. To graph the equation, first graph the y–intercept (0, 4). From the y–intercept, use the slope to find another point. If the slope is ¾ , from the y–intercept go up 3 steps and go right 4 step and then you're at another point on that line—for this line, the new point is (4, 7). Now you've got two points and can draw a line connecting them and our graph is complete.

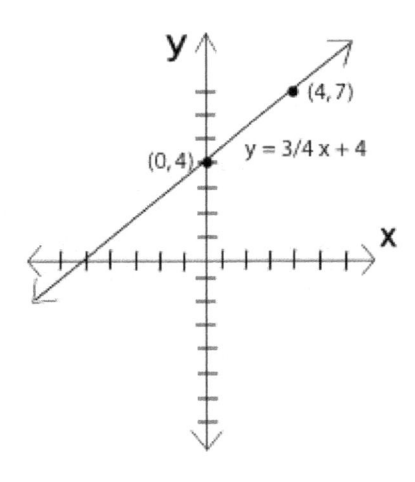

Parallel and Perpendicular Lines

Parallel lines are two lines that have no points of intersection; they never meet. **Parallel lines have the same slope.** So if you're presented two lines that have the same slope, they never meet (unless they happen to be the same line) and have no points of intersection (again unless they happen to be the same line in which case all their points intersect). **Perpendicular lines are lines that intersect at right angles to each other** e.g. when two perpendicular lines intersect, they will form a 90° angle.

Perpendicular lines have slopes that are the *negative inverse* of each other. If the slope of a line, for example, is 2, then the slope of a line perpendicular to that line will be the negative inverse of 2. The inverse of 2 (which expressed as a fraction is 2/1) is 1/2. Let's make it negative, −1/2, and we've got the slope of the line perpendicular to the line with slope 2. More pairs of perpendicular lines include 3/2 and − 2/3, and 8/9 and −9/8. Remember it's easy to take the inverse of a number when it's in the form of a fraction—so turn any slope into a fraction and then take the negative inverse to get the slope of a line perpendicular to it.

Note for those interested in science: with analytical geometry (formally developed in the 17th century by Rene Descartes) begins the possibility of modern science whose goal is the mathematization of nature—turning everything in nature into equations which enable us to make precise predictions. Many natural phenomena lend themselves fairly directly to be turned into geometrical objects e.g. we can turn the wind into line segments (actually a special type of line segment called a vector which is a line segment that also has a direction, it's pointing somewhere). Once we can turn geometrical objects into equations, then these equations allow us to make precise predictions about how these things i.e. nature and its objects including us behave (e.g. turn the vectors which represent the wind into equations which we can then solve to predict the weather)! Incidentally, calculus also developed out of analytical geometry—the idea of a derivative is giving the definition of a slope to curves (dy/dx is analogous to $\Delta y / \Delta x$)!!

Math Section: Lines Problem Set

Answers are in Appendix 1 on page 502.

Find the slope of the line that passes through each set of points below.

1. (1, 1) (3, 3)

2. (2, 0) (3, 0)

3. (−4, 5) (4, −5)

4. (3, 6) (3, −2)

5. (−2, −4) (−5, −10)

6. (6, −9) (−3, 4)

Write the equation of the line for a line with the given slope which passes through the given point.

7. m = 3   (10, 12)

8. m = ½   (−5, 7)

9. m = −2   (−2, −2)

10. m = 6   (−8, 11)

Identify the y–intercept and the slope of the following lines then graph them.

11. y = 1.5x − 10

12. $2y = 4x + 8$

13. $y = -2x - 4$

Write the equation of the line for a line *perpendicular to* the given slope which passes through the given point.

14. $m = 3/2$ (2, 0)

15. $m = -5$ (1, 1)

16. What's the value of h if the following equation describes a line with a slope of 5?
      $hx - 5y = 18.$

17. What's the value of k if the following equation describes a line with a slope of 2?
      $kx + 3y = 9$

Circles

Definition of a Circle, Radius, and Diameter

Let's first try to understand what a circle is—how we can define what a circle is precisely. One way to think of a circle is as the collection of all points equidistant from some fixed point. Let us fix a point—we'll call it the origin. This point, the origin, will be the center of our circle. Next, we'll pick some fixed distance which we'll call the radius. Finally, we can make a circle—every point that is the distance of the radius away from the origin will be a point in the circle. If we can draw all those points, then voila, we've got a circle.

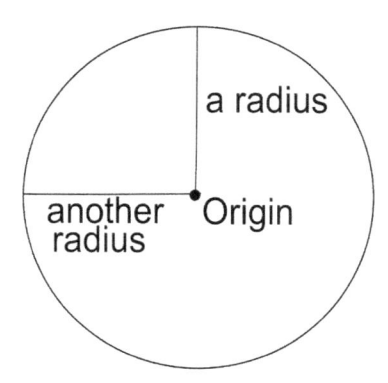

It's important to remember that a radius is any line segment that connects the center or origin of the circle to a point on the edge of the circle—and every radius has the same length. Some problems will depend on this insight!

The diameter of the circle is equal to double the radius (two times the radius) and is any line segment that connects two points on the edge of the circle while also passing through the origin of the circle.

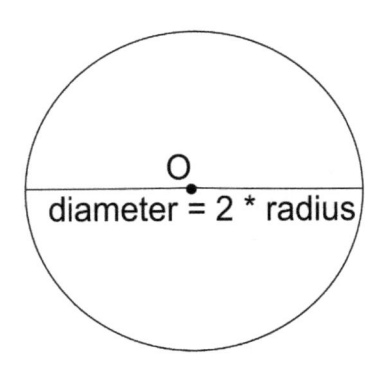

Also, remember that by definition a circle has 360 degrees—in other words to go in a complete circle we have to go 360°. A right angle, 90°, thus represents one fourth of a circle.

Area
Here's the formula to determine the area of a circle:
Area of a Circle = pi × radius squared = π r²
(remember it as pi r squared!)

Circumference
The circumference of a circle represents the distance around a circle—it's the special term for a circle's perimeter.

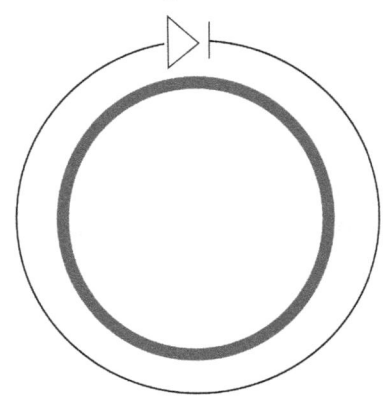

The formula for calculating the circumference of a circle is:
Circumference = 2 × pi × radius = pi × diameter = 2 π r = π d

Also, remember that pi or π is a constant that equals 3.14159...there's usually a π on most scientific calculators that stores its value.

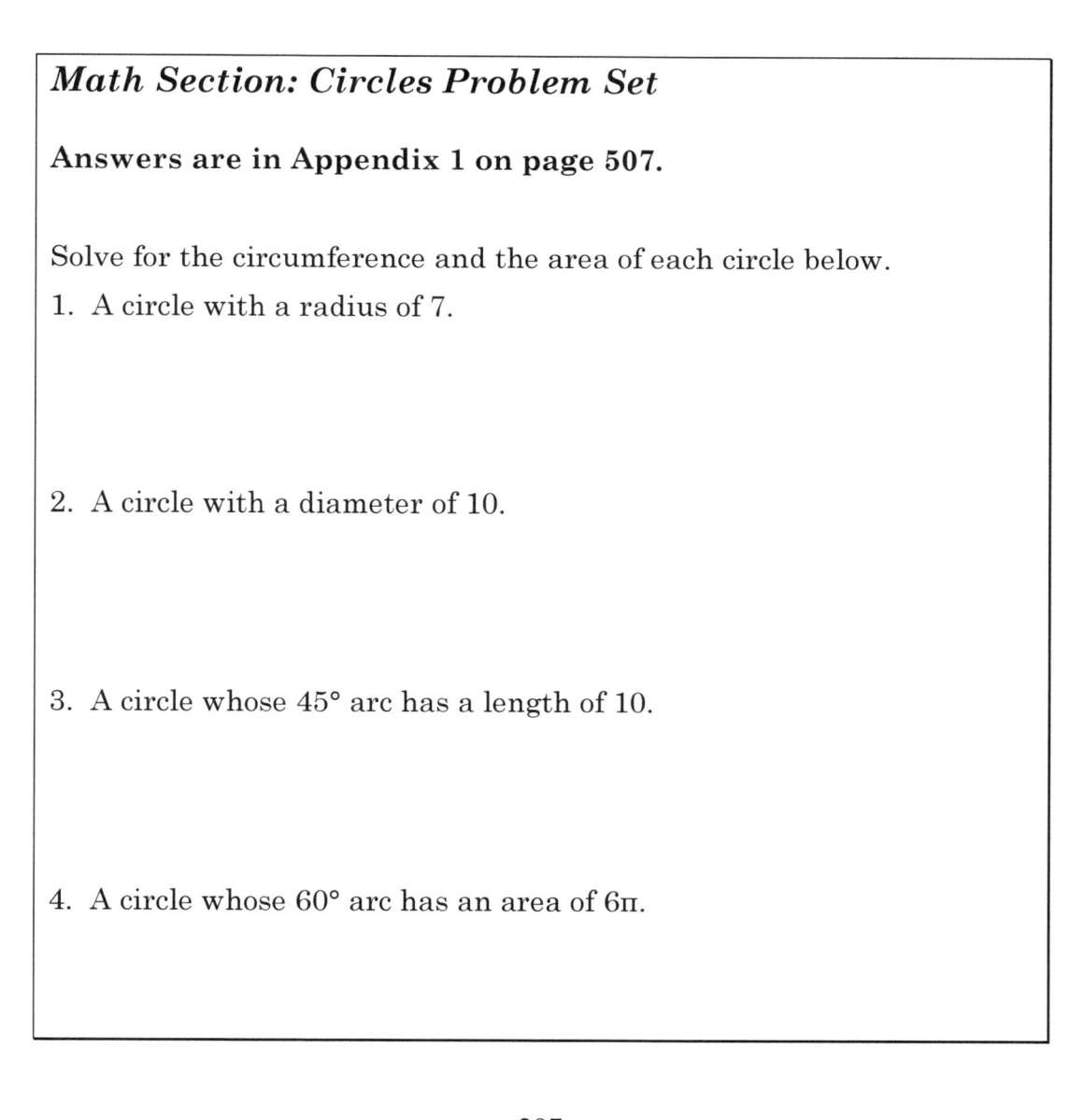

Math Section: Circles Problem Set

Answers are in Appendix 1 on page 507.

Solve for the circumference and the area of each circle below.

1. A circle with a radius of 7.

2. A circle with a diameter of 10.

3. A circle whose 45° arc has a length of 10.

4. A circle whose 60° arc has an area of 6π.

Volume of a Sphere and a Cylinder

The occasional SAT problem will ask you for the volume of a sphere or a cylinder. The equation for the volume of a cylinder where h is the height of the cylinder and r is the radius of the circular top (or bottom) of the cylinder is:

$$\text{Volume of a cylinder} = \pi \times r^2 \times h$$

A good way to remember this equation is to think of a cylinder as a lot of circles (all the same size) stacked on top of each other—specifically some height of circles. So to calculate the volume of a cylinder, we first calculate the area of the circle ($\pi \times r^2$), then multiply that by the height of how many circles we have (h).

$$\text{Volume of a sphere} = 4/3 \times \pi \times r^3$$

You'll learn how to derive this equation when you study calculus (don't worry about where the equation came from for now).

Math Section: Spheres and Cylinders Problem Set

Answers are in Appendix 1 on page 508.

1. What's the volume of a sphere which has a radius of 5?

2. What's the volume of a cylinder with a radius of 2 and a height of 2?

3. The volume of a cylinder with a radius of 4 is 96 π. What's the height of the cylinder?

4. What's the radius of a sphere that has a volume of 36π?

Special Right Triangles

There are several special right triangles you need to know. If you see an SAT problem with a right triangle, always check if it's one of our special right triangles. They're special in that we know the ratio of the sides in these triangles.

3:4:5 Right Triangles

Three–four–five right triangles are right triangles whose sides have the ratio 3:4:5. You'll generally be given two sides of such a triangle as well as be told that it's a right triangle…in which case you can figure out the third side using the ratio (3:4:5). Let's suppose you're given a right triangle with a hypotenuse of 20 and one base of 12, and asked to calculate the side of the remaining base. Since it's a right triangle, we'll first ask ourselves if it's a special triangle. Let's see if it's a 3:4:5 triangle. The hypotenuse is equal to 5 times a constant (5 × 4), and the base is also equal to 3 times the same constant (3 × 4). Since it's a right triangle and two sides fit into the ratio of 3:4:5, then it is a 3:4:5 triangle and the remaining side has to be 4 times the same constant (4 × 4)…thus the remaining side has a length of 16.

Below is a 3:4:5 triangle where k represents the constant of proportionality—the number that's multiplying each of the sides to make the triangle either bigger or smaller but doesn't change the ratio of the sides to each other.

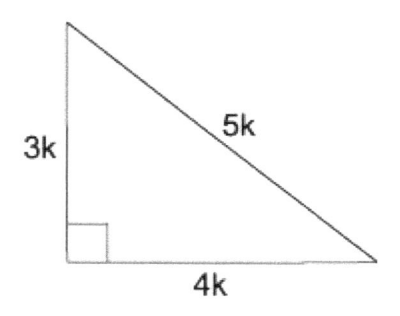

30°–60°–90° Right Triangles

Below is a 30°–60°–90° triangle—the sides are in the ratio of $k : k\sqrt{3} : 2k$ where k is the constant of proportionality or scaling factor. k is the number which makes the triangle either bigger or smaller but it doesn't change the ratio between the sides (since it's multiplied by each side). The best way to remember the triangle is to remember the sides opposite the angles: k (the shortest side) is opposite the 30° angle, $k\sqrt{3}$ is opposite the 60° angle, and 2k (the largest side and the hypotenuse) is opposite the right angle.

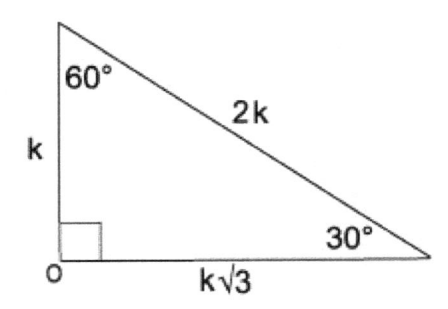

If you're given a 30°–60°–90° triangle and told the side opposite the 60° angle is $5\sqrt{3}$, then we can solve for the other sides of the triangle once we know the constant of proportionality. In this case, the side opposite the 60° angle is $5\sqrt{3}$ which in our proportion is $k\sqrt{3}$. So we have the equation, $5\sqrt{3} = k\sqrt{3}$. Dividing both sides by $\sqrt{3}$, we solve for k, the constant of proportionality, which is 5.

We now know the other two sides. The side opposite the 30° angle is k, simply the constant of proportionality, which is in this case 5. The side opposite the right angle is twice k or 10.

45°–45°–90° Right Triangles

There are two cases for the 45°–45°–90° right triangle: the case where you're given the length of the hypotenuse and the case where you're given the length of one of the bases.

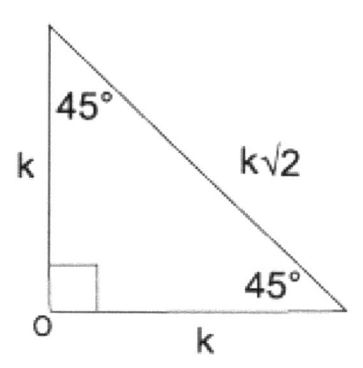

Use the above triangle when you're given the length of one of the bases which we call k. The length of the hypotenuse is then k times the square root of two. So if you're given a 45–45–90 right triangle in which one base is 5, you know the other base also has a length of 5 and its hypotenuse has a length of 5√2.

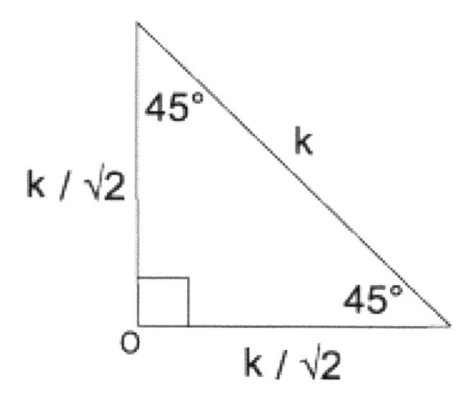

Use the above triangle when you're given the length of the hypotenuse. The length of the hypotenuse is in this case, k, which you have to divide by the square root of two to get the length of the two bases. If you're given a 45–45–90 right triangle in which the hypotenuse is 5, you know each base has a length of 5/√2.

Pythagorean Theorem

The Pythagorean Theorem gives us a relationship between the sides of *any* right triangle. Specifically, it says that the sum of the squares of the bases of a right triangle is equal to the square of the hypotenuse of the right triangle. In equation form, for any right triangle:

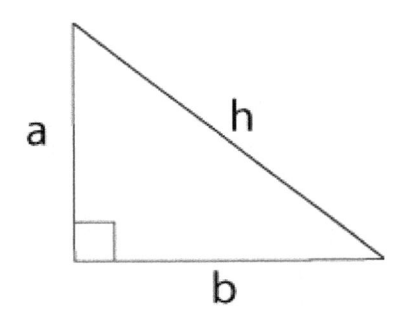

$$a^2 + b^2 = h^2$$

This is a very famous equation—you need to memorize it! Also, anytime you see a right triangle, write this equation down and think to yourself—I can use the Pythagorean theorem (to solve for sides of a right triangle).

Suppose you're given a right triangle, told the lengths of the two bases of the triangle are 5 and 12, and asked to find the length of the hypotenuse? We can use the Pythagorean theorem to solve this problem. Plug the two bases into the equation:

$$5^2 + 12^2 = h^2$$
$$25 + 144 = h^2$$
$$169 = h^2$$
$$h = \sqrt{169}$$
$$h = 13$$

We've thus found that the length of the hypotenuse is 13. We've also incidentally discovered another special right triangle—we already knew that there were 3:4:5 right triangles, now we know there are also 5:12:13 right triangles!

More on Triangles

A few things to remember about triangles:

The sum of the interior angles of a triangle is 180°. The three angles of a triangle always have to add up to 180.

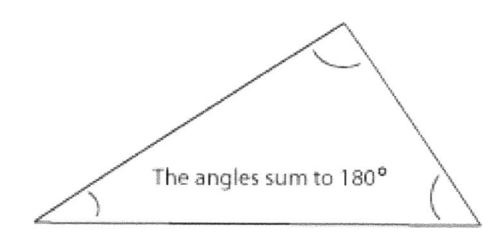

Any two sides of a triangle have to sum to be greater than the third side. Thus, the sides of a triangle can not be 4, 5, 10 (since 4 plus 5 is less than 10). To understand why this is true, draw three line segments in which two segments are together shorter than the third segment—we can't make a triangle from them because the two shorter sides aren't long enough to connect each other and both endpoints of the longest side.

Math Section: Triangles Problem Set

Answers are in Appendix 1 on page 509.

Fill in the remaining two sides for the following the 3:4:5 right triangles:

1. Base 1= 15   Base 2= ?   Hypotenuse= ?

2. Base 1= ?   Base 2= 28   Hypotenuse= ?

3. Base 1= ?   Base 2= ?   Hypotenuse= 55

4. Base 1= 42   Base 2= ?   Hypotenuse= ?

Using your knowledge of special triangles (particularly the 30:60:90 and 45:45:90 triangles), solve for x, y and z in the triangles below.

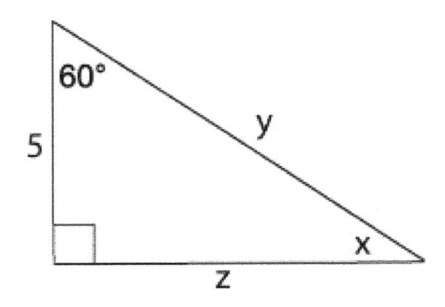

5.

6.

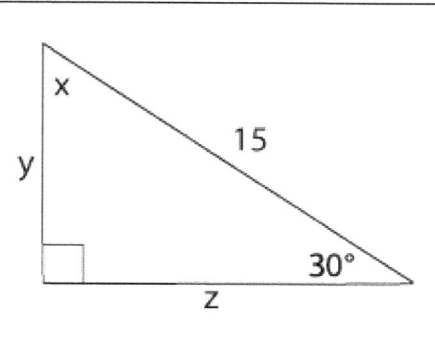

A right triangle with hypotenuse 15, angle 30° at bottom right, right angle at bottom left. Sides labeled x (top angle), y (left leg), z (bottom leg).

7.

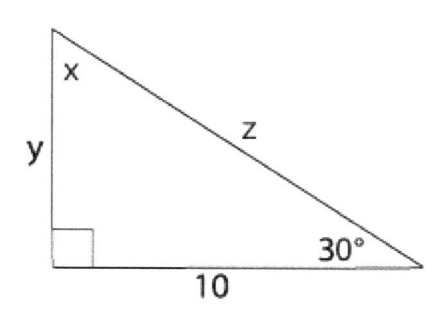

A right triangle with bottom leg 10, angle 30° at bottom right, right angle at bottom left. Sides labeled x (top angle), y (left leg), z (hypotenuse).

8.

A right triangle with both legs labeled $12/\sqrt{2}$ and hypotenuse labeled x.

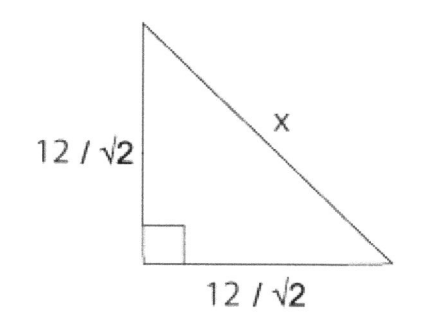

9.

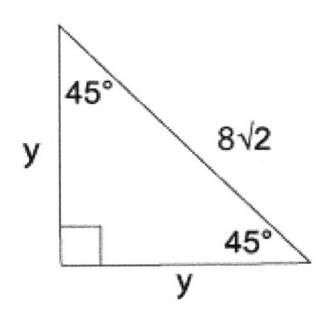

$$45°$$
$$y$$
$$8\sqrt{2}$$
$$45°$$
$$y$$

Solve the below problems (hint: use the Pythagorean Theorem):

10. What's the length of the hypotenuse in a right triangle with bases of length 8 and 15?

11. What's the length of the remaining base in a right triangle with a base of length 7 and a hypotenuse of length 25?

12. What's the length of the remaining base in a right triangle with a base of length 21 and a hypotenuse of length 29?

Optional: Proof of the Pythagorean Theorem!

This proof is one of the most beautiful things you'll ever see. The two squares below with the various triangles and squares represent a geometric proof of the Pythagorean Theorem. If you were an archaeologist and found such a diagram on some ancient clay tablet, you could deduce that that culture knew and had proven the Pythagorean theorem. See if you can figure out how the diagram below represents a "proof" of the theorem. Hint: try labeling each side of the triangle (e.g. a,b,h) remembering to use the same labels for all the triangles. If you can't see it, don't worry, the proof is explained on the next page.

Geometric Proof of the Pythagorean Theorem Explained.

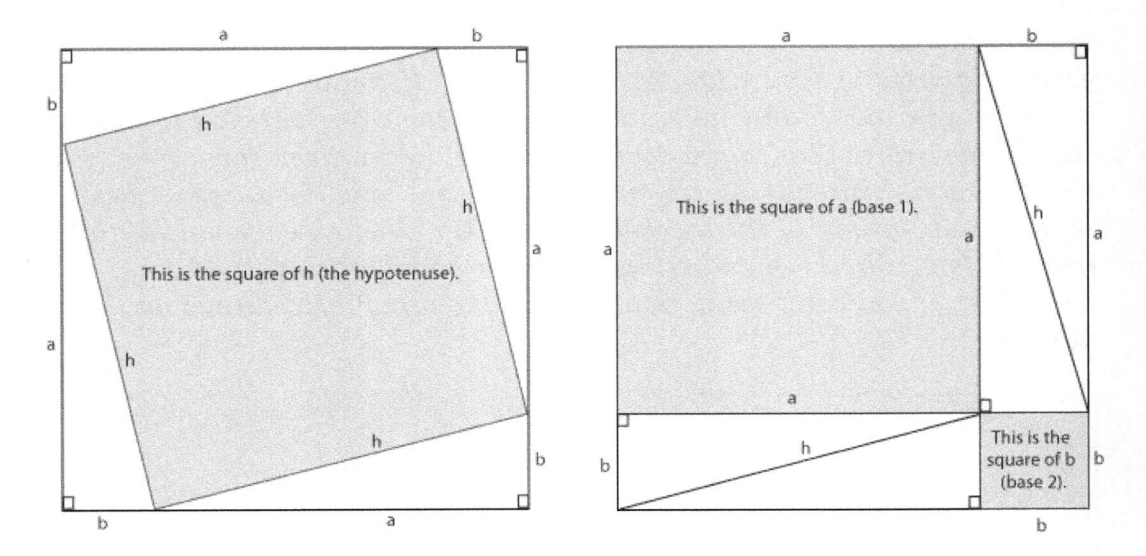

The area of both big squares (side length = a + b) is the same. The area of the right triangle of sides a,b,h is also the same. There are four right triangles in each of the big squares. Thus, the area of each big square minus the area of the four right triangles must be the same for both big squares. That means that the area of the remaining square of the hypotenuse in the left square has to be equal to the sum of the areas of the squares of the bases in the right square...which is the Pythagorean theorem. The theorem states that the square of the hypotenuse of a right triangle is equal to the sum of the squares of the bases of the same right triangle.

To recapitulate the proof, the big square minus the four triangles on the left leaves us with the single square of the hypotenuse. The big square minus the four triangles on the right leaves with the squares of the two bases. The squares of the two bases have to be equal to the square of the hypotenuse since both the left and right big squares have the same area and the four right triangles we removed from each one also have the same area. Thus the two small squares of the bases have to be equal to the square of the hypotenuse (which again is the Pythagorean theorem!).

Polygons

Sum of the Interior Angles of a Polygon

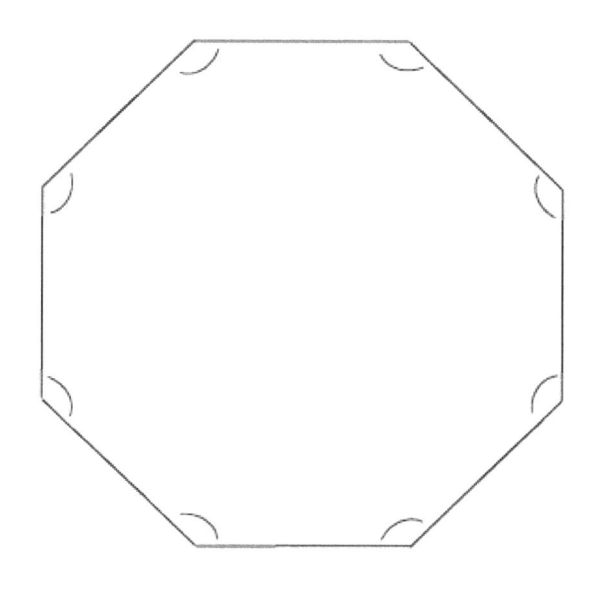

There are two ways to calculate the sum of the interior angles of a polygon: via a formula or by drawing triangles. Remember that any polygon will have as many interior angles as it has sides—so a pentagon has 5 interior angles and an octagon has 8 interior angles. To calculate the sum of those interior angles, there are two methods:

Formula:
Sum of Interior Angles of an n–sided Polygon = (180° × (n–2))

Example: What's the sum of the interior angles of an octagon?
    An octagon has 8 sides, so n = 8
    Sum = (180° × (n–2))
           = (180° × (8–2))
           = (180° × (6))
           = 1080°

Drawing Triangles Method to Calculate the Sum of the Interior Angles of a Polygon:

Draw triangles between the Vertices to Cover the Whole Space of the Polygon. Then, multiply the number of triangles you've drawn by 180° and you'll have the sum of the interior angles of that polygon.

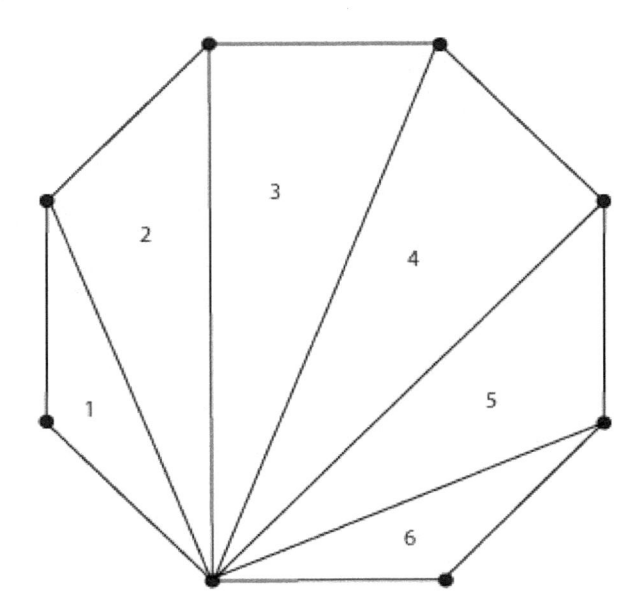

We drew triangles to figure out the sum of the interior angles of an octagon—in this case, we chose a vertex and drew triangles to every other vertex. We drew 6 triangles so the sum of the interior angles is equal to 6 × each triangle's interior angles = 6 × 180° = 1080°.

One important term to remember is 'Regular Polygon'—a regular polygon is one whose sides are of equal length and angles are of equal measure. If you need to calculate the measure of an angle in a regular polygon—you can divide the sum of all the angles by the number of angles i.e. the measure of every interior angle in an octagon will be 1080° divided by 8 or 135°.

Math Section: Polygons Problem Set

Answers are in Appendix 1 on page 510.

1. What's the sum of the interior angles in an 11 sided polygon?

2. In the figure below, what's the sum of its interior angles?

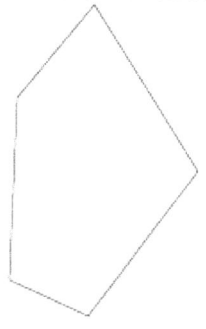

3. In a regular 7 sided polygon, what's the measure of each interior angle?

4. In the figure below, what's the sum of its interior angles?

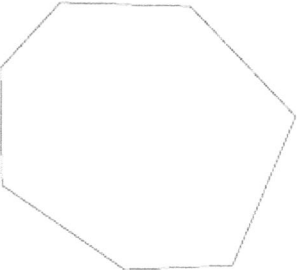

5. For a regular nonagon (9–sided polygon), what's the measure of each interior angle?

Solved Geometry Problems

Solved Geometry Problem 1

In the diagram below in which side CD = 5√3 and side BC = 5, what's the length of AB (for fun try to solve all sides and angles in the diagram)?

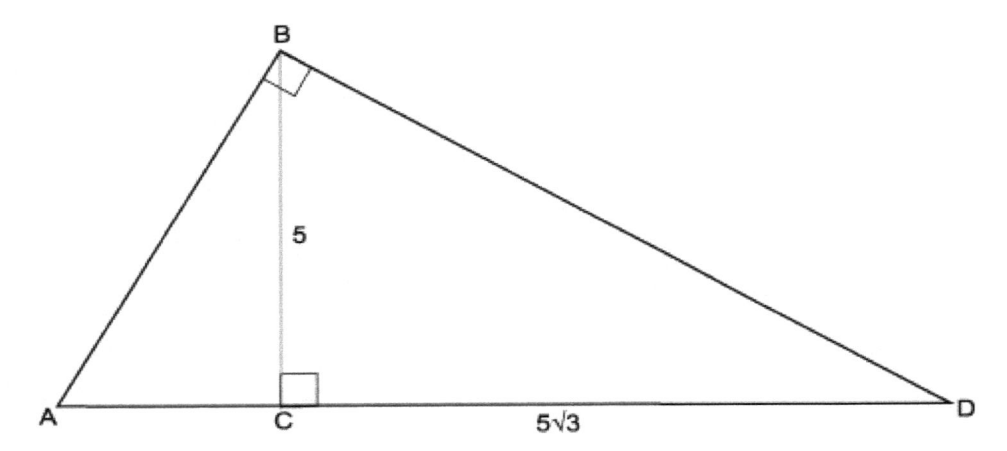

We've been given a diagram of right triangles and asked to solve for the length of the one of the sides. There are two things to solve in any triangle: its angles and its sides. Let's write in any information we can about right triangles and see what could help us solve its angles and side lengths.

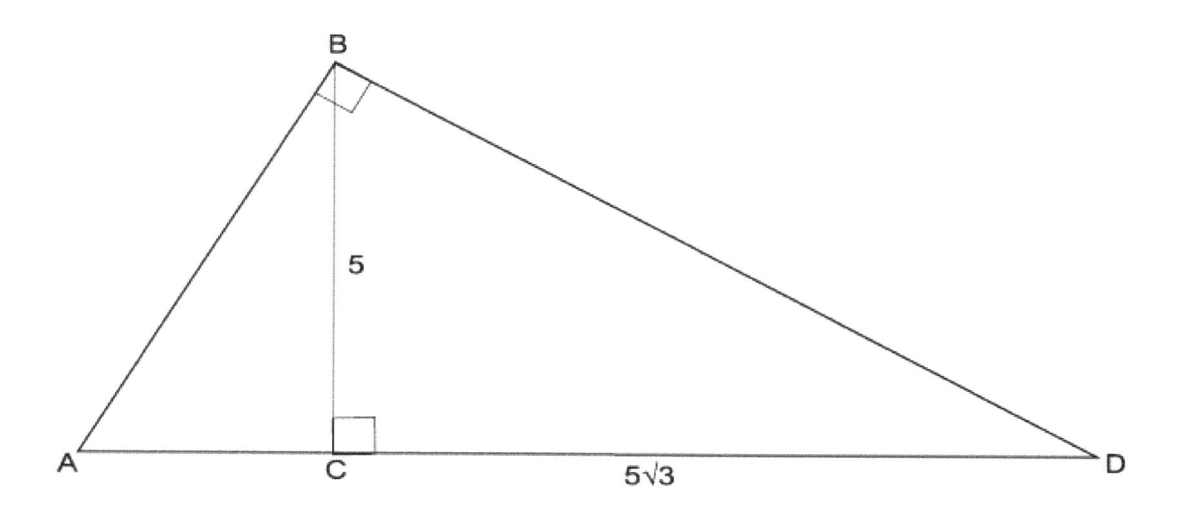

[Figure: Triangle ABD with B at top, A at bottom-left, D at bottom-right, and C on AD between A and D. BC is perpendicular to AD with BC = 5. CD = 5√3. Angle ABD at B is marked as a right angle.]

SIDES
Pythagorean Theorem: $a^2 + b^2 = h^2$

ANGLES
Special triangles
   30-60-90. $x : \sqrt{3}x : 2x$
   45-45-90. $x : x : \sqrt{2}x$
   3-4-5. $3x : 4x : 5x$

We could solve the side BD with the Pythagorean theorem...we know two sides of a right triangle, so we could use it to solve the third side. Let's first see, though, if triangle BCD is a special right triangle. Anytime you see a √3 in the side of a triangle, you should immediately think "this may be a 30–60–90 triangle." Indeed, BCD is a 30–60–90 right triangle—which makes solving for side BD faster than using the Pythagorean theorem. It also lets us fill in (very importantly) all the angles of triangle BCD—*fill in as much information as you can for any geometry problem even if you're not sure that it'll be helpful.*

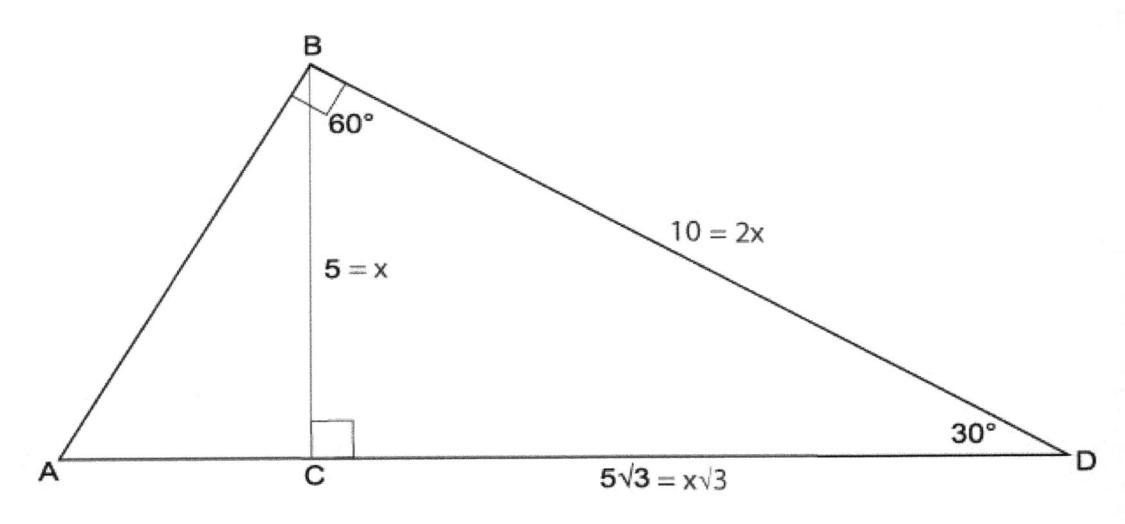

Pythagorean Theorem: $a^2 + b^2 = h^2$
Special Right Triangles
    30-60-90. $x : \sqrt{3}x : 2x$
    45-45-90. $x : x : \sqrt{2}x$
    3-4-5. $3x : 4x : 5x$

Since it's a 30–60–90 right triangle, let's fill in the angles. We know the angle opposite the smallest side is 30° and the other angle must thus be 60°. We know the side opposite the 30° angle has a length of x, the side opposite the 30° angle has a length of x√3, and the hypotenuse has a length of 2x. We wrote those in, and then solve for x (it solves itself practically) which is 5. Plugging 5 into 2x, we get the length of BD as 10.

We still have to solve AB, though. How do we solve the triangle ABC? We know one side of the triangle, BC, but that's not enough to help us solve AC or AB. Can we fill in any of the angles of triangle ABC? Yes! We know the measure of angle ABD and the measure of angle CBD. We can thus figure out the measure of ABC (30°), and then using ABC (180° − 90° − 30°) figure out the measure of angle CAB (60°). We've done it in the below diagram.

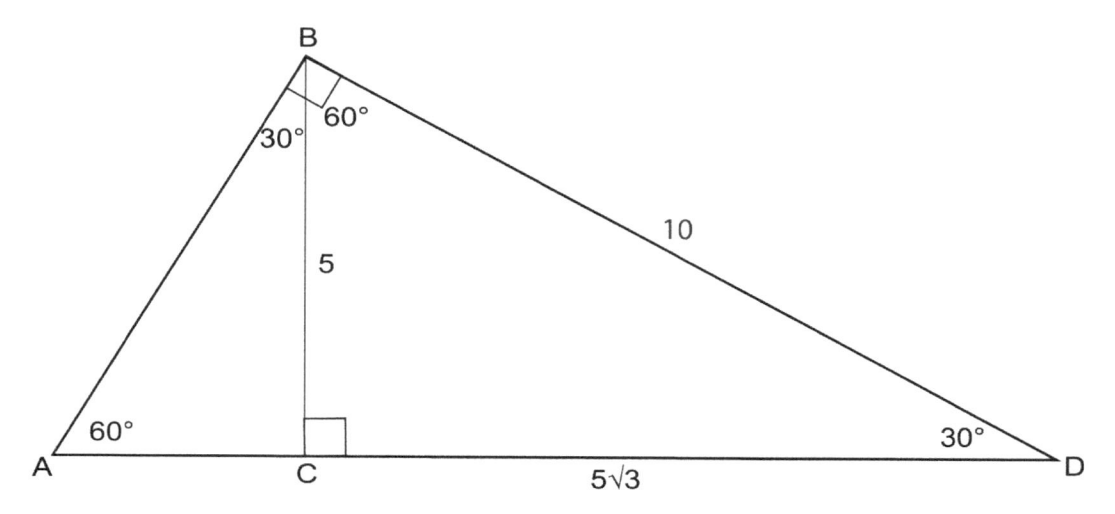

Pythagorean Theorem: $a^2 + b^2 = h^2$
Special Right Triangles
    30-60-90. $x : \sqrt{3}x : 2x$
    45-45-90. $x : x : \sqrt{2}x$
    3-4-5. $3x : 4x : 5x$

We can now solve for AB since we know one side of the triangle and that it's a 30–60–90 triangle. We know AB will be equal to 2x since it's the hypotenuse of a 30–60–90 triangle. We have to, though, figure out what x is. We know the side opposite the 60° angle is 5 and is also x√3. Using that, we can solve for x.

x√3 = 5
x = 5 / √3

AB is, then, equal to 2x or 10 / √3. To get rid of the square root in the denominator we can multiply the whole fraction by √3 / √3, and get the answer: 10 √3 / 3.

Here's the diagram with all sides and angles now solved!

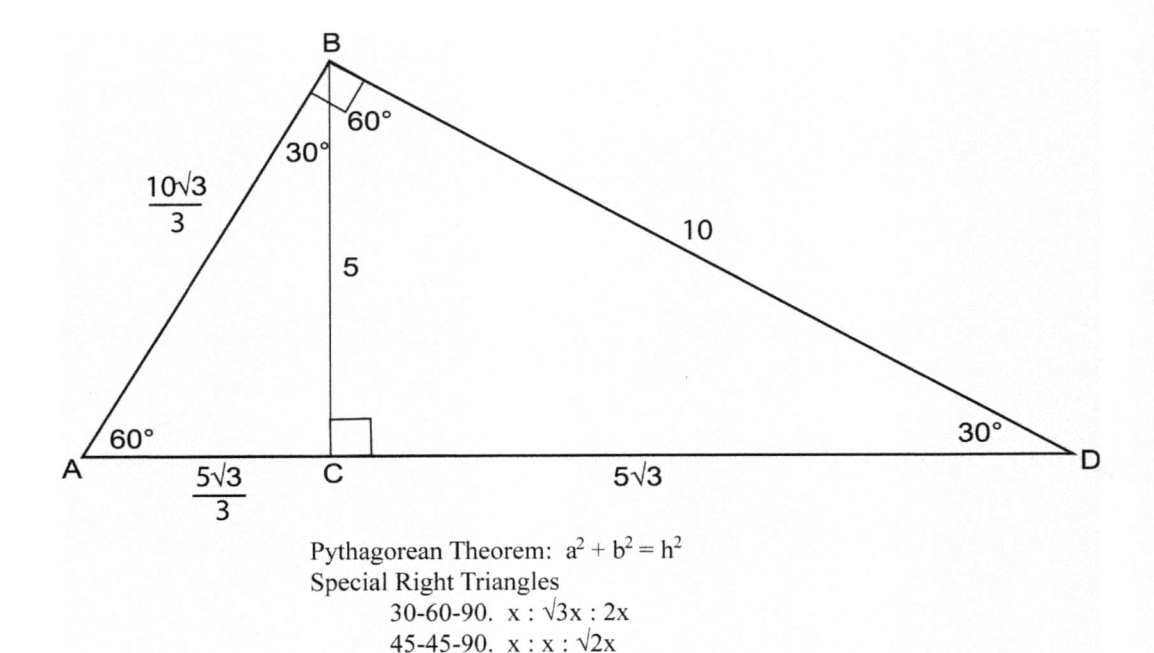

[Figure: Triangle ABD with point C on AD, BC perpendicular to AD. Angle A = 60°, angle at B above BC = 30°, angle at B to the right of BC = 60°, angle D = 30°. AC = 5√3/3, AB = 10√3/3, BC = 5, CD = 5√3, BD = 10.]

Pythagorean Theorem: $a^2 + b^2 = h^2$
Special Right Triangles
    30-60-90. $x : \sqrt{3}x : 2x$
    45-45-90. $x : x : \sqrt{2}x$
    3-4-5. $3x : 4x : 5x$

What were the key steps in this problem? Writing in all the side and angle information we could, and also being cognizant of our special triangles, in this case the 30–60–90 right triangle. *Write in everything you can and try to solve for any and everything you can (every angle, side, etc.) in geometry problems…and eventually you'll get the problem or the insight necessary to solve what the problem is asking for!*

Solved Geometry Problem 2

What's the measure of angle z in terms of x and y?

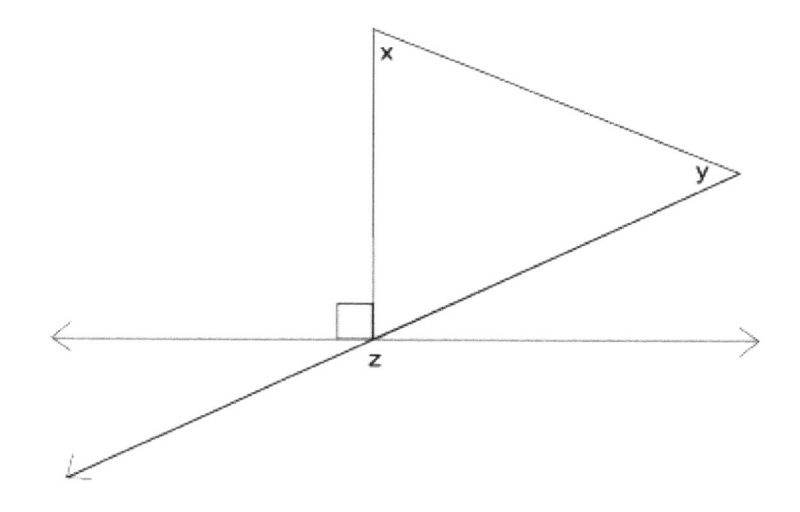

(A) 360 − 2x + y
(B) 180 − x − y
(C) 90 + x + y
(D) 90 + x − y
(E) 270 − x − y

In this problem, we have to define the other angles in the diagram in terms of x and y. Which angle can we start with? We have a triangle and two of the three angles are identified…so we can fill in that third angle since we know the sum of the three angles of a triangle is always 180°.

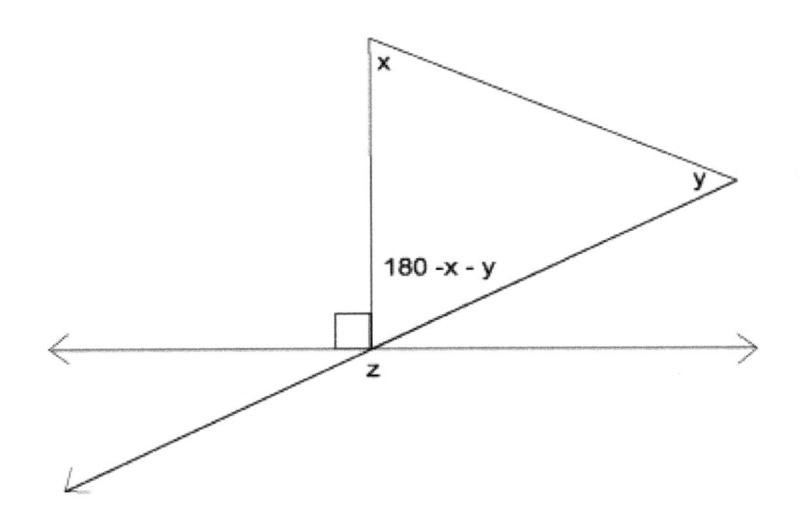

Now, let's fill in the other angles via complements, supplements and angle relationships (vertical and corresponding angles).

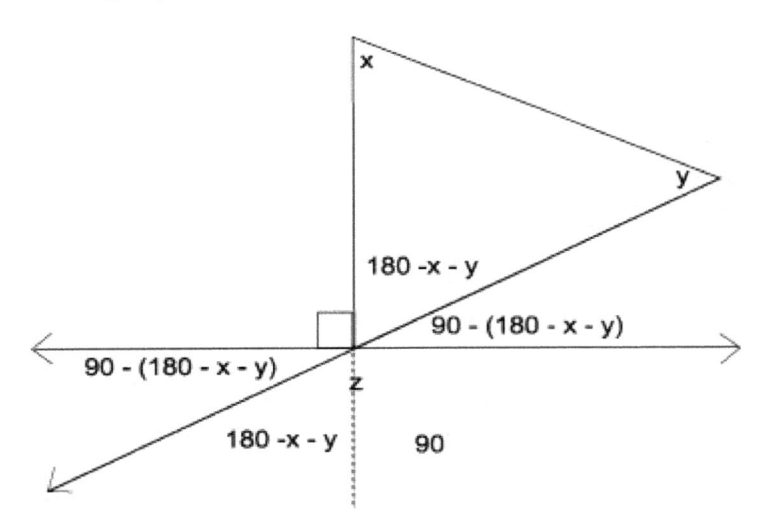

Since the angle below the triangle is the complement of (180°− x − y), then its measure must be equal to 90° − (180° − x − y) since complementary angles add to up to 90°. We can fill in the vertical angle opposite it, as well as the vertical angle opposite (180° − x − y)—

the dotted line drawn in the diagram above helps you see the vertical angle relationship clearly. Now we've got z which is the sum of 90° and 180° − x − y.

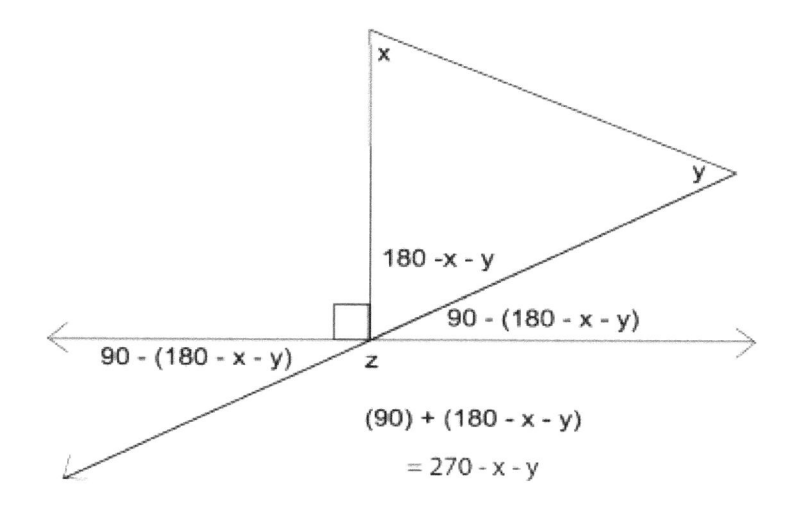

```
                            x
                            |
                            |\
                            | \
                            |  \
                            |   \
                            |    \
                            |     \  y
                            |     /
                            |    /
                            |   /
                            | 180 - x - y
                            |  /
                            | /  90 - (180 - x - y)
    ←―――――――――――――――――□―――/――――――――――――――→
           90 - (180 - x - y)  z
                              /
                             /
                            /
                    (90) + (180 - x - y)
                        = 270 - x - y
```

Angle z in terms of x and y thus equals 270° − x − y. We solved this problem by defining two angles (x and y—they were actually defined for us) and then "naming" or defining other angles in terms of those first angles. Whenever something is not given a value, give it a name such as x or y. Giving something a name helps you know and manage what entities you have to deal with. After naming x and y, we defined the other angles in terms of x and y…and therein solved the problem.

Alternative Method to Solve the Problem: Plug in Numbers!

If using x and y looks confusing to you...then plug in numbers for x and y and then solve for z. Plugging in numbers is very regularly helpful for algebra problems and occasionally even helpful for geometry problems! You'll still have to know that the angles of a triangle add to up 180° and the vertical angle relationships, but using actual numbers rather than variables often makes a problem easier to work through and tackle.

Let's pick 70° for x and 50° for y—for this problem (and most problems) we don't have to think too much about what numbers to pick, just try to pick angles that are reasonable and easy to work with (70 and 50 are easy numbers to work with). Using those angle measures, we can fill up the rest of the diagram.

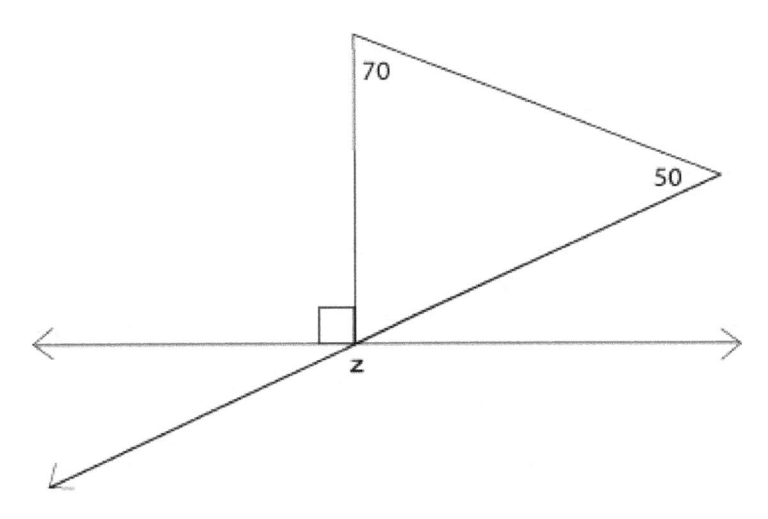

We start by filling in the third angle of the triangle (180° − 70° − 50° = 60°).

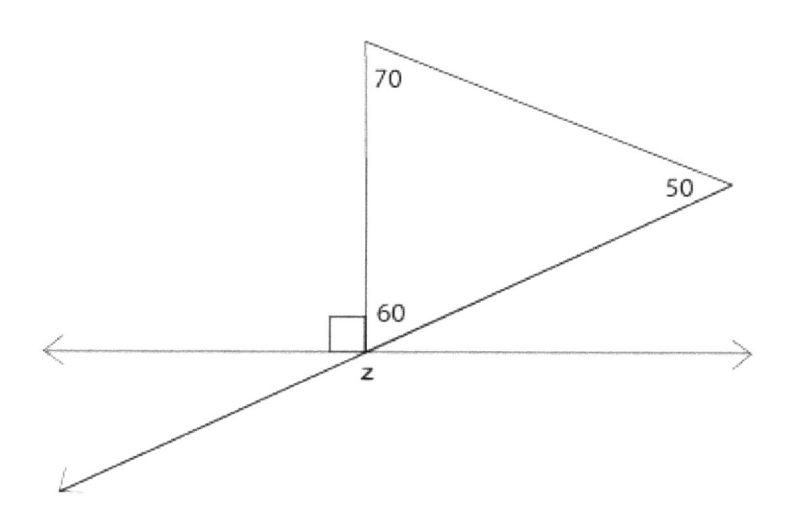

We can now fill in the complement of 60° (30°).

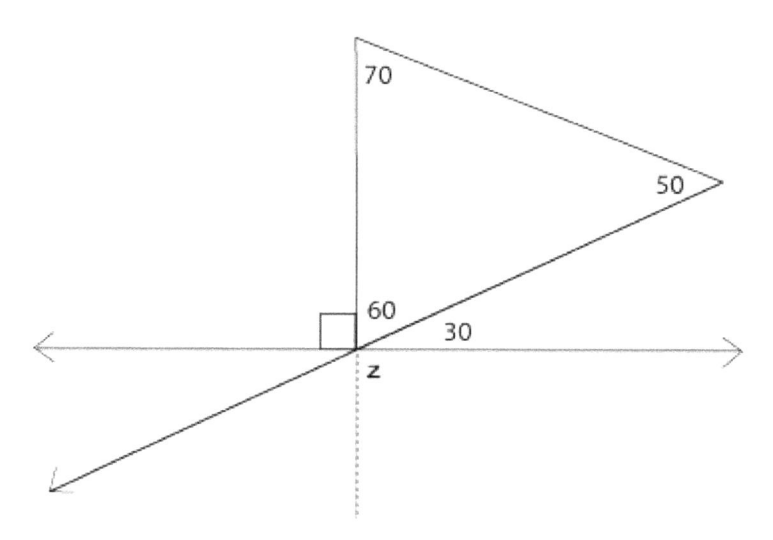

Let's now fill in the vertical angle relationships.

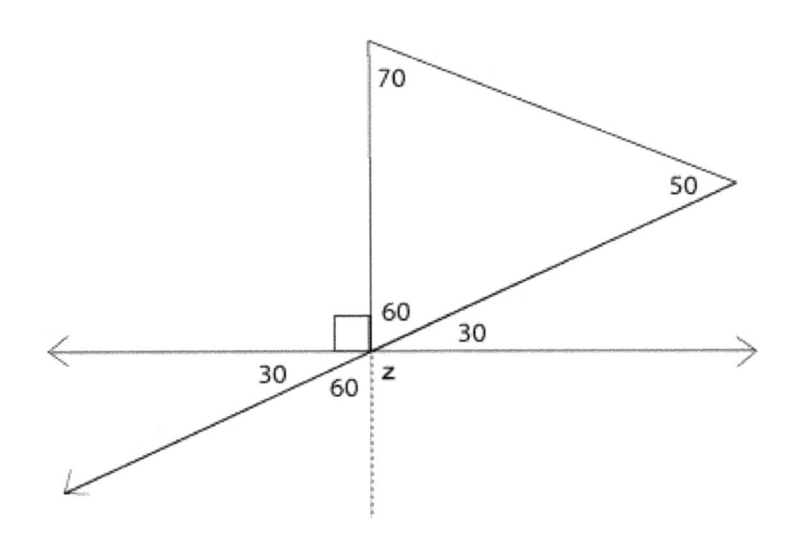

We've got z now: it's 60 + 90 or 150°.

We now have to plug in our numbers into the possible answer choices and see which choice produces 150°.

(A) 360 − 2x + y
(B) 180 − x − y
(C) 90 + x + y
(D) 90 + x − y
(E) 270 − x − y

Plugging in 70 for x and 50 for y yields:

(A) 360 − 2x + y   360 − 2 × 70 + 50 = 270
(B) 180 − x − y   180 − 70 − 50 = 60
(C) 90 + x + y   90 + 70 + 50 = 210
(D) 90 + x − y   90 + 70 − 50 = 110
(E) 270 − x − y   270 − 70 − 50 = 150

Choice (E) is what we calculated, 150°, and is correct!

Solved Geometry Problem 3: Using Measurement

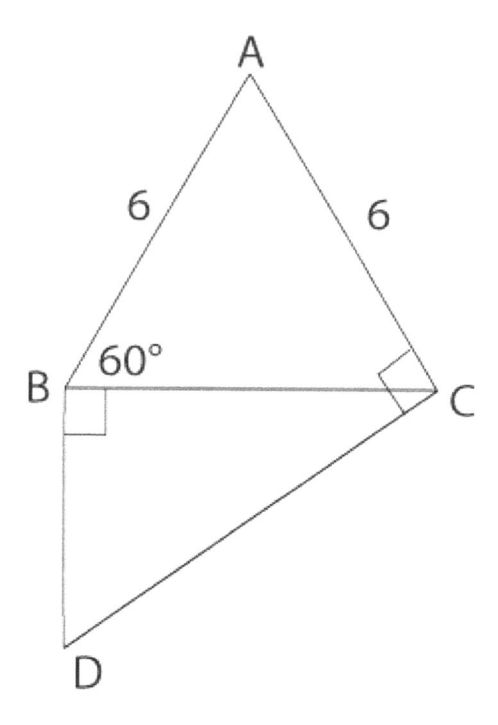

In the figure above, what's the perimeter of the quadrilateral ABDC?

(A) 20
(B) 12 + 6√2
(C) 12 + 6√3
(D) 12 + 8√3
(E) 28

Let's assume we've tried to use our knowledge of geometry to solve the problem but we didn't get anywhere...so then we have to measure. We'll count how many tick marks on our marked pencil is equal to the length of 6 units which is given to us and then from there we'll determine the lengths of BD and CD. If a diagram is not marked "not drawn to scale", then assume it is drawn to scale. If it's not drawn to scale, re–draw it so that it is drawn as closely to scale as you can, then measure! By the way, each space in the diagram given to you in the problem we'll call a unit, and each space on your pencil we'll call a tick mark.

We have to first take out our marked pencil whose tip should look something like this:

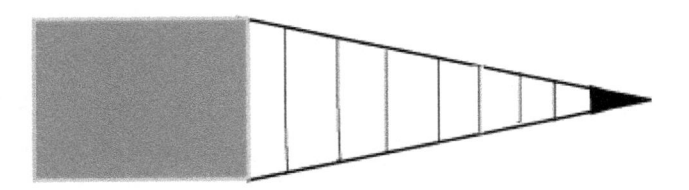

Notice that the tick marks are fairly accurately calibrated but not perfect—each tick mark is roughly the same distance from any other mark. Try the best you can.

We have to use that pencil to measure how many tick marks equal the length of 6 units in the diagram.

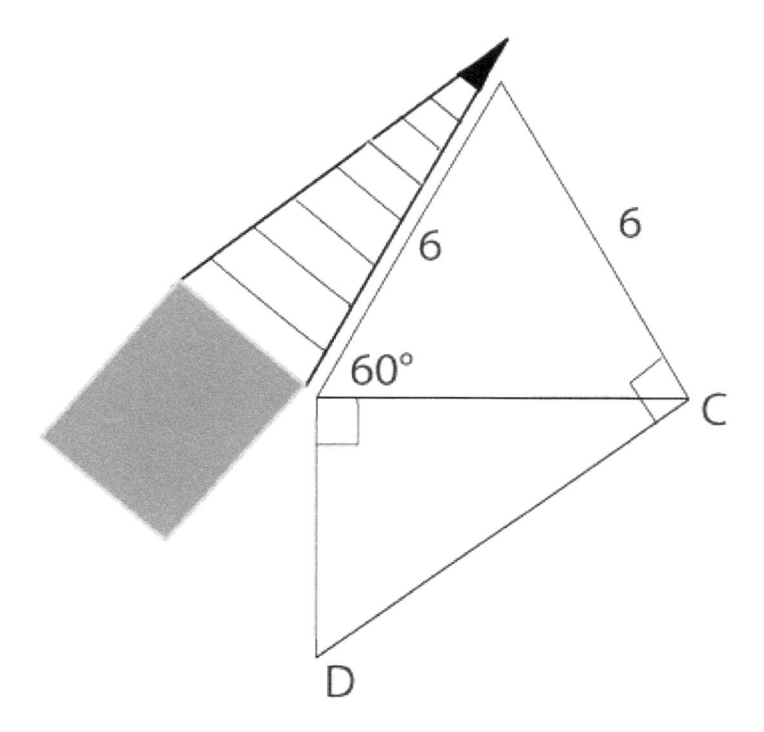

There are approximately 8.5 tick marks to the line segment of length 6 units. Now we have to measure how many tick marks there are in the two line segments we don't know (BD and DC—we know both AB and BC are 6 units in length).

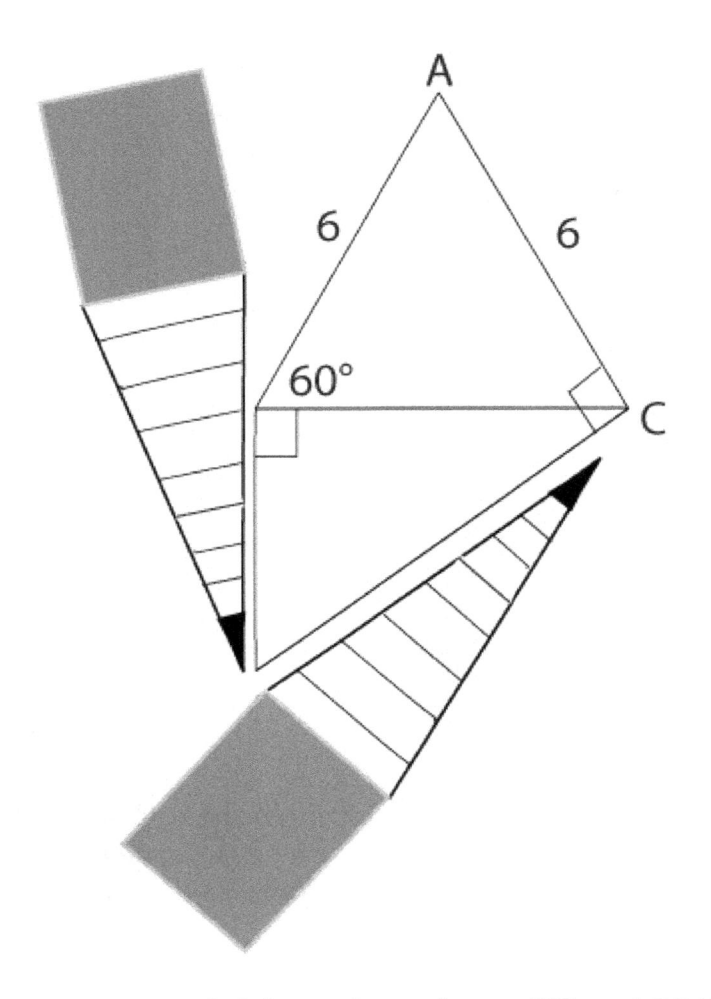

From here, we can count 6 tick marks make up BD and 10 tick marks make up DC (the pencil has 9 tick marks on it and it looks like that extra space represents one more tick mark). Using a simple ratio, we now can calculate the lengths of both BD and DC. Let's call the length of BD x, and the length of DC y. It's a direct proportion (if units go up, we know tick marks also go up) so we know to set up the proportion or ratio as a fraction (where the first fraction is the distance given to us, 6 units which we measured as 8.5 tick marks). For side BD, our fraction will be this:

$$\frac{6 \text{ units}}{8.5 \text{ tick marks}} = \frac{x \text{ units}}{6 \text{ tick marks}}$$

After cross–multiplying (anytime you have fractions in an equation, think *cross–multiply*), we get:

$36 = 8.5x$

$x = 4.2$

The length of BD as measured then is ~ 4.2 units.

Let's calculate DC:

$$\frac{6 \text{ units}}{8.5 \text{ tick marks}} = \frac{y \text{ units}}{10 \text{ tick marks}}$$

$8.5y = 60$

$y = 7.1$

The length of DC as measured then is ~ 7.1 units.

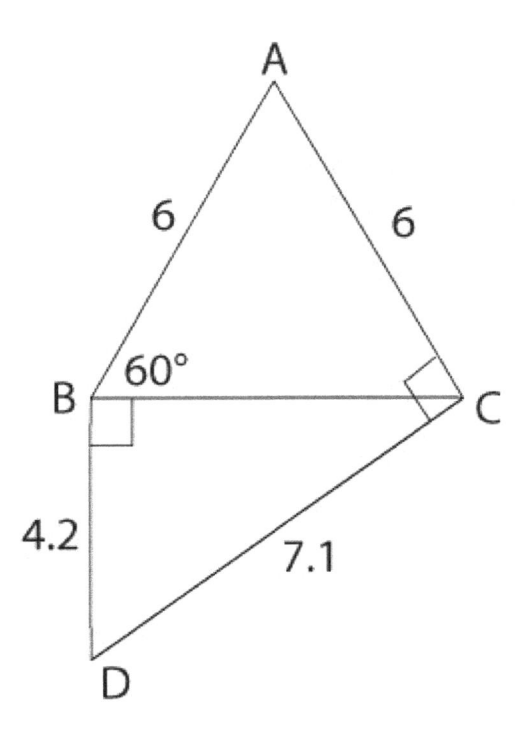

The perimeter of ABDC then equals 6 + 6 + 4.2 + 7.1 which totals 23.3. Let's see which answer choice is closest to 23.3.

    (A) 20

    (B) $12 + 6\sqrt{2}$ ~ 20.5

    (C) $12 + 6\sqrt{3}$ ~ 22.4

    (D) $12 + 8\sqrt{3}$ ~ 25.9

    (E) 28

The closest choice is (C)...so we have to pick it. And in fact, (C) is correct! Practice measurement—it can save you a lot of time and frustration occasionally when you're stuck on a geometry problem!!

Alternative Method to Solve the Problem: Using Geometry!

For those of you curious as to how to solve the problem using pure geometry...here goes.

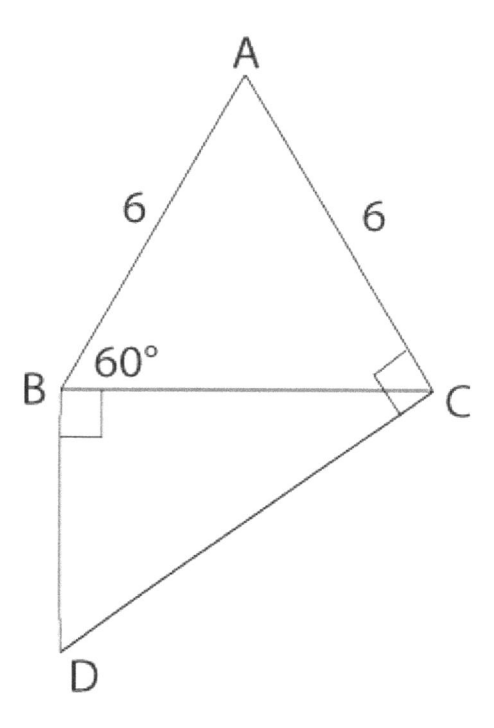

We have to try to fill in as many angles and side lengths in the diagram as we can. A key insight that can get us started is realizing that sides in a triangle that are of equal measure also have angles opposite them that are of equal measure. Thus, if AB and AC are the same measure (6), then angles ABC and ACB have to be the same measure (60°).

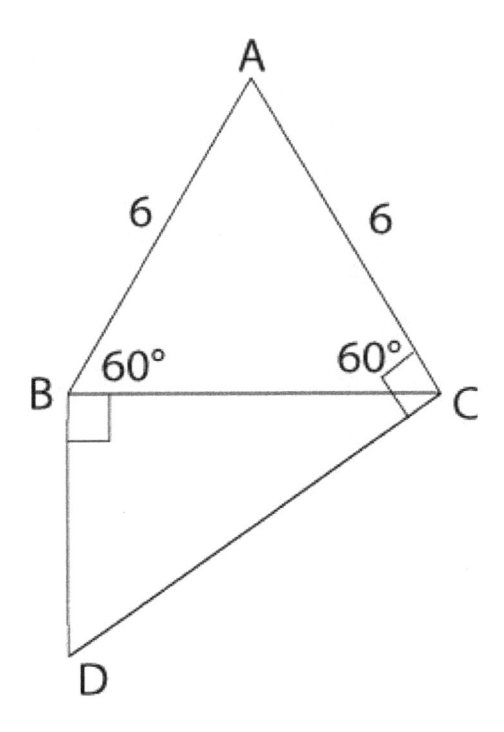

From there knowing that the angles of a triangle sum to 180°, we know angle BAC has to be 60°.

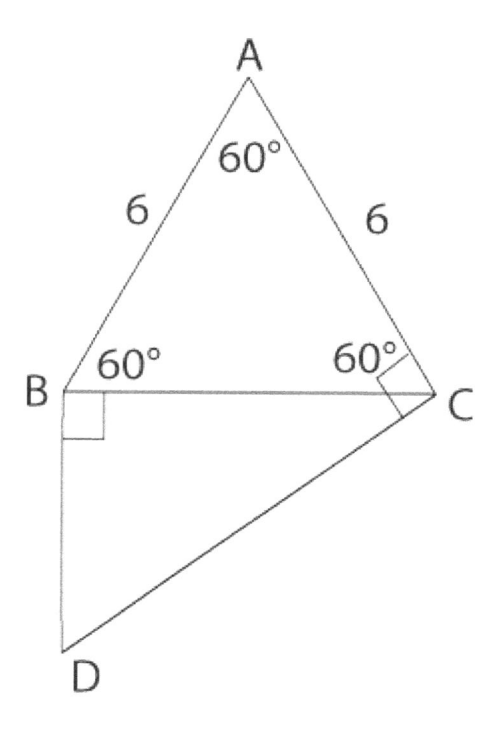

Then using that same initial principle regarding the equal measure of sides and their opposite angles—we know that since angle BAC is equal in measure to angle ABC, their opposite sides (AC and BC) have to be of equal length (6).

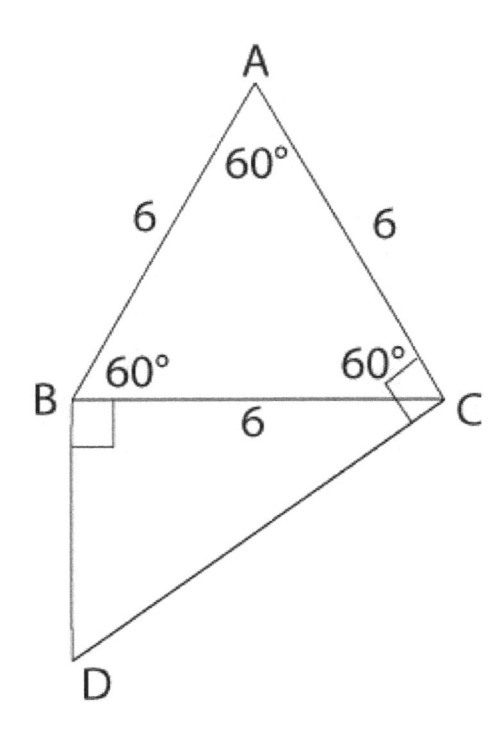

We've now solved triangle ABC…let's see what we can do with triangle CBD. We know that angle DCB is the complement of angle ACB—since the two together equal angle ACD which is indicated in the diagram to measure 90°. Angle DCB has to measure 30°, then. If DCB is 30°, then the remaining angle in triangle CBD has to be 60°.

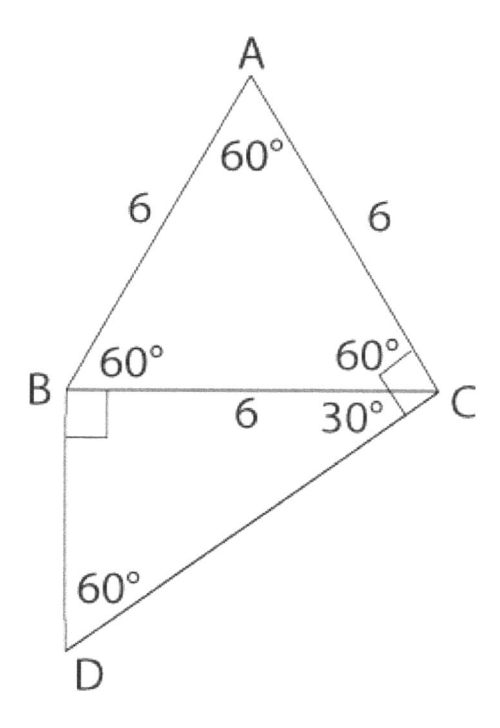

Triangle BCD is a 30–60–90 triangle and we know the measure of one of its sides: we can now solve the other two sides! Let's write in our 30–60–90 relationships into the diagram (1x: x√3 :2x) then solve for BD and DC.

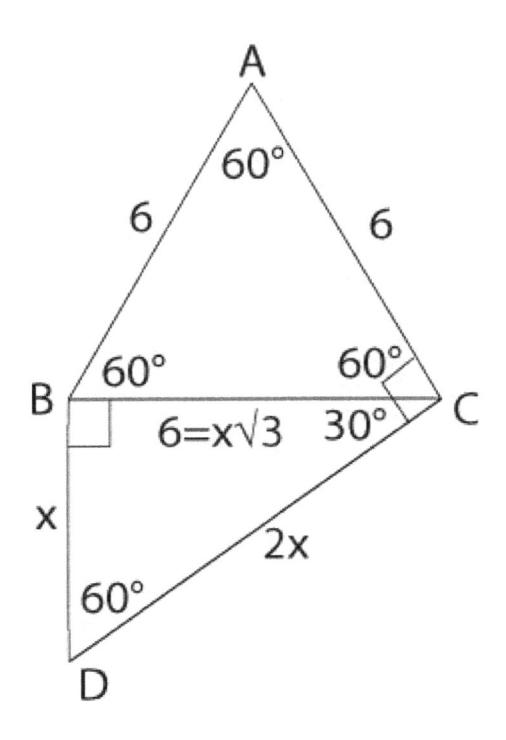

We have to solve for x:
  $6 = x\sqrt{3}$
  $x = 6 / \sqrt{3}$

To put x into proper form (no square roots in the denominator), we have to multiply it by $\sqrt{3} / \sqrt{3}$.

$$x = \frac{6}{\sqrt{3}} \times \frac{\sqrt{3}}{\sqrt{3}} = \frac{6\sqrt{3}}{3} = 2\sqrt{3}$$

Now we know BD has a length of 2 √3, and D has a length of 4 √3

ABCD's perimeter is equal to 6 + 6 + 2 √3 + 4 √3 = 12 + 6 √3 (answer choice (C)).

Again notice how we've solved our geometry problems: plugging in one deduction after another in detective–like fashion until we've finally got all the data and information we need to solve the problem. Don't try to solve the problem entirely at once or expect the insight to solve it will just pop into your head—*work on problems on paper step by step, deduction by deduction using your knowledge of angle/side and other relationships in geometric figures.*

Solved Geometry Problem 4: An Analytical Geometry Problem

A line with a slope of 4 passes through the point (1, z) and through the y–intercept of the function $y = x^2 + 16$. What is the value of z?

This is a multi–step problem. Let's first figure out the y–intercept of $y = x^2 + 16$. We have the equation and we know its y–intercept is the point at which x=0...so we can easily solve for the y–intercept.

$y = x^2 + 16$
$y = (0) + 16$
$y = 16$

The y–intercept of the function $y = x^2 + 16$ is thus 16.

We now know two points which the line passes through: (1, z) and (0, 16). We also know its slope is 4. We can plug this data into our equation for the slope of a line and then solve for y.

$$m = 4 = \frac{(y_1 - y_2)}{(x_1 - x_2)} = \frac{(z - 16)}{(1 - 0)} = \frac{z - 16}{1}$$

$4 = z - 16$
$4 + 16 = z - 16 + 16$
$20 = z$

We've solved the problem, z = 20.

Write down the various equations you know for solving analytical geometry problems that may be relevant to the problem at hand (e.g. the equation for slope, the point–slope equation of a line (y = mx +b)) and fill in data or solve for the data that can be plugged in to solve the equations ... until you've got your solution. Also, solve for any piece of information that could be relevant and that you know you can solve for e.g. we solved for the y–intercept of the given function initially which we knew we could solve for easily given what we were told in the problem.

Math Section: Measurement Problem Set

Use our measurement technique (the tick-marked pencil) to solve these problems. Afterwards, try to solve the problems using "pure" geometry.

Answers are in Appendix 1 on page 512.

1. In the diagram below in which B is the center of a circle which contains points A and C, what's the area of triangle BAC?

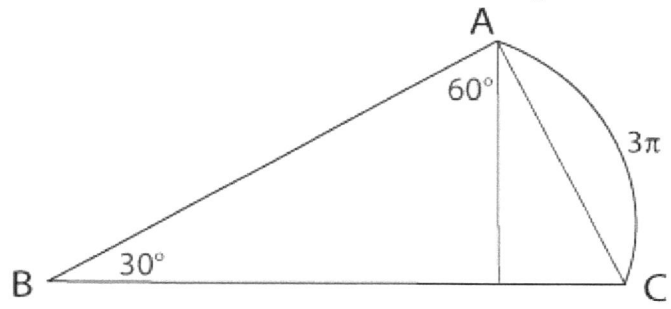

(A) 27
(B) 36
(C) 18π
(D) 64
(E) 81

2. If the length of line segment AB is equal to r, the radius of the circle, then what's the length of line segment BC?

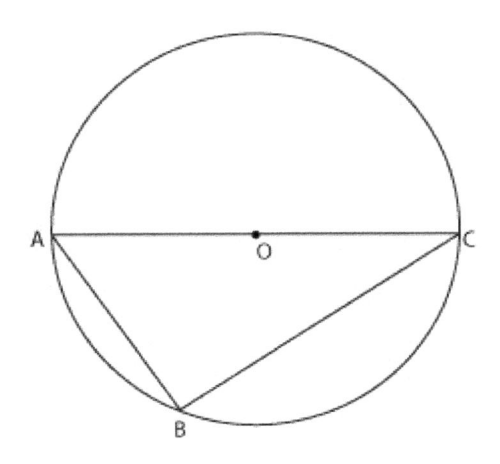

(A) r / √3
(B) r √3 / 2
(C) r √3
(D) 2r √3
(E) r + √3

3. In the diagram below, what's the area of the shaded region in the square BCED?

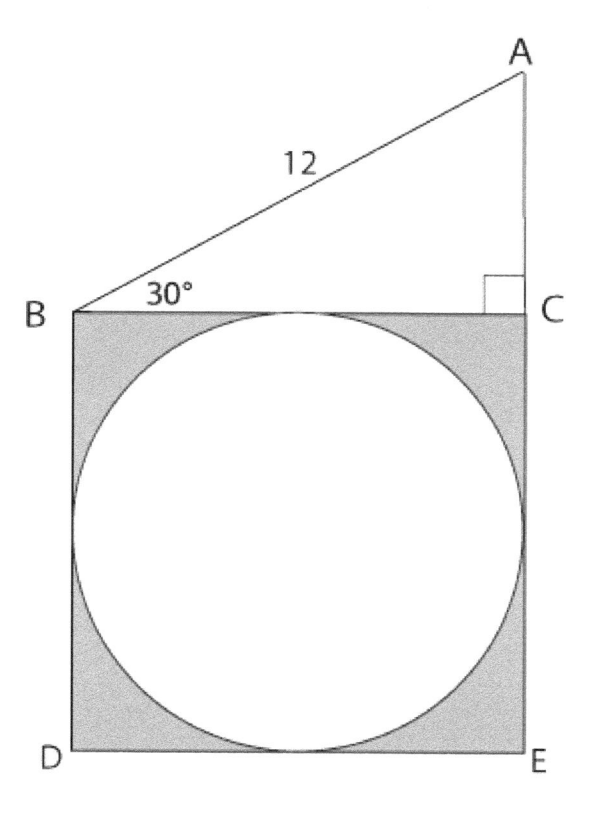

(A) $54 - 27\pi$
(B) $108 - 27\pi$
(C) $108 - 6\sqrt{3}\pi$
(D) $27\pi - 54$
(E) $144 - 36\pi$

Math Section: Geometry Problem Set

Use your system for solving geometry problems: write down everything you know, solve for as many unknowns in the problem as you can, and finally solve the question!

Answers are in Appendix 1 on page 514.

1. Given that m and n are parallel lines and that angle g measures 110°, what is the sum of angles f and j?

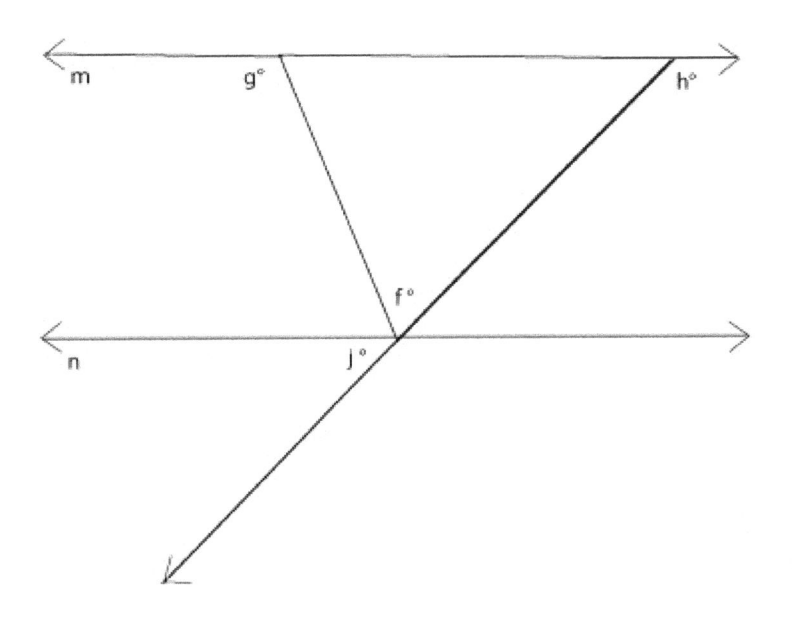

2. What's the measure of angle z in the parallelogram below equal to?

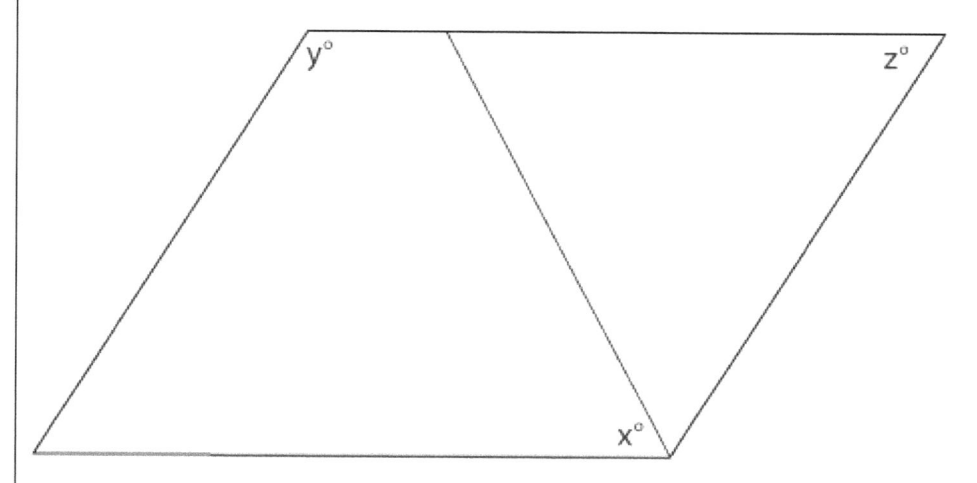

(A) $180° - y$
(B) $180° - x - y$
(C) $x + y$
(D) $y - x$
(E) $2y - x$

3. What's the sum of the exterior angles (marked in the diagram via circles) of the polygon below?

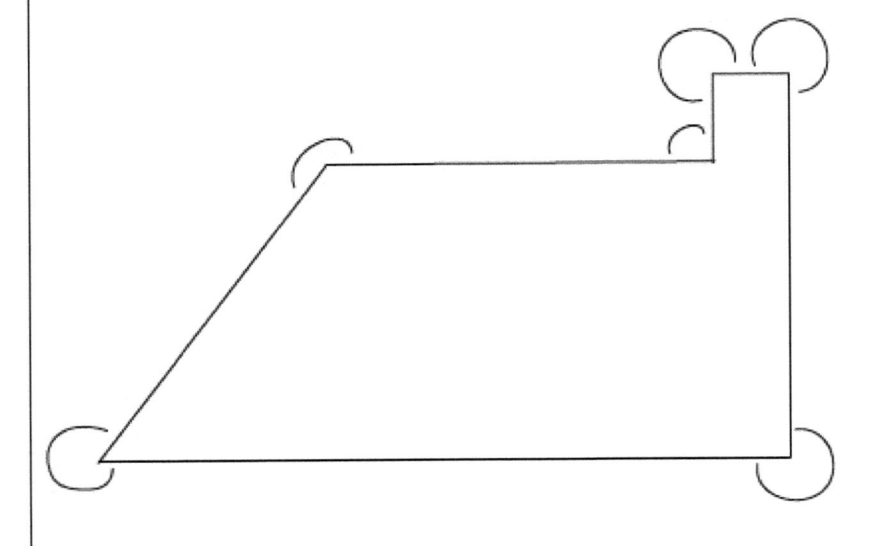

4. The rhombus ABDC has diagonal CB equal to 10. What's the ratio of its diagonal CB to the length of one of its sides (e.g. line segment CD)?

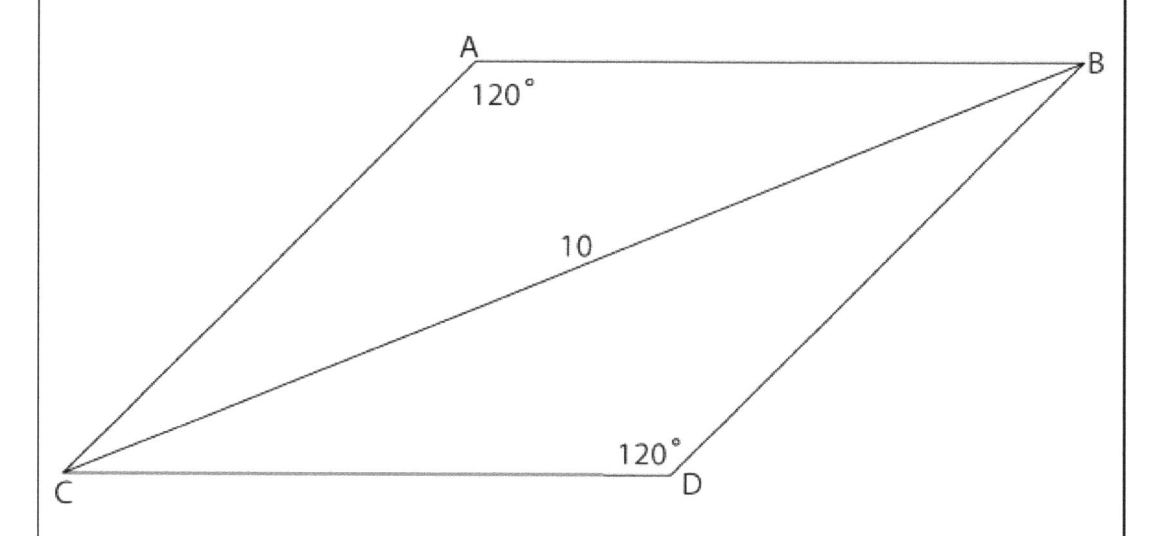

5. What's the maximum number of points on which a square can intersect a circle?

   (A) 2
   (B) 4
   (C) 6
   (D) 8
   (E) 10

Math Recapitulation

General

- ✓ Use your pencil—Work On Paper!!!! Keep Moving—don't dwell on any problems (circle unanswered problems and come back to them later).

- ✓ Double-check your work. One for reasonableness. Two for careless mistakes. Always. Especially on easy to medium problems—you can't afford to miss them.

- ✓ Make sure you're answering the question (and haven't just solved for an intermediate value).

- ✓ Practice, practice, practice—get additional SAT math books with problem sets on every type of problem on the test and practice, practice, practice!

Algebra/Arithmetic

- ✓ Plug-In Numbers.

- ✓ Work Backwards from the Answers.

- ✓ Pure Algebra Procedure:

- - Write down knowns and unknowns.
  - Write as many equations as you can until you have as many equations as you have unknowns. One way to generate an equation is to define one variable in terms of another variable.
  - Finally, when you have as many unknowns or variables as equations, solve.

- ✓ Plugging in numbers for arithmetic problems: when testing behavior use numbers that are positive/negative, integers/decimal, and greater than 1/less than 1.

- ✓ Write down all your work—it's easy to make careless mistakes when you have several steps in a problem.

Geometry

- ✓ Work from the Diagram: Write in Everything You Know and Work Step-by-Step, Deduction-by-Deduction.

- ✓ Plug-In Numbers.

- ✓ Measure. Use your tick marked pencil.

WRITING SECTION: Multiple–Choice Questions Overview

The multiple choice questions in the writing sections are the most content–based of the three sections in the SAT test. That means that you can, relative to other sections, more easily learn what's being tested in these questions and master them. We've seen the most consistent score improvements among students in the writing multiple choice sections.

There are three types of multiple choice questions in the writing section: sentence revision, sentence correction, and paragraph revision. We'll first review our techniques for approaching these problems as well as the grammatical rules tested, and then we'll tackle and analyze several problems.

We've found that students have an easier time becoming comfortable with sentence and paragraph revision questions than with sentence correction questions. This is probably because the sentence correction questions test formal grammar the most thoroughly of the three. For the sentence and paragraph revision questions, much of what's tested is style i.e. whether or not it sounds like bad writing.

In our chapters on the writing section, get ready to learn some basic techniques for approaching all these problems including most critically crossing out extraneous words and using your ear. We also review the grammar you need to know for the test. If you study the rules and review and complete practice test writing sections intensely, you'll quickly "tune yourself" to the types of grammatical errors tested and see score improvements.

Here are sample problems of each of the three types of writing multiple choice problems as well as key guidelines to keep in mind when tackling these problems. At the end of this chapter, we'll work through several more problems.

Sentence Correction Problems

In sentence correction problems, you're asked to correct any grammatical mistakes in a sentence. Either the sentence is correct as written or you have to change some underlined part of the sentence to make it correct. There will be a grammatical mistake 80% of the time in these problems. The other 20% of the time it's (E) or no error. These questions do not test your knowledge of style—no answer will be wrong because it's too wordy or sounds awkward. If an answer sounds wrong, for the easy and medium questions, pick that answer as it very likely is wrong (because of a grammatical not a stylistic problem). For hard questions, the final four or five sentence correction problems, if an answer choice sounds wrong, be certain that it is grammatically incorrect (by being able to identify the grammatical error)—some answers will sound awkward even though they're technically correct.

Sample Sentence Correction Problem

There <u>is</u> <u>between</u> the school and the church four different grocery
     A   B

stores <u>which is</u> quite <u>surprising</u>. <u>No error</u>
       C   D   E

Let's first see if we can cross out any extraneous modifiers or phrases: 'between the school and the church' is a prepositional phrase which sounds fine (i.e. there's no error with (B) between) and thus can be crossed out. Crossing out such unnecessary phrases helps your ear "hear" the grammar of the sentence better.

There <u>is</u> ~~between the school and the church~~ four different grocery
     A   B

stores <u>which is</u> quite <u>surprising</u>. <u>No error</u>
       C   D   E

Now that we've crossed out the prepositional phrase 'between the school and the church', the answer should pop out to you (you should "hear" it when you read the revised sentence out loud or to yourself). The answer is (A). The singular verb 'is' is not in agreement with the plural direct object 'four different grocery stores.' We have to change (A) is to 'are.'

Here are four key points to keep in mind when tackling sentence correction problems. These are the toughest problems in the section so they may take a bit of time and practice to crack, but they test the same grammar rules over and over so if you're attentive and practice, you'll learn to hear and detect those errors.

1. **Know your grammar!** Be able to analyze sentences grammatically and according to the commonly tested grammatical errors. Know the checklist of possible errors for each respective part of speech!
2. **Cross out Modifiers and Prepositional Phrases. Simplify the sentence.** If a modifier is not underlined and even if it is and it's correct and not crucial to the grammar/meaning of the sentence, then cross it out! Sometimes a modifier is necessary to the meaning of the sentence in which case you'll have to keep some or all of it—you can always try reading a sentence without the modifier or move the modifier around in the sentence to understand and hear the sentence better.
3. **20% or 1 in 5 of the answers should be E. No Error.** If you have many more or fewer E's, re–evaluate!
4. **Use your ear, but don't always rely on it.** Try to always identify the grammatical error—sounding a little bit funny isn't enough to make something wrong for sentence correction problems. This is important essentially for the hard questions. For the easy to medium sentence correction problems (the first 2/3rds of the problems), if it sounds wrong to you, it's very likely wrong (but it's still a good discipline to be able to identify the grammatical error). For the hard problems (the last ones),

make sure it doesn't just sound funny, but that there's also an error you can identify. These questions often have answer choices that are grammatically correct but sound funny. If you know your grammatical rules when something sounds funny but it isn't breaking any of the rules, you won't pick it.

Sentence Revision and Paragraph Revision Problems

Sentence Revision Problems.

These problems will ask you to revise a sentence for both style and grammar. In terms of grammar, there are roughly 20 or so commonly tested grammatical rules we'll cover in the grammar section. For style, correct answers will represent precise, concise and clear writing. You'll notice that many answer choices and sentences will sound clumsy, wordy, awkward, etc.—eliminate them based on style (they represent ineffective writing). Choice (A) is always the sentence as it is written.

Sample Sentence Revision Problem

There were only two choices <u>for him; try to continue</u> or admit defeat.

- (A) for him; try to continue
- (B) for him: try to continue
- (C) for him including trying
- (D) to continue
- (E) to continuing

Grammar is being tested, for example in (A) or (B) whether we need a colon or a semicolon. Style is also being tested, for example between (C) and other choices whether we need 'including' or not. Between (A) and (B), the colon is the preferred punctuation since the second part of the sentence is not an independent clause but rather a list of two choices. We can eliminate (A) and keep (B). Choices (D) and (E) sound awkward without 'for him'—eliminate them. Choice (C) has an error in verb parallelism: trying and admit are in two different tenses which is an error. Eliminate (C). We're left with (B) which is correct.

Paragraph Revision Problems

You'll be given a short passage (in which each sentence is numbered) to read and then asked to revise various sentences or combinations of sentences in order to make the passage better. Your revisions should be based on the ideas expressed or desired to be expressed in the passage as well as based on grammar and style.

Sample Paragraph Revision Problem

What's the best way to revise and combine sentences 7 and 8 (reproduced below)?

(7) Her early success made her excessively confident in her talent. (8) She failed to see that the world had changed.

- (A) Her early success made her excessively confident in her talent, and she failed to see that the world had changed.
- (B) Her early success made her excessively confident in her talent, because she failed to see that the world had changed.
- (C) She failed to see that the world had changed because of excessive confidence from her early success.
- (D) Her excessive confidence in her early success, though, has led her to fail to see that the world had changed.
- (E) Failing to see that the world had changed, her early success made her excessively confident in her talent.

This problem is mainly one of style and grammar—how do we most effectively combine the two sentences—but we also have to be sure to express the meaning of both sentences clearly as well. The answer choice that does this is (C).

(B) and (E) reverse or confuse the order of causality—for example, (E) needs 'had made her' for example to be correct. (D) is wordy. (A) doesn't connect the two sentences or show that because of the first sentence (her success), the outcome of the second sentence occurs (failing to see that the world had changed). (C) expresses the ideas of both sentences and combines them in their proper logical relationship using the logically correct conjunction 'because'.

Sentence Revision and Paragraph Revision Problem Key Points

Here are five key points to keep in mind for sentence and paragraph revision problems. We find most students become adept at solving these problems with practice without much difficulty. If you find yourself having a lot of trouble with them, sit down with your English teacher or someone who's a good writer who can explain why and how some sentences are poorly written or awkward and who can help you hear the awkwardness of wrong answer choices.

1. **20% or 1 in 5 of the answers should be** A. correct as written. If you have many more or fewer A's, re–evaluate!
2. **Use your ear.** Both the sentence and paragraph revision questions test style which is whether or not sentences and paragraphs represent clear, concise, effective writing. There aren't any easy rules we can teach you to help you identify what's clear writing and what isn't. Luckily, thanks to all the reading and writing you've done in school, you should already have a good ear for identifying what's well–written and what's awkward. So use it!! Use your ear to solve these questions. Whether an easy or hard problem, if something sounds quite

awkward in a sentence or paragraph revision problem, it's wrong.

3. **Eliminate answers based on similar structure.** Many questions will test multiple things at once—a common example would be to test if you know the correct punctuation for separating two independent clauses and if you have a sense of what a well–written sentence is (e.g. style). For such a problem, if you know that we can't separate two independent clauses with a colon and that if we're using a semicolon we shouldn't have a conjunction, you'd likely be able to eliminate a few of the answer choices fairly quickly (which differ only in how the independent clauses are separated). After that, you can decide which of the remaining choices is the best written (also remember *shorter writing is often better writing* when you're stuck).

4. **Read improved sentences out loud (during practice tests only!).** If you're having trouble with these problems, try reading them out loud when you take practice tests and even give yourself a bit more time for these sections. By the time the test date rolls around, you should be able to hear the mistakes when you read the sentences to yourself.

5. **Read the paragraphs in paragraph revision problems quickly at first.** Get to the questions quickly. The questions won't test your comprehension of the paragraphs, only your ability to edit those paragraphs and the sentences they're composed of.

Our Approach to the Writing Multiple-Choice Section

The same grammar rules are repetitively tested.

It's always the same set of roughly 20 rules. These rules must be learned and mastered. We go over the particular rules tested in the grammar review section. While our emphasis is on using your ear to detect what sounds wrong, you should be able to then explain why something is wrong using proper grammatical terms. This is crucial for harder sentence correction questions in which answer choices are deliberately made to sound wrong when they are actually correct.

You need to be able to identify and break a sentence into its components such as subject, conjunction, direct object, indirect object, prepositional phrases, other modifying phrases, adjectives, and adverbs. Further, you should be able to identify the various grammatical rules that are tested e.g. misplaced modifier, subject–verb agreement, pronoun case error, et cetera. When you review your practice tests and even while taking them, identify what specific rule is being broken and the part(s) of speech of the affected words. Practice breaking down sentences into parts of speech. We'll cover all of that in the grammar section; be sure to apply what you learn from that section to the problems you do in practice tests. You have to learn and master a bit of grammar…and as you practice learning those grammar rules, your ear will "tune" to them.

Use your ear to hear grammatical mistakes.

This method is crucial for all the problems in the writing section. For the harder sentence correction problems (the last third of the problems), using your ear must be combined with grammatical analysis e.g. you shouldn't pick an answer to a hard sentence correction problem as wrong just because it sounds wrong, you should be able to explain why it's wrong as well. For easy and medium problems, if something sounds wrong, it most likely is wrong so you can without any further analysis select that answer (though if you can state what the grammatical error is, that's best of course). For many of the sentence and paragraph revision problems, your ear is all you have to go by—many answers will simply sound awkward and that makes them wrong (there's no grammatical reason why they're wrong, they'll just be wordy, awkwardly phrased or confusing).

Cross out extraneous parts of the sentence so that errors are easier to hear.

You should practice crossing out modifiers, prepositional phrases, and other not terribly necessary words in the sentence in order to help your ear hear the core of the sentence. For example, one of the most commonly tested errors is subject–verb agreement; in these questions, some prepositional or other phrase will usually be inserted between the subject and the verb to make it sound like an object in the phrase is the subject of the sentence and fool your ear into thinking the sentence is correct. Crossing out such extraneous phrases helps your ear hear more clearly what's the subject and what's the verb and also that they don't agree. So cross out unnecessary modifiers and phrases. It also saves you time when you read sentences to yourself in your head.

Shorter is often better.

This rule isn't as important as the above ones, but it's important nonetheless particularly for the sentence and paragraph revision problems. Shorter writing is often better. This isn't always true, but it often is. When you're down to two choices and you're stuck, go with the one that sounds better but if they sound the same, go with the shorter one.

WRITING SECTION: Grammar Review

Parts of Speech: a Quick Review

It's crucial to know the parts of speech and the terms for the basic parts of speech. In tackling the writing multiple choice questions, you have to analyze and break down the sentences—to do that, you need to know what you're looking for, what to call it and how it behaves. To that end, learning the various parts of speech will give you insight into the components of sentences, how sentences work, and how to analyze them/break them apart.

Small Optional Note: Though you may find our definitions of many grammatical objects "obvious" and simple to understand, actually many are not. It's difficult, for example, to define what a subject of a sentence is. The most common definition (our definition in fact) is that the subject is what does the action in the sentence. The problem is that you can switch any sentence around to make the subject into the direct object of another sentence—both expressing the same action. The cook put garlic into the pot. Garlic was put into the pot by the cook. In the first sentence, the cook is the subject and in the second sentence garlic is the subject even though in both sentences it's the cook who's doing the action. Defining some parts of speech, thus, can be philosophically difficult...if you find this interesting, consider studying linguistics at some point. Linguistics is the study of language in general and one of its goals is to understand grammar and particularly to know if there's a universal grammar that underlies every language.

Noun—a person, place or thing.

    A *pickle* from *Brazil* told *me* to keep a green *complexion*.

"Brazil" is a place and thus a noun. "Me" is a person and thus a noun. "Pickle" and "complexion" are also things (complexion is an abstract thing) and thus nouns.

Subject—the noun which generally does the main action in the sentence.

> *She* gave me the book.

"She" is the subject of this sentence as she's doing the main action of giving me the book. In the previous example, "pickle" is the subject as it's doing the main action of telling me (to keep a green complexion).

Direct Object—the noun that's the direct recipient of the action or verb in the sentence.

> She gave me *the book*.

In this case, the direct recipient of this action of giving is "the book."

Indirect Object—the noun that is the indirect recipient of the action or verb in the sentence.

> She gave *me* the book.

In this case, the indirect recipient of this action of giving is "me" who receives the book, the direct object. The indirect object is often the object of a prepositional phrase. For example, we can rewrite the sentence so that me is part of a prepositional phrase: She gave the book to *me*.

Pronoun—a word that refers to or takes the place of some other noun or nouns.

> There's the goat. *It*'s running

'*It*' is a pronoun that refers to or represents the goat. You have to use a different pronoun if you're using a pronoun as a subject of a sentence or as an object of a sentence. This is called pronoun case. *I* am going to the store. The pronoun "I" is in the subject or subjective case as it's the subject of the sentence. Give it to *me*. The pronoun "me", though referring to the same person as "I", is in the object or objective case as it's an indirect object in the sentence.

There are first–person pronouns (I/we, me/us), second person pronouns (you/you), and third person pronouns (he/she/they, him/her/them).

Verb—a word that indicates some action or state of being.

> He *is jumping* over the elephant. She *feels* sad.

"Is jumping" and "feels" are the verbs of the respective sentences with "is jumping" representing an action and "feels" a state of being.

Adjective—a word that describes or modifies a noun.

> That *beautiful* book is on the *big* table.

Beautiful and big are adjectives describing or modifying the book and the table, respectively.

Adverb—a word that usually describes or modifies a verb, but can also describe or modify an adjective or adverb. Adverbs usually end in –ly.

> Why are you running so *quickly*? Sit down *comfortably*.

Quickly and comfortably are adverbs describing how the person is running and how the person should sit, respectively.

Phrase—some group of words that as a whole functions typically as a modifier and doesn't have a subject–verb structure.

> *Watching the light in the clouds*, he forgot what time it was.
> Jim, *the captain of the sailboat*, ran to tell me to zip up my pants.

"Watching the light in the clouds" is a phrase which modifies "he". "The captain of the sailboat" is a phrase and in this case it functions as a noun to tell us more about Jim—you could thus think of it as a modifier as well as a noun. The technical term for some phrase which re–states and describes the subject of a sentence is an appositive. Note that we could remove that phrase and the sentence would still be fine: Jim ran to tell me to zip up my pants.

Preposition/Prepositional Phrase—a preposition is almost always found as part of a prepositional phrase which consists of a preposition and an object and functions as a kind of modifier usually indicating some type of relationship.

> Examples of prepositional phrases include *above the car, below the table, on the door, in the bathroom, for you, to me, with her, from the giraffe, about their dissent*, et cetera.

Each of the previous examples is a simple prepositional phrase consisting of two parts: a preposition (above, below, on, in, for, to, with, from, etc.) and an object (car, table, door, bathroom, you, me, etc.). Note that pronouns in prepositional phrases must be in the object or objective case—thus it's correct to write "give it to us" NOT "give it to we" since us is in the objective case.

Independent Clause—a group of words that has a subject and verb and can stand alone as an independent sentence.

>When you're in Mangalore, *you shouldn't eat too many mangos.*

In this sentence, "you shouldn't eat too many mangos" is an independent clause as it has a subject and a verb and could stand alone as an independent sentence.

Dependent Clause—a group of words that has a subject and verb but can not stand alone as an independent sentence.

>*When you're in Mangalore*, you shouldn't eat too many mangos.

"When you're in Mangalore" is a dependent clause since it has a subject and verb but it can't stand alone as an independent sentence. Note that if "when" was removed, it would become an independent clause.

Punctuation for Dependent Clauses (specifically when to use a comma).

When the independent clause comes before a dependent clause, we usually don't separate them with a comma (unlike a sentence in which a dependent clause comes first). For example:

>When the dependent clause comes first, we have to use a comma.
>We usually don't separate clauses with a comma when the independent clause comes before the dependent clause.

Noun Clause—a clause that functions as a noun.

That he's younger than you is no reason to beat him.

What's the subject of this sentence? It's not a single word or thing but rather the whole clause "that he's younger than you." The verb is "is".

Conjunction—a word that functions to connect other words, groups of words, phrases, or clauses; the most used conjunctions are and, but, and or.

He should give the keys to me *or* to her.

Exercise: Practice Breaking Sentences Apart According to Their Parts of Speech

When you're completing writing sections, try breaking down sentences into their various parts of speech. Here are two examples:

The beautiful girl	in the pink dress	made of silk	ate	the chocolate cake	quickly.
subject/noun	prep. phrase	modifying phrase	verb	direct object	adverb

Running around trees	in the afternoon	was	his favorite activity.
subject/noun clause	prep. phrase	verb	direct object

Don't worry about breaking down sentences into more fine-grained categories (e.g. articles, helping verb, et cetera). You just need to be able to identify the critical parts of speech (particularly the subject, predicate, prepositional/modifying phrases and direct object) in any sentence quickly!

Take some sentences from this book and practice breaking them down (following the above examples):

Grammatical Errors Tested

We'll now review the grammatical rules that are tested in the writing section. As you complete and review practice tests, you'll develop a "grammatical ear"—you'll be able to "hear" what's wrong when you read these sentences to yourself. Help your "grammatical ear" by crossing out extraneous words and phrases. Working through practice tests with these rules in mind will develop your "grammatical ear" which will then do the work of identifying what's right and what's wrong.

Verb Tense

If there's more than one verb in a sentence, make sure that the tenses are relative to each other consistent and correct. Also be sure that the verb is conjugated correctly—use your ear. There's a common error of parallel verb tense which we treat separately.

Examples:

- Given: When he was young, he has three toy trucks.
- Corrected: When he was young, he *had* three toy trucks.

"When he was young" clearly puts this sentence in the past, so the verb needs to be in the past tense.

- Given: Even though the magazine gained readers since 1985, it was still losing money in 1990.
- Simplified: ~~Even~~ though the magazine gained readers ~~since 1985~~, it was still losing money ~~in 1990~~.
- Corrected: ~~Even~~ though the magazine *had* gained readers ~~since 1985~~, it was still losing money ~~in 1990~~.

The second part of the sentence makes it clear we're talking about two events both in the past. One event occurs earlier than the other which means we need the past perfect tense or "had gained." We can cross out a few prepositional phrases and the word "even" to simplify the sentence and try to hear more easily whether or not the two verbs fit together. Verb tense questions will often include many extraneous phrases and words—try to cross out extraneous modifiers and phrases to focus your ear on the essential aspects of the sentence and whether they're correct.

Parallelism

Parallelism or parallel structure is the idea that when we have a multiple terms which are serving a similar or analogous function in a sentence, they should all be in the same or parallel form. The most commonly tested parallel structure is multiple verbs applied to the same subject—the verbs must all be in the same tense. Parallelism also applies to lists of prepositional phrases used as modifiers for the same noun or verb. The SAT has a *strong* preference for parallel structure, so if you encounter a problem where parallelism is violated, it's an error. Studying some examples should make the idea of parallelism clearer.

Examples:

- Given: John Muir spent his life preserving natural beauty, fighting for the environment, and also was having a lot of fun.
- Simplified: John Muir spent his life preserving natural beauty, fighting for the environment, and ~~also~~ was having a lot of fun.
- Corrected: John Muir spent his life preserving natural beauty, fighting for the environment, and ~~also~~ *having* a lot of fun.

Since "preserving", "fighting," and "was having" are part of a list of verbs applied to "John Muir", they should be in the same tense.

Changing "was having" to "having" accomplishes that. Crossing out "also" helps us a bit in hearing and seeing the parallelism.

- Given: Every person must have a good character, good thoughts, and preserving purity of heart.
- Corrected: Every person must have a *good character*, *good thoughts*, and *a pure heart*.

"Good character" and "good thoughts" are both nouns while "preserving purity of heart" is a phrase and thus breaks the parallel structure of the list. We thus need to replace "preserving purity of heart" with a simple noun to preserve parallelism and "a pure heart" does the trick.

- Given: Your attitude demonstrated that you are afraid and having doubts.
- Corrected: Your attitude demonstrated that you are afraid and *have* doubts.

Since we have two verbs that modify the same subject separated by commas in a list, these verbs need to obey parallelism. "Are" and "are having", though, are in two different tenses so we have a parallelism problem. We put both into the simple present tense to make them parallel.

- Given: Jiff sailed around the lake, swam in the water, and from a tall rock he dove.
- Corrected: Jiff *sailed* around the lake, *swam* in the water, and *dove* from a tall rock.

In the corrected sentence, we have the parallel structure of verb followed by prepositional phrase, verb followed by prepositional phrase, etc. In the sentence as given, that structure is violated at the end when the prepositional phrase is followed by a subject and verb. That's corrected and put into proper parallel form in the corrected sentence in which we have three verbs in the same tense ('sailed', 'swam', 'dove'), each of which is followed by a prepositional phrase.

Subject–Verb Agreement

Subject–verb agreement is a commonly tested error in the writing section. Be prepared to face a question very much like the examples in which the subject and verb of a sentence are separated by some phrase intended to fool your ears into thinking the verb is correctly conjugated (when in fact it isn't).

These problems illustrate how important it is to cross out modifiers in order to use our ears to hear what's wrong with the sentence.

Examples:

- Given: Michael's face known to millions have been subjected to multiple cosmetic surgeries.
- Simplified: Michael's face ~~known to millions~~ have been subjected to multiple cosmetic surgeries.
- Corrected: Michael's face ~~known to millions~~ *has* been subjected to multiple cosmetic surgeries.

The small phrase "known to millions" which modifies "Michael's face" tends to fool our ear into thinking that "millions" is the subject of the sentence which "have" agrees with. "Michael's face", though, is the subject of the sentence and it's singular so we need "has". Notice how when we cross out the modifier "known to millions", "have" sounds quite wrong to our ears. Use your pencil—cross out extraneous modifiers then let your 'ears' do the rest of the work!!

- Given: John from the California Universities want to make the SAT test optional for potential students.
- Simplified: John ~~from the California Universities~~ want to make the SAT test optional for potential students.
- Corrected: John ~~from the California Universities~~ *wants* to make the SAT test optional for potential students.

Here again, a phrase (a prepositional phrase in this case) that's been put between the subject and verb fools our ear into thinking that the object of the prepositional phrase which is plural is the subject of the sentence. When we cross out that prepositional phrase, our ears pretty quickly realize that "John want" is not correct.

Noun–Noun Agreement (subject–object or noun–pronoun)

Nouns which refer to each other must agree in number and in gender. A noun which is an object in a sentence must agree with the subject if it refers to it. A pronoun must also agree with its antecedent (the noun the pronoun refers to).

Examples:

- Given: The best students among those who attend college hope that his or her higher future income will more than compensate for income lost while pursuing higher education.
- Simplified: The best students ~~among those who attend college~~ hope that his or her higher future income will more than compensate for income lost while pursuing higher education.
- Correct: The best students ~~among those who attend college~~ hope that *their* higher future income will more than compensate for income lost while pursuing higher education.

This is an example of a noun–pronoun agreement error. "His or her" refers to "students" which is a mismatch since the former is singular and the latter plural. The easiest fix for the sentence is to turn "his or her" into the plural "their" which brings the noun and possessive pronoun into agreement. Crossing out the phrase "among those who attend college" helps our ear pick out that "students" and "his or her" are not in agreement.

- Given: John and Bill are looking for a towel.
- Corrected: John and Bill are looking for *towels*.

This is an example of subject–object agreement error. Though the subject and object refer to different things, the plural subject in this case requires a plural direct object since presumably each of these fellows seeks his own towel. Thus, we need to make "towel" plural.

- Given: Graduates have certain responsibilities to his society.

- Corrected: Graduates have certain responsibilities to *their* society.

This is a noun–pronoun agreement in number error. The pronoun possessive must agree with its plural antecedent "graduates", thus the singular "his" has to be replaced with the plural "their."

Pronoun Agreement

This is the same error as noun–noun agreement, but we're discussing it separately so that you'll be sure to check for this error whenever you see a pronoun. Pronouns that refer to each other have to agree in gender, number and person.

Examples:

- Given: When someone has an urge, they should control it.
- Corrected: When someone has an urge, *he or she* should control it.

This is an error of pronoun agreement in number. 'Someone' is a singular pronoun and thus any subsequent pronouns that refer to it must be singular. Hence, we must change 'they' to 'he', 'she', or 'he or she' (the singular third person).

- Given: If you want to lead a good life, he has to concentrate on right thoughts.
- Corrected: If *he wants* to lead a good life, *he* has to concentrate on right thoughts.

In this case, we have two pronouns which refer to each other but are in different persons; 'you' is in the second–person and 'he' is in the third person. Pronouns which refer to each other have to be in the same person, hence we changed 'you' to 'he' to put both pronouns in the third–person.

Pronoun Case

If a pronoun is used as the subject of a sentence it needs to be in the subject or subjective case, and if it's used as the object of a sentence it needs to be in the object or objective case. You would say "I am going out", not "Me am going out", because when we speak in the singular first person as the subject of a sentence we use "I." Similarly, you'd say "give it to me" not "give it to I." In that case, "me" is the object of a prepositional phrase and we need our pronoun to be in the objective case. Pronoun case errors are commonly tested on the SAT—train your ears to pick up on them. All pronouns in a prepositional phrase must be in the objective case (since they're the objects of the preposition).

Pronoun Type	Subjective Case	Objective Case
First Person Singular	I	me
First Person Plural	we	us
Second Person Singular	you	you
Second Person Plural	you	you
Third Person Singular	he/she	him/her
Third Person Plural	they	them
Interrogative Pronoun	who/whoever	whom/whomever

Examples:

- Given: Between we and them, it doesn't make a difference.
- Simplified: Between we ~~and them~~, it doesn't make a difference.
- Corrected: Between *us* ~~and them~~, it doesn't make a difference.

Here the pronoun is the object of a preposition (forming a prepositional phrase) so the pronoun has to be in the object or objective case. For the first person plural pronoun in the objective case, we need 'us' not 'we' (we is the subject or subjective case). 'Them' is correct as 'they' is the third person plural subjective case pronoun and them is the objective case pronoun. Notice that crossing out 'and them' makes it even clearer to our ears that 'we' is wrong.

- Given: James told you and I to come at 3.
- Simplified: James told ~~you and~~ I to come at 3.
- Corrected: James told ~~you and~~ *me* to come at 3.

Simplifying this sentence helps our ears hear that "I" is not correct ("James told I" sounds wrong). Since "you and I" is the direct object of the sentence, both pronouns must be in the objective case. "You" is the same for both objective and subjective cases, but "I" needs to change to "me" which is the first person objective pronoun.

- Given: Sharon and her need to come back to visit me.
- Simplified: ~~Sharon and~~ her *need* to come back to visit me.
- Corrected: Sharon and *she* need to come back to visit me.

Isolating "her" and making it into a singular subject of the sentence helps our ears pick out that "her" is wrong (if we make the subject only "her" or "she", we have to change the verb from "need" to "needs" so that it sounds correct—you should do that so you don't get distracted when you're trying to hear if "her" is correct). "Sharon and her" is the subject of the sentence, but "her" is in the objective case. We need to change it to "she" which is in the subjective case.

- Given: To who should I address the package?
- Corrected: To *whom* should I address the package?

Who is in the subjective case and whom is in the objective case. Here, "who" is the object of the preposition "to" so we need the objective case of the pronoun or "whom."

Pronoun Ambiguity

Sometimes there will be more than one possible antecedent (the noun that the pronoun is referring to) for a pronoun—for the SAT if it's ambiguous, that's an error. There shouldn't be any ambiguity as to what noun a pronoun is referring to. These errors aren't as regularly tested as some others but do occasionally show up.

Examples:

- Given: John told Bill that he needs to understand why knowledge is important.
- Corrected: 'He' needs to be replaced with either "John" or "Bill"—whomever John is speaking of. At this point it's ambiguous.

Misplaced Modifier

Modifiers, particularly phrases which are modifiers, should be as close as possible to what they modify. We read sentences in such a way that the modifier modifies the noun closest to it, so the SAT counts it as a mistake if a modifier is closer to an alternate noun rather than the noun the modifier is intended to modify.

Examples:

- Given: After reading his final novel, Nabokov became my favorite writer.
- Corrected: Nabokov become my favorite writer after I read his final novel.

- Given: Festooned by sunlight escaping from the trees, my eyes caught sight of the road I had lost.
- Corrected: My eyes caught sight of the road, festooned by sunlight escaping from the trees, that I had lost.

Both given sentences begin with an introductory phrase that's meant to modify. In the first case, it's 'me' who's just read Nabokov's final novel, but putting 'Nabokov' immediately after the phrase 'after reading his final novel' leads one to think that it's Nabokov who's just read his own final novel. The corrected version makes it clear who's just read the novel.

In the second sentence, the 'festooned by...' phrase modifies the 'road' not 'my eyes' which makes the given sentence incorrect. We have to insert the modifying phrase 'festooned by...' right after 'road' in order to make it clear what it's modifying.

General Conjunction Errors

Be certain that the correct conjunction is being used as this error is tested in all three problem types. For instance, if a sentence begins with one idea then argues against that initial idea, you'll need a conjunction such as 'but' or 'although.' If one part of a sentence is a cause for the next part, you need the conjunction 'because.' The conjunction needs to express the logical relationship between the two parts of the sentence.

Example:

- Given: Then Jane was shopping frantically, Jack was blithely unconcerned.
- Corrected: *While* Jane was shopping frantically, Jack was blithely unconcerned.

'While' makes the sentence sensible, adding the logic that at the same time when Jane was shopping, Jack was unconcerned.

Correlative Conjunction Errors

There are occasionally errors in using a conjunction or preposition in which two words or phrases are always found together. Such conjunctions are called correlative conjunctions (conjunctions which consist of two words or phrases in different parts of the sentence which go together). Prepositions which require a certain conjunction include between (and), and both (and).

Some examples of correlative conjunctions or preposition+conjunction are:

- Either/Or
- Whether/Or

- Neither/Nor
- Between/And
- Not only/But also
- Both/And

So if you see some part of a correlative conjunction in a sentence, say 'either' or 'neither', then you should see 'or' or 'nor' later in the sentence. If the other word is not in the sentence, then there's an error.

Example:

- Given: Between apples or oranges, I wasn't sure which would be healthier to eat.
- Corrected: Between apples *and* oranges, I wasn't sure which would be healthier to eat.

'Between' requires 'and', so the first sentence which uses 'or' is not correct.

- Given: Neither black or green are my favorite colors.
- Corrected: Neither black *nor* green *is* my favorite color.

There are actually two errors there: 'Neither' requires 'nor,' and when both subjects separated by an or/nor statement are singular the verb should also be singular.

- Given: There were not only several types of desserts and also a cheese platter.
- Corrected: There were not only several types of desserts *but* also a cheese platter.

The given sentence should sound awkward as using 'not only' prompts us to expect 'but' later in the sentence. Replacing 'and' with 'but' corrects the sentence and conveys the appropriate sense.

Double Negative/Redundancy

There are occasional errors in which redundant words or double negatives are used. Double negatives are self-explanatory and pretty easily detected. Redundancy is when you have more than one word or phrase expressing the same thing.

Examples:

- There's a *high probability* that I'll *likely* skip going to my Senior Prom.
- I *feel* that *in my opinion* FDR was just another politician.
- Don't call me after *eleven pm at night*.
- She *couldn't hardly* control herself after she found out she won the election.

The first three sentences are examples of redundancy. 'High probability' and 'likely' express the same thing as do 'feel' and 'in my opinion' hence they're redundant terms and one or the other word or phrase should be deleted. In the third sentence, one knows that eleven pm is night-time so adding 'at night' is not necessary. The final sentence is a double negative since we have both 'not' and 'hardly'; we could correct it by changing 'couldn't hardly' to 'could hardly' or 'couldn't.'

Proper Comparisons

When we compare any two things, we have to compare apples and apples. We can't compare apples and oranges. Improper comparisons are common errors so *be sure to check for a proper comparison anytime things are compared in a sentence.*

Example 1:

- Given: I don't find Calvino's novels as entertaining as James Joyce.
- Corrected: I don't find Calvino's novels as entertaining as James Joyce*'s novels.*

We have to compare apples and apples. We can't compare 'novels' with 'James Joyce'—these are two totally different things (books and a person). We have to compare 'Calvino's novels' with 'James Joyce's novels.'

Example 2:

- Given: Jeeves is better than me at setting the table.
- Correct: Jeeves is better than *I* at setting the table.

This example also falls under the pronoun case errors. We've put it here because thinking about it as a comparison helps to frame proper thinking about the sentence. We should read the sentence so that the two parts are being compared and thus should have a parallel grammar so that the sentence becomes 'Jeeves is better than I *am...*' (the 'am' is implicit). Since we have to compare oranges and oranges, if it's 'Jeeves is' then it also has to be 'I [some verb],' and anytime it's a pronoun doing an action, that pronoun has to be in the subjective case hence 'I' not 'me.' The 'am' of 'I am,' by the way, is implicit—though there isn't any 'am' in the corrected sentence, it's implicitly "there."

Small Note on "than": *One more quick note, for some sentences using 'than I' or 'than me' implies a very different meaning for the sentence. 'Dean likes Thom better than me' we would interpret as meaning: 'Dean likes Thom better than Dean likes me.' 'Dean likes Thom better than I' we would interpret as meaning: 'Dean likes Thom better than I like Thom.' This isn't particularly important for the SAT test but we thought we'd mention it here so that you don't think objective pronouns should never follow 'than.'*

Comparisons: More/Most

When you compare two things, you use 'more' or an adjective ending in –er.

When you compare three or more things, then you can say one is the 'most' (something) or use an adjective ending in –est.

Examples:

- Liza is the *more* studious of the two sisters.
- James is the *most* difficult of the four brothers.
- Between the two of them, Elsa is prett*ier*.
- Frank is the bigg*est* of the four.

All four above sentences are correct. Since there are only two sisters, we say one is the 'more' studious or 'prettier' (–ier) of the two. There are four brothers, though, so we say one is the 'most' difficult or the 'biggest' (–est).

Idiomatic Errors/Wrong Preposition

If a preposition is underlined in a sentence correction problem, there's one possible error: prepositional idiom. It may be the wrong preposition for that usage or context. For instance, we say that you're studying *for* the SAT not *about* the SAT. There's not an extremely compelling reason why we use for instead of about, it's simply how we speak—that's called an idiomatic usage of a word. On the SAT test, particularly in sentence correction problems, there may be idiomatic errors with prepositions.

Example:

- Given: What's the use for more paper when I'm sick of taking notes.
- Corrected: What's the use *of* more paper when I'm sick of taking notes.

'For' should sound a little bit awkward in the first sentence; 'of' should sound correct. For this type of error, you have to trust your ear as there's no easy way to analyze the meaning of a preposition and determine whether it does or doesn't quite fit.

Incorrect Word

Occasionally a similarly spelt or similar-sounding word will be substituted for the correct word, particularly in sentence correction problems. Here are several such word pairs: be sure to keep the words straight!

- Accept/Except

Accept—to receive
Except—to leave out/left out

I *accept* your apology. *Except* for surfing the internet, I've given up all other diversions while I prepare for the SAT.

- Affect/Effect

Affect—(verb) to act on or produce a change in; (secondary) to pretend or to feign
Effect—(noun) the result

Her moving speech *affected* the election; it likely had the *effect* of securing Moss's victory.

- Aggravate/Irritate

Aggravate—to make worse
Irritate—to annoy or to make angry

The situation was *aggravated* when he pointed out that she was having a bad hair day which *irritated* her.

- Allusion/Illusion

Allusion—a reference or indirect mention of something or some past event
Illusion—a false perception of reality

His *allusion* to the propaganda of the first world war with the phrase 'baby–killing Huns' was meant to help remove the *illusion* held by the audience that Islam today represented a threat to world peace.

- All ready/Already

All ready—prepared
Already— prior to some other time; the present time (to express surprise or impatience)

Is it time *already*? A half hour later with the family still not *all ready*. People, let's go *already*.

- Altogether/All together

Altogether—wholly or entirely or utterly
All together—some group of people or things which are together

The television stopped working *altogether* when the whole family was *all together* and ready to watch the wedding video.

- Ascent/Assent

Ascent—(noun) upward movement; movement from some lower to a higher state
Assent—agreement

The trekking team was in *assent* that any further *ascent* up the mountain was too dangerous.

- Complement/Compliment

Complement—something that completes; a full quantity or amount; (verb) to make complete
Compliment—an expression or action of praise or commendation

I paid my mom the *compliment* that the delicious potatoes were the perfect *complement* to the equally tasty green bean casserole. A full *complement* of deserts was the meal's superb finish.

- Conscience/Conscious

Conscience—the sense of right and wrong
Conscious—aware

I was *conscious* of his ill intentions. My *conscience* told me to avoid him and to avoid any conflict.

- Council/Counsel

Council—a group that governs or advises
Counsel—(verb) to advise; (noun) legal advisor

His legal *counsel counseled* him to accept responsibility and admit to his indiscretion before the city *council*.

- Elicit/Illicit

Elicit—to bring out or draw out
Illicit—illegal

The mother's discovery of *illicit* materials in her daughter's purse *elicited* an excoriating speech from the mother. The daughter's subsequent suffering *elicited* sympathy from her father.

- Eminent/Imminent/Immanent

Eminent—famous, well–known, well–respected
Imminent—about to happen
Immanent—within something, existing within, inherent

As war was *imminent*, the *eminent* philosopher tried to return the nation to sanity with the remark that, "our capacities to will and to think are *immanent* powers of the mind."

- Fewer/Less

Fewer—use for some quantity that can be counted
Less—use for non–countable quantities

I have *fewer* pencils than you. She is *less* hard–working than he is.

- Incredible/Incredulous

Incredible—hard to believe, very surprising
Incredulous—suspicious, doesn't believe what someone else has said or claims

If there was a man with wings, yes that would be *incredible*, but given your big grin I'm simply *incredulous*.

- Lay/Lie

Lie—to speak or write falsely
Lay—to recline or to place

I *lied* when the judge asked me if I had committed the crime. I have *laid* on fields of soft grass for hours without thoughts passing through my mind.

- Principal/Principle

Principal—most important, first in rank; (noun) head of a school
Principle—a rule of conduct or action

The *principal principle* a *Principal* should teach students is the golden rule: do unto others as you would have them do unto you.

- Prosecute/Persecute

Prosecute—to charge and take someone to court on grounds of some crime
Persecute—to harass or to oppress

He claimed that he was *persecuted* because he was gay and went on to *prosecute* the assailants.

- Stationery/Stationary

Stationery—paper for writing
Stationary—standing or being still

I was *stationary*, not sure of what to write. Before me on the table was the *stationery* on which I would soon pen the most important letter of my life.

- Then/Than

Then—next, or at that time
Than—comparing

I was given two years to complete my thesis which was better *than* Greg who was given one year, but *then* I won a year and half fellowship to train for the Olympics and ended up with only six months in which to write my thesis.

- Their/They're/There

Their—belonging to them
There—indicating a location
They're—they are

They're over *there* with *their* books.

Sentence Fragments

There are occasionally sentence fragment errors in the test—a sentence fragment is something that's supposed to be a sentence but it's missing something and thus is not technically a sentence. When you read a sentence fragment, you'll usually feel like something is missing. Your ear will usually detect these errors; below are a few examples of sentence fragments to help train you.

Examples:

- Then I went to bed.
- Because he isn't afraid of being alone.
- At the fair, a lot of rides.
- Such as the full moon and the sky full of stars.
- Feeling the paper for dampness.
- Running around the park and then back home.
- To be a famous opera singer or to become a great baseball player.

All of the above are sentence fragments. The first two sentences could pass as "sentences" in certain fiction writing, but for the SAT and grammatically, they are sentence fragments and thus errors. To be complete sentences, the second sentence requires some other thought to complete the 'because' and the first sentence needs to tell us what came before 'then.' The next two sentences and the final sentence don't have any action or verb. The second and third to last sentences don't have a subject.

Singular Nouns

There are several nouns which may seem plural but are in fact singular. Here are the most common singular nouns to be aware of:
- Anyone
- Everyone
- Anybody
- Everybody
- Each
- Either
- Every
- Nobody
- Neither
- Collective nouns: group, corporation, committee, research, news, data, baseball team, etc.

Those are all singular nouns!!!

Examples:

- Given: Every girl who have a car should speak up.
- Corrected: Every girl who *has* a car should speak up.

- Given: Anybody who are ill are permitted to skip the event.
- Corrected: Anybody who *is* ill *is* permitted to skip the event.

- Given: Anyone who's taken a standardized test knows that they have to prepare for it.
- Corrected: *Anyone* who's taken a standardized test knows that *he or she has* to prepare for it.

- Given: Everyone going to the party need invitations.
- Simplified: Everyone ~~going to the party~~ need an invitation.
- Corrected: Everyone ~~going to the party~~ *needs an invitation.*

- Given: The team which won all the matches are very happy.
- Simplified: The team ~~which won all the matches~~ are very happy.
- Corrected: The team ~~which won all the matches~~ *is* very happy.

In the first two examples, your ear should pick up that using the plural form of the verb sounds awkward—both anyone and anybody are singular nouns and require verbs in the singular form. In the middle example, there's a noun–noun agreement problem. 'Anyone' is singular so that subsequent nouns that refer to it must also be singular. In the last two examples, crossing out modifiers also helps us to hear that there's a subject–verb agreement problem: the singular subjects need verbs in the singular form.

Adjective where an Adverb is necessary or vice versa

Sometimes, an adjective or adverb will be used when the other is needed. Remember that an adjective is used to modify nouns, and an adverb is used to modify basically anything else other than nouns (primarily verbs and adjectives). Many adverbs end in –ly.

Examples:

- Given: John did good at the swim meet.
- Corrected: John did well at the swim meet.

- Given: He gave a brilliantly and precise answer.
- Corrected 1: He gave a *brilliant* and precise answer.
- Corrected 2: He gave a *brilliantly precise* answer.

- Given: At the meet, he swam his laps quick.
- Simplified: At the meet, he swam ~~his laps~~ quick.
- Corrected: At the meet, he swam ~~his laps~~ *quickly*.

'Well' is an adverb while 'good' is an adjective. In the first example, how he 'did' is being modified, so we need an adverb (since a verb is being modified). In the second example, there are two modifiers for the noun 'answer' hence we need two adjectives. 'Brilliant and precise' corrects the sentence since they're both adjectives. We can alternatively keep 'brilliantly' but instead of making it modify 'answer,' we have to make it modify the adjective 'precise' (remember adverbs modify adjectives but not nouns). In the last example, when we cross out 'his laps', our ears immediately pick out that 'he swam quick' is incorrect. Since we're describing how we swam, we're modifying a verb and need an adverb ('quickly').

Punctuation Errors

Punctuation errors are tested regularly in the sentence and paragraph revision problems. You need to know how to separate two independent clauses for example. Punctuation errors are almost never tested in the sentence correction problems, however. So if you suspect a punctuation error in a sentence correction problem, triple–check it as they're rare.

Separating Two Independent Clauses

An independent clause is a clause with a subject and verb which could stand alone as an independent sentence. There are only two ways to separate two independent clauses in a single sentence: use a semicolon (;), or use a comma and a conjunction.

> *Semicolon Example:* This is the first independent clause; this is the second independent clause.

> *Comma and Conjunction Example:* This is the first independent clause, and this is the second independent clause.

There's also always the option of having two separate sentences.

> *Two Separate Sentences:* This is the first independent clause. This is the second independent clause.

So if two independent clauses are separated by just a comma or by a colon or by a conjunction and a semicolon, that's a punctuation error. Independent clauses have to be separated by a semicolon or by a comma and a conjunction.

Colons

A colon (:), the punctuation symbol of two dots on top of each other, is used to introduce a list or place emphasis on some point. A colon can introduce a list of elements, or introduce and put emphasis on a phrase, noun, or sentence which is a conclusion or consequence of the first part of the sentence.

Examples:

- There are three things that I do every week: practice tests, problem sets, and intense test reviews.
- I have one key goal for the next two months: improve my SAT score by 200 points.
- One personal quality will enable me to achieve my goal: dedication.

The first example has a colon introduce a list of items namely the three things to do every week. The second and third examples have the colon introduce and place a lot of emphasis on a particular word or phrase following it.

Commas

Correct Comma Usage.

Commas have many uses including:
1. Separating two independent clauses along with a conjunction (comma and conjunction),
2. Separating elements in a list of items,
3. Separating an introductory phrase or non–essential modifiers from the rest of the sentence.

Examples:

- He gave me a present for my birthday, but it was a used book that I had already read.
- Don't read, chew gum, or talk to other students during the test.
- After the sun sets, we'll run to the lake to see the moon.
- John, the guy in French class with spiked hair, said that we won.

The first sentence correctly separates two independent clauses with a comma and a conjunction. The second sentence correctly separates a list of verbs (read, chew gum, talk) with commas. The third sentence correctly separates an introductory phrase from the rest of the sentence. The fourth sentence correctly separates a non–essential modifier (in this case an appositive) from the rest of the sentence.

Incorrect Comma Usage.

Do not use a comma to:
1. Separate the subject and the verb,
2. Separate any essential part of the sentence,
3. Separate any two things in a sentence where there are only two things (e.g. two nouns, two verbs, etc.),
4. Separate an independent clause from its dependent clause when the independent clause comes first in the sentence.

Examples:

- Given: When my car broke down, a girl in a blue dress, gave me a lift to the test.
- Corrected: When my car broke down, a girl in a blue dress gave me a lift to the test.

- Given: You should meditate, to have peace of mind.
- Corrected: You should meditate to have peace of mind.

- Given: I'll be running, and swimming today.
- Corrected: I'll be running and swimming today.

- Given: I don't care where you go, if you leave now.
- Corrected: I don't care where you go if you leave now.

The first sentence incorrectly separated the subject and verb with a comma. The second sentence incorrectly separated an essential part of the sentence with a comma. The third sentence incorrectly separated two verbs with a comma. The last or fourth sentence incorrectly separated an independent clause from a dependent clause following it. Note that if the dependent clause had come first then it should have been followed by a comma (e.g. this would've been correct: if you leave now, I don't care where you go.).

Grammar Checklist: Possible Errors by Part of Speech

This is a list of possible errors for the various parts of speech. You may read a difficult sentence correction problem and it will sound correct—use this list to check every underlined word to make sure that it is in fact correct. For example, if an underlined word is a verb, then you immediately know there are three possible errors to quickly check for (tense, agreement, parallelism).

- ✓ **Noun**
  - Agreement with other nouns
  - Agreement with verb(s)
- ✓ **Verb**
  - Tense
  - Agreement with subject
  - Parallel structure
- ✓ **Preposition**
  - Idiom
- ✓ **Adjective or Adverb**
  - Correctly used (do I need an adverb here instead of an adjective?)
  - Misplaced (misplaced modifiers)
- ✓ **Conjunction**
  - Logically correct conjunction or correlative conjunction pair
- ✓ **Pronoun**
  - Case—subjective (I, you, he, we) vs. objective (me, you, him, us)
  - Agreement—should agree in gender and in number with what it's referring to
  - Ambiguity—are there multiple nouns which the pronoun could be referring to (which could be its antecedent)

- Person—are the pronouns that refer to each other in the same person i.e. all in first person, in second person, or in third person

A few other quick checks:

- ✓ **Comparison.** Is the word 'than' in the sentence? Is a comparison being made, if so is it properly made? Is it between apples and apples?

- ✓ **Modifier (Phrase).** Is there any ambiguity/is it as close as possible to what it's supposed to be modifying?

- ✓ **Parallelism for Lists of Words or Phrases.** Are all words or items in a parallel form?

Writing Section: Grammar Review Problem Set

Make sure you've mastered the grammar we've just reviewed by (1) identifying the error in each sentence and (2) correcting the error.

Answers are in Appendix 1 on page 518.

1. I was going up the hill quick.

2. James is the most hardworking of the twins.

3. Juanita is the more well–read in her class.

4. The boat collapsing in the harbor.

5. The corporation in the islands have several worthless assets on the books.

6. We are going to be at the roof.

7. He went to the store then he needed milk.

8. I had only one thought in my mind; run away.

9. I had gone to the store when I was remembering that I left the door open.

10. The principal of excepting an award is to pretend to be incredible when the award is immanent.

11. I gave the librarian the books I was returning: I took the books I had just checked out.

12. With the hammering of the final nail, the table was fixed by Lu Bingfeng.

13. Fred told James that he got the sale.

14. The postcards on the table, are going to be mailed tomorrow.

15. Between you and I, this is fantastic news but we have to be hush–hush about it.

16. If Jill and Bill in this heat is going to take a hot shower, then he's crazy.

17. Don't even think about smoking, drinking or take drugs.

18. Between the hurricane or the blizzards, there was nowhere safe to go for vacation.

19. It's not that I don't appreciate Marino's passes, it's just that I prefer Elway.

20. You haven't got hardly any time left.

WRITING SECTION: Multiple–Choice Questions Solved and Analyzed

Let's use our knowledge of grammar and our techniques to tackle some problems. As we solve these problems, pay attention to how we're using the techniques and thinking about the problems. Emulate our thought process and approach when you solve problems in practice tests.

- ✓ *Use Your Ear.*
- ✓ *Cross out Modifiers and Prepositional Phrases. Simplify the sentence.*
- ✓ *Shorter is (usually) Better.*
- ✓ *Remember our Checklist of Possible Errors.*

Sentence Revision Problems

In sentence revision problems, you have to choose which answer choice makes the sentence both grammatically correct as well as the best sentence stylistically. Answer choice (A) represents the sentence as written and should be correct approximately 20% of the time. Many times you'll eliminate answers that sound wrong even though there's no grammatical error. These problems test your sense of style as much if not more than your knowledge of grammar and punctuation.

Solved Problem 1

The easiest way to get from point a to point b on a map is not a straight line but <u>rather a curved line since the curvature of the earth</u>.

  (A) rather a curved line since the curvature of the earth.
  (B) a curved line because of the curvature of the earth.
  (C) a curved line from the curvature of the earth.
  (D) even a curved line because the earth's curvature.
  (E) the earth's curvature makes a curved line.

Let's solve this problem quickly. Try reading each of the choices and determine which one sounds the best. If an answer sounds awkward, eliminate it.

Choice (A) sounds awkward because of 'since'—since has something to do with time but the sentence doesn't have events at different times. (B) sounds pretty good and uses the correct conjunction, 'because', which expresses the proper meaning (unlike 'since' in (A) and 'from' in (C)). 'From' in (C) is awkward—even though it does express something close to a correct meaning, it sounds awkward and thus we should eliminate (C). (D) sounds awkward with 'even' and it sounds like there are words missing after '...curvature.' Eliminate (D). Finally, eliminate (E) as it sounds awkward when read with the first part of the sentence. We expect to find out that it's a 'curved line' right after 'but' since 'a straight line' is just before 'but'.

We're left with (B) which is the correct answer. Make sure that you can hear how (A), (C), (D), and (E) sound awkward and therefore are wrong. For some answers like (A) we can identify precisely what makes the choice wrong, but for others like (C) it's more idiomatic and all we can say is that it sounds awkward.

Solved Problem 2

The critics preferred 1960s European films <u>over</u> the Americans.

- (A) over
- (B) than did
- (C) to the films of
- (D) more than
- (E) over the films coming out of

What's the purpose of the underlined word 'over'? Comparison!!! 'Over' and other words of its ilk like 'than' are important words: when you encounter them, think *comparison*. When you think comparison, ask yourself am I comparing apples to apples? In the sentence as written, we aren't; we're comparing '1960s European films' to the 'Americans'. Thus, we can eliminate (A) which represents the sentence as written. We can eliminate (B) along the same lines—an improper comparison. (C) sounds all right and it's a proper comparison, films are compared to films, so let's keep it. Choice (D) gives a different meaning to the sentence that's a bit strange—that the critics preferred 1906s European films more than the Americans presumably liked them (we can either interpret the sentence that way or consider it as a wrong comparison of films and Americans). Eliminate (D). Choice (E) is wordy and also sounds awkward. Eliminate (E).

We're left with (C)—it's a proper comparison and it's the correct answer. Note that 'more than the films of' may sound better than 'to the films of', the correct answer, but it's not one of our choices and choice (D) as written gives the wrong meaning to the sentence. We have to pick the choice that corrects the sentence's error out of the choices given (but it may still not be perfect)—that choice here is (C).

Solved Problem 3

Sophocles wrote over a hundred plays of which seven survive<u>, the best do demonstrate</u> a brilliant dramatist.

- (A) , the best do demonstrate
- (B) ; the best demonstrate that he was
- (C) demonstrating
- (D) that demonstrate
- (E) and are demonstrating that he was

The first thing we notice in (A) and (B) are the punctuation: (A) begins with a comma and (B) with a semicolon. (A) doesn't sound quite right. The problem is that two independent clauses are separated by a comma which is wrong; two independent clauses can only be separated by a comma and a conjunction or by a semicolon. (B) is correct as the two independent clauses are separated by a semicolon. (B) sounds fine as well—let's keep it.

(C) has an advantage that it's quite short, a single word, but unfortunately it's ambiguous what "demonstrating" refers to—whether that the seven demonstrate that Sophocles was a brilliant dramatist or that writing over a hundred plays demonstrates that. Due to this ambiguity, we can eliminate (C). (D) sounds a bit awkward and also suffers from the same ambiguity problem as (C): we're not sure if it's the over a hundred plays written or the seven surviving 'that demonstrate.' Both (C) and (D) also have the problem that we end up having 'plays demonstrate a brilliant dramatist' which is not accurate—the plays demonstrate that the author was a brilliant dramatist. We can't equate plays with dramatist directly (it's like comparing apples and oranges).

(E) could've worked but it has a grammatical error commonly tested on the SAT: verb parallelism. When the same subject has multiple verbs in a list, all the verbs must be in the same tense. In this problem, we have 'survive' but then in (E) we get 'are demonstrating—two different verb tenses which violates parallelism. Thus we can eliminate it. (E) also sounds quite awkward. We're left with (B); it's precise in that it claims that 'he' or Sophocles is a brilliant dramatist, and it sounds good. Let's pick it...and it's correct.

Solved Problem 4

When someone picks up a guitar and plays a song, <u>you follow</u> a popular music tradition begun by traveling Renaissance musicians.

(A) you follow
(B) they are following
(C) you are following
(D) he or she is following
(E) it will follow

Let's analyze (A). The first word 'you' is a pronoun. From our checklist, we know we could have an agreement, an ambiguity, a case, or a person error. 'You' refers to 'someone'; there's no other person in the sentence so there's nothing else it could refer to so there's no ambiguity error. Both are also singular and without gender so there's no agreement error. Are the pronouns in the same person? No, 'you' is in the second person while 'someone' or any pronoun with 'one' is in the third person. Thus, we have a pronoun error. We can eliminate (A) and (C) which both use 'you.' We further know that the pronoun must refer to a person so 'it' is out; eliminate (E). Since someone is singular, (B) is eliminated as 'they' is plural.

We're left with (D), let's make sure it's correct. 'Someone' is singular, without gender and in the third person, while 'he or she' is singular, of both genders, and in the third person. 'One' can later link to either 'he', 'she' or 'he or she', so there's no gender error in (D). Read the sentence with 'he or she is following' plugged in to make sure you hear that (D) is correct.

If the person, case, gender, etc. analysis is confusing, don't worry—the key thing is to hear that 'someone' and 'you' don't go together but that 'someone' and 'he and she' do...use your ear!

Solved Problem 5

First discovered drunk in a gutter reciting verse, <u>the article analyzes the growing reputation of the now–esteemed poet.</u>

  (A) the article analyzes the growing reputation of the now–esteemed poet.
  (B) the now–esteemed poet and his growing reputation are the subjects of the article.
  (C) the subject of the article is the growing reputation of the now–esteemed poet.
  (D) the now–esteemed poet is greatly discussed including his growing reputation in the article.
  (E) the now–esteemed poet whose reputation is growing is discussed much in the article.

There's one critical point of grammar tested in this question: misplaced modifiers! The introductory phrase 'first discovered...reciting verse' clearly has to modify a person.

Using the principle that what's modified should come as close to the modifier as possible, the main clause of the sentence should begin with the person being modified. This eliminates (A)—the modifier 'first discovered...' can not modify 'the article.' This eliminates (C) as well—it's not modifying 'the subject...'.

We're left with (B), (D) and (E). All three begin with 'the now-esteemed poet' which can't be used to eliminate any of them (since all three have it!) and which is a person and thus coheres with the introductory modifier.

We should be leaning slightly towards (B) since it's shorter than (D) and (E), but we need to read and review the three choices. Both (D) and (E) sound awkward. In (D), 'is greatly discussed including' is awkward, and in (E) 'is discussed much' makes the sentence awkward. (B) is simple and clear...and the correct answer.

Solved Problem 6

When you cry while watching a film, you interpret the various events that you see as though it were happening to you through mirror neurons.

- (A) that you see as though it were happening to you
- (B) you see and interpret them happening to you
- (C) that you're seeing then feel they were happening to you
- (D) you see as though they were happening to you
- (E) you see and they are happening to you

Let's simplify the sentence before we evaluate the choices:

~~When you cry while watching a film~~, you interpret ~~the various~~ events that you see as though it were happening to you through mirror neurons.

Simplifying the sentence helps us to hear the correctness or incorrectness of the answer choices more clearly and saves us from having to read the full sentence multiple times.

Choice (A) should sound wrong to you—'it' is incorrect as its antecedent is the plural 'events.' (B) sounds awkward since 'interpret' gets repeated in it (interpret is used earlier in the sentence). The 'then' in choice (C) gives an incorrect meaning to the sentence (we don't interpret the events then feel the events happening to us rather feeling that the events are happening to us is how we interpret them according to the sentence); eliminate (C).

(D) sounds decent enough on a first read—let's keep it. It also expressed the correct meaning—we interpret the events as though they were happening to us (but they're not hence the 'though'). Choice (E) sounds awkward and also has a punctuation error: two independent clauses are separated by a comma (we need a comma and a conjunction or a semicolon to separate independent clauses). (E) is eliminated. We're left with (D), and it's correct.

Sentence Correction Problems

For sentence correction problems, you have to identify where the error is in the sentence if there is an error (if there isn't an error, choose (E) No error which will be correct approximately 20% of the time). If there is an error in the sentence, you have to pick which underlined word or set of words makes that sentence incorrect and which could be changed to make the sentence correct. In these problems, *errors will be identifiable grammatical errors.* In other words, something that's wrong won't be wrong just because it sounds awkward but it will sound awkward because it represents a grammatical error.

Solved Problem 1

Several admirals, including the Chief <u>himself</u>, <u>has ordered</u> various
                                         A   B
ships <u>to flank</u> the tiny island <u>in the Pacific</u>. <u>No error</u>.
        C   D   E

(A) sounds correct so let's eliminate it. There is actually an error there in that 'including the Chief himself' is part of the subject and it's separated by a comma from the verb 'has ordered.' Neither of the commas is underlined, though, so we can't do anything about that error (you have to ignore it!). (B) is a verb that's underlined—from our checklist, we have to check for 1. subject–verb agreement, 2. verb tense, and 3. parallelism. Let's simplify the sentence to check first for subject–verb agreement (if that's okay, we'll then check for verb tense errors). Admirals is plural thus it's a plural subject. Let's cross out 'including the Chief himself' to simplify the sentence—this is crucial particularly for checking subject–verb agreement.

Several admirals, ~~including the Chief himself~~, <u>has ordered</u> various
                                         A   B
ships <u>to flank</u> the tiny island <u>in the Pacific</u>. <u>No error</u>.
        C   D   E

Hopefully, the subject–verb agreement error pops out when you read the corrected sentence to yourself—'Several admirals has ordered' should sound quite wrong! 'Has ordered' is singular and thus needs to be changed to 'have ordered.' The error is in (B) which can be changed to 'have ordered' which would correct the sentence.

Remember to always cross out extraneous phrases, phrases which you know are correct and don't affect the meaning of the sentence, to help your ear pick out errors!

Solved Problem 2

The Professor of the short course on music appreciation <u>taught</u> basic
                                                                             A

chord progressions, conducted performances <u>of simple pieces</u>, and
                                                                                          B

<u>students had</u> a chance <u>to compose</u> pieces themselves. <u>No Error.</u>
    C   D   E

Let's assume on a first pass this reads fine to you. It's a pretty long sentence—we can almost certainly cross out multiple extraneous modifiers and phrases. Let's do that before analyzing the answer choices.

The Professor ~~of the short course on music appreciation~~ taught ~~basic~~
                                                                                A

chord progressions, conducted performances <u>of ~~simple~~ pieces</u>, and
                                                                                      B

<u>students had</u> a chance <u>to compose</u> ~~pieces themselves~~. <u>No Error.</u>
    C   D   E

We were able to cross out a lot—not just prepositional phrases but some adjectives as well ('basic' and 'simple'). It should make analyzing the sentence easier—particularly choice (A)! Analyzing choice A, 'taught' is a verb and thus has three checks we have to go through: subject–verb agreement, tense, and parallelism. After crossing out the prepositional phrases, we can hear that the verb agrees with the subject. 'the professor taught' sounds correct. All the verbs are in the past tense so that's correct. With parallelism, we have a problem though. The sentence reads '...taught, conducted, and students had...' which isn't parallel. Since we can't change both taught and conducted, we have to pick answer choice (C). We have to change 'students had' to a verb with the original 'the Professor' as the subject. We can change 'students had' to 'gave students' which corrects the sentence (...taught chord progressions, conducted performances, and gave students... is parallel). The answer thus is (C).

Solved Problem 3

Aspirations of the nouveau riche <u>demonstrates that</u> wealth
                                          A
<u>creates lavish desires</u> of a nature quite different from what one <u>ever</u>
         B   C
imagined when living <u>in poverty</u>. <u>No error.</u>
                          D   E

Let's first try to simplify the sentence by crossing out prepositional phrases and modifiers which aren't essential. We'll need to analyze (D) first as it is a prepositional phrase. The only error with a prepositional phrase is one of idiom—it could be the wrong preposition. In this case, we do say 'in poverty' so it is correct...we can eliminate (D) and cross out 'when living in poverty' (we'll cross out that whole phrase which is extraneous). We can also cross out 'lavish' as it's the correct word and it otherwise doesn't affect the sentence.

Aspirations ~~of the nouveau riche~~ <u>demonstrates that</u> wealth
                                              A

<u>creates</u> ~~lavish~~ desires of a nature quite different from what one <u>ever</u>
   B   C

imagined ~~when living in poverty~~. <u>No error.</u>
                   D   E

We crossed out two prepositional phrases, a dependent clause which included a prepositional phrase and an adjective. At this point the error in the sentence should pop out to your ear: (A) 'demonstrates..' is singular while the subject 'Aspirations' is plural. The answer is (A) and we can correct the sentence by changing 'demonstrates that' to 'demonstrate that.'

Subject–verb errors are common, and crossing out unnecessary modifiers and phrases particularly prepositional phrases help our ears pick those errors out.

Solved Problem 4

<u>While typing</u> on the computer I <u>heard</u> screams, unexpected in respect
      A   B

<u>with</u> my isolation <u>in the woods</u>. <u>No Error</u>.
   C   D   E

Let's assume that on a first read, the sentence reads okay, and we have to analyze each possible error or answer choice. First, can we eliminate any extraneous modifiers or phrases?   Yes, one prepositional phrase.

<u>While typing</u> ~~on the computer~~ I <u>heard</u> screams, unexpected in respect
     A   B
<u>with</u> my isolation <u>in the woods</u>. <u>No Error</u>.
 C   D   E

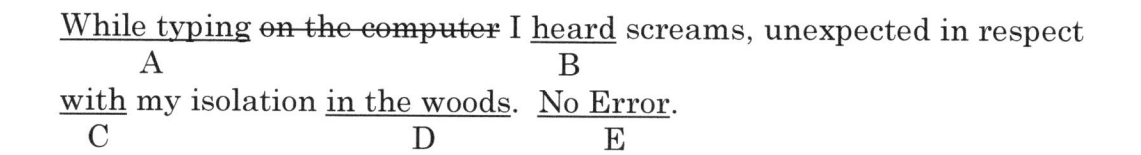

Let's now analyze the choices. Is there anything wrong with 'while typing'? Sounds fine and it agrees with the other verb—while typing I heard makes logical sense. How about 'heard'—go through the checklist (subject–verb agreement, tense, parallelism)—no problems. What about 'with'—as a preposition, there's one possible error; it could be the wrong preposition e.g. an error of idiom. It in fact is. 'With' sounds funny because we generally say 'in respect to'. The answer thus is C, and to correct the sentence, we need to change 'with' to 'to'.

Solved Problem 5

<u>From my perspective</u>, the green satin dress and the black velvet dress
       A
<u>are</u> both pretty, <u>but</u> the green one is <u>the most</u> elegant. <u>No Error</u>.
 B   C   D   E

Let's assume on a first pass the sentence reads fine, so we have to analyze each choice. (A) is a prepositional phrase—so the preposition could be idiomatically wrong. In this case, though, 'from' is the correct preposition and 'from my perspective' makes sense in the context of the sentence. Eliminate (A). Choice (B) is a verb—let's first check subject–verb agreement. 'Are' is plural and so is the subject—so they're in agreement. 'Are' and the later verb are both in the present tense—so no tense problem. There are no other verbs so there can't be any parallelism error. Eliminate (B). For choice (C), does the second part of the sentence say something that's different from the first part? Yes, it states a difference between the two dresses while the first part of the sentence states a similarity of the two. Thus, 'but' is the correct conjunction and we can eliminate (C). For answer choice (D), we have a comparison being made since 'most' is there. Is the comparison between two or more than two persons or things? It's between two things, so then we need…more! For comparisons of two persons or things, we have to use 'more.' So (D) is the correct answer and should be changed to 'the more' to correct the sentence. We use most only in comparisons of three or more persons or things.

Paragraph Revision Problems

In paragraph revision problems, you're asked to revise sentences and paragraphs. You should edit the sentences and paragraphs for grammar mistakes and awkwardness in style in order to realize well–written sentences and paragraphs that flow. There will always be a few paragraphs with each sentence numbered followed by multiple questions.

Solved Problem 1

Passage

(1) Famous for his invention of a printing press that rarely broke down and worked better than existing presses. **(2)** This invention greatly pleased the wealthy. **(3)** The constant requests for his machine kept him very busy—his heart, though, desired a new adventure. **(4)** After much deliberation, he finally spun a globe deciding to go wherever his finger landed. **(5)** It landed on the Ivory Coast, a country in West Africa. **(6)** In a village in Africa, he was inspired by the erratic winds to build a windmill. **(7)** It was able to be moved so as to always face the wind.

Which of the following is the best version of the underlined portion of sentences 6 and 7 below?

In a village in Africa, he was inspired by the erratic winds to build <u>a windmill. It was able to be moved so as to always</u> face the wind.

- (A) a windmill that could always
- (B) a windmill that could thus be moved to always
- (C) a windmill, and it would
- (D) a windmill. It could always be moved so as to
- (E) a windmill that could be moved so as to always

Let's first simplify the sentences:

> ~~In a village in Africa~~, he was inspired by the erratic winds to build <u>a windmill. It was able to be moved so as to always</u> face the wind.

Upon reading the simplified sentences, you should feel that there's a logical connection between the windmill and the feature of being able to be moved to face the wind—specifically that the inventor designed the windmill *to move to face the wind* (because of the erratic winds—that phrase is important to the meaning of the sentence, which is why we didn't cross it out). Using that insight, we can eliminate choices which separate the clauses which don't express that logic—particularly (C) and (D). Those choices, (C) and (D), state the facts of the inventor building the windmill and the windmill being moveable as unrelated, separate facts. Eliminate (C) and (D).

We're now left with (A), (B), and (E) which all express the idea that the windmill was designed expressly to be moveable. Which one is best? On a first pass, (A) is short and works. Let's keep it. 'Thus' in (B) sounds awkward—there is no first point from which another point is being made so 'thus' is not needed and makes (B) incorrect. Eliminate (B). Choice (E) sounds a little wordy with 'so as to' but not awkward nor wordy enough to eliminate it.

We're left with (A) and (E). Which to choose? Choice (E) tells us that the windmill can be moved to the face the wind—(A) lets us know that the windmill can always face the wind but we don't know how. Choice (A) thus leaves out a key aspect of the invention: it was designed to be moved to be able to always face the wind. Choice (E) is the better choice, then, and it's correct.

Solved Problem 2

Passage

(1) Famous for his invention of a printing press that rarely broke down and worked better than existing presses. **(2)** This invention greatly pleased the wealthy. **(3)** The constant requests for his machine kept him very busy—his heart, though, desired a new adventure. **(4)** After much deliberation, he finally spun a globe deciding to go wherever his finger landed. **(5)** It landed on the Ivory Coast, a country in West Africa. **(6)** In a village in Africa, he was inspired by the erratic winds to build a windmill. **(7)** It was able to be moved so as to always face the wind.

In context, which is the best way to deal with sentence 1?

Famous for his invention of a printing press that rarely broke down and worked better than existing presses.

- (A) Change "that" to "which".
- (B) Change "of" to "he invented".
- (C) Insert "At first becoming" at the beginning of the sentence.
- (D) Insert "He became" at the beginning of the sentence.
- (E) Change "worked" to "works".

It's critical to notice that the sentence as written is a sentence fragment. We have to correct that.

Choice (A) doesn't save the sentence from being a fragment—eliminate it. It's also a quite minor change that wouldn't likely improve any sentence very much. Choice (B) saves the sentence from being a fragment—'he invented' becomes the subject and verb of the sentence. It, however, uses 'invented' almost directly after the word 'invention' which sounds awkward. Lightly cross out (B) for now. Choice (C) doesn't save the sentence from being a fragment—it actually turns the sentence a long introductory modifying phrase which is not a good thing. Eliminate (C). Choice (D) gives us a subject and verb: 'he became.' It saves the sentence from being a fragment, and it reads well—put a check next to (D). Choice (E) doesn't save the sentence from being a fragment and it introduces an error of parallelism. 'Worked' is actually correct as it's in the same tense as the verb in parallel with it, 'broke down'. Eliminate (E). We have to pick (D), and it's correct.

Solved Problem 3

Passage

(1) Famous for his invention of a printing press that rarely broke down and worked better than existing presses. **(2)** This invention greatly pleased the wealthy. **(3)** The constant requests for his machine kept him very busy—his heart, though, desired a new adventure. **(4)** After much deliberation, he finally spun a globe deciding to go wherever his finger landed. **(5)** It landed on the Ivory Coast, a country in West Africa. **(6)** In a village in Africa, he was inspired by the erratic winds to build a windmill. **(7)** It was able to be moved so as to always face the wind.

Which of the following is the best version of the underlined portion of sentence 4?

After much deliberation, he finally spun a globe <u>deciding to go wherever his finger landed.</u>

(A) then decided to go wherever his finger would land.
(B) having decided to go wherever his finger would land.
(C) and decided to go wherever his finger would land.
(D) deciding to go to where his finger landed.
(E) and decided to go to the place where his finger would land.

Let's try to eliminate choices that sound particularly awkward or wordy. Choice (E) qualifies as wordy—'to the place'—is redundant

414

(when you go somewhere you're by definition going to some place). Let's eliminate it.

To analyze the remaining choices, we need to realize the logic of the sentence. Does he spin the globe then decide to go where his finger lands? Or has he already decided to go where his finger lands when he spins the globe? The most logical assumption is the latter—he doesn't spin a globe then in an instant decide to go where his finger lands, but rather he spins it with the intention of stopping the globe with his finger and going to where his finger lands. The introduction 'after much deliberation' and 'finally' clue us in that that's the order of events—only after thinking a long time did he spin the globe and presumably he had spent the time thinking about whether or not to travel somewhere. Only choice (B) preserves this logic—that he had decided to go to where his finger would land before he spun the globe. Choices (A) and (C) express the logic that he spun the globe and then decided to go somewhere (namely where the globe landed). Choice (D) also expresses the idea that he spun the globe and then in that instant decided to go where his finger would land. Choice (B) is thus the correct answer.

Solved Problem 4

Passage

(1) Famous for his invention of a printing press that rarely broke down and worked better than existing presses. (2) This invention greatly pleased the wealthy. (3) The constant requests for his machine kept him very busy—his heart, though, desired a new adventure. (4) After much deliberation, he finally spun a globe deciding to go wherever his finger landed. (5) It landed on the Ivory Coast, a country in West Africa. (6) In a village in Africa, he was inspired by the erratic winds to build a windmill. (7) It was able to be moved so as to always face the wind.

Which sentence is the best to add after sentence 7 (to the end of the passage)?

(A) He loved traveling and created inventions that served people around the world.
(B) His next invention was in the field of telecommunications.
(C) This invention for the poor complemented his printing press for the rich.
(D) He was, thus, a humble person who served the public good.
(E) It was a satisfying achievement for an inventor already rich from his new printing press.

One of these sentences should conclude the passage, so we know that the sentence should summarize the passage a bit and have some concluding aspect to it.

We can thus eliminate any sentences that mention a new idea or that mention a detail. Let's eliminate (B) which mentions a new, not terribly important fact which has no connection to the preceding sentences. Let's also eliminate (D) which describes his character which no other sentences in the passage do (thus the 'thus' isn't correct since it doesn't connect to the previous sentences and also isn't supported by the previous sentences).

Out of (A), (C), and (E), which is the better conclusion? Choice (A) includes the claim that the inventor 'loved traveling' which isn't supported by the passage—he was seeking an adventure, but that doesn't necessarily mean he loves traveling. It's an inference without support in the passage—let's lightly cross out (A). Choice (C) is a bit awkward in its use of 'complemented' in that the two inventions don't really work together directly—let's also lightly cross it out. We're left with (E) and it reads well (even thought it's long). It expresses the key point that when the inventor left for Africa, it was not with the intention to make money—and having worked to make another successful invention in a very different context from his first success would indeed be 'satisfying.' The answer, thus, is (E).

Writing Section Multiple Choice Question Problem Sets

Apply the methods and techniques you've just learned from the previous Writing Section chapters to solve these problems. Be sure to write in this book, crossing out words, et cetera—as using your pencil, working on paper, and making precise pencil marks are critical to solving these problems quickly and reliably.

Sentence Correction Problem Set

Answers in Appendix 1 on page 522.

1. <u>Watching films</u>, eating good food, <u>listening</u> to great songs, and <u>make</u>
       A   B   C
   jokes were the four precepts of his guide <u>to</u> good living. <u>No Error</u>
                                                 D   E

2. To master the dance step, I have <u>practiced</u> <u>on</u> an approach
                                            A   B
   <u>to keeping</u> my hand steady while my head <u>moves</u>. <u>No error</u>
      C   D   E

3. Sloths <u>had to have</u> <u>had</u> multiple adaptations over millions of years
           A   B
   because <u>it survives</u> primarily on leaves which are a poor source
                C
   <u>of energy and nutrition</u>. <u>No error</u>
         D   E

4. I <u>had told</u> you both not <u>to go outside</u>, but <u>between you and she</u>, the
   　　A　　　　　　　　　B　　　　　　　　C
   orders <u>weren't followed</u>. <u>No error</u>
   　　　　　　D　　　　　　　　E

5. If we <u>could</u> flap our arms and fly <u>at</u> the speed of falcons, the average
   　　　　A　　　　　　　　　　　　　B
   person <u>won't</u> need to use a car <u>very often</u>. <u>No error</u>
   　　　　　C　　　　　　　　　　　　　D　　　　　　E

6. <u>Between</u> <u>you and me</u>, I have always <u>found</u> Salesman the <u>more</u>
   　　A　　　　　B　　　　　　　　　　　　C　　　　　　　　　　D
   compelling film of the two. <u>No error</u>
   　　　　　　　　　　　　　　　　　E

7. The island <u>manufactures</u> large blocks of feta cheese which <u>is</u> usually
   　　　　　　　A　　　　　　　　　　　　　　　　　　　　　　　　　B
   <u>exported to</u> Greece <u>for consumption there</u>. <u>No error</u>
   　　C　　　　　　　　　　　　D　　　　　　　　　　　E

8. In contrast <u>to Kafka</u>, Mann's prose <u>is</u> <u>neither</u> sparse <u>nor</u> short.
   　　　　　　　A　　　　　　　　　　　　　B　　C　　　　　　　D
   <u>No error</u>
   　E

9. When Charley, late at night <u>searching</u> for detritus to make art,
                                  A
   <u>removes</u> posters from walls, onlookers would <u>inquire</u> as to his
      B   C
   authority to <u>take them</u>. <u>No error</u>
                     D   E

10. The recognition <u>awarded to</u> popular music groups <u>have boosted</u> the
                         A   B
    <u>interest</u> of people of all ages <u>in music</u>. <u>No error</u>
        C   D   E

11. <u>After</u> seventeen years <u>of writing</u>, Joyce <u>released</u> his novel
        A   B   C
    Finnegans Wake to an <u>utterly</u> baffled public. <u>No error</u>
                             D   E

12. <u>When</u> you <u>don't</u> report a crime, it is <u>as though</u> no crime <u>never</u>
        A   B   C   D
    happened. <u>No error</u>
                   E

Sentence Revision Problem Set

Answers in Appendix 1 on page 526.

1. Over 50% of all unique plant species are found in the Amazon; <u>only 4% in Madagascar</u>.

    (A) ; only 4% in Madagascar
    (B) in comparison to 4% in Madagascar
    (C) , and compared to Madagascar with only 4%
    (D) , while Madagascar has only 4%
    (E) ; but only 4% are found in Madagascar

2. It is the knights' sacred duty during the arduous and long journey to feed the princess, to protect her, <u>and entertaining her.</u>

    (A) and entertaining her.
    (B) and to entertain her.
    (C) and entertained her.
    (D) and have her entertained.
    (E) and to have her entertained.

3. The Cardinal insisted that Alexander VI should be deposed on the ground that he had paid for the papacy<u>, whereas</u> spiritual office obtained in that way was ipso facto void.

    (A) whereas
    (B) even if
    (C) for
    (D) any
    (E) and any

4. The former police officer spent fourteen years working from a small office in the basement of his home searching tirelessly and thoroughly for his eldest daughter whom he believed kidnapped.

   (A) kidnapped
   (B) has been kidnapped
   (C) had been kidnapped
   (D) was being kidnapped
   (E) as kidnapped

5. Kids were allowed to wait in line, they were not allowed to ride the adult rides.

   (A) Kids were allowed
   (B) Though kids were allowed
   (C) They allow kids
   (D) Allowing kids
   (E) For allowing kids

6. The enumeration of such procedures is out of place in the encyclopedia and belongs rather to a medical treatise.

   (A) and belongs rather to
   (B) and rather for
   (C) rather than
   (D) and instead belongs in
   (E) instead belonging to

7. Their actions have motives far more complex _if_ we are inclined to suppose.

    (A) if
    (B) because
    (C) for
    (D) around which
    (E) than

8. Afraid of being mobbed by her admirers, <u>a disguise was worn by the famous chanteuse</u> to attend the rock concert.

    (A) a disguise was worn by the famous chanteuse
    (B) in disguise the famous chanteuse was
    (C) wearing a disguise was the famous chanteuse
    (D) the famous chanteuse wore a disguise
    (E) the famous chanteuse disguised

9. On a cool Sunday morning, we discovered that there were daisies to be found <u>with</u> the meadow.

    (A) with
    (B) into
    (C) for
    (D) throughout
    (E) from

10. The two books belonged to both Janet and Rene, but they were not found.

    (A) they were not
    (B) they had been
    (C) they are being
    (D) Janet and Rene were not to be
    (E) Janet and Rene are

Paragraph Revision Problems

Answers in Appendix 1 on page 531.

(1) Susan B. Anthony, the famous women's rights activist, was a precocious child. (2) As a child learned to read and write at age three. (3) In 1826, when she was six years old, the Anthony family moved from Massachusetts to Battenville, New York. (4) Susan was sent to attend a local district school, where a teacher refused to teach her long division because of her gender. (5) Under her father's tutelage, though, she would learn long division and much more. (6) Upon learning of the weak education she was receiving at the local school, her father promptly removed her. (7) He moved her to a group home school where he taught Susan himself.

(8) Susan's first job was as a teacher at Eunice Kenyon's Friends' Seminary in New Rochelle, and then at the Canajoharie Academy in 1846, where she rose to become headmistress of the Female Department. (9) Her family at one point was in financial ruin. (10) At the Seminary, she earned as did all other woman roughly one fourth what men earned for the same work. (11) The disparity in wages inspired her first brush with women's rights: advocating wage equivalence for women and men performing the same duties at the Seminary.

1. What must be done to sentence 2?

    (A) begin it with the words "It was"
    (B) replace "As a child" with "who" and combine with sentence 1
    (C) add "even before" to the end of the sentence and combine it with sentence 3
    (D) change "learned" to "taught herself"
    (E) add a comma to the end of the phrase "As a child"

2. Which sentence should be deleted?

   (A) 1
   (B) 6
   (C) 8
   (D) 9
   (E) 11

3. The primary purpose of the second paragraph in the passage on Susan B. Anthony is to

   (A) provide background information about her
   (B) present a theory about her childhood
   (C) tell a story relevant to how she became an activist
   (D) describe her character in detail
   (E) explain her later career

4. What should be done with sentence 5?

   (A) delete "and much more"
   (B) delete ", though,"
   (C) combine it with sentence 4 by deleting ", though," and changing "gender. Under her" to "gender, but under her"
   (D) place it after sentence 3
   (E) place it after sentence 7

Writing Recapitulation

- ✓ Use your ear—train your ear through reading sentences out loud during practice tests. Your ear will pick out grammatical and stylistic errors (awkward writing).

- ✓ Cross out prepositional phrases and other unnecessary modifiers...this helps you analyze the essential aspects of the sentence.

- ✓ Know SAT grammar (the grammar tested on the SAT) and the parts of speech. Know the grammar checklists for each part of speech—use the checklists when analyzing sentence correction problems. Be able to break down sentences into their respective parts of speech.

- ✓ 20% of sentence revision problems are correct as initially written, choice (A), and 20% of sentence correction problems have (E) No error. If you have far fewer or more than 20% of the answer choices as (A) or (E), check over your work.

- ✓ Eliminate based on differences—if multiple answer choices have the same words or phrase in them, look at what's different and use differences between the answers to eliminate choices.

- ✓ Don't spend an inordinate amount of time reading the paragraphs of paragraph revision problems...get through the passage quickly and get to the questions.

- ✓ Shorter writing is often more effective writing.

- ✓ Practice, practice, practice—doing many problems and reviewing them carefully will help train and tune your ear to pick out SAT grammar! These problems are the most content-based on the SAT test so practice really will make perfect for these problems.

WRITING SECTION: Essay

The essay does not affect your numerical writing section score greatly, so working on the essay is of less concern to us than working on the multiple choice questions. Moreover, we've found it's much easier to realize substantial improvements on the multiple choice questions than on the essay. You should set a minimum goal of getting an aggregate 8 or greater score on your essay (out of 12 possible points; your essay will be scored by two readers who will rate it between 1 and 6). If you're self-preparing for the SAT, ask an English teacher or an experienced writer you know to rate your essay(s) after showing them rated essays from *the Official SAT Study Guide* (there are several actual SAT essays with ratings to give you an idea of what's expected from your essay in *the Official SAT Study Guide*).

Here are our guidelines and tips on how to prepare for the essay, how to write, and what to write.

Your Four Musts

1. **Your essay MUST be well over a page in length.** You should fill up *at least* a page and a quarter of space with your essay—ideally a page and a half to three quarters of space. If you're having trouble writing that long of an essay in 25 minutes, *use larger handwriting*. There's a strong correlation between the length of your essay (that is, how much space on two pages you use up) and your score. Try not to write a full two page essay unless you have important points to make or your handwriting is naturally large, as having time to revise your essay is crucial. Your essay should also have a minimum of four paragraphs with each paragraph having at least three sentences except for the introduction and conclusion which can be shorter. If you find yourself writing two or three paragraph essays and paragraphs with two to three sentences, work with one of your

teachers on developing your ideas more fully into a longer essay. Again, your essay should be roughly a page and a half in length—if your essays are consistently less than that, *use larger handwriting so that your essays are consistently a page and a half in length*!

2. **Your essay MUST answer the question!!!** If not, you risk getting a score of 0, a risk you absolutely can not afford to take. If you're not sure that your idea is on–topic, come up with another idea.

3. **You MUST write a well–organized essay (ideally 4 or 5 paragraphs).** Most successful essays will be of the standard 4 or 5 paragraph variety: an introduction with a thesis statement at the end, 2 or 3 main body paragraphs each of which develops a single point, and a short and sweet conclusion. Your paragraphs should express well a single point and the ideas should fit together to make a single argument, support a thesis, or describe an event or feeling.

4. **You MUST make an outline before you start writing.** Your outline doesn't have to be detailed, it could be just your thesis and three points you're going to make in each of the three body paragraphs, but you need to have planned out what points you're going to make and what you intend to write. Try to spend *at least* 3 minutes preparing an outline (no more than 5 or 6 minutes), then approximately 15 minutes writing the essay and 5 minutes revising. Don't read the prompt and immediately start writing—make an outline!!

Introductions and Conclusions

1. **Can't Come Up With an Introduction: Use the Background Information or Quote in the Box.** If you're having trouble thinking of an introduction or even if you're just short on time, use the background information in the box (which is above the prompt or assignment itself) as introduction material. Rewrite the ideas from the box in your own words and discuss them slightly to lead up to your thesis.

2. **First Two Paragraph Perfection.** The readers will likely spend all of 3 minutes reading your essay so first impressions are crucial. Be sure there are no glaring mistakes particularly in the first two paragraphs and try to have a strong first two paragraphs.

3. **Primacy/Recency.** Many argue in rhetoric that the first and last things you say or write are what the reader will remember. Bearing this in mind reinforces the idea of making sure your introduction and conclusion have no glaring errors and are well written.

4. **Short and Sweet Conclusion.** You don't have a lot of time, so if you've made your point and you don't have an idea for a conclusion, don't be afraid to write a short and sweet conclusion. It should be at least 2 sentences and at least 1 sentence should be well–written and catchy so that the reader once again leaves with the point you're trying to make. You can extend or question the ideas slightly but don't bring up any new points in the conclusion.

Essay Content

1. **Avoid Controversy.** Avoid discussion of controversial topics like abortion, current politics or world events, sex education, et cetera.

2. **A Stockpile of Generic Literary and Historical Examples.** Try to have/prepare a list of literary and historical examples you know well which you can use to support a thesis. Most topics are quite open–ended and examples from literature and history can easily fit into them. Try to know a few novels and historical events really well and have them ready for incorporation into your essays. For example, if you know the events of the Civil War or the novel Wuthering Heights, be capable of writing some sort of Civil War based or Wuthering Heights related essay on any topic.

3. **High Scoring Essays are Often Personal Essays.** Personal essays when germane to the topic and examples from your personal life are great to use. Multiple SAT essay graders have told us the best essays they've read were personal essays on topics such as playing the saxophone, skateboarding, and working in a health clinic. Don't be afraid, on the contrary welcome the chance, to write a personal essay. Since you know your personal life much better than any novel or historical event, that you can write a better essay on something from your own life isn't surprising—knowing an event really well and being able to describe it precisely (whether it's a personal event or a historical one) makes for great writing. So if some part of your life is relevant to an essay, by all means write about it.

Writing Tips

1. **Use One "Impressive" Word.** If possible try to use one or two more difficult words if and only if you're sure that you're using the words correctly. Do not try to use too many impressive words as it will come off as precisely that—that you're trying to show off. Just one word which is used precisely will have a great effect (that you have a good vocabulary and that you can express yourself with words effectively).

2. **The PRO (Precision, Revision, Organization) Hallmarks of Writing.** Revision (for the SAT essay, try to use the last 5 minutes of your time to revise your essay), Precision (careful word/phrase choice), and Organization (a clear, logical organization of the essay in which facts/ideas/discussions support a main thesis or topic). For a full explanation of the PRO method for essay writing see Appendix 3 which is a full exposition on our approach to essay writing, the PRO+CUPED method.

3. **CUPED Method for Logical Reasoning/Argument Formation.** CUPED stands for Conclusions, Unstated premises, Premises, Evidence, Definitions. It's a method for forming the logical argument or logical framework of an essay. A full explanation of CUPED is in Appendix 3 of this book.

4. **Practice writing precise, detail–type sentences.** If you decide to study the PRO+CUPED method we've developed, or just want to improve your essay writing in general, do practice writing precise sentences. It's difficult to express a thought simply and in a detailed, precise way in a single sentence. It takes practice. For example, consider "King Lear was fooled by the fulsome speeches of Goneril and Regan." That sentence isn't too bad, but it could be more precise: how exactly was Lear fooled, what kind of speeches were given, why? Trying again, "Goneril and Regan praise their father the King lavishly not out

of love or affection but in order to inherit through flattery the best parts of his kingdom." The new sentence though a bit long is in the active voice and it's more specific as to the motivation and methods of the sisters Goneril and Regan.

5. **Active voice!** Avoid the passive voice. Instead of writing, "Food was eaten by us", use "We ate the food." Make the subject of the sentence, the thing or person or persons that do the actions (and hence active)! More engaging writing is generally in the active voice.

Outline Creation Practice

Practice creating outlines for different essay prompts to get used to the open–ended nature of the essay. You can find many actual prompts from SAT tests online at the College Board's website as well as use prompts from their various published practice tests in the Official SAT Study Guide.

Examples:

Assignment: Do we need other people in order to understand ourselves?

> **Introduction:** Story about myself and how I always thought that I was a courageous person but when another person was being bullied, I was afraid and didn't stick up for him.
>
> **Thesis:** Yes, we need other people in order to understand ourselves, because we react to other people and thus come to know who we ourselves are. Shakespeare's tragedies MacBeth and King Lear present us with examples of such self–discovery.

I. MacBeth comes to know that he's capable of murder for the sake of ambition through the goading of his wife Lady MacBeth.

II. King Lear comes to know that he's capable of being rash and being fooled because of the speeches from his daughters.

Conclusion: Summarize key points from the plays and how they support the thesis. Link back to the introductory story, was rudely surprised that I wasn't courageous as I thought I was. But in a later moment, someone tried to bully me and I wasn't afraid. People can through knowing themselves come to change and become also the person they thought they always were.

You don't have to write so much in your outline but try to have the key points and some details there. Just writing "didn't face up to bully" for the introduction is enough for you to know what to write about. The introduction and the conclusion in the above example are linked together which is nice when it works out. Also, the personal story is a good touch. It's also quite possible that the whole essay could have been about that single event when I didn't stand up for someone else who was being bullied. The thesis in the above example was two sentences long with the first sentence being the thesis, what the essay's about, and the second sentence telling us where we're going or how we're supporting that idea.

Assignment: Is the world changing for the better?

Introduction: Imagine going out and everyone looked like you. Imagine traveling to another country and it was just like your country—everyone spoke the same language, had the same beliefs, used the same products... This is happening.

Thesis: The world is becoming the same everywhere which is not a change for the better. The U.S.A. as an example has lost diversity as a country as all the cities become the same and this lost diversity is a loss.

I: Stores, products and culture everywhere in the U.S.A. are the same. Give examples: malls, same drinks, food, same films and music.

II: Lack of cultural and product diversity is bad, because it makes the world a dull place. Discuss why not being the same everywhere is a great thing.

Conclusion: Summarize thesis. Link back to the introduction—have to act to preserve diversity or the world will become the same everywhere.

This essay has a two–step argument. It first presents evidence that the world is changing—that things are becoming the same everywhere—and then it goes on to argue that becoming the same is a bad thing. Thus, we reach a thesis which is that the world is changing and that it's becoming a worse place (which combined answers the assignment). We have to be careful with point II. as we can't just assert that less diversity is bad; we have to prove that becoming less diverse hurts the world by making it more dull or the same and then discuss a bit why being dull or the same is a bad thing.

Practice: Write outlines on your own.

Write outlines for essay prompts to get in the habit of quickly putting together arguments and essays for these types of prompts. Try to write multiple outlines for each prompt—use examples from your own life for a first outline and then write another outline with examples from history or from literature. Pick one or no more than a few plays or novels to know really well which you can fit into most essay topics.

Concluding Thoughts

Congratulations, you've made it through the SAT Master Class! These are the methods and techniques that I've developed over the several years I tutored SAT students in New York City. I developed these approaches and methods after being disappointed with other books and finding their approaches ineffective. I hope you're feeling confident that with hard work you can achieve your score goals...because you can!

If this is the first time you're reading the book, you should have a good idea of how our methods and techniques work. To really know and be able to use them, you have to put them into practice. Actively implement these techniques and ideas while you're taking practice tests. You can keep the book open while you do practice tests to try to model your thought process and approach to problems on ours here in the book. Also use the compact outline in Appendix 2 to help jog your memory and to review our techniques.

To reinforce what you've learned and to make sure you've got everything down, you'll need to re-read or skim over chapters in the book. If you find you need extra help, try to get help from a teacher or a tutor if there are any available where you live (even your mom or dad or anyone else who's been through the test may be able to help you—two heads are almost always better than one).

Train hard and work thoughtfully and honestly not just for the SAT but for all work you take up in life. Good luck.

APPENDIX 1: Problem Set Answers

Critical Reading Section: Sentence Completion Problem Set Answers

Single-Blank Questions.

1. (A) concatenated

2. (B) benevolent

3. (C) peremptory

Note: watch out for words that are related to the sentence's topic, e.g. extralegal and political are words that are related to passing a bill—never automatically pick them; always check that their meaning coheres with the sentence

4. (D) lustrous

5. (E) treacherous

6. (A) pilloried

7. (B) homogenous

8. (C) lugubrious

9. (D) unsavory

Note: watch out for words that go together e.g. affirmative proposition (choice (B))—just because two words often go together often doesn't mean that they're correct on an SAT problem, you have to check the meanings of the terms and the sentence.

10. (E) abdicate

Double-Blank Questions.

11. (A) gaiety .. sadness

12. (D) energetic .. exhibition

13. (D) insurrection .. indifferently

14. (C) hesitated .. approved

15. (E) disorder .. inexplicable

16. (B) silenced .. pleased

Note: a key word in the sentence that needs to be made meaningful is "unattractive." While other answer choices make the sentence coherent, for example choice (D) makes sense, it doesn't nor do other choices make the word "unattractive" sensible except for the correct answer (B).

17. (E) reproach .. unnerve

18. (B) entreaties .. coaxed

19. (C) obliteration .. cowed

20. (A) paramount .. advancement

Critical Reading Section: Reading Passage Problem Set Answers

Your completed problem set should have various words in the answer choices marked out with precise pencil marks just like the solved problems in the chapter (if they don't...re–do the problem set).

1. (B). discovered

Plug the answer choices into the sentence (or at least the part of the sentence where 'hit on' appears). Discovered should sound sensible and considerably more sensible than the other choices.

2. (D). Didn't realize that agriculture could generate substantial quantities of produce

3. (C) A reminder of mortality

By traveling in the city in which all the narrator's former friends and acquaintances are gone, the narrator is reminded that he or she too is mortal and will one day die and have all his or her thoughts and actions forgotten.

4. (A) The author's friends are no longer in the city

5. (A) system of law

Instead of natural compassion ensuring that people obey contracts and engage in trade ethically, a system of law was created to ensure that people behave appropriately.

6. (C) regretful dissatisfaction

The author's attitude towards society and laws is negative as revealed in comments such as "...subjected the rest of mankind to perpetual labor, servitude, and misery..." but full condemnation is a bit too strong as the author also recognizes and observes the value and purpose of laws and society.

7. (B) defend themselves

These lines support the answer as to why when one group of people organized into a society, all other peoples had to similarly organize: "We may easily conceive how the establishment of a single society rendered that of all the rest absolutely necessary, and how, to make head against united forces, it became necessary for the rest of mankind to unite in their turn." The rest of mankind that's not united into a society thus has to unite in order to defend itself against the single united society. If the rest of mankind does not unite, the united society would overpower the rest of mankind and conquer or abuse them.

8. (E) a path of exploration for historical art and architectural works

The key phrase in the first sentence "when engaged through cultural artifacts" gives strong support that the passage is about exploring historical art and architectural works. Choice B's a plan of travel is too general as the passage discusses exploring history and meaning rather than just a place itself and certain travel related terms like "side–steps" are used metaphorically not literally.

9. (B) visiting less appreciated artworks

While we usually associate being sentimental as being a negative thing, the author in the passage associates sentiment with being adventurous and treading outside conventional lines. The author uses "sentiment" to mean an emotional appreciation of a historical period, place or time, and thus, "sentiment...encourages these side–steps..." which would include most likely visiting less appreciated artworks.

10. (B) organized and hodgepodge

The author describes Louis XIV's gardens as possessing "sober majesty" which would be consistent with being organized, while Louis XV's gardens are a "tangle of warring elements" which is consistent with being a hodgepodge.

11. (C) one that follows an internal logic consistently

We don't know what constitutes a consistent style exactly from the passage, but we know that the author's major criticism of Louis XV's gardens wasn't that it had curves that that it's curves were "dissolute and irrational" i.e. didn't have a consistent logic dictating how the curves and the gardens should be designed and placed together. We know, moreover, from the passage that the author is against mixing styles and wild experimentation.

12. (A) the author will not adorn additional wonders to bees and the beehive

The author in that sentence and the subsequent sentences is indicating to the reader that he or she is against exaggeration and will report only the truth plainly.

13. (B) biology enthusiasts

The passage is written in a casual style and the author states that his scientific and beekeeping results will be published in a later "technical work" so it's not for experts (eliminating choices (A) and (E)). Truth seekers is too vague so biology enthusiasts is the best choice.

14. (C) personification

The author describes the beehive as one would describe human cities e.g. "acquiring wealth" or "induce in them habits of conquest and idleness"...hence the author's using personification or treating non-human things or living creatures as though they were human.

15. (A) visiting flowers is hard work

Notice that choice (E) is very close...but there's no sense in the passage that creating honey by one's self is actually a "waste." It takes a lot of time for bees to make honey themselves but that doesn't mean that such time is wasted and the author who seems to be against bee conflicts wouldn't likely consider creating honey a waste.

Math Section: Overview Problem Set Answers

Math Section: Plugging–In Numbers Problem Set

You should've used plugging-in to solve the problems...for extra practice, try re-solving them using just algebra and or follow our algebraic solutions for some of the problems below.

1. (D) $1/(ab - a + 1)$

Here's how to solve the problem using algebraic manipulation (we hope you solved it by plugging in numbers for a and b):

Reduce the following where b and a are not equal to either 1 or –1:

$$\frac{\frac{1}{(b-1)}}{a + \frac{1}{(b-1)}}$$

$$= \frac{\frac{1}{(b-1)}}{\frac{a(b-1)}{(b-1)} + \frac{1}{(b-1)}}$$

$$= \frac{\frac{1}{(b-1)}}{\frac{ab-a}{(b-1)} + \frac{1}{(b-1)}}$$

$$= \frac{\frac{1}{(b-1)}}{\frac{ab-a+1}{(b-1)}}$$

We can now cancel out the (b – 1) terms since they're both the denominators of the respective fractions:

= $\dfrac{1}{ab - a + 1}$

2. (B) $(52 \times x \times y \times g) / 100$

3. (D) 120

Here's how to solve it via algebra:

If k percent of 50 is equal to 60 divided by m, then what's the value of km?

First we translate the problem's English into a mathematical equation:

$\dfrac{k}{100} \times 50 = \dfrac{60}{m}$

Now we solve the equation.

$\dfrac{50k}{100} = \dfrac{60}{m}$

Since we have an equation with two fractions, we think: Cross-Multiply!

50km = 60 × 100
50km = 6000
km = 6000/50
km = 120

Notice we can't solve for either k or m individually (k or m could still be any value), but we KNOW that the product km must equal 120!

4. (B) j^2/m

Here's how to solve the problem via algebraic manipulation:

If $x^{11} = j$ and $x^{15} = m$, what must be equal to x^7?

We have to try to manipulate the exponents so we are left with x^7.

We can solve it via dividing the two givens: $x^{15} / x^{11} = x^4$ SO $m/j = x^4$
  (remember the exponent division rule: subtract the exponents)

We can then get to x^7 via $x^{11} / x^4 = x^7$
Plugging in j for x^7 and m/j for x^4 we get $j / (m/j) = x^7$

$j / (m/j)$ simplifies to j^2/m
(to see how turn the fraction into division so that it becomes j divided by m / j. Then turn division of two fractions into the multiplication of j by the reciprocal of m / j...that's how we multiply fractions!)

5. **(A) 3/8**

If $7a / (8x - 3y) = ¾$, then $14a / (32x - 12y) = ?$

To solve it algebraically we multiply the numerator by 2 (7a × 2 = 14a) and the denominator by 4: $[((8x - 3y) \times 4) = 32x - 12y]$ SO we also have to multiple 3/4 by 2/4 which yields 6/16 or 3/8.

6. **(D) 5.**

7. **(D) j + ((n +xm)/100)**

8. **(B) y**

Let's solve the problem algebraically: If $5x + y = 9$ and $x + y = 5$, then $4x = ?$

We need to subtract the second equation from the first equation (anytime you see two equations with two variables, think *'I can add/subtract the equations to eliminate a variable and solve for the remaining variable'*).

```
   5x + y = 9
 −  x + y = 5
   4x + 0 = 4
```

444

4x = 4.
x = 1

Let's plug 1 in for x into an equation to solve for y.

x + y = 5
1 + y = 5
y = 4.

If 4x = 4, then y = 4x as well since y = 4.

9. (C) 35

10. (E) 2x + 9

Wole is six years older than Jean who is twice as old as Doris whose current age is x. In three years, Wole will be how old?

Doris = D = x.
Jean = J = 2x
Wole = W = J + 6 = 2x + 6

In three years then Wole will be 2x + 6 + 3 years old or 2x + 9 years old.

Math Section: Working Backwards Problem Set

1. **(C)** 2

2. **(A)** 9

4. **(E)** $1200

A computer previously for sale at 75% of its retail price is discounted an additional 25% to a final price of $675. What was its original price?

To solve the problem via algebra, use the concept of percentage off:
O = the computer's original price
S = the computer's first sale price
N = the computer's new sale price

N = $675
N = S × .75
S = O × .75
So via manipulation we get:

O = S / .75
S = N / .75

S = $675 / .75 = $900
O = S / .75 = $900 / .75 = $1200

5. **(B)** 8

6. **(D)** 10

7a − 15 = 4a
3a = 15
a = 5   so 2a = 10

7. (E) 25

Method 1: Form an Equation.

If we call the first integer is x, then the next six consecutive integers will be x+1, x+2, x+3, x+4, x+5, x+6

The sum of 7 consecutive integers = x + (x+1) + (x+2) + (x+3) + (x+4) + (x+5) + (x+6)
154 = x + (x+1) + (x+2) + (x+3) + (x+4) + (x+5) + (x+6)
154 = 7x + 21
133 = 7x
19 = x

The integers are then 19, 20, 21, 22, 23, 24, 25

Double-check does check out since 19 + 20 + 21 + 22 + 23 + 24 + 25 = 154

Method 2: Work Backwards from the Answer Choices

Assume that (C) 20 is the last integer and see if it summed with its previous six integers equals 154...if it's too big, then try (A) or (B) or if it's too small try (D) or (E).

8. (D) 2.5

If $x^2 - 3x + 15 = 5x$, then what is one possible value of x/2 =

$x^2 - 3x + 15 = 5x$
$x^2 - 8x + 15 = 0$
$(x - 3)(x - 5) = 0$
x is equal to 3 or 5...x/2 is equal to 1.5 or 2.5

Math Section: Algebra Problem Set Answers

Math Section: Algebra Concepts Problem Set

1. Classify each of the following numbers as an integer and or a rational number:

   5 is an integer and rational number

   0 is an integer and rational number

   .78932 is a rational number

   −3 is an integer and rational number

   ½ is a rational number

   −2.669 is a rational number

Remember every integer is also a rational number (but not vice versa, not all rational numbers are integers)!

2. Identify the variable and coefficient for each polynomial expression below:

   variable x, coefficient 4   for $4x^{-3}$

   variable y, coefficient −82   for $-82y^6$

   variable y, coefficient 1   for y

   variable z, coefficient 22   for $22z^4$

Note that when no coefficient is explicitly written as is the case for 'y', then the implicit coefficient is always 1.

3. Solve the following absolute values:

$\|-8\|$	=	8
$\|9 - 8 \times -3\|$	=	$\|9 + (24)\| = 33$
$\|(-7 \times 6 / 3 + 1)\|$	=	$\|(-42 / 3 + 1)\| = 13$
$\|(-9 + 3) / -3\|$	=	$\|(-6) / -3\| = 2$

4. Explain what a function is and how both the below equation and table each represents a function.

A function is a special type of mapping between two sets of items. A function is special in that every item in the domain or set of inputs can map to one and only one value in the range or the set of outputs. One way of figuring out which input is matched to which output is via a formula which is usually an equation of the form f(x) = something. Another method is via a table which lists x and f(x) values.

$f(x) = x^2 - x + 2$

We can generate y or f(x) values for the function via plugging in x values into the equation...so f(1) is obtained by plugging in 1 for x into the formula $x^2 - x + 2$ which results in 2. f(2) similarly obtained is 4.

x	y
1	2
2	4
3	8
4	14
5	22

The table directly lets us find x and y values. So the function's value is 4 when the input is 2, or the function gives us a 22 when the input is 5. We can also solve for input if we're given outputs e.g. if we're told the output (or f(x) or y value) is 8, then we know the input or x value is 3.

5. What's the degree of each of the below equations:

$x^4 - y^6 = 85$

the degree is 6.

$x^2 - x^3 + x^4 = 98$

the degree is 4.

$$x^2 + 2x^2 - 4x^2 = -9.5$$
the degree is 2.

6. What does the degree of an equation tell us?

The degree of an equation tells us how many possible solutions (how many possible values could be substituted for the variable which satisfy the equation or make it true) there can be for the equation.

7. What's the one difference between manipulating an inequality versus manipulating an equation?

When we multiply or divide both sides of an inequality by a negative number, the sign flips!

Math Section: System of Equations Problem Set

We hope you solved these problems using both the substitution and adding/subtracting equations methods! We've solved 1. and 2. via the substitution methods, and the remaining problems via adding/subtracting equations.

Problems Solved via Substitution:

1. $x = 51/23 = 2.22$
              $y = -191/345 = -.55$

$17x - 15y = 46$
$24x + 60y = 20$

Let's isolate the variable y in the second equation and then plug it into the first equation:

$60y = 20 - 24x$
$y = (20 - 24x) / 60$
$y = (5 - 6x) / 15$

Plugging in that for y in the first equation gives us an equation with a single variable, x, which we can now solve for:
17x − (15 × ((5 − 6x) / 15)) = 46
The fifteens cancel out...
17x − (5 − 6x) = 46
17x − 5 + 6x = 46
23x = 51

2.   x = .5 = 1/ 2
     y = 7/ 8

3x + 4y = 5
5x + 12y = 13
Let's isolate the variable x in the first equation and then plug it into the second equation:

x = (5 − 4y) / 3

Plugging it in for x into the second equation:
5((5 − 4y)/3) + 12y = 13
25/3 − (20y/3) + 12y = 13
16y/3 = 14/3

Multiplying both sides by 3 gives us:
16y = 14
y = 14/16 = 7/8

3.   y = 6.5
     x = 207.5 / 15 = 13.83

15x − 25y = 45
35y − 15x = 20

Let's isolate x in the first equation and plug in what it's equal to for x in the second equation:
15x = 45 + 25y
x = 3 + 5y/3

Plugging into the second equation
35y − 15 (3 + 5y/3) = 20
35y − 45 − 75y/3 = 20

10y = 65
y = 13/2 = 6.5

Problems Solved via Adding/Subtracting Equations:

4.   x = 1485/253 = 5.87
     y = –363/253 = –1.43

–11x – 22y = –33
 4x – 15y = 45

[–11x – 22y = –33] × 4
[4x – 15y = 45] × 11

–44x – 88y = –132
 44x – 165y = 495

Adding both equations yields:
– 253y = 363

5.   x = –2.4
     y = –.4

–20x + 20y = 40
[10x + 40y = –40] × 2

We multiplied one of the equations by 2 so that when we add the equations below the x terms will cancel out.
–20x + 20y = 40
20x + 80y = –80
100y = –40
y = –40 / 100 = –.4

6.   x = 0
     y = –2

16x – 16y = 32
[3x + 8y = –16] × 2

452

Above we multiplied one of the equations by 2 so that when we add the equations below the y terms will cancel out.

16x − 16y = 32
3x + 16y = −32
19x = 0
x = 0

7.   (B) 5

If $x + 2y − z = 2$ and $2x + y + z = 13$, then $x + y = ?$

Add both equations:
x + 2y − z = 2
2x + y + z = 13
3x + 3y = 15

Divide the resulting equation by 3:
x + y = 5

Solving problems in which you have solve for the sum or difference of two variables (e.g. x + y in this problem) is much easier by adding/subtracting equations vs. the substitution method!

8.   (E) 23

If $3x − 2y − z = 12$ and $x + y + z = 11$ then, $4x − y = ?$

Add both equations:
3x − 2y − z = 12
x + y + z = 11
4x − y = 23

Math Section: FOIL Problem Set

1. $(x - 4)(x + 8) =$ $x^2 + 4x - 32$

2. $(x - 7)(x - 8) =$ $x^2 - 15x + 56$

3. $(x + 5)(x + 5) =$ $x^2 + 10x + 25$

4. $(x - 9)(x + 9) =$ $x^2 - 81$

5. $(x - 3)(x - 4) =$ $x^2 - 7x + 12$

6. $(x + 7)(x + 6) =$ $x^2 + 13x + 42$

7. $(x - 2)(x + 2) =$ $x^2 - 4$

8. $(x + 7)(x - 4) =$ $x^2 + 3x - 28$

Math Section: Advanced FOIL Problem Set

1. $(2x - 7)(x - 2) =$ $2x^2 - 11x + 14$

2. $(2x - 3)(3x + 3) =$ $6x^2 - 3x - 9$

3. $(3x - 6)(4x + 11) =$ $12x^2 + 9x - 66$

4. $(4x + 5)(6x + 7) =$ $24x^2 + 58x + 35$

5. $(x - 8)(2x + 3) =$ $2x^2 - 13x - 24$

6. $(2x + 6)(3x - 17) =$ $6x^2 - 16x - 102$

7. $(x + 3)(x^2 - 5x + 12) =$ $x^3 - 2x^2 - 3x + 36$

8. $(2x + 2)(x^2 - 17x + 15) =$ $2x^3 - 32x^2 - 4x + 30$

9. $(x - 5)(2x^2 - 8x + 31) =$ $2x^3 - 18x^2 + 71x - 155$

Math Section: Factoring Problem Set

1. $x^2 - 5x + 6 = 0$
(x − 3) (x − 2) = 0

2. $x^2 + 18x + 45 = 0$
(x + 15) (x + 3) = 0

3. $x^2 - 2x - 15 = 0$
(x + 3) (x − 5) = 0

4. $x^2 - 5x + 6 = 0$
(x − 3) (x − 2) = 0

5. $x^2 + x - 20 = 0$
(x − 4) (x + 5) = 0

6. $x^2 - 7x - 30 = 0$
(x − 10) (x + 3) = 0

7. $x^2 + 8x + 12 = 0$
(x + 6) (x + 2) = 0

8. $x^2 - 2x - 3 = 0$
(x + 1) (x − 3) = 0

9. $x^2 + 11x - 12 = 0$
(x + 12) (x − 1) = 0

10. $2x^2 + 16x - 18 = 0$
(2x − 2) (x + 9) = 0

11. $3x^2 + 20x + 25 = 0$
(3x + 5) (x + 5) = 0

12. $4x^2 - 10x - 14 = 0$
(2x − 7) (2x + 2) = 0

Math Section: Translating English into Equations Problem Set

1. Four less than a number is the sum of three plus the square of two.
$$-4 + x = 3 + 2^2$$

x = 11

2. The product of five and another number is equal to the absolute value of the difference of five hundred and seven hundred.

$5 \times x = |500 - 700|$

$5x = 200$
x = 40

3. A number is divided by 8, and the result is the same when that number is subtracted from seven.

$x / 8 = 7 - x$

$x = 56 - 8x$
$9x = 56$
x = 56 / 9

4. Twice the sum of three integers is equal to twice the sum of negative sixteen and two of the integers. Find the value of any one of the three integers.

$2(x + y + z) = 2(x + y + -16)$

$2x + 2y + 2z = 2x + 2y + -32$
$2z = -32$
z = -16

One of the integers is -16.

5. With attendance at night lecture totaling fifty, there are sixteen more women than men. How many men and how many women attend night lecture?

M + W = 50
W = M + 16

Let's solve the system of equations by adding them which cancels out the M terms letting us solve for W.
M + W = 50
−M + W = 16
2W = 66
W = 33

There are 33 women and 17 men at the lecture.

Math Section: Inequality Problem Set

Be sure to always remember to flip the inequality sign when you multiply or divide an inequality by a negative number!

1. x < 0

−x − 1 > −1
−x − 1 + 1 > −1 + 1
−x > 0
(−x) × −1 < 0 × −1   (multiplying by a negative number triggered a sign flip)
x < 0

2. y ≥ 1

$\dfrac{-3y}{-3} \leq \dfrac{-3}{-3}$

y ≥ 1

3. x ≥ 5

5x − 15 ≥ 25 − 3x
8x ≥ 40
x ≥ 5

4. x < –11.5

–2x – 8 > 15
–2x > 23
x < –11.5   (dividing by a negative number triggered a sign flip)

5. x < –4

–7x – 8 > 20
–7x > 28
x < –4   (dividing by a negative number triggered a sign flip)

6. x – y > 8
y < x – 8

[Graph showing the line y = x – 8 as a dotted line with the region below it shaded, labeled "y < x - 8"]

7. $17y < -9 + 3x$
y < -9/17 + (3/17)(x)

[Graph showing line y < -9/17 + (3/17)(x) on xy-axes]

8. $-2y \leq -16 - 4x$
Multiplying both sides by -1: $2y \geq 16 + 4x$
y ≥ 8 + 2x

[Graph showing line y ≥ 8 + 2x on xy-axes]

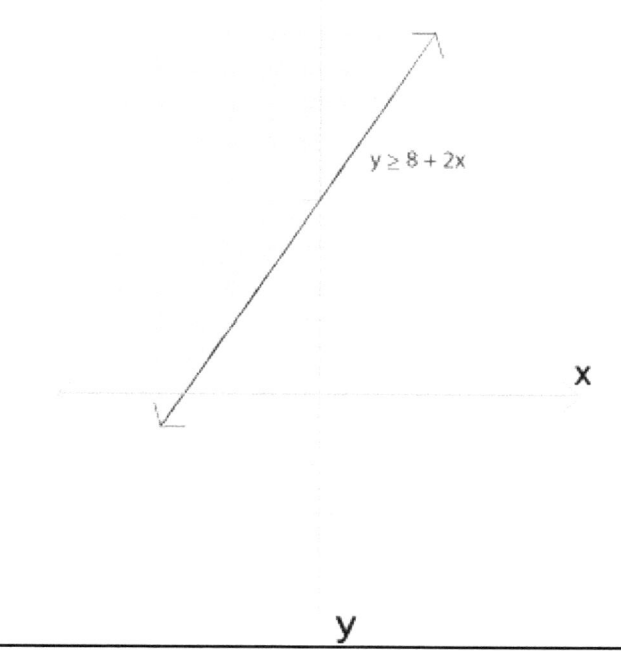

Math Section: Rate and Percentage Mixture Problem Set

1. 4.375 pounds

5 pounds of a solution is 25% saline by weight. How many pounds of salt should we add to make it 60% saline by weight?

	Initial	Final
Water	75% → 3.75 pounds	40% → 3.75 pounds
Salt (Salinity)	25% → 1.25 pounds	60% → 1.25 pounds + x
Total	5 pounds	5 pounds + x

We can set up an equation from the table, namely that 40% of the total volume which represents the water in the solution must equal 3.75 pounds.

.4 (5 + x) = 3.75
2 + .4x = 3.75
.4x = 1.75
 x = 1.75 / .4 = 4.375 pounds

2. 37.6 miles per hour

Your office is 50 miles away. You spend 200 minutes commuting everyday. Due to heavy traffic, your speed coming home is 25 miles per hour. What's your speed in the morning going to work?

	Distance =	Rate ×	Time
Going	50 miles	x	y
Coming	50 miles	25 mph	z
Total	100 miles	---	3.33 hours

Let's first solve for z:

50 miles = 25miles per hour × z
z = 2 hours

Then we can solve for y:

z + y = 3.33 hours

2 hours + y = 3.33 hours
y = 1.33 hours

Finally, we can solve for the speed going:

50 miles = x × 1.33 hours
x = 37.6 miles per hour

3. 47.5%

12 gallons of a mixture are 45% cow's milk and 30% goat's milk by volume. If we add 4 gallons of goat's milk to the mixture, what percentage of the resulting mixture will be cow's milk?

	Initial	Final
Cow's Milk	45% → 5.4 gallons	Initial → 5.4 gallons
Goat's Milk	30% → 3.6 gallons	Initial + 4 gallons → 7.6 gallons
Total	12 gallons	Initial + 4 gallons → 16 gallons

Final % Cow's Milk = 7.6 gallons / 16 gallons = .475

4. 9.5 hours

You drive at 55 miles per hour to a concert at night. You're only able to travel back home from the concert at 40 miles per hour. If the distance from your home to the concert venue is 220 miles, how much total time did you spend traveling to and from the concert?

	Distance =	Rate ×	Time
To the concert	220 miles	55 mph	x
Back from concert	220 miles	40 mph	y
Total	440 miles	---	x + y

Let's set up as many equations as we can—we need at least two.

220 miles = 55mph x x
220 miles = 40mph x y
Solving, we get: x = 4 hours; y = 5.5 hours; x + y = 9.5 hours

Math Section: Proportions/Ratios Problem Set

1. 2 days

It takes 10 girls 5 days to clean the garage. How long will it take 25 girls to clean the same garage?

When girls goes up, days goes down—hence it's an inverse proportion.

$X_1 \times Y_1 = X_2 \times Y_2$

10 girls × 5 days = 25 girls × Y days
Y = 50 girl-days / 25 girls = 2 days

2. 7 minutes

It takes 16 minutes to fill the bucket with 800 liters of water. How long will it take to fill the bucket with 350 liters of water?

When minutes goes up, volume goes up—hence it's a direct proportion.

$X_1 / Y_1 = X_2 / Y_2$

16 minutes / 800 liters = X minutes / 350 liters

X minutes = 5600 liter-minutes / 800 liters = 7 minutes

3. 3 cakes

A cake requires 3 eggs and a hundred grams of sugar. How many cakes can you make with 10 eggs and five hundred grams of sugar?

We have to figure out which is our limiting factor, whether it's eggs or sugar and what's the maximum number of cakes we can make with our limiting factor.

Since we need 3 eggs to make a cake, we could make a maximum of 3 cakes with 10 eggs (leaving 1 egg left-over). Since we need 100 grams of sugar to make one cake, we could make 5 cakes with 500 grams of sugar.

Eggs are thus our limiting factor and we can make a maximum of 3 cakes.

4. 231 dried apricots

In a mixture of dried fruit, there are 2 banana chips to 3 dried apricots to 5 prunes. How many dried apricots are in such a mixture of 770 pieces of dried fruit?

2B : 3A : 5P

To make the mixture, we have to add groups of 10 pieces of dried fruit in order to preserve the ratio (for every 2 banana chips, we have to also add 3 dried apricots and 5 prunes for a total of 10 pieces of dried fruit). 770 pieces of dried fruit thus consists of 77 (770 / 10) groups of dried fruit.

If there are 77 groups of dried fruit and there are 3 apricots in each group, there are 77 times 3 or 231 apricots in the mixture.

5. 15 days.

If it takes 5 boys 6 days to mow the golf course, how long will it take 2 boys to mow the whole golf course?

If boys goes up, days to mow goes down—hence it's an inverse proportion.

X1 × Y1 = X2 × Y2
5 boys × 6 days = 2 boys × Y days
30 boy-days / 2 boys = Y days
Y days = 15 days

6. 5 chocolate bars

We have a bag of chocolate bars. There were 15 children at the party and each child was going to get 6 chocolate bars. Three more kids showed up, however, and there are now 18 children at the party. If we give each child the same number of chocolate bars, what's the maximum number of chocolate bars we can give to each child?

15 children × 6 chocolate bars per child = 90 chocolate bars

90 chocolate bars / 18 children = 5

We can thus give each child 5 chocolate bars.

7. 6 marbles.

There are 10 blue marbles and 9 red marbles in a jar. What's the least number of marbles we can ADD to the jar to get the ratio of blue marbles to red marbles to be 3:2.

Original: 10 blue : 9 red

Desired Ratio: 3 blue   : 2 red
Multiples of the Desired Ratio: 6 blue   : 4 red
                                             9 blue   : 6 red
                                             12 blue : 8 red
                                             15 blue : 10 red

The closest desired ratio we could get to only by adding marbles is 15 blue to 10 red. To get to that ratio, we need to add 5 blue marbles and 1 red marble.

8. 9

x is directly proportional to y such that when x = 10, y = 6, what does y equal when x = 15?

Direct Proportion: $X_1 / Y_1 = X_2 / Y_2$
$10 / 6 = 15 / Y_2$
Cross-Multiply to get: $10 Y_2 = 6 \times 15 = 90$
So $10 Y_2 = 90$, then $Y_2 = 90/10 = 9$.

9. 200

z is directly proportional to q such that when z = 20, q = 5, what does z equal when q = 50?

Direct Proportion: $X_1 / Y_1 = X_2 / Y_2$
$z_1 / q_1 = z_2 / q_2$
$20 / 5 = z_2 / 50$
$z_2 = (20 \times 50) / 5$
$z_2 = 200$

10. 9/4 liters of vinegar

The volume of vinegar to oil in a certain salad dressing is 3 to 5. To make 6 liters of the dressing, how many liters of vinegar do we require?

3 liters of vinegar : 5 liters of oil
3 liters of vinegar and 5 liters of oil thus makes 8 liters of salad dressing.

Vinegar = 3/8 of the volume of the dressing
Oil = 5/8 of the volume of the dressing

For 6 liters of dressing, vinegar will be 3/8 of the volume or 3/8 × 6 liters = 9/4 liters.

Math Section: *Function Graph Problem Set*

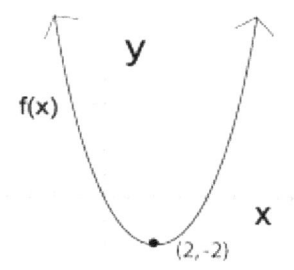

Using the above graph of f(x) with vertex at the point (2,−2), draw the following shifted functions:

1. Draw the graph of f(x) + 3

Your graph should be of the same parabola shifted up 3 so that the new vertex is (2, 1)

2. Draw the graph of f(x − 4)

Your graph should be of the same parabola shifted to the right 4 so that the new vertex is (6, −2)

3. Draw the graph of f(x) − 2

Your graph should be of the same parabola shifted down 2 so that the new vertex is (2, −4)

4. Draw the graph of f(x + 7)

Your graph should be of the same parabola shifted to the left 7 so that the new vertex is (−5, −2)

Graphs of the first four problems:

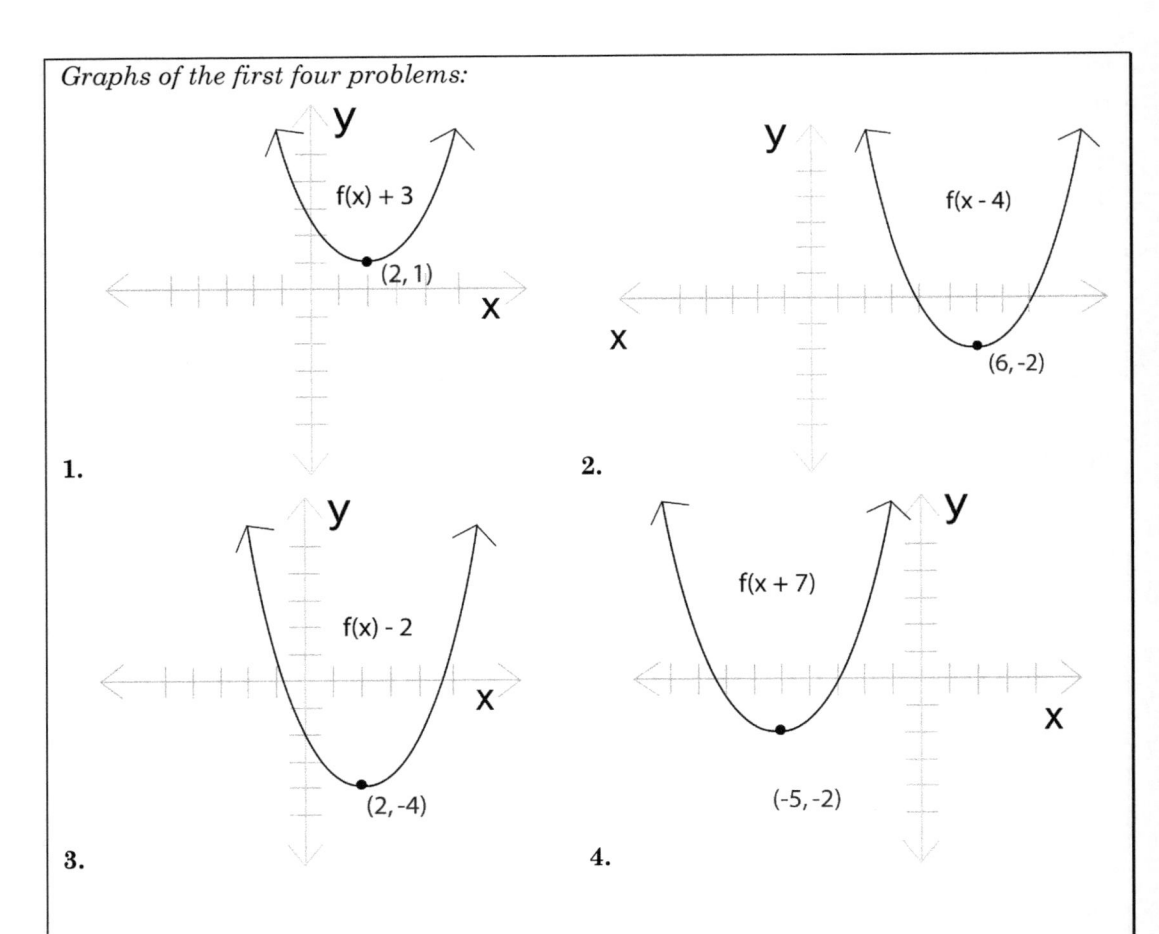

1. f(x) + 3, vertex (2, 1)

2. f(x - 4), vertex (6, -2)

3. f(x) - 2, vertex (2, -4)

4. f(x + 7), vertex (-5, -2)

5. 2 points

For f(x) over the domain of −2 < x < 6, for how many values of x does f(x) = −1?

We have to first find all the points at which f(x) or y = −1 (remember f(x) and y refer to the same thing!). Using the graph of f(x), draw the horizontal line y = −1 and see that there are two points of the parabola which are intersected (the approximate points (1, −1) and (4, −1)). So there are two points in which f(x)= −1: (1, −1) and (4, −1). Are these points within the domain of −2 < x < 6? Yes, both x-values of 1 and 4 are less than 6 but greater than −2.

Math Section: Functions of Functions Problem Set

For the two functions:
$f(x) = 4x^2 - 7x + 16$
$g(y) = 17 - y$

1. 508

Solve for f(g(5))

$g(5)$ = 17 − 5
       = 12

$f(g(5)) = f(12)$

$f(12)$ = 4 × 12² − 7 × 12 + 16
        = 576 − 84 + 16
        = 592 − 84
        = 508

2. − 469

Solve for g(f(− 10))

$f(-10)$ = (4 × [(−10)²]) − (7 × −10) + 16
        = (4 × 100) − (−70) + 16
        = (400) + 70 + 16
        = 486

$g(f(-10)) = g(486) = 17 - y = 17 - 486 = -469$

3. f(g(y)) = 4y² − 129y + 663

What's the composite function f(g(y)) = ?

For a composite function problem, we have to plug in one function instead of a number or value into another function. In this case, we have to plug in g(x) into f(x). So anywhere where there's an x in the function f(x), we have to plug in g(x) or 17 − y. We get:

$f(x)$ = 4x² − 7x + 16

467

g(y)   = 17 − y
To solve for f (g(y)), we have to plug in 17 − y for every x in f(x), so we get:

f(g(y)) = 4 (17 − y) ^{2} − 7(17 − y) + 16
         = 4 (189 − 34y + y²) − (109 − 7y) + 16
         = 756 − 136y + 4y² − 109 + 7y + 16
         = 4y² − 129y + 663

4. g(f(x)) = −4x² + 7x + 1

What's the composite function g(f(x)) = ?

f(x)   = 4x² − 7x + 16
g(y)   = 17 − y
We have to plug in f(x) in for each y in the g(y) function, so we get:
g(f(x)) = 17 − (4x² − 7x + 16)
          = −4x² + 7x + 1

For the three functions:
f(x) = −x² + 10x − 8
g(z) = 5z + 15
h(x) = 25 − x

5. −15,608

Solve for f(g(h(2)))

We start with the innermost function h(2) and work our way out:
  h(2) = 25 − 2 = 23

g(h(2)) =
g(23) = 5 × 23 + 15 = 115 + 15 = 130

f(g(h(2))) =
f(g(23)) =
f(130) =
f(130) = −(130)² + 10(130) − 8
       = −(16,900) + (1300) − 8
       = −16,900 + 1300 − 8
       = −15,608

6. $f(g(h(2x))) = -100x^2 + 2700x - 18{,}208$

Solve for $f(g(h(2x)))$

$f(g(h(2x))) =$

$h(2x) = 25 - 2x$
$g(h(2x)) =$
$g(25 - 2x)$ 　　$= 5(25 - 2x) + 15$
　　　　　　　　$= 125 - 10x + 15$
　　　　　　　　$= 140 - 10x$

$f(140 - 10x) = -x^2 + 10x - 8$
　　　　　　　$= -(140 - 10x)^2 + 10(140 - 10x) - 8$
　　　　　　　$= -(100x^2 - 2800x + 19{,}600) + (1400 - 100x) - 8$
　　　　　　　$= -100x^2 + 2800x - 19{,}600 + 1400 - 100x - 8$
　　　　　　　$= -100x^2 + 2700x - 18{,}208$

7. $f(g(h(x))) = -25x^2 + 1350x - 18208$

What's the composite function $f(g(h(x))) = $?

First, we plug in $h(x)$ into $g(x)$.

$g(z)$ 　$= 5(25 - x) + 15$
　　　$= 125 - 5x + 15$
　　　$= 140 - 5x$

Then we'll plug in $g(h(x))$ into $f(x)$.
$f(x)$ 　$= -x^2 + 10x - 8$
　　　$= -(140 - 5x)^2 + 10(140 - 5x) - 8$
　　　$= -(25x^2 - 1400x + 19600) + 1400 - 50x - 8$
　　　$= -25x^2 + 1400x - 19600 + 1400 - 50x - 8$
　　　$= -25x^2 + 1350x - 18208$

Math Section: Inverse Functions Problem Set

1. $f^{-1}(x) = (x - 8) / 10$

$f(x) = 10x + 8$
$y = 10x + 8$

Inverse function:
$x = 10y + 8$

$x - 8 = 10y$
$y = (x - 8) / 10$

2. $g^{-1}(x) = (81 - x) / 5$

$g(x) = 81 - 5x$

$x = 81 - 5y$
$5y = 81 - x$
$y = (81 - x) / 5$

3. $f^{-1}(x) = (18 - x) / 3$

$f(x) = -3x + 18$

$x = -3y + 18$
$x - 18 = -3y$
$y = (18 - x) / 3$

4. $f^{-1}(x) = 21 - x/2$

$f(x) = 42 - 2x$

$x = 42 - 2y$
$2y = 42 - x$
$y = 21 - x/2$

5. $f^{-1}(x) = x + 3$

$f(x) = x - 3$; $x = y - 3$; $y = x + 3$

Math Section: Function Tables Problem Set

1. f(5) = 1

2. g(3) = –3

3. g(f(4)) = g(2) = –4

4. f(– g(2)) = f(– –4) = f (4) = 2

5. x = 8

        x – f((–2 × g(5))^2) = g(f(3)) × g(f(2))
        x – f((–2 x –1)^2) = g(3) × g(4)
        x – f((2)^2) = –3 × –2
        x – f(4) = 6
        x – 2 = 6
        x = 8

6. y = 7

        g(f(4)^2) = y – 4 × –g(3) + f(3)
        g(2^2) = y – 4 × – –3 + 3
        g(4) = y – 4 × 3 + 3
        – 2 = y – 12 + 3
        – 2 = y + –12 + 3
        – 2 = y + –9
          7 = y

Math Section: Fractions in Equations Problem Set

1. x = 2 or –2

    $\dfrac{5x}{15} = \dfrac{8}{6x}$

    30x² = 120
    x² = 4

2. x = (√2) / 2 or (–√2) / 2

    $\dfrac{4}{9x} = \dfrac{48x}{27}$

    432x² = 108
    x² = 1/2

3. x = √15 or –√15

    $\dfrac{14x}{9} = \dfrac{70}{3x}$

    42x² = 630
    x² = 15

4. x = 1/6 or –1/6

    $\dfrac{3}{32x} = \dfrac{27x}{8}$

    24 = 864x²
    24 / 864 = x²
    1 / 36 = x²

5. x = 3 or –3

    $\dfrac{8x}{81} = \dfrac{16}{18x}$

    144x² = 1296
    x² = 9

Math Section: Absolute Value Problem Set

1. x = 6 or -12

$|x + 3| = 9$
Becomes: (x + 3) = 9   AND   –(x + 3) = 9

(x + 3) = 9
x = 6

–(x + 3) = 9
–x – 3 = 9
–x = 12
x = -12

2. x > 4   and   x < –1

$|2x - 3| > 5$
Becomes: (2x – 3) > 5   AND   – (2x – 3) > 5

2x > 8
x > 4

–2x + 3 > 5
–2x > 2
 x < –1

3. x = 4/3 or 14/3

$|3x - 9| = 5$
Becomes: (3x – 9) = 5   AND   – (3x – 9) = 5

(3x – 9) = 5
3x = 14
x = 14/3

– (3x – 9) = 5
–3x + 9 = 5
–3x = –4
x = 4/3

4. x < 90 or x > –60   so –60 < x < 90

$|15 - x| < 75$
Becomes: $(15 - x) < 75$ AND $-(15 - x) < 75$
$(15 - x) < 75$
$x > -60$

$-(15 - x) < 75$
$-15 + x) < 75$
$x < 90$

5. x = –10

$|x| = 58 - 38 + x$
$x = 20 + x$
$0 = 20$ …no solution
OR
$-x = 20 + x$
$-2x = 20$
$x = -10$

6. x = 4.5 or -4.5

Math Section: (mostly) Arithmetic Problem Set Answers

Math Section: PEMDAS Problem Set

1. 1

$8 - 4 + 5 \times 3^2 / -15 = $??

$= 8 - 4 + 5 \times 9 / -15$
$= 8 - 4 + 45 / -15$
$= 8 - 4 + -3$
$= 4 + -3$

2. 7

$(15 - 3) \times 2 / -2 + 3 - 4^2 \times -1 = $??

$= 12 \times 2 / -2 + 3 - 16 \times -1$
$= 24 / -2 + 3 - 16 \times -1$
$= -12 + 3 + 16$

3. 49 / 30

$(24 / 6 \times -5 / 10 - 5)^2 / (12 \times 3 - 12 / 2) = $??

$= (4 \times -5 / 10 - 5)^2 / (36 - 12 / 2)$
$= (-20 / 10 - 5)^2 / (36 - 6)$
$= (-2 - 5)^2 / (36 - 6)$
$= (-2 + -5)^2 / (30)$
$= (-7)^2 / (30)$
$= 49 / 30$

4. 0

$(3 \times 15 / 9 - 5) + (12 / 3 - 8 / 2) = $??

$= (45 / 9 - 5) + (4 - 8 / 2)$

$= (5 - 5) + (4 - 4)$
$= 0 + 0$

5. **− 4.5**

$(-3 \times 4 / 2 - 1)^2 + 2 / 4 - 8 / 4 \times 3^3 =$??

$= (-12 / 2 - 1)^2 + 2 / 4 - 8 / 4 \times 27$
$= (-6 - 1)^2 + 2 / 4 - 8 / 4 \times 27$
$= (-6 + -1)^2 + 2 / 4 - 8 / 4 \times 27$
$= (-7)^2 + 2 / 4 - 8 / 4 \times 27$
$= 49 + 2 / 4 - 8 / 4 \times 27$
$= 49 + .5 - 8 / 4 \times 27$
$= 49 + .5 - 2 \times 27$
$= 49 + .5 - 54$

6. **−21**

$(((2 - 3 + 4^2) \times -2) - 8) + (5 \times 4 - 9 / 3) =$??

$= (((2 - 3 + 16) \times -2) - 8) + (20 - 9 / 3)$
$= (((15) \times -2) - 8) + (20 - 3)$
$= ((-30) + -8) + (20 - 3)$
$= (-38) + (17)$

Math Section: Radicals/Roots/Powers Problem Set

1. $5^{8/3} = 25 \sqrt[3]{25}$

$5^{2/3} \times \sqrt[3]{(125^2)} = ??$

$= 5^{2/3} \times \sqrt[3]{((5^3)^2)}$
$= 5^{2/3} \times \sqrt[3]{(5^6)}$
$= 5^{2/3} \times 5^{6/3}$
$= 5^{8/3}$

2. 2^{47}

$\sqrt[4]{(32^{11} \times 128^{19})} = ??$

$= \sqrt[4]{((2^5)^{11} \times (2^7)^{19})}$
$= \sqrt[4]{((2^{55} \times (2^{133})))}$
$= \sqrt[4]{(2^{188})}$
$= 2^{188/4}$
$= 2^{188/4}$
$= 2^{47}$

3. $3^{7/3} = 9 \sqrt[3]{3}$

$243^{1/3} \times \sqrt[3]{9} = ??$

$= (3^5)^{1/3} \times \sqrt[3]{9}$
$= (3^{5/3}) \times 9^{1/3}$
$= (3^{5/3}) \times (3^2)^{1/3}$
$= (3^{5/3}) \times (3^{2/3})$
$= 3^{7/3}$

4. $2^3 = 8$

$\sqrt[5]{128} \times \sqrt[10]{((8 \times 32)^2)} = ??$

$= \sqrt[5]{(2^7)} \times \sqrt[10]{((2^3 \times 2^5)^2)}$
$= \sqrt[5]{(2^7)} \times \sqrt[10]{(2^6 \times 2^{10})}$
$= \sqrt[5]{(2^7)} \times \sqrt[10]{(2^{16})}$
$= 2^{7/5} \times 2^{16/10}$
$= 2^{7/5} \times 2^{8/5}$
$= 2^{15/5}$

5. 18 $^3\sqrt{3}$ = 2 × $3^{7/3}$

$18^{1/3} \times 9^{2/3} \times 12^{1/3}$ = ??

= $(2 \times 3^2)^{1/3} \times (3^2)^{2/3} \times (2^2 \times 3)^{1/3}$
= $(2^{1/3} \times 3^{2/3}) \times (3^{4/3}) \times (2^{2/3} \times 3^{1/3})$
= $2^{1/3} \times 2^{2/3} \times 3^{2/3} \times 3^{4/3} \times 3^{1/3}$
= $2^{3/3} \times 3^{7/3}$
= $2 \times 3^{6/3} \times 3^{1/3}$
= $2 \times 3^2 \times 3^{1/3}$
= 18 $^3\sqrt{3}$

6. 16 = 2^4

$^2\sqrt{32} \times 4^{3/4}$ = ??

= $(2^5)^{1/2} \times (2^2)^{3/4}$
= $2^{5/2} \times 2^{6/4}$
= $2^{5/2} \times 2^{3/2}$
= $2^{8/2}$

7. $3^{9/4}$ = 9 $^4\sqrt{3}$

$^4\sqrt{27} \times 27^{1/2}$ = ??

= $^4\sqrt{(3^3)} \times (3^3)^{1/2}$
= $(3^3)^{1/4} \times (3^3)^{1/2}$
= $3^{3/4} \times 3^{3/2}$
= $3^{3/4} \times 3^{6/4}$
= $3^{9/4}$

8. 2^{50}

$^2\sqrt{(2^{20} \times 4^{40})}$ = ??

= $(2^{20} \times 4^{40})^{1/2}$
= $2^{20/2} \times 4^{40/2}$
= $2^{10} \times 4^{20}$
= $2^{10} \times (2^2)^{20}$ = $2^{10} \times 2^{40}$

Math Section: New or Made–Up Operators Problem Set

1. −8

4 ■ −3 = ?   where x ■ y = x×y + x

4 × −3 + 4 =

−12 + 4

2. 46

7 ♠ (6 ♠ 5) = ? where x ♠ y = 2x − 4y

7 ♠ (2 × 6 − 4 × 5)

7 ♠ (12 − 20)

7 ♠ (−8)

(2 × 7) − (4 × −8)

(14) − (−32)

14 + 32

3. Yes.

Is (−4 ◉ −2) = (−2 ◉ −4)   where x ◉ y = y^x −4

$-2^{-4} - 4 = -4^{-2} - 4$

1 / 16 − 4 = 1 / 16 − 4

4. z

(z + 1) ☼ 1 = ?   where x ☼ y = xy − y

(z + 1)×(1) − 1 =

z + 1 − 1 =

z

5. x − 5y + 200

(x ╬ (y ╬ 8))　　where x ╬ y = x − 5y

x ╬ (y − 5×8)

x ╬ (y − 40)

x − (5 × (y − 40))

x − 5y + 200

6. −100

(5 □ (5 □ (5 □ 5)))　where x □ y = x² − 5y

(5 □ (5 □ (5² − 5×5)))

(5 □ (5 □ (25 − 25)))

(5 □ (5 □ 0))

(5 □ (5² − 5 × 0))

(5 □ (25 − 0))

5 □ 25

5² − 5 × 25

25 − 125

7. x = 1

Solve for x in this equation: x ┬ −5 = 7 ┬ x　　where x ┬ y = x² − 2xy + y²

x ┬ −5 = 7 ┬ x
x² − (2×x × −5) + (−5)² = (7)² − (2 × 7 × x) + x²
x² − (−10x) + 25 = 49 − 14x + x²
x² + 10x + 25 = 49 − 14x + x²
24x = 24

8. 702

6 ↑ (8 ↑ 9)　　where　x ↑ y = xy + 5x

6 ↑ (8 × 9 + 5 × 8)

6 ↑ (72 + 40)

6 ↑ (112)

6 × 112 + 5 × 6

672 + 30

480

9. 0

$((-5 \blacksquare 5) \text{ x } (\text{ x } \blacksquare \text{ x}^2))$ where $x \blacksquare y = x^3 - xy$

$(-5^3 - (-5 \times 5)) \times (x^3 - (x \times x^2))$

$(-125 - (-25)) \times (x^3 - (x^3))$

$(-125 + 25) \times (x^3 - x^3)$

$(-100) \times (0)$

Math Section: Elementary Number Theory Problem Set

1. 74

The positive integer x is a two–digit number. When it is divided by 11, the remainder is 8, and when it is divided by 15, the remainder is 14. What is the value of x?

To solve this problem, the fastest approach is to write out all the two-digit numbers which leave a remainder of 8 when divided by 11...then from that list find the term that leaves a remainder of 14 when divided by 15.

The two-digit numbers which have a remainder of 8 when divided by 11 are:
19
30
41
52
63
74
85
96

When divided by 15, only 74 results in a remainder of 14.

2. 28

Jim has 123 cents. Jonah has 104 cents. Buying an artificial start tattoo costs 7 cents. Jonah and Jim each want to buy the same number of tattoos. What's the maximum number of tattoos Jim and Jonah can buy respectively (using only their own money) so that each individual owns the same number of tattoos?

Jonah is the limiting factor since he has less money than Jim. Jonah can but a maximum of 14 tattoos (he'll then have 6 cents leftover). So Jim and Jonah to have the same number of tattoos each could buy a total of 28 tattoos.

3. (a) 2. (b) 12. (c) 4.

What's the Greatest Common Factor of the following sets of numbers:

(a) 156 and 178?

$156 = 2^2 \times 3 \times 13$

178 = 2 × 89

The two terms have only 2 in common.

(b) 24, 36 and 48

$24 = 2^3 \times 3$
$36 = 2^2 \times 3^2$
$48 = 2^4 \times 3$

The GCF will thus be composed of 2^2 and 3 ($2^2 \times 3 = 12$) which are the prime factors we find in each of the terms.

(c) 196 and 132

$132 = 2^2 \times 3 \times 11$
$196 = 2^2 \times 7^2$

The two terms both have two 2s in them so the GCF is 2^2 or 4.

4. (D) 84

56^{30} is divisible by all the following except:

$14 = 2 \times 7$
$16 = 2^4$
$28 = 2^2 \times 7$
$84 = 2^2 \times 3 \times 7$
$112 = 2^4 \times 7$

$56 = 2^3 \times 7$
SO $56^{30} = 2^{90} \times 7^{30}$

Thus all the other terms which are composed of 2s and 7s will be factors of 56^{30} except for 84 which includes a 3 in it—there are no 3s in 56^{30} so it's impossible for any number which contains a 3 as one of its prime factors to divide 56^{30}.

5. 75. 12^{75} is the largest multiple of 12 that's a factor 360^{50}.

What's the largest possible value for n for which 12^n is a factor of 360^{50}?

$360 = 2^3 \times 3^2 \times 5$

$360^{50} = (2^3 \times 3^2 \times 5^1)^{50}$
$\phantom{360^{50}} = 2^{150} \times 3^{100} \times 5^{50}$

$12 = 2^2 \times 3$

Twelve is thus composed of 2 twos and a three. For every 3, we need two 2s. For 360^{50}, then, 2^{150} is our limiting factor…the biggest multiple of 12 we can form that will "be in" 360^{50} is 12^{75} which would be composed of 2^{150} and 3^{75} (which leaves 3^{25} left-over).

6. (a) 5472. (b) 720. (c) 1344.

What's the least common multiple of the following sets of numbers:

(a) 32, 36 and 38

$32 = 2^5$
$36 = 2^2 \times 3^2$
$38 = 2 \times 19$

To build our LCM, let's first put 32 into the LCM which means adding 2^5
LCM = 2^5
Next, we need to put 36 into our LCM…we already have two twos, so need to add two threes:
LCM = $2^5 \times 3^2$
Next, to finally put 38 into it…we have to add a 19:
LCM = $2^5 \times 3^2 \times 19$

The LCM thus is 5472.

(b) 40, 45 and 48

$40 = 2^3 \times 5$
$45 = 3^2 \times 5$
$48 = 2^4 \times 3$

The LCM is composed of $2^4 \times 3^2 \times 5 = 720$

(c) 42, 56 and 64

$42 = 2 \times 3 \times 7$

$56 = 2^3 \times 7$
$64 = 2^6$

The LCM is composed of $2^6 \times 3 \times 7 \ = \ 1344$

Math Section: Sequences Problem Set

1. 2

Always write out of the first few terms of the sequence:
2, 2, 2, 2…

This was a bit of a trick question—the sequence will also result in 2!

2. 3

Always write out of the first few terms of the sequence. Here, we've italicized the successive odd terms.
5, 2, *3*, 0, *3*, 0, *3*, 0, *3*, …

We've discovered that this is a repeating sequence after the first two terms. The 57th term is an odd term so it will be 3.

3. –56

Again, we start by writing out the first several terms of the sequence:

0, 2, *–2*, 0, *–4*, –2, *–6*, –4, *-8*…

We have two arithmetic sequences: a sequence of even terms going down by two and a sequence of odd terms also going down by two.

We need to find the 57th term in the sequence of both evens and odds which will be the 29th term in the sequence of odd terms written below:

0, –2, –4, –6, –8…

n^{th} term = first term + k(n – 1)
29th term = 0 + –2(29 – 1)
       = 0 + –56
       = –56

4. 1/ 27

81, 27, 9, 3, 1…

486

The pattern is that every successive term is obtained by multiplying its preceding term by 1/3. This is a geometric sequence!

Nth term in a geometric sequence = first term x k^{n-1}
8th term = $81 \times 1/3^{8-1}$
= $81 \times 1/3^7$
= 1/27

5. 20

Let's write out the first several terms of the sequence:

20, −20, −21, 21, 20, −20, −21, 21, 20, −20...

This is a repeating sequence. The four terms 20, −20, −21, 20 repeat over and over forever.

To find the 45th term, we have to divide 45 by the number of terms that repeat, in this case 4, and the remainder will tell us which term it will be.

45 divided by 4 leaves remainder of 1. Thus, it's the 1st term in the repeating sequence or 20.

6. 67

−20, −25, −35, −55, −95, −175, ...

From the problem, we can write equations for x and y using the terms given in the sequence:

(−20 × x) + y = −25
(−25 × x) + y = −35

We can solve the above two equations as a system of equations:

[(−20 × x) + y = −25] −1
= 20x − y = 25

Let's add the two equations:

20x − y = 25
−25x + y = −35

Yields −5x = −10
5x = 10
x = 2

Plugging in x = 2, we can solve for y:

(−20 × 2) + y = −25
−40 + y = −25
y = 15

x + y = 15 + 2 = 17

7. 9

We have to write out several terms in the sequence but we have to go backwards since the rule tells us not how to get successive terms (n + 1) but rather preceding terms (n − 1).

... 12, 17, 22, 27, 32, 37, 42, 47...
13th 14th 15th 16th 17th 18th 19th 20th

This is an arithmetic sequence since each term is the previous term plus give, let's figure the first term in the sequence using our equation for arithmetic sequences:

Nth term = 1st term + k(n − 1)
13th term = x + 5(13 − 1)
12 = x + 5 (13 − 1)
12 = x + 5 × 12
12 = x + 60
x = −48

Now we have to solve for n when the term equals −8.

−8 = −48 + 5 (n − 1)
40 = 5n − 5
45 = 5n
n = 9

The 9th term in the sequence thus equals −8.

8. 7

The equation, T(n) = T(n – 1) × 3, tells us that each succeeding term is the product of its preceding term and three. Thus if T(1) = 1/27, then T(2) will equal 1/27 × 3, then T(3) will equal T(2) × 3, et cetera.

T(2) = 1/27 × 3 = 1/9
T(3) = 1/9 × 3 = 1/3
T(4) = 1/3 × 3 = 1
T(5) = 1 × 3 = 3
T(6) = 3 × 3 = 9
T(7) = 9 × 3 = 27

Here's an alternative method to solve the problem using our formula for finding the nth term in a geometric sequence.
Nth term = first term × k^{n-1}
Nth term = 1/27 × 3^{n-1}
27 = 1/27 × 3^{n-1}
27 × 27 = 3^{n-1}
3^3 × 3^3 = 3^{n-1}
3^6 = 3^{n-1}
So n – 1 = 6, then n = 7.

9. 2077

This is an Arithmetic Sequence.
$8.70 = $1.50 + ((n – 1) × $.10)
7.20 = .1n – .1
7.30 = .1n
n = 73

In the 73rd year beginning with 2005 (which is 2005 + 72 or the year 2077), a cup of coffee will cost $8.70.

10. $117.39

This is a Geometric Sequence Problem.
Cost in 2055 = $(1.1)^{50}$ × $1.00 = $117.39

489

Math Section: Percentage Problem Set

1. 1000

If 15% of a number is equal to 300% of 50, then what is that number?

.15 × x = 3.00 × 50
x = 150 / .15
x = 15,000 / 15
x = 1000

2. $24

Shirts regularly priced at $40 each are marked down by 20%. If you were to buy three shirts, how much would you save in total (in dollars)?

Savings per shirt = $40 × .20 = $8
Total savings = 3 × $8 = $24

3. 605

If a baby's caloric intake grows an average of 10% each month, and in March a baby was eating 500 calories a day, how many calories would the baby eat in May?

March—500
April—500 + (500 × .1) = 500 + 50 = 550
May—550 + (550 × .1) = 550 + 55 + 605

4. −10%

A photo's height was reduced by 25% and its length increased by 20%. By what percentage, whether negative or positive, did the area of the photograph change?

Original Area = 1 × 1 = 1
New Area = .75 × 1.2 = .9 of the Original Area

Math Section: Percentage Pay/Percentage Off Problem Set

We hope you solved each problem using Percentage Pay (instead of Percentage Off)!

1. **$71.43**

A shirt after a 30% discount costs $50. What was its original price?

Original price × percentage pay = sales price
Original price × .70 = $50
Original price = $50/.70 = $71.43

2. **51.03%**

You can buy a car at 70% of its list price in January with the price decreasing by an additional 10% every month thereafter. What percentage of list price would you pay to buy the car in April?

Price in the Preceding Month x Percentage Pay = Price in the Succeeding Month

List Price × .70 = January Price
January Price × .90 = February Price
February Price × .90 = March Price
March Price × .90 = April Price

April Price   = .9 × March Price
              = .9 × (.9 × February Price)
              = .9 × (.9 × (.9 × January Price))
              = .9 × (.9 × (.9 × (.7 × List Price)))
              = .9 × .9 × .9 × .7 × List Price
              = .5103 × List Price

3. **10,000**

Average sales × 1.20 = 60,000
Average sales = 60,000 / 1.20 = 50,000

The Rolling Stones would thus have to sell 10,000 copies above the mean sales of 50,000 to match the Beatles.

4. $291,588

(((Original Price × .95) × .95) × .95) = $250,000
Original Price = $250,000 / (.95 × .95 × .95)

Math Section: Combinatorics Problem Set

1. 84 possible groups of photographs and frames.
We need combinations.
6 slots. 9 × 8 × 7 × 6 × 5 × 4 = 60,480 permutations.
combinations = 60,480/6! = 60,480 / (6×5×4×3×2×1) = 84 combinations

2. 2 slots for colors. 3 slots for accessories.
        (6 × 5)   ×   (7 × 6 × 5)   = **6300 possible dolls**

3. 225 three-digit numbers

There are three possible ways we could have a three-digit number with 8:
8 __ __
__ 8 __
__ __ 8

Since we can't put an 8 in either of the empty slots, there are 9 choices for the remaining digits except for the first digit for which there are 8 choices since the three-digit numbers can't begin with a zero.

1 × 9 × 9 = 81
8 × 1 × 9 = 72
8 × 9 × 1 = 72

There are then 225 three digit numbers which have exactly one digit equal to 8.

Notice that the 8s become 1 when we actually calculated the possible permutations because there was only a single or one choice for that particular slot (it had to be filled with an 8) hence we put a 1 there.

4. 3 × 4 × 5 = 60 possible routes

5. 81

How many integers are there with different digits in the integers between 10 and 99 inclusive of 10 and 99?

Method 1. Combinatorics.

We can use combinatorics to calculate how many possible 2-digit numbers fulfill the desired criteria. For the first slot, there are 9 possibilities (the digits 1 through 9, we can't use 0), and for the second slot there are 10 possibilities (the digits 0 through 9). The condition, though, is that both digits can not be the same. Thus whatever digit gets used in the first blank can not be put into the second blank, so there are now not 10 but rather 9 possibilities for the second blank. The total number of permutations or integers with different digits will be 9 * 9 or 81.

Method 2. Counting.

It's not too difficult to count the integers between 10 and 99 with the same digits and then subtract those from the total number of integers between 10 and 99.

11, 22, 33, 44, 55, 66, 77, 88, 99 = 9 integers with the same digits

90 integers between 10 and 99 including both 10 and 99

There are then 90 – 9 or 81 integers with different digits.

6. 165

You have to write a report on 3 different historical figures, and you have 11 historical figures to choose from. How many different combinations or groups of historical figures could you write about? There are three slots so:

$$\frac{11 \times 10 \times 9}{3!}$$

Math Section: Probability Problem Set

1. 11/18

(Green sock AND Green sock)   OR   (Red sock AND Red sock)
    (7/9 × 6/8)   +   (2/9 × 1/8)

= 42/72 + 2/72
= 44 / 72 = 22/36 = 11/18

Notice that both the numerator and the denominator decrease by 1 in the fractions because the problem is without replacement. Also note again that the ANDs become multiplication signs and the ORs plus signs.

2. 3/25

(Red AND Red AND Red) OR (Blue AND Blue AND Blue) OR (Yellow AND Yellow AND Yellow)

(6/15 × 6/15 × 6/15) + (5/15 × 5/15 × 5/15) + (4/15 × 4/15 × 4/15)
= (6/15)³ + (5/15)³ + (4/15)³

= 216/3375 + 125/3375 + 64/3375
= 405 / 3375
= 81 / 675
= 3 / 25

Note that since this is a with replacement problem, the fractions don't change.

3. 28 / 3003 = 4 / 429

Probability no "c" guests get a slice =
        Number of combinations in which "d" and "e" guests get all 6 slices
        Total number of combinations

6 cake slices = our slots

__ × __ × __ × __ × __ × __

There are 8 persons whose names don't begin with "c." We have to give all the slices of cake to 6 of these 8 in order to calculate the probability that none of the persons with a name beginning with "c" get a slice.

8 × 7 × 6 × 5 × 4 × 3 = 20,160 = number of permutations in which "d" and "e" get all the slices of cake

20,160 / 6! = 28 = number of combinations in which "d" and "e" get all the slices of cake

The total number of combinations is calculated using all the 14 guests:
Permutations = 14 × 13 × 12 × 11 × 10 × 9 = 2,162,160
Combinations = 2,162,160 / 6! = 3003

The probability thus is 28 / 3003.

Key insight: there are two ways to calculate the probability of event X: calculate p(X) or calculate p(not X) i.e. you can calculate the probability of event X happening or the probability of X not happening and subtract it from 1 (since p(X) + p(not X) = 1). In this problem it's easier to calculate directly the probability that only guests with name beginning with "d" or "e" get a slice of cake—which is the same thing as calculating the probability that none of the "c" named guests get a slice. Another way to calculate the probability is to subtract the number of combinations in which "c" named persons get a slice of cake but that's quite difficult (you'd have to first figure out how many possible combinations exist in which 1 "c" name person gets a piece, then 2 "c" name persons, etc.—tedious and tough).

Small Note: You may have noticed that you could also have gotten the correct probability by dividing the permutations (20,160 / 2,162,160)…that is correct but if your insight is that we need combinations, it's better to avoid shortcuts and model problems properly.

4. 7 socks.

If you picked just 6 socks, it's possible that you would have picked 6 red socks. If you pick 7 socks though, you must have *at least* one sock of each color and thus at least one blue sock.

Math Section: Statistics Problem Set

1. The least and greatest possible 5-day average rainfalls are 9 inches and 10.2 inches.

It rained every day the past five days and the daily rainfall varied between 2 inches and 15 inches. The median rainfall was 10 inches, and the mode was 15 inches. What is the least and greatest possible 5–day average or mean daily rainfall?

There are five terms in this set with the end terms being 2 and 15, and the middle term being 10. We've, from the problem, then got: 2, __, 10, __, 15. 15 is the mode so it must occur twice so we can fill in the fourth blank: 2, __, 10, 15, 15. The possible values for the second blank are then 3 through 9: 2, 3–9, 10, 15, 15.

The mean could vary from (2 + 3 + 10 + 15 + 15) / 5 to (2 + 9 + 10 + 15 + 15) / 5…which varies the mean from 9 inches to 10.2 inches.

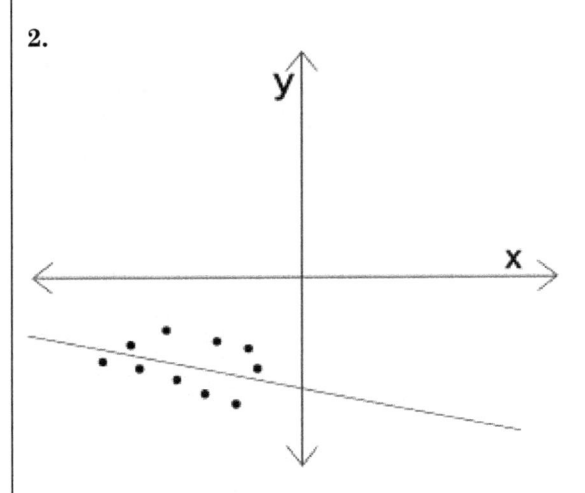

2.

3. The Mode is 5.

The median of a set of 5 integers is 5. The average of the set of integers is 4.8. The range of the set is 3. The mode appears three times in the set. What's the mode of this set of integers?

We know the middle term is five. We know the end terms have a difference or range of 3 so they could be 8 and 5, 7 and 4, 6 and 3, or 5 and 2. We further know the sum of the five terms is 24 since the average of the five terms is 5 (4.8 × 5 = 24). So we have to try to construct a set that meets that criteria with a sum of 24.

Let's write out our possibilities:
2, _, 5, _, 5
3, _, 5, _, 6
4, _, 5, _, 7
5, _, 5, _, 8

In the first and last case, we can fill in one more term that has to be 5!:
2, _, 5, 5, 5
5, 5, 5, _, 8
Since the sum of the 5 terms has to be 24, neither can work, since we would need 7 for the first option which is not between 2 and 5, or 1 for the second option which is not between 5 and 6. So the end terms can not be 2 and 5 nor 5 and 8

We're left with:
3, _, 5, _, 6
4, _, 5, _, 7

In the first case, 3 + 5 + 6 equals 14, so we need the remaining two terms to add up to 10...5 and 5 work and so does 4 and 6, but using 5 and 5 gives us a mode of 5 which appears three times which is what the problem requires. In the second case, 4 + 5 + 7 equals 16 so we need the remaining two terms to sum to 8...there aren't any possibilities that work...so the answer is that the mode is 5 and our sequence is 3, 5, 5, 5, 6!

4. Mode: 0
Median: 3
Mean: 32 / 7

Note: to find the median, the set of numbers must be written in order of the least to greatest (in that list where the elements are arranged in ascending order, the middle term will be the median)!

5. Mode: 1
Median: 1 = middle two terms summed/2 = (1 + 1) / 2
Mean: 27 / 8

Math Section: Averages Problem Set

1. 11.

What is the average of the following set of terms: 7, 11 – x, 12, 14 + x ?

7 + 11 – x + 12 + 14 + x = 44 (the x terms cancel out)

The average then is 44 divided by the number of terms which is 4…so the average is 44 / 4 = 11.

2. 96°

To qualify as 'flame retardant' for country X, a jacket needs to survive an average temperature of 90° C without catching fire over four trials. In the first three trials, the jacket has withstood an average of 88° before catching fire. Up to what temperature does the jacket need to withstand heat in its fourth and final trial in order to qualify as 'flame retardant'?

Average of 90° over 4 trials implies that:

90° = sum of four trials / 4
sum of four trials = 360°
The sum of the four trial temperatures is thus 360°.

If the jacket has withstood an average of 88° in the first three trials, the sum of the first three trials' temperatures is 264°. The fourth trial must make that sum 360° so it can be calculated as 360° minus 264° which means the jacket must withstand a temperature of 96° in the fourth trial.

3. The average of all five numbers is 24.

From the definition of an average as the sum divided by the number of elements we get:

$$\frac{x + y + z}{3} = 20$$

and

$$\frac{a + b}{2} = 30$$

498

By manipulation

x + y + z = 60
and
a + b = 60

SO x + y + z + a + b = 120

Then the average of all five numbers must be 120/5 or 24.

4. The sum of the additional three integers must be 240.

The average of six integers is 50. We want to add three more integers to the original six to raise the average to 60 for all nine integers from 50 for the six integers. What, then, should the sum of three additional integers be?

$50 = \dfrac{\text{sum of six integers}}{6}$

Sum of six integers = 6 × 50 = 300

$60 = \text{average of 9 integers} = \dfrac{\text{sum of nine integers}}{9}$

Sum of nine integers = 9 × 60 = 540

The sum of the additional three integers = 540 − 300 = 240.

Math Section: Geometry Problem Set Answers

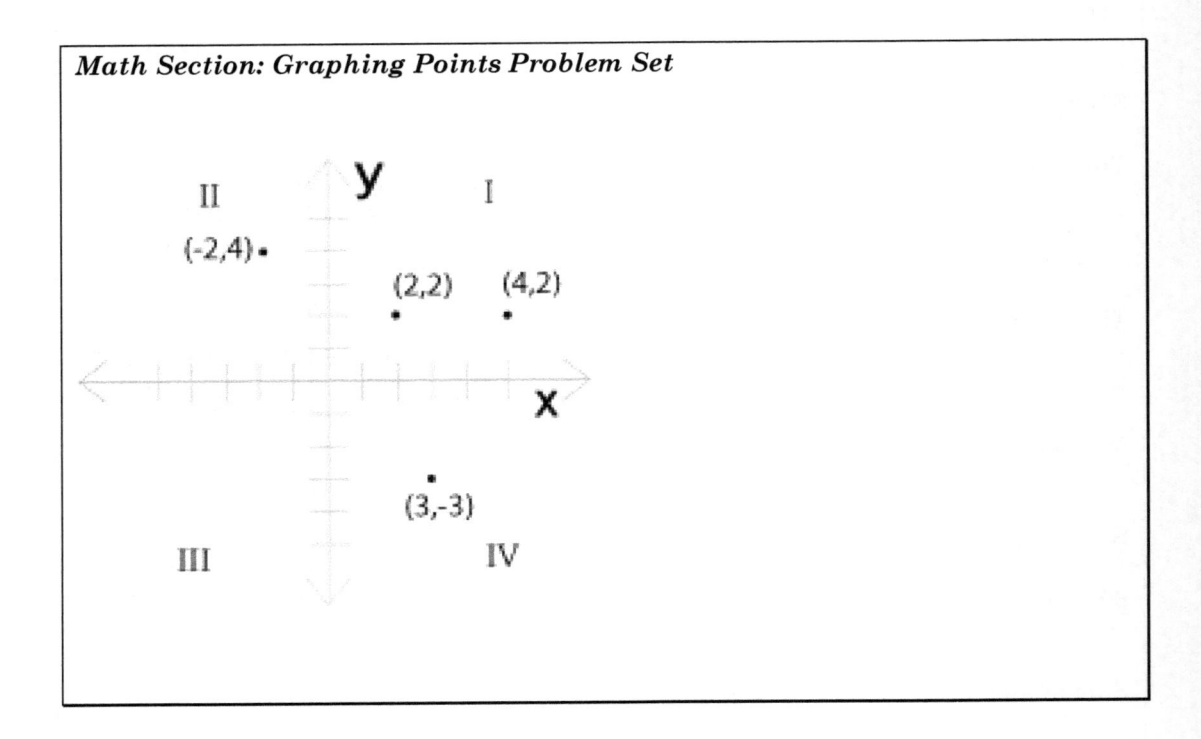

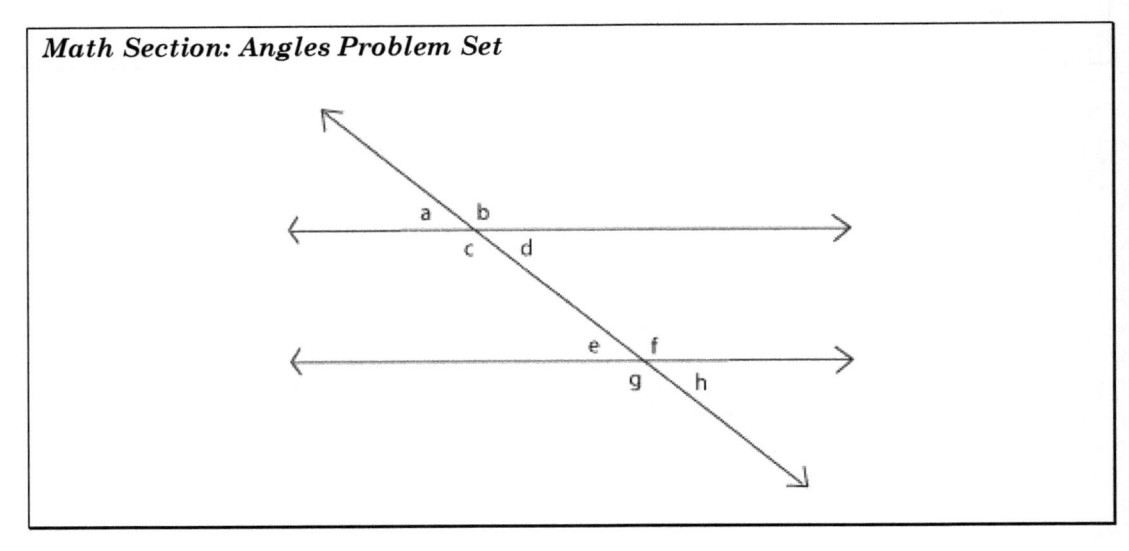

Math Section: Graphing Points Problem Set

II (-2,4)

I (2,2) (4,2)

IV (3,-3)

III

Math Section: Angles Problem Set

a b
c d

e f
g h

1. If Angle b= 150°, then

Angle c is a vertical angle and thus 150°
Angle g is an opposite exterior angle and also 150°
Angle d is its supplement and equals 30°
Angle h is also a supplement and equals 30°

2. 280°

If Angles d, e, and g sum to 220°, what's the sum of Angles f and c?

Angles e and g are supplements so they have to sum to 180°, so all three angles will sum to 180° + Angle d which equals 220°...so Angle d must equal 40°. Angles f and c are supplements of Angle d and thus measure 140° each or 280° in total.

3. 405°

If Angles h and e are complements, then what's the sum of Angles a, d, e, f, and g?

Angles h and e have to equal each other since they're vertical angles—if they're complements, they have to be equal and thus 45° each. Their supplements which include Angles f and g, will measure 135° each. The sum of Angles a, d, e, f, and g is then   45° + 45° + 45° + 135° + 135°.

Math Section: Lines Problem Set

1. m = 1

(1, 1) (3, 3)

m = (3 − 1) / (3 − 1) = 2 / 2 = 1

2. zero slope

(2, 0) (3, 0)

m = (0 − 0) / (3 − 2) = 0 / 1 = 0

Note: Remember a line with zero slope is a horizontal line, and a line with no slope (i.e. you'll get a fraction where the denominator is zero and thus undefined) is a vertical line.

3. m = −5/4

(−4, 5) (4, −5)

m = (5 − −5) / (−4 − 4)
= 10 / −8
= −5/4

4. No Slope

(3, 6) (3, −2)

m = (−2 − 6) / (3 − 3)
= −8/0 = undefined
No slope (hence a vertical line).

5. m = 3

(−2, −4) (−5, − 10)

m = (−10 − −4) / −4 − −2)

= –6 / –2
= 3

6. m = 13 / –9

(6, –9) (–3, 4)

m = (4 – –9) / (–3 – 6)
= 13 / –9

Write the equation of the line for a line with the given slope which passes through the given point.

7. y = 3x – 18

m = 3   (10, 12)

y = mx + b
12 = 3 × 10 + b
12 = 30 + b
b = –18

8. y = ½x + 9.5

m = ½   (–5, 7)

y = mx + b
7 = ½ x –5 + b
7 = –2.5 + b
b = 9.5

9. y = –2x – 3

m = –2   (–2, –2)

Let's solve the problem using the definition of a slope. The y-intercept will always be in the form (b, 0). So plugging in (b, 0) and the point we know (–2, –2), we can solve for b.

m = $y_2 - y_1$

503

$$-2 = \frac{\overset{x_2 - x_1}{-2 - 0}}{-2 - b}$$

$(-2) \times (-2 - b) = -2$
$(-2 - b) = 1$
$b = -3$

10. y = 6x – 59/6

m = 6   (–8, 11)

$$6 = \frac{11 - 0}{-8 - b}$$

$(6) \times (-8 - b) = 11$
$(-8 - b) = 11/6$
$b = -8 - 11/6 = -59/6$

11. b = – 10;   m = 1.5
y = 1.5x – 10

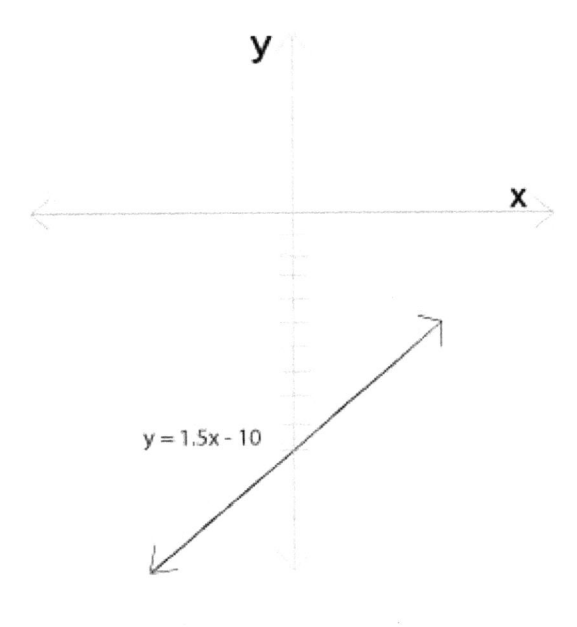

y = 1.5x - 10

12. b = 4; m = 2
2y = 4x + 8
y = 2x + 4

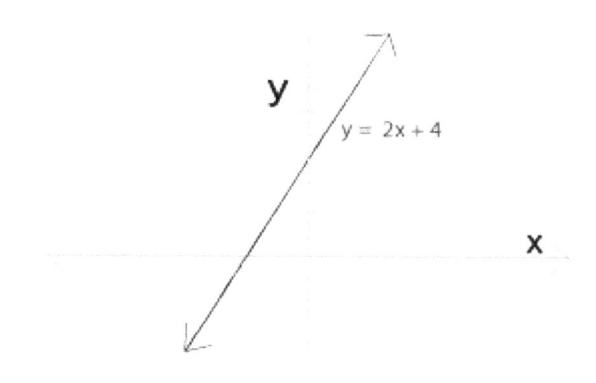

y = 2x + 4 graph

13. m = –2; b = – 4
y = –2x – 4

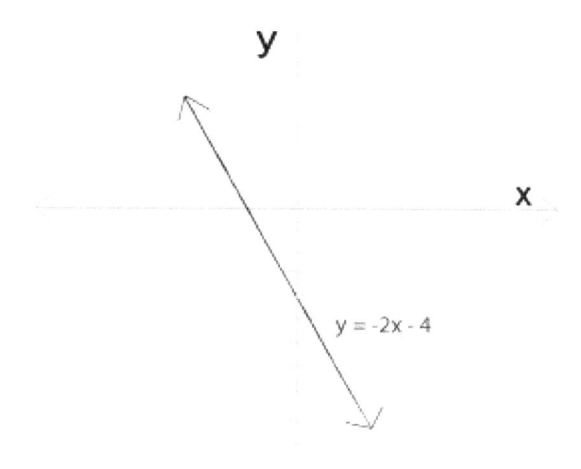

y = -2x - 4 graph

14. y = –2x/3 + 4/3

m = 3/2   (2, 0)

m of a perpendicular line is the negative reciprocal: –2/3
y = –2x/3 + b
0 = –2x2 / 3 + b

505

b = 4/3

15. y = x/5 + 4/5

m = –5   (1, 1)

m of a perpendicular line is the negative reciprocal: 1/5
y = x/5 + b
1 = 1 / 5 + b
b = 4/5

16. h = 25

What's the value of h if the following equation describes a line with a slope of 5?
hx – 5y = 18.

When dealing with equations of lines, we always want to get the equations into y = mx + b form, so let's do that first.

5y = hx – 18
y = hx / 5 – 18 / 5

Since the slope equals 5 and for any equation in y = mx + b form, m is the slope, then h/5 is m in the equation above and it must equal 5:
h / 5 = 5
h = 25

17. k = –6

What's the value of k if the following equation describes a line with a slope of 2?

kx + 3y = 9
3y = 9 – kx
y = 3 + –kx / 3
thus m = –k / 3 and we're told the slope is 2 so we get:
–k / 3 = 2
k = –6
k = –6

Math Section: Circles Problem Set

1. C = 14π   A = 49π

A circle with a radius of 7.

C = 2 π r   A = π r²
C = 2π × 7   A = π(7)²
C = 14π   A = 49π

2. C = 10π   A = 25π

A circle with a diameter of 10.

C = 2 π r   A = π r²
C = 2π × 5   A = π (5)²
C = 10π   A = 25π

3. C = 80   A = 162.3 π

A circle whose 45° arc has a length of 10.

If a 45° arc has a length of 10 then the 360° circle will have a circumference or length of 80 (since 45° represents 1/8th of the distance around the circle).

C = 2πr = 80
r = 80/2π = 12.74
A = π r² = π (12.74)² = 162.3 π

4. C = 12π   A = 36π

A circle whose 60° arc has an area of 6π.

A 60° arc represents 1/6th of the circle, so the area of the whole circle will be 36π.

A = π r²
36π = π r²
r² = 36
r = 6

C = 2πr = 2π × 6 = 12π

Math Section: Spheres and Cylinders Problem Set

1.   4/3 π r³ = 4/3 π 5³ = 4/3 π 125 = 500π / 3 = **500π/3**
2.   π r² h = **8π**
3.   **h = 6**

96 π = π r² h
 = π 4² h
 = π 16 h
h = 96 / 16 = 6

4.   **r = 3**

4/3 π r³ = 36π
4/3 r³ = 36
r³ = 27

Math Section: Triangles Problem Set

1. **Base 1 = 15 Base 2 = 20 Hypotenuse = 25**

2. **Base 1 = 21** Base 2 = 28 **Hypotenuse = 35**

3. **Base 1 = 33 Base 2 = 44** Hypotenuse = 55

4. Base 1 = 42   **Base 2 = 56   Hypotenuse = 70**

5. x = 30°
y = 10
z = 5√3

6. x = 60°
y = 7.5
z = 7.5√3

7. x = 60°
10 = y√3
y = 10/√3
y = 10√3 / 3
z = 20√3 / 3

8. x = 12

9. y = 8

10. 17

$8^2 + 15^2 = 17^2$

11. 24

$7^2 + 24^2 = 25^2$
$49 + 576 = 625$

Tip: to do mental math like 24^2 in your head, break the problem down into simpler multiplication problems and add the products
e.g. 24^2 = (20 * 24) + (4 * 24) = (20 * 24) + (4 * 20) + (4 * 4) = 480 + 80 + 16

12. 20

$20^2 + 21^2 = 29^2$

Math Section: Polygons Problem Set

1. Sum of interior angles = 1620°

Using our formula:
Sum of interior angles = (n − 2) (180°)
Sum of interior angles = (11 − 2) (180°)
Sum of interior angles = (9) (180°)

2. Sum of interior angles = 3 triangles × 180°/triangle = 540°

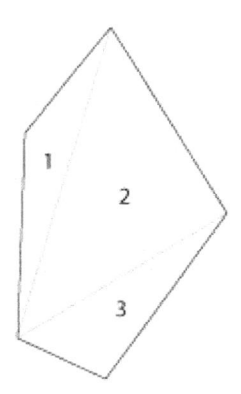

3. approximately **128.6°** or **900°/7**

Sum of interior angles = (n − 2) (180°)
Sum of interior angles = (7 − 2) (180°)
Sum of interior angles = (5) (180°)
Sum of interior angles = 900°

A regular heptagon has interior angles which are all equal.

Each interior angle in a regular heptagon = 900° / 7

4. Sum of interior angles = 5 triangles × 180°/triangle = 900°

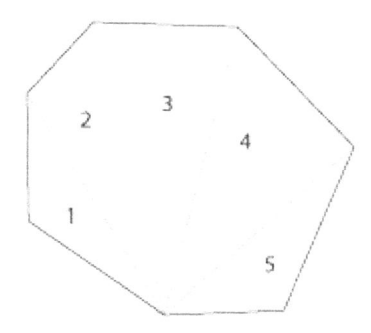

5. 140°

Sum of interior angles = (n − 2) (180°)
Sum of interior angles = (9 − 2) (180°)
Sum of interior angles = (7) (180°)
Sum of interior angles = 1260°

Each interior angle in a regular nonagon = 1260° / 9

Math Section: Measurement Problem Set

We hope you used our measurement technique to solve these problems!

1. (E) 81
This arc is a little tricky to measure using a pencil! Divide 3 pi in half and just measure half the arc (and so convert the tick marks that represent half the arc are equal to 3/2 pi units in the diagram). Then measure the height and base of triangle BAC in tick marks, convert them into units and then calculate the area of the triangle (remember the formula for the area of a triangle is 1/2 base times height).

Solving the problem using Geometry:
First we have to convert arc length into circumference (360 = 30 × 12) so circumference is 3pi × 12 = 36pi. Then from our formula for the circumference of a circle (C = 2pi r), we can calculate the radius to be 18. We know now side BC has a length of 18. Key Point to Remember: *every line segment from the center of a circle to a point on the circle is a radius* so line segment BA also has a length of 18. We know a side in a 30:60:90 triangle so we can solve for the remaining two sides including the height of triangle of BAC which has to be 9. The area of the triangle is 1/2 base times height or ½ times 18 times 9 or 81.

This doesn't help us solve this problem...but this may be critical in solving other problems so remember it: *the angles opposite two equal sides in a triangle are also equal.* Thus if AB and AC are both 18, then angles BAC and ACB have to be equal as well. Since the third angle in the triangle is 30 and those two angles are equal, then BAC and ACB have to each have a measure of 75 degrees.

2. (C) r √3

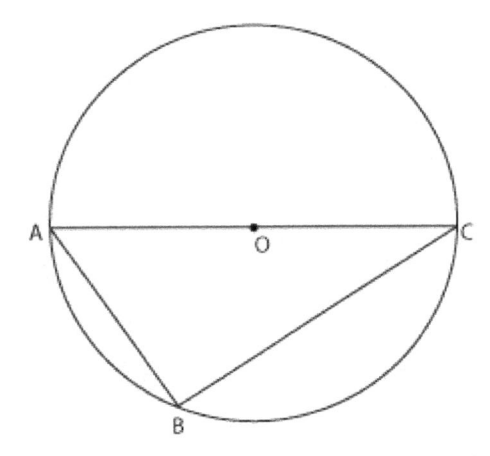

To solve geometrically, notice that OA is also of length r and that you can draw a line segment OB which is also of length r. Thus, you can draw an equilateral triangle

OAB and you should fill in its angles as each 60°. We can fill in the measure of angle AOB as 60° and from that its supplement angle BOC must be 120°. Since OB and OC are equal, then the angles opposite them are also equal and measure 30° each. We know now that triangle ACB has angle BAC equal to 60°, angle ACB equal to 30°, and angle ABC equal to (60° + 30°) 90°. Since side AC equals 2r and is opposite the 90° angle in triangle ABC, then side BC opposite the 60° angle is equal to r√3.

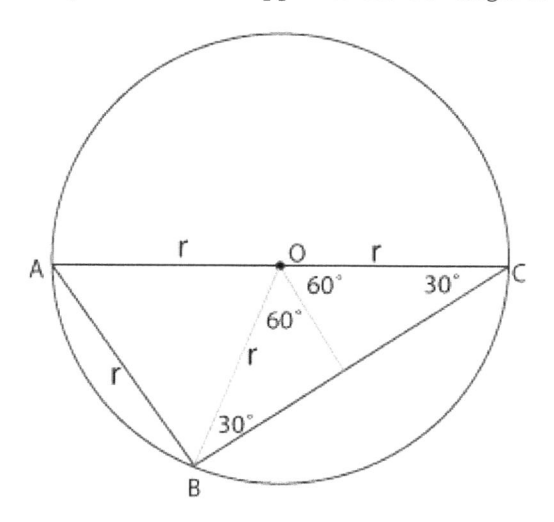

Alternate geometric solution: if you notice that AC is equal to 2r, that AB is equal to r, and that angle ABC equals 90° because it's inscribed by a 180° arc...then you can immediately realize that ABC is a 30:60:90 triangle and thereby solve for BC.

3. **(B)** 108 – 27π

To solve geometrically, notice that triangle ABC is a 30:60:90 triangle. Thus, AC equals 6 and BC equals 6√3. The area of the square is then 108 and the area of the circle 27π, and the area of the shaded area their difference.

Math Section: Geometry Problem Set

1. 110°

First fill in angle g with 110°. Then mark j's vertical angle; let's call that k. Angles f and k then sum to equal g since g and the angle resulting from f and k are opposite interior angles.

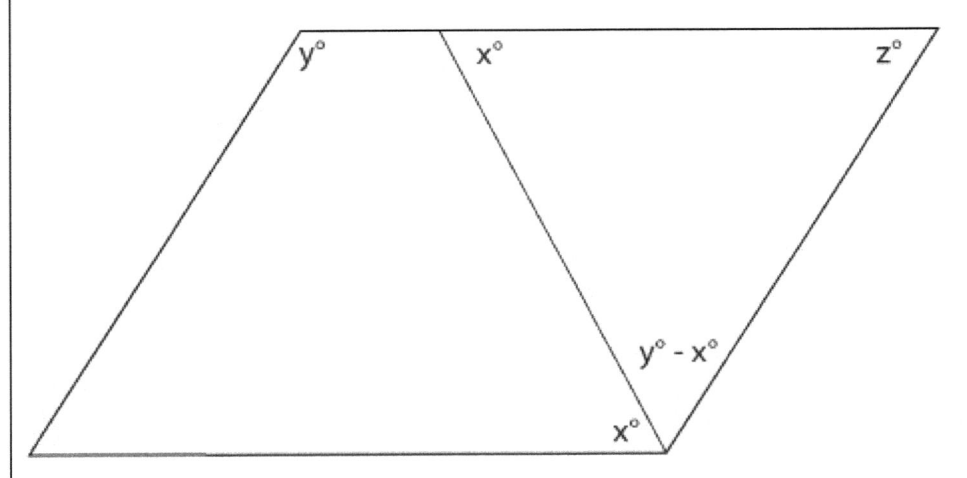

2. (A) 180° − y

We can fill in x at the top since it's an opposite interior angle. We can fill in y − x since we know that that full angle in the parallelogram is equal to y. From the triangle, we know 180 − x − (y − x) = z. A simpler way to solve the problem is that since it's a parallelogram, z and y are supplements…so z is equal to 180 minus y.

3. 1440°

What's the sum of the exterior angles (marked in the diagram via circles) of the polygon below?

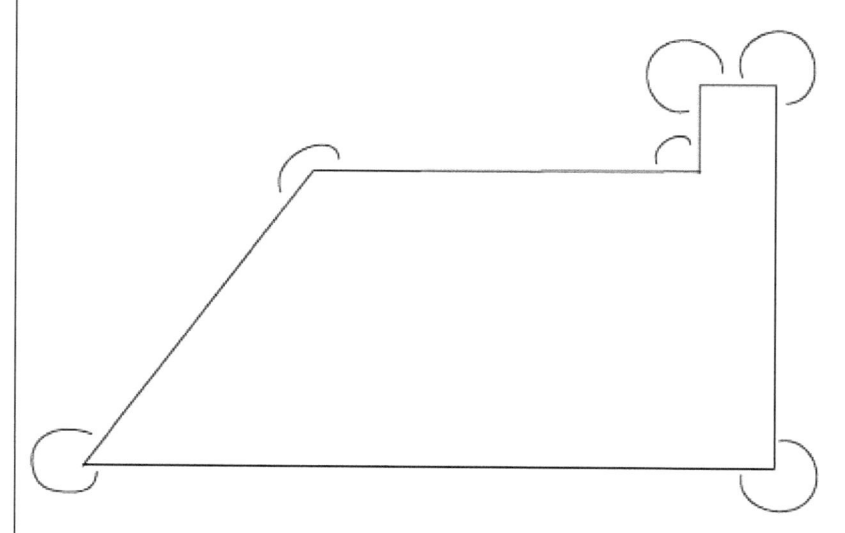

The sum of the exterior angles of any n-sided polygon will be equal to 360° × n minus the sum of its interior angles…since each exterior angle is equal to 360° minus that vertex's interior angle.

(360° × 6) − (n − 2)(180°)
(2160°) − (6 − 2)(180°)
(2160°) − (4 × 180°)
(2160°) − (720°)
1440°

To calculate the sum of the interior angles, you could also alternatively have drawn in (four) triangles.

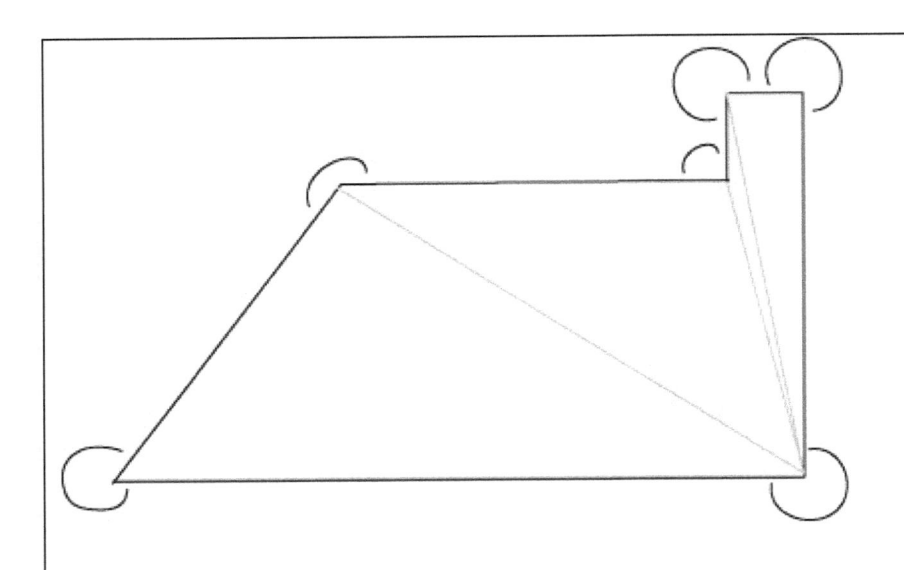

4. 10 to 10√3 / 3

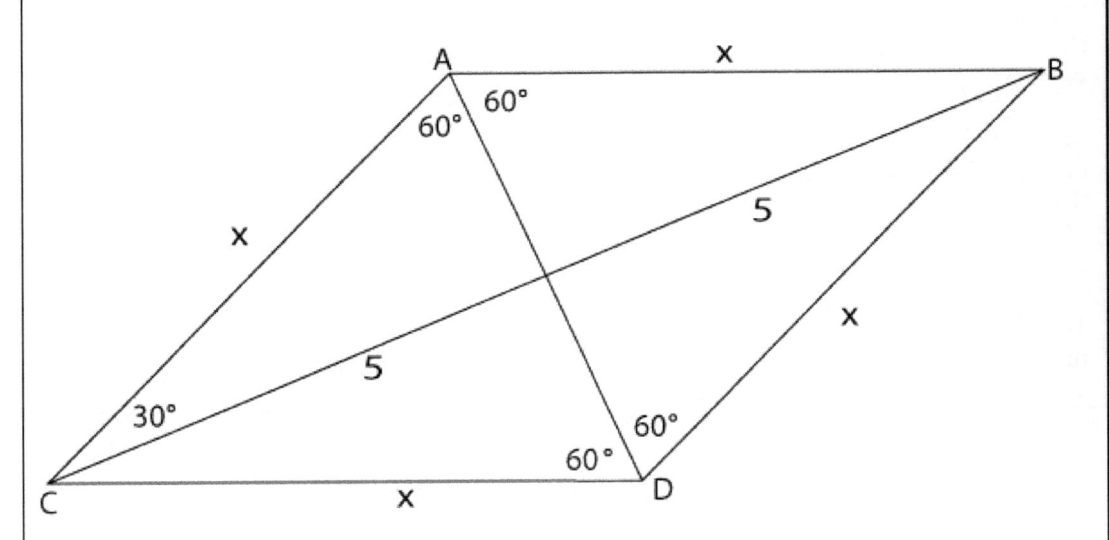

A Rhombus has four sides of the same length. We can label each side in the rhombus x—the same variable since all four sides have to be of equal length. Drawing in the diagonals, we get two isosceles triangles and can break them up further into four 30–60–90 triangles. From the 30:60:90 triangle, we know that x/2 × √3 = 5. Solving for x, we get 10 / √3.

Note we could have used measurement for this problem as well.

5. (D) 8.

Try to draw a square inscribed in the circle (4 points of intersection), not inscribed but inside the circle (no points of intersection), and then not inscribed but mostly inside the circle (8 points of intersection), and a square that has the circle inscribed in it (4 points of intersection). Try to exhaust all possibilities when solving a problem of this type e.g. the circle could be inscribed in the square (smaller circle, larger square), it could inscribe the square (larger circle, smaller square), or it could be neither but sort of over-lapping a similarly sized square (similarly sized circle and square—this diagram gives us the correct answer).

Writing Section: Grammar Review Problem Set Answers

1. I was going up the hill quick.

Adjective/Adverb Error. "Quick" describes how I was going up the hill so it modifies "going" which is a verb and requires an adverb or quickly.

2. James is the most hardworking of the twins.

Improper Comparison. Most is used for three or more people or things (so more is needed).

3. Juanita is the more well–read in her class.

Improper Comparison. More is used for only two people or things (so most is needed).

4. The boat collapsing in the harbor.

Sentence Fragment. There's no verb in the sentence.

5. The corporation in the islands have several worthless assets on the books.

Subject–Verb Agreement/Singular Nouns. Corporation is a singular noun and thus requires a singular verb (has instead of have).

6. We are going to be at the roof.

Preposition Idiom. We say on the roof not at the roof.

7. He went to the store then he needed milk.

Conjunction. "Then" should be because.

8. I had only one thought in my mind; run away.

Colon Usage. A semicolon is used to separate two independent clauses, but a colon is used to provide emphasis to a phrase or to introduce a list. In this case, a colon should be used instead of the semicolon to emphasize "run away."

9. I had gone to the store when I was remembering that I left the door open.

Verb Tense. "Was remembering" doesn't work with "had gone", we need "remembered."

10. The principal of excepting an award is to pretend to be incredible when receiving the award is immanent.

Wrong Words. We meant to use or at least should have used principle, accepting, incredulous, and imminent! The sentence should read: the principle of accepting an award is to pretend to be incredulous when receiving the award is imminent.

11. I gave the librarian the books I was returning: I took the books I had just checked out.

Separating Two Independent Clauses. We need a semicolon (or a comma and a conjunction or a period) to separate two independent clauses.

12. With the hammering of the final nail, the table was fixed by Lu Bingfeng.

Misplaced Modifier. Lu Bingfeng did the hammering not the table thus the sentence should read with the hammering of the final nail, Lu Bingfeng fixed the table.

13. Fred told James that he got the sale.

Pronoun Ambiguity. We don't know if it was Fred or James who got the sale and to whom he refers to.

14. The postcards on the table, are going to be mailed tomorrow.

Comma Usage. A comma should not separate a verb from its subject. To correct this sentence, the best option is to remove the comma, though if the fact of the postcards being "on the table" is sufficiently unnecessary to the meaning of the sentence then the whole prepositional phrase could be set off in commas ", on the table."

15. Between you and I, this is fantastic news but we have to be hush-hush about it.

Pronoun Case. "You and I" is the object of the preposition between so both pronouns must be in the objective case; I is in the subjective case and thus incorrect, it needs to be me.

16. If Jill and Bill in this heat is going to take a hot shower, then he's crazy.

Subject–Verb Agreement. *Jill and Bill is plural but "is" is singular and needs to be replaced with "are"; crossing out the prepositional phrase "in this heat" makes this error clear.*

Noun–Noun Agreement. *Jill and Bill is plural third–person, but in the next phrase "he's" is in the singular third person, "he's" needs to be changed to "they're."*

17. Don't even think about smoking, drinking or take drugs.

Parallelism. *"Take drugs" is not in a parallel form with smoking and drinking, it should be changed to "taking drugs."*

18. Between the hurricane or the blizzards, there was nowhere safe to go for vacation.

Correlative Conjunction. *"Between" requires "and."*

19. It's not that I don't appreciate Marino's passes, it's just that I prefer Elway.

Proper Comparison. *We can only compare apples to apples. In this case, "Marino's passes" are being compared to "Elway" which is an improper comparison. We should change "Elway to "Elway's passes."*

20. You haven't got hardly any time left.

Double Negative. *"Haven't" is already negative so "hardly" should be cut out.*

Writing Section: Sentence Correction Problem Set Answers

1. <u>Watching films</u>, eating good food, <u>listening</u> to great songs, and <u>make</u>
       A   B   C
   jokes were the four precepts of his guide <u>to</u> good living. <u>No Error</u>
                                                                             D   E

(C). Parallelism. We need to change 'make' to "making" to preserve the parallelism of the sentence ('watching', 'eating', and 'listening').

2. To master the dance step, I have <u>practiced</u> <u>on</u> an approach
                                                    A   B
   <u>to keeping</u> my hand steady while my head <u>moves</u>. <u>No error</u>
       C   D   E

(B). Prepositional Idiom (Preposition Error). This isn't quite a prepositional idiom error but rather a case of a superfluous preposition. It's not the case that we should use another preposition instead of 'on;, but rather that we don't need 'on' at all.

3. Sloths <u>had to have</u> <u>had</u> multiple adaptations over millions of years
               A   B
   because <u>it survives</u> primarily on leaves which are a poor source
               C
   <u>of energy and nutrition</u>. <u>No error</u>
          D   E

(C) Noun–Pronoun Agreement. 'It survives' refers to 'sloths' which is plural thus it needs to be changed to "they survive."

4. I <u>had told</u> you both not <u>to go outside</u>, but <u>between you and she</u>, the
      A   B   C
   orders <u>weren't followed</u>. <u>No error</u>
              D   E

(C). Pronoun Case. The error is in the prepositional phrase 'between you and she.' Since 'you and she' is the object of the phrase, it must be in the object or objective case...she is in the subjective case and must be changed to "her."

5. If we <u>could</u> flap our arms and fly <u>at</u> the speed of falcons, the average
           A   B
   person <u>won't</u> need to use a car <u>very often</u>. <u>No error</u>
              C   D   E

(C). Verb Tense. We need the conditional tense here—since we began with 'if...could', the next phrase needs a verb similarly in the conditional tense, in this case "wouldn't."

6. <u>Between</u> <u>you and me</u>, I have always <u>found</u> Salesman the <u>more</u>
          A   B   C   D
   compelling film of the two. <u>No error</u>
                                      E

(E). No error. 'Between' is the appropriate preposition, and 'more' is also the appropriate term for a comparison between two things.

7. The island <u>manufactures</u> large blocks of feta cheese which <u>is</u> usually
                    A   B
   <u>exported to</u> Greece <u>for consumption there</u>. <u>No error</u>
          C   D   E

523

(B). Subject–Verb Agreement. Crossing out the prepositional phrase 'of feta cheese' simplifies the sentence to 'large blocks...which is' which should sound wrong to your ears. Blocks is plural and needs the plural verb "are."

8. In contrast <u>to Kafka</u>, Mann's prose <u>is</u> <u>neither</u> sparse <u>nor</u> short.
                A   B   C   D

   <u>No error</u>
     E

(A). Proper Comparison. We can only compare apples and apples, authors and authors or prose and prose, but not an author and prose...thus we can't compare 'Kafka' to 'Mann's prose' and need to change 'to Kafka' to "to Kafka's prose" or "to Kafka's writing."

9. When Charley, late at night <u>searching</u> for detritus to make art,
                                     A
   <u>removes</u> posters from walls, onlookers would <u>inquire</u> as to his
     B   C
   authority to <u>take them</u>. <u>No error</u>
                    D   E

(B). Verb Tense. The verbs 'removes' and 'would inquire' are inconsistent—we need to change 'removes' to the past tense or change 'would inquire' to the present tense. We can only change 'inquire' but not 'would' since only 'inquire' is underlined, so we have to change 'removes' to "removed."

10. The recognition <u>awarded to</u> popular music groups <u>have boosted</u> the
                         A   B
    <u>interest</u> of people of all ages <u>in music</u>. <u>No error</u>
         C   D   E

(B). Subject–Verb Agreement. If you cross out the modifier 'awarded to popular music groups', then the subject–verb agreement error should be clearly heard. The sentence should read "the recognition…has boosted."

11. <u>After</u> seventeen years <u>of writing</u>, Joyce <u>released</u> his novel
        A   B   C
    Finnegans Wake to an <u>utterly</u> baffled public. <u>No error</u>
                              D   E

(E). No error. The sentence is correct—the introductory modifier 'after seventeen years of writing' modifies Joyce which correctly comes immediately after the modifier. 'After' is the correct preposition, 'released' is the correct verb tense, and 'utterly' is an adverb correctly modifying the adjective 'confused.' The sentence is correct as written.

12. <u>When</u> you <u>don't</u> report a crime, it is <u>as though</u> no crime <u>never</u>
       A   B   C   D
    happened. <u>No error</u>
                    E

(D). Double Negative. Since we already have 'no crime', having another negative 'never' gives us a double negative error. We need to change 'never' to "ever."

Writing Section: Sentence Revision Problem Set Answers

1. Over 50% of all unique plant species are found in the Amazon; <u>only 4% in Madagascar</u>.

    (A) ; only 4% in Madagascar
    (B) in comparison to 4% in Madagascar
    (C) , and compared to Madagascar with only 4%
    (D) , while Madagascar has only 4%
    (E) ; but only 4% are found in Madagascar

(D). Proper Comparison. While we do separate independent clauses with a semicolon as is done in (A), we need an appropriate conjunction to separate them which makes (B), (D), and (E) more appropriate. Since "and" isn't an appropriate conjunction, we can eliminate (C). We only need a comma and conjunction to separate independent clauses (not a semicolon and conjunction) so (E) is incorrect. Between (B) and (D), (B) sounds a bit awkward leaving (D) as the best choice.

2. It is the knights' sacred duty during the arduous and long journey to feed the princess, to protect her, <u>and entertaining her.</u>

    (A) and entertaining her.
    (B) and to entertain her.
    (C) and entertained her.
    (D) and have her entertained.
    (E) and to have her entertained.

(B). Parallelism. Verbs in parallel (subject followed by 'to feed', 'to protect'...) need to be in the same tense and form...so we need "to entertain."

3. The Cardinal insisted that Alexander VI should be deposed on the ground that he had paid for the papacy, whereas spiritual office obtained in that way was ipso facto void.

   (A) , whereas
   (B) even if
   (C) , for
   (D) , any
   (E) , and any

(A). Correlative Conjunction. The conjunction that has an appropriate meaning—that because the papacy had been paid for therefore the office is void—is whereas. Using a conjunction such as 'and' doesn't imply that the latter claim (the voiding of the papacy) is because of the first claim (that the papacy had been paid for).

4. The former police officer spent fourteen years working from a small office in the basement of his home searching tirelessly and thoroughly for his eldest daughter whom he believed kidnapped.

   (A) kidnapped
   (B) has been kidnapped
   (C) had been kidnapped
   (D) was being kidnapped
   (E) as kidnapped

(C). Verb Tense. This sentence has a lot of verbiage which we hope you crossed out as you answered it to get to the 'core meaning' of the sentence. The correct verb tense needs to be in the past perfect tense ("had been kidnapped) since presumably her kidnapping happened before his search began. If you cross out multiple prepositional phrases then you can hear how (C) is correct: The former police officer spent fourteen years ~~working from a small office in the basement of his~~

~~home~~ searching ~~tirelessly and thoroughly~~ for his ~~eldest~~ daughter whom he believed <u>had been kidnapped</u>.

5. <u>Kids were allowed</u> to wait in line, they were not allowed to ride the adult rides.

    (A) Kids were allowed
    (B) Though kids were allowed
    (C) They allow kids
    (D) Allowing kids
    (E) For allowing kids

(B). Forming a Dependent Clause/Correlative Conjunction. The two clauses are separated by a comma so the first clause about the kids in line has to be a dependent clause (because we can not separate independent clauses with only a comma). We can thus eliminate (A) and (C) which would result in independent clauses. From what's remaining, (B) sounds the best and has the correct correlative conjunction "though."

6. The enumeration of such procedures is out of place in the encyclopedia <u>and belongs rather to</u> a medical treatise.

    (A) and belongs rather to
    (B) and rather for
    (C) rather than
    (D) and instead belongs in
    (E) instead belonging to

(D). Prepositional Idiom and Transition. While we need a term such as "rather" or "instead" to give the proper sense to the sentence, the use of "rather" in (C) conveys the opposite of the intended meaning.

The remaining choices are all awkward with the exception of (D) which also uses the correct preposition "in."

7. Their actions have motives far more complex <u>if</u> we are inclined to suppose.

    (A) if
    (B) because
    (C) for
    (D) around which
    (E) than

(E). Correct Correlative Conjunction. We need a correlative conjunction which expresses the logic of the sentence appropriately, and for this question it's "than."

8. Afraid of being mobbed by her admirers, <u>a disguise was worn by the famous chanteuse</u> to attend the rock concert.

    (A) a disguise was worn by the famous chanteuse
    (B) in disguise the famous chanteuse was
    (C) wearing a disguise was the famous chanteuse
    (D) the famous chanteuse wore a disguise
    (E) the famous chanteuse disguised

(D). Misplaced Modifier. The introductory phrase "afraid of being mobbed by her admirers" modifies the chanteuse so 'the chanteuse' needs to come right after that modifier which it does in choices (D) and (E). Of those two, (D) is the correct one.

9. On a cool Sunday morning, we discovered that there were daisies to be found <u>with</u> the meadow.

    (A) with
    (B) into
    (C) for
    (D) throughout
    (E) from

(D). Prepositional Idiom. We would say that there are flowers 'throughout' the meadow rather than use any of the other prepositions.

10. The two books belonged to both Janet and Rene, but <u>they were not</u> found.

    (A) they were not
    (B) they had been
    (C) they are being
    (D) Janet and Rene were not to be
    (E) Janet and Rene are

(D). Pronoun Antecedent Ambiguity. We have to re–state "Janet and Rene" explicitly since it's otherwise ambiguous whether "they" refers to them or the two books.

Writing Section: Paragraph Revision Problem Set Answers

(1) Susan B. Anthony, the famous women's rights activist, was a precocious child. (2) As a child learned to read and write at age three. (3) In 1826, when she was six years old, the Anthony family moved from Massachusetts to Battenville, New York. (4) Susan was sent to attend a local district school, where a teacher refused to teach her long division because of her gender. (5) Under her father's tutelage, though, she would learn long division and much more. (6) Upon learning of the weak education she was receiving at the local school, her father promptly removed her. (7) He moved her to a group home school where he taught Susan himself.

(8) Susan's first job was as a teacher at Eunice Kenyon's Friends' Seminary in New Rochelle, and then at the Canajoharie Academy in 1846, where she rose to become headmistress of the Female Department. (9) Her family at one point was in financial ruin. (10) At the Seminary, she earned as did all other woman roughly one fourth what men earned for the same work. (11) The disparity in wages inspired her first brush with women's rights: advocating wage equivalence for women and men performing the same duties at the Seminary.

1. What must be done to sentence 2?

   (A) begin it with the words "It was"
   (B) replace "As a child" with "who" and then combine it with sentence 1
   (C) add "even before" to the end of the sentence and combine it with sentence 3
   (D) change "learned" to "taught herself"
   (E) add a comma to the end of the phrase "As a child"

(B). Sentence 2 as written is a fragment since there's no subject in the sentence. The best revision for the sentence is to combine it with sentence 1 which already mentions that she "was a precocious child." Adding the additional details that Susan "learned to read and write at age three" explains how she was precocious.

2. Which sentence should be deleted?

   (A) 1
   (B) 6
   (C) 8
   (D) 9
   (E) 11

(D). Sentence 9 is chronologically out of place and not relevant to either story of her childhood education nor her teaching experience...and so should be deleted.

3. The primary purpose of the second paragraph in the passage on Susan B. Anthony is to

   (A) provide background information about her
   (B) present a theory about her childhood
   (C) tell a story relevant to how she became an activist
   (D) describe her character in detail
   (E) explain her later career

(C). The paragraph does provide background information about her, but that's not its primary purpose. No theory is presented in the paragraph nor is her character described in detail. While the story tells us her first encounter with activism for women's rights, it doesn't explain why or how she made a career out of promoting women's rights and what other women's rights she struggled for making choice (E) is too strong a claim. The paragraph basically tells the story of her first teaching job which was her first experience with discrimination against women—an experience presumably of some importance to her later, extensive work for women's rights.

4. What should be done with sentence 5?

- (A) delete "and much more"
- (B) delete ", though,"
- (C) combine it with sentence 4 by deleting ", though," and changing "gender. Under her" to "gender, but under her"
- (D) place it after sentence 3
- (E) place it after sentence 7

(E). Sentence 5 is related to sentence 7. It's at the group home school where Susan comes under her father's tutelage and learns long division and more. Sentence 5 should logically come immediately after sentence 7.

APPENDIX 2: Outline of the Master Class Methods for Easy Reference

Overall Guidelines

I. Bubble in groups with a dull pencil—bubble 5 or 10 answers at a time. You're less prone to making bubbling mistakes and will also save a bit of time. Having a dull point on your pencil makes filling the circles faster.

II. Eliminate and Guess. For any section, if you eliminate even one answer, you MUST guess.

III. When Stuck, Move On. If you're stuck on a problem, come back to it later...often, when you come back to a question later, the answer will become clearer to you. Time is absolutely crucial, and you don't have time to agonize over any problem. Circle the numbers of questions you're stuck on or unsure of and come back to them when you're done the rest of the questions.

IV. Work on paper...try to move your thoughts to paper, that allows your brain to move on. Also, the more detail/information you have for a question written down and thus preserved in your work, the less time you waste in re–thinking a problem you come back to.

V. Provisions—take many, at least four pencils (two to do your work with, one dull pencil to bubble with, one marked pencil to use as a ruler), a silent watch, silent candies to eat quietly during the test, juice, and snacks for the break. For the pencil to use as a ruler, accurately make 1mm tick marks on one pencil tip to use just as a ruler for geometry problems.

VI. Sign up for tests as well in advance as possible—slots fill quickly at convenient locations and the usual, minimum advance notice to sign–up is six weeks.

Math

I. Overview
   A. Three Key Problem–Solving Methods (there are usually at least 2 ways to solve every math problem on the test)
      1. Plugging In Numbers—whenever you see variables, you can (almost always) plug in numbers (particularly when variables are in the answer choices)
      2. Work Backwards from the answer choices—in other words, plug in the answer choices. Always start with the middle choice so that you have to try a maximum of three choices.
      3. Measurement—for geometry problems, instead of calculating the answer using the geometry, you can for some problems measure the answer using a tick marked pencil.
   B. Checking Reasonable–ness/Double–Checking Work (ideally with Different Methods)
   C. Work on Paper—never meditate on a problem. Solve math problems by working them out on paper...write down the givens, then your ideas, then try to write equations.
   D. Guessing Strategy—if you can't solve the problem, try to eliminate answers, if you eliminate any answers, you must guess. If you get an answer for a grid–in problem grid it in even if you're uncertain because you don't lose any points for incorrectly answered grid–in problems.
   E. Re–read the Question (before you circle it). What are you being asked for? Every question is worth a single point so invest a few seconds double–checking/triple–checking every easy and medium question to make sure you've got them.
   F. Easy, Medium, Hard Questions—the math sections are ordered such that the easiest questions are first then the medium ones then the hard ones. Use this to your advantage. If an easy question seems easy, that's fine because it's supposed to be easy. If the last question in the section seems really easy, that should raise a red flag—it's not supposed to be easy.

G. Under 600 Scorers Should Skip Hard Questions—if you're scoring below 600, focus your time on the easy and medium questions and getting all of them, so omit roughly the last third of the problems in the math section—at least until you're certain you've gotten all of the first two–thirds of questions correct.
H. Calculator—for computationally intensive problems, don't be afraid to use your calculator to check things. Round to nearest thousandth.
I. Practice, practice...there are twenty or so types of problems that are tested, the more you practice them, the more adept you'll be at solving them.

II. Algebra
   A. Plugging in Numbers for Variables...is a key technique. You must practice it. 3 steps: 1. Pick my numbers. 2. Plug into problem/solve problem in terms of my picked numbers. 3. Solve answer choices in terms of my picked numbers
   B. Working Backwards from Answers...is a key technique. You must practice it.
   C. Top scorers will solve algebra problems algebraically and then double–check them by working backwards or using substitution.
   D. Method, work in steps: write down givens, unknowns; define variables, try to define variables in terms of other variables if there are more then 2 (or 3 variables); write down equations. Need as many equations as variables. For hard algebra problems, you're going to have to use this method because there are too many steps to "see" the solution all at once.
   E. Factoring Quadratic Equations/Multiplying Polynomial Expressions (FOIL) [$x^2-y^2=(x-y)(x+y)$]. Middle term is a sum, the 3rd term a product.
   F. Translating English into Equations
   G. Manipulating Inequalities—sign flips if divide/multiply by a negative number, graphing filled or dotted line depending on

greater than/less than and equal to or just greater than/less than
- H. Rate, Mixture and Other Types of Applied Algebra Problems: keep units as a double-check; conversion fractions—units of desired answer indicate how to set up fractions; use a table for these problems
- I. Solving Systems of Equations using substitution or preferably adding/subtracting equations
- J. Functions—inverse functions, functions of functions, linear functions, the graph of functions and how it can be altered, vertical-line test.
- K. Two Fractions in an Equation—think cross-multiply
- L. Absolute Value Equations—turn into two equations (negative/positive answer).
- M. Degree of equation—the number of possible solutions to the equation and the number of points of interception on x-axis.
- N. Terms to know: coefficient. variable. absolute value. inequality. equation. polynomial. function. variable. constant. degree of an equation.

IV. Geometry
- A. Work from the diagram—fundamental technique—if the diagram is too small or clearly not at all drawn to scale, redraw it. Put in as much information as you can no matter whether you think it's useful or not: keep putting in information, try solving for angles, sides, write down any and all equations that apply to the shapes, et cetera...and gradually the insight necessary to solve the problem will come to you.
- B. Measure—use your marked pencil as a ruler and a makeshift protractor to make measurements of lengths and angles, often this can get you the answer precisely, and usually it can help you narrow it down to two choices.
- C. Coordinate Geometry—graphing points, the four quadrants, alternate interior/exterior/vertical angles, complementary/supplementary angles.

D. Equation of a line—slope, y–intercept, other forms of linear equations besides point–slope form; definition of m or slope; graphing linear equations.
E. Parallel/Perpendicular Lines—slopes are negative reciprocals
F. Triangles
   1. Pythagorean Theorem ($a^2 + b^2 = h^2$)
   2. Sum of Angles of a Triangle/Exterior Angle Relationships
   3. Special Triangles—3–4–5; 30–60–90; 45–45–90
G. Circles—definition, degrees, area, circumference, volume of a sphere, diameter, definition of the radius (a line segment from center of circle to a point on the circle; remember all radii have the same length)
H. Sum of Angles of n–sided Polygons—(180x(n–2)) (equivalent to drawing in triangles)
I. Regular Polygons—polygons whose sides are of equal length and angles are of equal measure

V. Arithmetic
   A. Order of Operations (PEMDAS or P/E/MD/AS)
   B. Radicals/Roots/Powers: exponent rules, fractional exponents, radical form and fractional exponent form
   C. Made–up Operators
   D. Natural, Whole, Integers, Rational, Irrational and other numbers
   E. Prime and Composite Numbers/Elementary Number Theory (Fundamental Theorem of Arithmetic) and Applications/Multiples/Factors
   F. Sequences and Series: arithmetic, geometric and repeating sequences; always write out first few terms of a sequence to find its pattern
   G. Ratios and Inverse and Direct Proportions
   H. Percentage Problems: definition of a percentage, and two ways to think about percentages: percentage pay, percentage off.
   I. Tests—try fractions less than one, negative/positive numbers, large/small numbers.

VI. Probability/Statistics
   A. Basic Combinatorics: Combinations/Permutations. Make a diagram with slots and possibilities; calculate combinations by dividing permutations by slots factorial.
   B. Probability Problems: definition of a probability; and/or statements; with or without replacement.
   C. Statistics—Mean, Median, Mode, Line of best fit, Standard Deviation (meaning of it)
   D. Averages: know the definition of average—be able to write that as an equation to solve problems e.g. what does X need on the fourth test to bring test up.

Critical Reading

I. Overview
    A. Overview: Sentence Completion Problems and Reading Passages
    B. Eliminate, eliminate, eliminate. Our fundamental strategy is to eliminate as much as we can as precisely as we can.
    C. Meaningful marks. Hard cross–out for definitely wrong. Light for maybes. Question marks for answers you don't understand. Checks if seem correct. Cross out only those words/terms that actually make the answer wrong.
    D. Precision. (watch out for rationalizing) Precision is a fundamental technique in reading passage problems—find the answer in which every word/phrase is made meaningful and thus true by the passage. Give words a precise, clear and unimaginative meaning...and when that's done to an answer choice if it is supported by the passage, odds are it's the correct answer (arrive at this answer by eliminating other choices).
    E. Guessing Word Meanings/Using Word Roots: Suffixes and Prefixes
    F. Build your vocabulary through good habits—anytime you encounter a word you don't know, write it down, look it up and start it using it that day and henceforth in your working vocabulary.

II. Sentence Completion Problems
    A. Eliminate! Our techniques are used not so much to find the correct answer, but more so to eliminate wrong answers.
    B. Precise Pencil Marks to preserve your thought e.g. if you eliminate one word of a pair just cross out that one word. Use light and dark marks to indicate relative degree of confidence in elimination.
    C. Two Blank Questions—blank by blank elimination.
    D. Two Blank Questions—is there a synonymous or antonymous or no relationship between blanks (use to eliminate choices as pairs)

E. Filling in Your Own Words. Cover up answer choices to avoid being biased. Fill in the blanks with your own words. Your own words can be a bit clumsy or even a phrase. Read the sentence to yourself carefully to make sure it makes sense. Eliminate words which are far away (in meaning) from your words.
F. Single Blank Questions: Identify+Underline Critical Words that are the Source of Meaning of the Blank, then draw arrows from the blank to the words which give meaning to that blank. This method is useful for tough double blank questions as well.
G. Identifying Positive/Negative Blanks. Identify blanks as requiring a positive or negative or neutral word and eliminate using that datum. Can try to "guess" if a word "sounds" positive or negative, also use etymological tools.
H. Simplify Sentences—if the sentence is a bit bulky, cross out unnecessary modifiers and prepositional phrases.
I. Practice, practice, practice—the first time you try to use these techniques to eliminate answers it may take a long time, but with practice these techniques become second-nature.
J. Leave Unfamiliar Words Alone—do not be in fact afraid to pick answers with words you don't know if the others have been eliminated.
K. Watch out for words that reverse meaning e.g. however, but, not...
L. Hard Double–Blank Questions—answer choices with two really easy words can generally be eliminated

III. Reading Passages
   A. Elimination and Precision: two fundamental techniques. Use the idea of precision to eliminate answers. Think: what can I eliminate, how can I eliminate this?
   B. Skimming versus Reading—if you tend to drift off or get bored, immediately go to the questions.

C. Only the Ideas—you're only expected to get the main ideas from reading a passage, once you've got them, no need to read anymore (also no need to memorize facts)
D. Read fact-based passages relatively quickly—there's no need to memorize facts, just know where they are.
E. Read narrative type passages relative to fact-based passages a bit slower and more carefully.
F. Never re-read a passage—try to get to the questions relatively quickly. Use your pencil to guide your eyes and keep them moving (also the pencil is then right there to underline key words, circle main ideas).
G. Order Strategy. Answer line-number questions first. Save main-idea questions for the end.
H. Underline/Summarize Facts, Opinions, Arguments, Changes in Tone, Critical Words.
I. Meaning In Context/Most Nearly Means—plug the answer choices into the sentence in question and see if any make sense. Circle the phrase or words or sentence in the passage that give meaning to the word in question.
J. Line Number Questions—always read a few lines above and a few lines below the line numbers cited in order to get the context of the lines (and sometimes the correct answer is sitting right there a few lines before or after the line numbers in question)
K. Outside the Scope of the Passage—most common wrong answer.
L. Practice—write the line number in the passage which eliminates/supports each answer choice.
M. Practice—write a small summary of the passage/identify its thesis or theses...if you practice this, by the time the real test rolls around, you will do this automatically.

Writing

I. Overview
  A. A few grammar rules are always tested...these rules must be learned and mastered.
  B. Use your Ear—if it sounds wrong, it probably is wrong. Cross out extraneous parts of the sentence to hear errors more easily.
  C. Shorter is often Better—shorter writing is often better...not always but often.

II. Grammar—the common errors tested.
  A. Subject–Verb–Object Error
  B. Verb Tense
  C. Parallelism (usually verb tenses, could also apply to adjectives)
  D. Noun–Noun Agreement: object–subject or noun–pronoun agreement
  E. Pronoun Ambiguity
  F. Pronoun Case
  G. Prepositional Idiom
  H. Incorrect Word (e.g. principal instead of principle)
  I. Punctuation—how to separate two independent, two dependent or one of each clauses...use of semicolon, comma and a conjunction; use of colon
  J. Sentence Fragment
  K. Misplaced Modifier
  L. Proper Comparison
  M. Redundancy
  N. Double Negative (e.g. not hardly)
  O. Singular nouns (e.g. anyone)
  P. Irregular verbs
  Q. Adjective where an Adverb is necessary or vice versa
  R. Conjunctions—logically correct conjunction (e.g. because for a causal relation between two clauses)

S. Correlative Conjunctions (e.g. either/or; neither/nor; between/and)

III. Sentence Correction
   A. Cross out Modifiers and Prepositional Phrases—if it's not underlined and even if it is and it's the correct idiom and there's a preposition and an object, then cross it out., or if the modifier is unnecessary, cross it out to simplify the sentence..
   B. 20% of the answers should be E. No Error—if you have many more or fewer E's, re–evaluate!
   C. There has to be an error—sounding a little bit funny isn't enough. This is important essentially for the hard questions. For the easy to medium sentence correction problems, if it sounds wrong to you, it's very likely wrong. For the hard problems (the last ones) in particular, make sure it doesn't just sound funny, but that there's an error you can identify OR that it sounds distinctly wrong.
   D. Checklist of potential errors e.g. if a verb is underlined, then there are three possible errors which you should check...
      a. Noun—agreement, with other nouns and with verbs
      b. Verb
         i. tense
         ii. subject agreement
         iii. parallel structure
      c. Preposition—idiom
      d. Adjective or Adverb—correctly used, is it misplaced
      e. Conjunction—logically correct
      f. Pronoun
         i. case—subjective (I, you, he, we) vs. objective (me, you, him, us)
         ii. agreement—should agree in gender and in number with what it's referring to
         iii. ambiguity—are there multiple nouns which the pronoun could be referring to
         iv. person—are the pronouns consistent and in the correct person e.g. in first person, second person, or third person

IV. Sentence/Paragraph Improvement
   A. 20% of the answers are going to be A. correct as written.
   B. Eliminate, eliminate, eliminate.
   C. Use your ear
   D. Eliminate based on differences between answers...e.g. A. and B. may have the exact same words but one may have a comma and the other a semicolon... eliminate one of them based on the necessary punctuation mark.
   E. Read Improved Sentences out loud at first—good way to practice (by the time the test date rolls around, you should be able to hear them in your head).

V. Essay
  A. Does not affect numerical score greatly…make sure though you're scoring at least an 8 (4 from each grader).
  B. A Page and a Half—essay must be at least a page and a half long…if you have trouble writing that long an essay, use larger handwriting…
  C. Make sure your essay answers the question!!!!
  D. First Two Paragraph Perfection—make sure there are no glaring mistakes in the first two paragraphs especially.
  E. Primacy/Recency—in rhetoric, the first and last things you say or write are considered to be what the reader will remember…this reinforces the need to make sure your introduction and conclusion have no glaring errors and are well written.
  F. Avoid Controversy—try not to have a controversial thesis.
  G. Use One or Two "Impressive" Words…not more than two generally. Do not use a word if you're not sure you're using it correctly and appropriately.
  H. Outline—you must spend at least 3 minutes preparing an outline, ideally 5 minutes, then 15 minutes writing the essay and 5 minutes revising.
  I. Three Hallmarks of Writing—Revision, Precision (careful word/phrase choice), and Organization (a clear, logical organization of the essay in which facts/ideas support a main thesis)
  J. CUPED Method for Logical Reasoning/Argument Formation—conclusions, unstated premises, premises, evidence, definitions
  K. 5 paragraph essay—introduction (thesis statement), 2 or 3 main body paragraphs each of which develops one point, short and sweet conclusion
  L. Generic literary and historical examples—try to prepare a list of literary and historical examples you know somewhat well which you can use to support a thesis.
  M. Personal Essays/Examples are Fantastic—if some part of your life that means something to you is involved in the essay, by all means write about it…

N. Practice writing outlines for different topics to get used to the open–ended nature of the topics.
O. Practice writing detail–type sentences.
P. Active voice! (avoid the passive voice)
Q. Introduction—if you're ever stuck or even if you're just short on time, use the background information in the box for the introduction, rewrite the idea(s) from the box in your own words and discuss them slightly to lead up to your thesis (try this strategy for a catchy introduction—present x then argue against x...doesn't this sound correct? The problem is it isn't correct because of Y and Z. ...)
R. Conclusions—don't bring up any new points. You can summarize briefly what you've argued and try to extend the idea slightly with a question but without trying to analyze the issue any further, just point to a direction where the argument could continue. If you can tie your conclusion to your introduction, that's a nice touch. The conclusion can and should be short and sweet.

APPENDIX 3: How to Write an Essay: the PRO+CUPED METHOD

Analytical Writing: the PRO+CUPED Approach

Do you want to learn to write? Do you want to love to write? Try PRO CUPED (pronounced just like Pro Cupid, being for the Roman God of Love). Use PRO, an acronym for Precision Revision and Organization, for your analytical writing process (to become a writing "Pro"), a process which is a form of structured thinking. Use CUPED to structure that thought. Our PRO+CUPED approach is a means of structured thinking that lends itself as a foundation for writing critical or analytical essays.

PRO (Precision Revision Organization) encapsulates the pith of what we teach our writing students: be Precise, have a logical Organization to your argument and essay (via CUPED, another didactic device we've devised), and Revise Revise Revise. Keep these ideas in mind in your critical or analytical writing assignments to produce focused, effective writing. CUPED, which stands for Conclusion(s), Unstated premise(s), Premise(s), Evidence, and Definition(s), is a method of logical reasoning to use to form the argument structure and then the outline of your essays.

O is for Organization

OPR wasn't very catchy so we went with PRO even though Organization then Precision then Revision is the order you should follow in writing an essay. Organization means two things: both the organization of your essay (e.g. the topic of each paragraph) and the logical framework of the argument you're going to make in your essay. The latter is the crux of your essay. Once you've put together your argument, then you can organize an essay around it.

It's absolutely essential to make an outline and think through the logical framework of your analytical essay before you start writing it. One reason is that analytical writing is a form of structured thinking, not free thinking! You need to think through what you want to say, why you want to say it, why you believe it's true, and how to make the argument clear before you begin writing. For really long assignments like a thesis or a dissertation, you'll be overwhelmed if you start writing without a logical structure for your whole work (the conclusions or the overall thesis as well as intermediate conclusions for each chapter and how those fit together) and outlines for each chapter. Having an outline for your essay also breaks down the writing process and makes it manageable. You'll be able to pick up a week old essay and see which points haven't been put to paper and pretty quickly start writing them.

The standard method for organizing an essay is a roman numeral outline. Here each paragraph is represented by a roman numeral (I, II, III, etc.), each point in the paragraph is represented by a capital letter below that numeral (A, B, C, etc.), and every supporting fact or detail is represented by a lower–case arabic numeral below the letter (1, 2, 3, etc.). If you're not familiar with this type of outline, read this (for more help do a search as there are many other websites that teach how to make an outline).

Before you put your outline together, you need to identify your argument and analyze it. In our approach, we recommend our students first set up an argument via CUPED and then use that argument to make the outline for their essay. CUPED is a method not for the writing process in general, but rather for the specific process of making an argument, a logically reasoned framework for your essay. This argument or framework will be (fairly easily) turned into an outline which then (not quite as easily) gets turned into your essay.

Organization: Using CUPED

An argument is comprised of five parts according to CUPED: conclusion(s), premise(s), unstated premises, evidence, and definitions. The conclusion is basically what you want to argue—usually your thesis. Premises, whether stated or unstated, are basically assumptions that you make upon which you build the argument. The premises are the reasons or assumptions that when accepted lead with ineluctable logical force to the conclusion. Evidence is simply evidence (facts, logic, etc.) that support your premises. Definitions are precise definitions of the terms you're using in your premises. (Note: Our method is similar of course to formal elementary logic and Toulmin's logic—we find CUPED an easier to learn and a more powerful framework for generating new thoughts than those others, but if you're interested in delving deeper into logical reasoning, those are good places to start).

The best way to get to know CUPED is by putting together and then breaking apart arguments. Take a simple argument, let's say to argue for a new dam to be built on a river in your city:

Premise 1: My city needs more environmentally-friendly energy.
Premise 2: Dams are a source of environmentally-friendly energy.
Conclusion: My city should build the XYZ dam because it will be a source of environmentally-friendly energy.

The conclusion is in this case an action we hope to implement, building a dam, that's what we're arguing for. We hope you scratched your head a bit after reading the argument as even though there's nothing wrong with it (the conclusion follows from the premises), but it can't be that simple to justify a decision to build a dam? Let's try to see what may be missing. From CUPED, our U or unstated premises are missing. Let's try to add some by brainstorming some considerations that are left out of the argument.

Are there alternative clean power sources? Are there any disadvantages to building a dam?

Aha, those questions instantly inform us that the previous argument assumes that there aren't any adverse effects from building a dam and that there are no other clean power alternatives. Let's guess at an unstated premise to add to the argument (by the way, unstated is a good term when you analyze others' arguments, when you analyze your own argument, it's more like discovering premises you hadn't realized you'd assumed—but to avoid confusion, we'll call all non–initial premises unstated premises). We can combine the two points regarding adverse effects and energy alternatives to dams into a single unstated premise.

Unstated Premise 1: Building a dam has fewer adverse effects than other environmentally–friendly energy sources for the city.

We now have a better argument that leads to a more thorough conclusion—remember, adding a new premise will often force you to change (the wording of at least) your conclusion.

Premise 1: My city needs more environmentally–friendly energy.
Premise 2: Dams are a source of environmentally–friendly energy.
Unstated Premise 1: Building a dam has fewer adverse effects than other environmentally–friendly energy sources for my city.
Conclusion: My city should build the XYZ dam because it will be a source of environmentally–friendly energy and has fewer adverse effects than alternatives.

We have a reasonable, basic argument now with premises, unstated premises, and a conclusion. Let's add some definitions and evidence.

Premise 1: My city needs more environmentally–friendly energy.
    Evidence 1: The city's population is growing by 5% a year, but at peak hours the energy usage is 98% of capacity.
    Evidence 2: There is a lot of pollution in the city.
Premise 2: Dams are a source of environmentally–friendly energy.
    Definition 1: Environmentally–friendly means it doesn't promote global warming.

Evidence 1: Dams don't generate any greenhouse gases.
Unstated Premise 1: Building a dam has fewer adverse effects than other environmentally–friendly energy sources for my city.
Evidence 1: Coal and Gas plants generate greenhouse gases.
Evidence 2: Nuclear power plants generate radioactive materials.
Conclusion: My city should build the XYZ dam because it will be a source of environmentally–friendly energy and has fewer adverse effects than alternatives.

If you've imbibed reasoning with premises and conclusions, we hope that you're filling in many gaps in the above argument. For instance, there is a gap in Premise 2's evidence: we need to add a new premise that "greenhouse gases promote global warming." The easiest way to effectively do this is to alter the definition to add "doesn't create greenhouse gases which promote global warming." You could alternatively add another premise to the argument (but it's not that important to the whole argument) or you could embed a premise inside the second premise say (but that gets confusing)—try to keep the argument as precise as possible but also with as clear a structure as possible.

Leaving aside the gaps, the above argument is reasonably developed, and you probably see that what we've now got is basically a Roman Numeral Outline. Let's change a few words around to turn it into an outline for an essay.

I. Introduction
Thesis: My city should build the XYZ dam because it will be a source of environmentally–friendly energy and has fewer adverse effects than alternatives.
II. My city needs more environmentally–friendly energy.
    A. *The city's population is growing by 5% a year, but at peak hours energy usage is 98% of capacity.*
    B. *There is a lot of pollution in the city.*
III. Dams are a source of environmentally–friendly energy.
    A. *Environmentally–friendly means it doesn't promote global warming.*

    B. Dams don't generate any greenhouse gases
IV. Building a dam has fewer adverse effects than other environmentally–friendly energy sources for my city.
    A. Coal and Gas plants generate greenhouse gases.
    B. Nuclear power plants generate radioactive materials.
V. Conclusion

You're now just about ready to write your essay. There are a few little things we ought to correct, though, Generally when you have an A., you should have a B.—so we should try to add some more evidence to paragraph II. (we'll let it slide for now). The other things missing are some ideas for an introduction and conclusion. Other than those points, you've got a pretty good blueprint for your essay in the above outline. You could start writing it now.

To illustrate how thinking in terms of premises and conclusions and CUPED is very powerful and important, let's look at the argument again. What important terms are inadequately defined, for instance? How about environmentally–friendly? Doesn't that encompass more than just global warming? What about protecting rivers and wildlife? That itself, though, begs the question, based on what premise (i.e. why?) should we protect wildlife and the environment? Let's look deeper into other effects from energy generation. We've considered adverse effects, but could there be other positive effects from other types of energy such as coal or nuclear (perhaps they're cheaper)? We're missing, thus, premise(s) that deal with potential beneficial effects of various energy sources.

When you begin thinking carefully through your premises, conclusions, definitions and evidence, things can get complex. Writing critical essays, making good arguments, and logical reasoning are not easy tasks, but they're essential in order to write a well–argued essays.

There are two things to take away from what we've done. One is that putting together an argument via CUPED is a form of structured thinking. We saw how we started with a very simple argument and through asking questions motivated by CUPED's argument structure, we ended up adding more premises leading to a more sophisticated and more accurate argument by the end of the process. Two is that the final form of our argument (of premises, evidence, definitions, conclusion) got turned into an outline pretty easily (which then needs to be turned into an essay).

P is for Precision

Thanks to the organization phase, we've got an outline for our essay. Now for the precision phase. Precision is an easier concept to explain than organization. More persuasive essays will generally be more precise. They can be more precise in three ways. They can have very precise evidence (facts, figures, etc.) supporting their premises. They can have a precise argument (precise premises and definitions). They can have precise details.

Making your argument more precise is essentially part of the organization phase of writing. It's important, though, in this phase to re–think your argument and see if it could be made more precise. In the example from above, we discovered that our premises and definitions could be made more precise. Environmentally–friendly wasn't very precisely defined. There were still some missing, unstated premises regarding the possible advantages of various types of power generation. There were also some so–called premises which weren't integrated into the argument. For instance, nuclear power plants generate radioactive waste, but there isn't anything in the argument that indicates that such waste is either good or bad. We'd have to make our definition of environmentally friendly more precise so as to prohibit not just greenhouse gases but also radioactive waste. When you get to the precision phase of writing an essay, take another look at your argument, make sure the premises are all related to each other and the conclusion. Be sure your argument is comprehensive, and that your definitions are precise and coherent.
When you're sure your argument and outline are strong, then we need to fill in the evidence. Your evidence should be as precise as possible. This is based on the assumption we make in writing essays that the

more precise support we have for our conclusion, the better received it will be (a reasonable premise, right?). For the our dam essay outline, some evidence is vague and not very persuasive—take "a lot of pollution in the city" for example. We need some specific facts or data to support that purported fact.

We could cite an increasing incidence of asthma among youth as evidence of air pollution, or a higher rate of birth defects as evidence of drinking water/river pollution. Presenting facts which are only weakly related to your premises are also imprecise and not persuasive. For instance, citing that I find myself coughing a lot as anecdotal evidence that there's a lot of pollution in the city is far less persuasive than the results of a proper scientific study. In terms of our outline, this would be putting and filling in arabic numerals in our outline, a 1 and 2 under each A and B.

Be precise in your description of the details. This is a crucial point for other types of writing such as fiction or personal essay writing. but is also extremely important to keep in mind in analytical writing. Look at the difference between these two examples from fiction writing:

Example One. Still missing his old girlfriend, Jack forgot to cross the street and instead looked at a pile of leaves.
Example Two. Stopped by a pile of brown leaves in front of him—spring was a long time ago, she wasn't coming back—Jack stood there, looking down, and didn't notice the lights change.

Details and precision make a big difference in the effect of these sentences. The first example throws you off in a distracting way when you find out about the pile of leaves *after* he forgets to cross the street, since the proper causal order is the opposite—that looking at the pile of leaves (first/cause) led him to miss the traffic light change (second/effect). The second example uses careful word choice to express what's happened to Jack. The first word "stopped" for instance alludes to the traffic light which is stopping traffic as well as to what's happened to Jack's life (we would guess) since she left him. Describing the leaves as brown also keys the reader in that it's autumn; in the first example, we don't know when it's taking place. Knowing that the leaves signify autumn also motivates Jack's memory of spring and then her in the second example. In the first example, there's no reason that's clear to the reader as to why in that moment Jack thought of his girlfriend and why he'd be transfixed by a pile of leaves.

Even though these two examples are from fiction writing, they make it clear how careful attention to word choice and precise details, in this case when telling a story, makes the writing much more effective. This applies to any writing whether you're analyzing MacBeth's character or explaining why someone should study mathematics. In the former case, just describing MacBeth as power–hungry or ambitious isn't very persuasive, but if you present specific quotes ("I have no spur To prick the sides of my intent, but only vaulting ambition which o'erleaps itself and falls on th'other.") and actions (killing his guest Duncan in order to become the King of Scotland), it'll be much harder for your reader to disagree with you. In the latter case, just saying mathematics is beautiful isn't persuasive as well, but presenting examples of specific and easily grasped proofs that are beautiful (say a geometric proof of the Pythagorean theorem) forces a reader to accept your point.

Precision is critical to keep in mind when writing your essay. It's a good idea to take your outline and add in as many precise details as possible at this point. In our build the dam essay, there are many places in which more precision in argument and precise facts are needed. We need to get quantified pollution levels for the city, the benefits and harms of various energy generation methods, an analysis of the city's growth, projections thereof and how well the different energies could meet and sustain energy for that growth.

Once you fill in more precise evidence in your outline, you're ready to write the first draft of your essay. Sit down with your outline and simply write it out. Some writers work carefully revising each paragraph as they write. Others prefer to write the whole thing out without rereading what they've written. Figure out what works for you, but whatever method you choose…you'll have to revise your essay.

R is for Revision

Writing is a process. "PRO" is a way to think about and structure that process. Once you've got a full draft completed of your essay (unless it's due tomorrow), you're not done yet. You need to revise, revise, revise.

When you revise your essay, you'll need to ask yourself, is this argument well made? Are there any gaps in my argument? Am I making the case as precisely as I can? Are there any premises or points that I make which aren't integrated into the whole paper? In other words, you'll continue to analyze your essay from the organizational and precision perspectives we've already discussed.

You'll also need to of course check out writing fundamentals—the "interior decorating" phase of writing an essay. Try to make long sentences shorter. Make sure that there aren't any grammatical errors, awkward phrases, confusing sentences, spelling errors, or any other problems with your writing. Always read every draft you write out loud—if an essay flows when you hear it, it will likely read well.

Also try to have someone (ideally a pretty experienced writer) read your essay. Many teachers are happy to read and comment on drafts (be sure to get drafts to them well in advance of an essay's due date). It's crucial to get feedback from someone other than yourself: of course your essay will sound pretty good to you, the question is how others find it! You need to get a perspective as to how persuasive and how clear your essay is. Another person can also point out gaps or flaws in your reasoning and argument.

Try to space out revisions of an essay over multiple days. It's important to have some distance between drafts—you need to come back to your essay with a fresh mind. You'll figure out how you work as well. Some writers find that they fill in gaps in revisions; others find that revising is like tending to a Japanese garden, removing everything that's not necessary. The deadlines imposed by your teachers may not allow that, but try your best to start early to have adequate time to prepare multiple drafts.

Short Notes on Introductions and Conclusions

Introductions have to engage the reader. Your introductions should pull the reader into your essay. The key rule for introductions then is don't be dull. Also, usually your key conclusion(s) or the main point of the essay is presented at the end of your introduction in the form of a thesis statement. It doesn't have to be there, but somewhere early in your essay there should be a sentence or two (or three) that expresses clearly what the thrust of your essay is.

For essay conclusions, don't be afraid to be short and sweet. You shouldn't spend the entire conclusion summarizing your essay, though you should briefly re-state the key points and your conclusions. Try to express your conclusion(s) and points in a final, powerful way. Conclusions are the last thing your reader will read and should be memorable. If it's possible to link your conclusion to your introduction, try it, it often works well. For essays of a more philosophical nature or tone, you can in a conclusion extend your ideas a bit; ask questions about them that could be the basis for further essays and explorations. Don't try to answer any questions you pose (in any detail that is) or analyze any problems you may raise in your conclusion, that's veering off-topic. The key guidance we'll leave you with for conclusions is to express your key points memorably without being repetitive.

The Last Word

Paul Erdos, a famous itinerant 20th century mathematician, once quipped that "a mathematician is a machine that turns coffee into theorems." Since the analytical writing process doesn't rely on bursts of late-night creativity, we don't have to become caffeine-addicts to become analytical writing machines.

Skip caffeine, but stay PRO CUPED. You'll need CUPED to construct your argument or the logical framework for your essay and PRO to guide you in the writing process. You have to turn that argument into an outline, and turn that outline into an essay. Lastly, revise, revise, revise that essay, ideally with the benefit of others' feedback.

APPENDIX 4: Word Roots and Origins

Negative Prefixes

Mal–, male– (latin) = "bad, ill–intentioned"

Dismal – bad or inept or causing bad or gloomy feelings
Malicious – having ill intentions
Malfeasance – wrongful actions by public or other officials
Malign – to speak badly of someone

Mis– "hate, badly, wrong"

Miscreant – a villain or depraved person (literally means 'wrong' + creant 'believing')
Misogynist – someone who hates or dislikes women
Miscast – to be wrongly cast

Dis– "apart, away from"

Dissonant – sounding harsh or inharmonious (literally sounds which sound apart from each other)
Disinter – to take a body away or apart from a grave or place of interment
Disseminate – to spread widely or scatter

De– "remove from, down"

Delineate – to trace the outline of (literally to put *down* the lines of)
Defame – to malign, discredit or disparage (literally to *remove* someone's reputation)

Descend – to come down from a higher place to a lower place; to climb *down*
Devalue – to reduce in value; to *remove* value from

Anti– "against, opposite of", occasionally also means "before"

Antithesis – two words or concepts which are *against* each other or *opposites* of each other
Antonym – a word that means the *opposite of* some other word
Antihero – a protagonist who by not having heroic qualities is *against* the hero typecast
Antipathy – strong feelings *against* someone or something
Antagonize – to behave in a hostile way towards someone (anti– against + –onize to struggle; so literally a struggle against someone)
Anticipate – to realize *before* (something happens)
Antiquate – to be out–dated i.e. to have been useful *before* but not now

Contra– "against"

Contravene – to act *against* or counter to a rule or law; to violate
Contradict – to speak *against* what someone else has claimed (contra– against + –dict to speak)

Un– / Non– "not"

Unseen – *not* seen
Unfair – *not* fair
Noninterference – *not* interfering
Nonpayment – *not* paying

A– An–   "without, not"

Amoral – *without* morality or immorality

Atheist – *without* god
Atypical – *not* typical
Anonymous – *without* a name
Anarchy – *without* a government

Positive Prefixes

Bene–, Bon– "good"

Benefit – something that promotes well–being or is *good*
Benediction – a blessing (bene– good + –dict speaking so literally to speak well of)
Benevolent – expressing *good*will (literally to wish well)
Bonus – something *good* received in addition to what was expected or due
Bona fide – sincere, presented or done in good faith (literally bona *good* + fide faith)

Eu– "good, well"

Euphemism – the use of a less offensive term in place of an offensive term
Eulogy – speech or writing in praise of someone (–logy means speech as well as study of)
Euphony – good sounding, harmonious (–phony refers to sound)
Euthanasia – to put to death painlessly usually to end suffering (–thanasia refers to death)

Other Common Prefixes

Ambi– Amph– "both, more than one, going around"

Ambidextrous – equally capable with *both* hands
Ambivalent – having *more than one* feeling; being drawn to *more than one* thing, person, idea, etc.
Ambiguous – having *more than one* possible meanings
Amphibian – originally an animal living *both* on land and in water
Ambience – the atmosphere or mood *around* a person or place
Ambitious— greatly desirous of power or distinction. Originally meant *going around* to get votes

Ante– "before"

Antecedent – something that came *before* something else
Anterior – to come *before* something else spatially
Antedate – to come *before* some other event

Auto– "self"

Autodidact – someone *self*–taught
Automatic – something that moves by it*self*
Autonomy – *self*–governing

Bi– "two, double, both"

Bipartisan – with *both* parties
Bilingual – speaking *two* languages
Biennial – happening every *two* years

Bio– "life"

Biology – the study of *living* things (bio– life + –ology study of)
Biography – a book about someone's *life* (bio– life + graphy writing)
Symbiotic – a mutually beneficial relationship between two *living* things (sym– together + bio– life)

Re– "back, again"

Recreation – amusement or play (originally and literally the re–creation of the spirit or mind of childhood through amusement or diversion)
Recession – when the economy goes *back* to older levels
Recluse – someone who lives away from the world; literally lives in *back* of shutters or behind closed shutters
Revise – to see or read something *again* in order to correct it
Revive – to make live *again*
Retain – to keep *back* for oneself
Renaissance – a re–birth; ideas and learning born *again*

Extra– "outside, beyond"

Extraordinary – *beyond* or *outside* the ordinary
Extract – to take something *outside* itself or its normal place
Extradite – to take someone who's *outside* his home country back home for arrest
Extrasensory – *beyond* or *outside* the senses
Extrapolate – to go *beyond* the literal meaning of what's said or written

Fore–   "before"

Foresight – to see or expect something *before* it happens
Foreshadow – to hint at something *before* it happens
Forestall – to extend the period *before* some event happens

Forthright – to speak openly and directly *before* being directly prodded

Hetero–   "different"

Heterosexual – to sexually prefer the *different* gender from one's own
Heterodox – to have *different* ideas relative to the orthodox or normal views
Heterogeneous – to be *different* e.g. some group of things in which the elements are *different* from each other

Homo–, Hom–   "same"

Homosexual – to sexually prefer the *same* gender as one's own
Homogenous – having the *same* consistency or nature
Homonym – having the *same* sound

Hyper– "excessive"

Hyperactive – *excessively* active
Hyperbole – *excessive* exaggeration
Hyperglycemia – having *excessive* sugar or glucose levels

Hypo– "under, beneath, less than"

Hypodermic – *under* the skin
Hypochondriac – someone excessively concerned about their health; literal meaning was *under* the breastbone which was believed to host the melancholic spirit so literally *under* the spell of melancholy
Hypocritical – to express ideas which one doesn't have or believe; literally being separate *beneath* or under one's public or outer persona
Hypoacidic – *less than* the normal acidity level
Hypoglycemia – *less than* the normal glucose or sugar levels

Inter– "between"

Interject – to insert *between* statements
Intersperse – to spread out *between* a large space or among many things
Interloper – to interfere in others' affairs; literally to enter *between*
Intermittent – to occur *between* some intervals of time
Interstate – *between* states

Omni– "all"

Omnipresent – being in *all* places
Omnipotent – having *all* powers

Pan– "all, everyone"

Pantheon – some group of worshipped people or things; literally *all* those considered gods
Pandemic – widespread, occurring to *everyone*
Panoply – a full suit of armor or some impressive array; literally having *all* armors
Panorama – a view in *all* directions
Pandemonium – chaos or tumult everywhere; literally the place of *all* the demons

Post– "after"

Posthumous – known or released *after* death
Posterity – all those who continue to or come to live *after* one's death
Posterior – located behind as opposed to anterior; literally coming *after*
Postnatal – after birth

Pre– "before"

Preface – a short essay *before* the main text
Prevail – to win or gain victory; to be strong *before* or in front of others
Prerequisite – a course that must have been taken *before* taking this course
Premonition – having a *thought* of an event before the event actually occurs
Precocious – having skills or knowledge at an age much *before* one is expected to have such skills or knowledge
Prejudgment – a judgment formed *before* knowing the full facts

Retro–   "backward"

Retrograde – moving *backwards* generally in an abstract sense
Retromingent – to urinate from behind; literally to urinate *backwards*

Sub– "under"

Subsistence – to barely survive; literally *under* existing
Subpoena – a legal order to appear in court; literally *under* penalty e.g. under penalty of law if you don't appear in court
Subversive – a person in a society or organization that is tending to overthrow or upset the usual order; literally to turn from *under*neath
Subterranean – *under* the surface of the earth

Trans–   "across"

Transaction – an agreement or exchange between two or more people; literally an action *across* e.g. across multiple persons
Transcend – to pass beyond some limits; literally to climb *across* e.g. to climb *across* the usual restraints or ideas or limits
Transgress – to violate a law or accepted behavior; literally to step *across* e.g. step *across* usually accepted rules

Transition – passage from one state to another, passing *across* one or more states

Common Suffixes

–archy   "government"

Anarchy – without a *government* ('an' means without)
Monarchy – *government* by one; more generally refers to any government by a king, queen, or some ruler ('mon' comes from mono)
Oligarchy – *government* by the few; a *government* controlled or ruled by a few persons, groups, or a particular class

–cracy   "government"

Meritocracy – *government* or any system ruled by merit or the merit of the individuals
Bureaucracy – *government* by bureaus or various departments; has come to mean a system of management for a government or organization which has lots of unnecessary procedures and rules which impede getting work done
Pornocracy – *rule* by prostitutes or harlots ('porn' refers to prostitution)

–cide "kill"

Infanticide – to *kill* an infant
Genocide – to *kill* a group of people based on their ethnicity (gen– comes from genus meaning race or type)
Regicide – to *kill* a king (reg from regis/rex meaning king)
Spermicide – to *kill* sperm

–otomy "cutting"

Lobotomy – to *cut* into a lobe of the brain
Tracheotomy – to *cut* into the trachea or windpipe (to make an opening for breathing)

–logy "study of", occasionally "writing"

Geology – the *study of* the earth
Ornithology – the *study of* birds
Psychology – the *study of* the mind
Chronology – the sequential order of a set of past events (chron– time + –ology words/writing)
Trilogy – a series of three works usually literary or dramatic works

More Roots

Anthro– "human, man"

Anthropology – the study of *humankind*
Anthropomorphic – ascribing *human* attributes to non–human things (morph means shape or form so literally giving a human form to other things)
Misanthrope – someone who dislikes *humankind* or people in general

Dem– (greek, noun: demos) "people"

Democracy – government by the *people* ('dem' people + 'cracy' government)
Pandemic – across many *people* ('pan' across + 'dem' people)

Chron– "time"

Synchronize – to cause to occur at the same *time* (syn– together + chronize time)
Anachronism – something that appears or is represented outside of its proper historical *time* (ana– not + chron– time)

Circum– "around, on all sides"

Circumference – the distance *around* a circle; the perimeter of a circle
Circumspect –cautious; considering likely consequences carefully (circum– on all sides + –spect to see; so literally to see all the sides of an issue)

Corps   "body"

Corporeal – related to the physical *body*
Corpulent – fat (corp– body + –ulent full of)
Corporation – a type of organization in which a group of individuals can act as a single group or *body*

Culp– "blame"

Culprit – the person responsible for a crime; the *blame*worthy person
Culpable – *blame*worthy; deserving *blame*

Cryp– "hidden"

Cryptography – the study of codes and *hiding* secrets
Apocryphal – of doubtful authenticity

Dict– "to say, to tell, to speak"

Dictionary – a book with the meanings of words in it (diction– speech + –ary pertaining to)
Predict – to *tell* what will happen in the future (pre– before + –dict say)
Verdict – the decision of a judge or jury in a court case (ver– true + –dict to say)
Indict – to formally accuse someone of a crime

Equa– "equal, even"

Equidistant – equally distant or spaced
Equation – in mathematics, a statement which states the equality of two expressions
Equanimity – calm temper and composure (equ– even + –animity mind or spirit)

Gn– Gno– "know"

Agnostic – someone who believes that one can't *know* if there is or isn't a god (a– not + gno know)
Prognosis – a prediction or forecast of the course of a disease (pro– before + gno know)

Idio– "one's own"

Idiosyncrasy – a characteristic, habit, or temperament peculiar to an individual person (idio– one's own + –syn together + –crasy mixture)
Idiom – an expression whose meaning can not be literally translated or understood from the literal meanings of the words composing the expression

Log–, Loq–, Loqu–, Loqui– (latin) = "to talk, speak"

Logorrhea – *talking* excessively and often incoherently (logo– word + –rhea discharge)
Colloquial – informal *speech*
Grandiloquent – pompous, excessively lofty *speech*
Loquacious – *talk*ative, garrulous
Eloquent – *speaking* well, expressing one's self effectively and forcefully

Luc–, Lum–, Lus–   "light, shine"

Lucid – easily understood; clearly perceived or understood
Translucent – permitting light to pass through (trans– through + lucent shine)
Elucidate – to explain, to make clear
Lustrous – shining, luminous, brilliant

Morph– "shape, form"

Amorphous – without *shape*
Metamorphosis – a change from one *form* into another *form*

Mort– "death"

Immortal – someone or something that will never *die*
Morbid – pertaining to *death*
Moribund – something that will soon *die*

Nov–, Neo–   "new"

Innovate – to introduce a *new* idea or change
Neophyte – someone who's *new* to some activity or discipline

Neologism – a *new* word
Renovate – to make *new* again; to restore to freshness or an earlier state of perfection

Phil– "love"

Philosophy – the search for wisdom and truth (philo– love + –sophy knowledge)
Bibliophile – someone who collects (or *loves*) books
Hydrophilic – someone or something that *loves* water
Philanderer – a man who habitually has casual love affairs

Phob–, –Phobic, –Phobia "fear"

Hydrophobic – *afraid* of water or something that's repulsed or repelled by water
Acrophobia – a *fear* of heights
Claustrophobia – a *fear* of enclosed spaces
Xenophobia – a *fear* of foreigners or things foreign

Phon–, Phono–, Phone–, –Phony   "sound"

Phonograph – a machine that reproduces *sound*, more popularly known as a record player
Cacophony – discordant or harsh *sounds* (caco– bad + –phony sound)
Symphony – a musical composition for an orchestra (sym/syn– together + –phony sound)

Sacr–, Sanct–   "sacred"

Sanctimonious – being hypocritically righteous or religious
Sacrifice – to offer a living creature or object to a deity (sacri– sacred + –fice make)

Sacrilege – to violate something sacred or held sacred
Sanctuary – a sacred or holy place; a safe place of refuge

Spec– (latin, verb: spectere) = " to see, to look"

Spectacle – something to be seen or watched, usually a large, impressive event
Inspect – to *look* at and examine carefully

Thei–, Theo–   "god"

Atheist – someone who doesn't believe in god (a– without + –thei god)
Theology – the study of a system of religious beliefs and teachings
Theocracy – rule by religious leaders, religious authority, or divine guidance
Apotheosis – elevation of someone to divine stature; a supreme or great example

Ver– "truth"

Veracious – honest; *truthful*
Verisimilitude – appearing to be true (very– true + –similitude similar)
Verity – the state of being *true*

APPENDIX 5: SAT Subject Test Preparation Guidance

Unfortunately, the College Board has released very few actual SAT Subject tests, so you have to rely on independent vendors' books to prepare for these tests. The College Board has released at least a single test for every test they offer in the book *The Official Study Guide for All SAT Subject Tests*. For some tests, there may be a single book with multiple tests for example for the history tests there's *The Official SAT Subject Tests in U.S. & World History Study Guide* and for the math tests there's *The Official SAT Subject Tests in Mathematics Levels 1 & 2 Study Guide*. Online, there are also pdf files with sample questions at the College Board's SAT Subjects website at: http://www.collegeboard.com/student/testing/sat/about/SATII.html

Due to the paucity of actual College Board tests and materials, we recommend our students supplement the College Board materials and tests with *at least* two books from independent vendors (e.g. REA, Kaplan, etc.). Use reviews from Amazon to help guide you as to which particular books are reliable as well as browse them yourself at a bookstore. You should read both the independent vendors' books even though doing the practice tests is the most crucial reason to purchase the books—reading the books which summarize the subject usually won't take very long.

What's absolutely crucial, though, is doing practice tests. You should take at least two full practice tests a week, ideally one from each of the independent vendor's books. After taking the tests, review them carefully just as you reviewed your SAT I practice tests (according to our recommendations we hope). Study and review those areas which you find yourself doing poorly in or which you haven't covered in your course.

After a few weeks of preparation using independent vendors' tests, you should be ready to take the College Board tests—both from the books and from the online question packet. Review those questions carefully and make sure you know those questions and content covered quite well. Your scores on the College Board tests will be the most indicative on your score on test day, so wait a few weeks to be sure you're ready when you take them and again be certain that you know the topics covered on the College Board tests extremely well.

We have found that students who are doing well on 'REA' tests, 'Barron's' tests, and 'Kaplan' tests...for example... on test day do well on the College Board test. Don't rely on a single independent vendor's book, though, as they are invariably off—use 2 or more!

APPENDIX 6: The Four Components of College Admissions

There are four key components to college admissions: your classes and grades, your standardized test scores, your extracurricular activities, and your essays.

For more competitive colleges (hereafter referred to as the MCCs), components one and two are essentially givens: you have to have them in order to even be in the running. Admissions for these schools thus hinges on your essays and your extracurricular activities.

Here's a brief overview of how each component impinges on your chances for admission at the MCCs (the most competitive colleges) and how to excel in each component.

Component One: Your Classes and Grades.

MCCs will expect you to have taken the most challenging courses offered by your school and to have gotten high grades in those classes. This doesn't mean you need to take 5 AP classes a year—but it also means that you should usually try to take an AP course when it's available instead of the regular course.

By high marks, we mean almost straight "A"s. You can get an occasional B or even C and still get admission to the most competitive schools—but the vast majority of your grades must be "A"s for the MCCs. Taking primarily less challenging courses at your school will severely hurt your chances for admission to an MCC even if you have straight "A"s in all of them. The occasional lower grade and easier course is fine, but if you consistently take easier courses (perhaps in order to always get an "A"), you'll seriously hinder your chances at admission at the MCCs.

You may find yourself with a trade–off at some point between taking an easier course and getting a higher grade. We'd recommend not worrying too much in these circumstances about college admissions, but rather pick the option that fits best with your full schedule and your goal. If you're particularly worried about BC calculus and you've got two other AP courses, AB Calculus is probably a good bet. If you feel your schedule isn't that challenging (no other AP courses say) and you really love math, then you probably would want to challenge yourself with BC calculus even though you expect it to be a bit rough.

To summarize, neither your grades in themselves nor the difficulty of your coursework in itself will affect your college admissions chances—rather the two of them in conjunction will be the first thing that admissions officers will consider. Consistently low grades or less challenging coursework will likely nix your chances for admission to MCCs.

The best path for course/grade optimization is the "middle path"—try to take as many challenging courses as you can but not when your grade in the course(s) will be a "C" or lower. Don't take extremely challenging courses and end up with a "C" average; but also don't take extremely easy courses and end up with an easy "A" average.

Component Two: Your Standardized Test Scores.

Your SAT or ACT scores for the MCCs are much like your classes and grades: a hurdle every candidate must clear. For the top MCCs, say the 10 or so most competitive colleges in the country, we recommend our students get a score of 700 or higher on each section of the SAT I and on each SAT Subject test that they take. 700 is a hurdle—once you're over it, you're over it and it doesn't matter by how much you clear it. In other words, getting 750 on all your subject tests or even 800 is not going to improve your admissions chances for the MCCs very much (beyond having 700). Once you've cleared the hurdle, your activities and essays become the deciding factor. So there's no need to kill yourself for a perfect 2400.

Most MCCs require 2 SAT Subject Tests. We recommend taking as many SAT Subject tests as you can (even more than 2) in which you're confident you'll score 700 or better. Taking say 5 different Subject Tests and getting over 700 on each one is impressive. We don't recommend, though, that anyone take more than 2 SAT Subject Tests on any single test date—taking 3 on a single day is a rather taxing we've found.

The ACT is a great option for students who don't like taking standardized tests as many colleges will accept the ACT test in lieu of the SAT I and SAT Subject Tests. For students who are having trouble with the SAT tests, we recommend trying the ACT test as well (even though it's very similar to the SAT) since you've got nothing to lose.

For MCCs other than the top ten, you don't have to get 700+ on each section of the SAT I and each Subject Test. Check what the average test scores are for the colleges you're interested in and try your best to be a bit higher than the average scores—and if you're a bit lower than average, don't worry, just make sure your essays and activities are really good.

Component Three: Extracurricular Activities.

Go deep, not wide. Don't join ten or fifteen clubs (well, you're young, explore, but don't list all ten of them on your college application), try rather to have two or three activities in high school in which you're deeply involved. If there isn't any group or activity at your school that you're interested in, join some activity outside of your school, be active in other ways, or start your own group or club.

Be creative and follow your heart. There are many ways to be productive (or at least what a college admissions officer will perceive as productive) while pursuing those things you love. Whatever you do, though, be dedicated and committed. If you're interested in poetry, start a poetry recitation club or a collaborative surrealist poetry–

writing group. If you love cinema, start a cinema blog but be sure to write about films other than the weekly box office hits—you have to try to really get to know cinema which is more than Tom Cruise and Indiana Jones.

Here are two examples of exceptional students we've worked with who were admitted to MCCs. One young girl authored a paper which was published in a medical journal and was also a committed dancer. One of our young fellows was a dedicated poet, a drummer in a band, and started a club to provide new services to students while raising money for non–profit organizations. One key thing to notice is that they had only a few activities and for each activity they clearly demonstrated a serious commitment and achievement.

You need to come off in your college application as a productive, serious person...not someone who sits around watching sitcoms and playing Xbox all day. Make sure when you write your activities that you come off that way; if you've participated in many activities or changed your activities in high school, that's fine but try to present the best two, three, four or five activities you've participated in such that you come off as a serious, hard–working and active person (which you are...we hope).

Component Four: Your Essays.

For MCCs, if you're okay but not really strong in components one, two and three, superb essays may be the trick to gain admission in some of those colleges. If you're really strong in components one through three, but write poor essays or send in an essay with spelling or grammatical errors, you can very likely find yourself getting a rejection.

First thing to keep in mind, then, is make sure your essays have no spelling or grammatical mistakes. Secondly, make sure they're coherent, decently written (even if dull or uninspired) essays. You need to show at a minimum that you can write an essay that has an introduction, a conclusion, and body paragraphs that each express some point.

That's a minimum. Ideally, you should aim to have a unique, well-written, focused essay that expresses some aspect of who you are and expresses it well. To aim for that, do read our essay writing process that we've developed over our history and that we follow with our students. It outlines how we work with students to get not just adequate essays, but inspired writing from them. We also discuss what not to write about there.

A Few, Parting Words.

When you get these four components together, you're golden. There's no other secret really to college admissions. Good luck. Study hard. Challenge yourself. Be prepared, be active, and be creative. Do remember, which college you go to doesn't determine who you are or what you do in life so don't get stressed, just keep a good conscience and do your best.

APPENDIX 7: Turn Out a Great College Application Essay.

How to Turn out a Poor Essay

The basic way to do this is to quite simply not listen to us (we being the college experts whether Yale Tutors or another tutor or your guidance counselor or English teacher or any other so–called expert). We often run into students who are loathe to heed our advice. We had, for example, a student who wanted our help putting final touches on his essays and personal statements i.e. fixing up sentence structure, word choice, etc. We cut the session short so as to save him money and told him that his essays were not sufficiently compelling. We advised him to write some more essays and we could take things from there. He didn't like our advice and cited how much his mother laughed at one essay and how much his sister appreciated another essay. He ended up not trusting our advice and judgment (he didn't write any other essays), and was not admitted to the schools he applied to.

The moral of the story is not that you can't trust your sister and your mother! Rather, it's that there are many people who can appreciate writing one way or another, but that doesn't mean that they have a good idea of what's unique and interesting and well–written from the perspective of a college admissions committee. You need to get feedback on any essay you write from an "expert," someone who's read a lot of high school student or college application essays and has some idea of what admissions committees are looking for. It's very hard to have a good perspective on your own writing. This is particularly true for personal writing—what you're experiencing may be very important to you, but it could also be something everyone goes through and so not interesting for any particular person to read (since they've been through that; it won't express anything unique about you). An editor will give you perspective and guide you.

A second common pitfall we run into is the summer essay. Many of our students come to us in the early fall with a college essay they've been working on for months which they gingerly hand over to us. After three minutes (we've read a lot of essays), we have a tough job: to tell our student that we know there are better essays inside him or her. To counter this phenomenon, we have a process we now use with our students...

How to Turn out a <u>Great</u> Essay

The First Step: Put Together a List of Colleges You Want to Apply to and Get Their Essay Topics

This step is fairly obvious—you'll need to know what the essay topics are before you can write on them. If you're having trouble with your list, you can start work on the topics for the common application (a single college application accepted by hundreds of colleges).
From this list, try to figure out how many essay topics overlap and where they overlap. If you're filling out ten college applications, you shouldn't have to write ten separate full essays—there should be a lot of overlap (you're allowed to send the same essay to multiple colleges). We're usually able to get our students down to two or three longer essays that they'll have to write and send in to colleges.

The Second Step: Make a List of Potential Events, Experiences, Persons, Things, etc. to Write About.

Brainstorm by yourself or with someone as to what are potential things you could write about for your college essays. Try to have at least three ideas for each essay you'll have to turn in. If you're able to quickly put together an outline of a potential essay, do it. If you're further able to discuss these topics and or your outlines with an "expert", also do it. The expert would already be able to guide you away from the essay on how you're ready to create world peace to an essay on why you don't like to help your mother wash the dishes.

Topics to avoid are anything political, anything really broad in nature like world peace or world hunger, anything controversial like abortion or sex education, and any topic that anyone could write the essay on that you intend to write. You need to pick topics on which you can write an essay that no one else in the world can write; an essay that depends on who you are, your thoughts and your experiences.

The Third Step: Free-Write Several Essays.

Here you need to put, say, three 2-hour blocks into your schedule for the week. For each block, sit in front of a computer (or with pen and paper) with some idea in mind (from step two) written at the top of the screen and start writing about it. Don't worry about sentence structure or organizing your thoughts into proper paragraphs. Focus on expressing what you're thinking or feeling accurately. Do this until you have at least a single page filled up, and try to keep going on the topic (writing more and more) for at least two hours. If you're having trouble writing anything, brainstorm and write examples or related thoughts to your initial idea at the top of the page. Do not get up from the computer until you've filled up at least one page.

Repeat this free-writing essay exercise until you have several different essay-like writings. After two weeks, you should have six pieces of writing which is pretty good.

The Fourth Step: "Expert" Advice on What's Sincere, Compelling and Interesting.

Take your essay-like writings from the third step (your six pieces, say) and give them to an "expert". We need the "expert's" perspective now. Ask the "expert" to tell you what particular ideas, sentences, paragraphs, or even entire essays express something interesting and compelling. The "expert" needs to look for what parts of your essays expressed something sincere and unique, that he or she wants to read more about. It could be a single sentence or it could be an entire piece you've written. The "expert" may find a single observation compelling in an otherwise boring essay, and that observation could be the kernel of a new and actually compelling essay.

Here are some examples. From a fairly typical essay about a student's summer volunteer work with a medical clinic in Latin America, the student had a single sentence on his visit to the home of a sick person and her silence upon seeing how this person lived. We told her to try to turn that single sentence or self-observation into an essay—write just about that single visit and not the whole trip. Another example is an essay on a college visit which was a bit nauseating in its praise of the college. There was one interesting bit, though, on impromptu student-to-student teaching. We asked the student to write more on that experience and anything else on how that college fosters students teaching other students and generally studying together or socially (and why that was an attractive thing). We believe the student ended up with a much more compelling, thought-out essay on what made that college and his own interest in attending it unique.

The Fifth Step: Perfect the Essay

Now that you have the raw material or rough draft of a great or even a few great college essays, you have to make them perfect. Now is the time to use the spell check and even the buggy grammar check in your word processor and more importantly the grammar and style check skills of your "expert" and or any other competent writer. Pay attention to word choice, sentence structure, and the general flow of the essay. At this point, you can obsess a bit about every little detail. The sentences should flow together well, and you should use one or two more difficult vocabulary words in the proper context and accurately (don't use more than one or two or it'll be obvious you're trying to show off). Revise an essay then sleep on it for a day or two before doing another revision—time will give you perspective on your writing. This is actually the easiest part of the whole process even though it may take the longest amount of time and require a bit of painstaking attention to detail.

To Recapitulate

In this one little area of writing a college essay, don't trust your mother's judgment unless she happens to be an admissions officer. Don't get attached to any particular essay you write. Write multiple free–written essays to start with. Don't start perfecting your essay or even revising it until you're certain your raw ideas and writing are unique and compelling. Try to find someone who has experience with essay writing in general and particularly college essays to get their perspective on your writing. Aim to be sincere, thoughtful, precise and observant in your essay. Be sure that your essay is uniquely yours—no one else in the world should really be able to write it other than you; it shouldn't be generic in anyway.